SEXUAL ORIENTATION AND HUMAN RIGHTS

SEXUAL ORIENTATION AND HUMAN RIGHTS

*The United States Constitution,
the European Convention,
and the Canadian Charter*

ROBERT WINTEMUTE
School of Law
King's College London

DAMAGED

CLARENDON PRESS · OXFORD

Oxford University Press, Great Clarendon Street, Oxford OX2 6DP
Oxford New York
Athens Auckland Bangkok Bogota Bombay
Buenos Aires Calcutta Cape Town Dar es Salaam
Delhi Florence Hong Kong Istanbul Karachi
Kuala Lumpur Madras Madrid Melbourne
Mexico City Nairobi Paris Singapore
Taipei Tokyo Toronto
and associated companies in
Berlin Ibadan

Oxford is a trade mark of Oxford University Press

Published in the United States
by Oxford University Press Inc., New York

First published 1995
First issued in paperback (with corrections) 1997

British Library Cataloguing in Publication Data
Data available

Library of Congress Cataloging in Publication Data
Wintemute, Robert.
Sexual orientation and human rights: the United States
Constitution, the European Convention, and the Canadian Charter /
Robert Wintemute.
p. cm.
Includes bibliographical references.
1. Gay rights. 2. Human rights. 3. Sexual orientation.
4. Gays—Legal status, laws, etc. I. Title.
HQ76.5.W56 1995 323.3'264—dc20 95–33042
ISBN 0-19-825972-7
ISBN 0-19-826488-7 (pbk)

Printed in Great Britain
on acid-free paper by
Bookcraft Ltd., Midsomer Norton, Somerset

Preface to the Paperback Edition

Since June 1995, when my editors were forced to call a halt to my updating, there have been many developments. A brief summary of the more important ones follows.

In the United States, the Supreme Court decided its first two cases of sexual orientation discrimination since *Bowers* v. *Hardwick* in 1986 and *San Francisco Arts & Athletics, Inc* v. *US Olympic Committee* in 1987. In the first case, *Hurley* v. *Irish-American Gay, Lesbian and Bisexual Group of Boston*,[1] the Court unanimously upheld the First Amendment right of organizers of the Boston St. Patrick's Day Parade to exclude a gay, lesbian, and bisexual organization that sought to march under its own banner, in spite of a Massachusetts statute prohibiting sexual orientation discrimination in public accommodations. The tone of Justice Souter's opinion was entirely respectful and neutral, focussing on the interference with the organizers' 'autonomy to choose the content of [their] own message',[2] and stressing both the absence of state action (i.e. the parade's being privately organized)[3] and the absence of any attempt to exclude openly gay, lesbian or bisexual individuals marching with other parade units.[4] *Hurley* thus represents a relatively narrow constitutional exception to the protection provided by anti-discrimination legislation like the Massachusetts statute, and should apply only to privately organized parades and similar expressive activities.[5]

In the second case, *Romer* v. *Evans*,[6] the Court (by 6-3) struck down Amendment 2, the 'pro-discrimination' amendment to Colorado's Constitution.[7] It was able to do so (to my surprise), not by relying on the Colorado Supreme Court's problematic 'right to participate equally in the political process', nor by reconsidering *Hardwick* on the right of privacy, nor by declaring sexual orientation a suspect or quasi-suspect classification, but by finding that Amendment 2 bore no 'rational relationship to a legitimate governmental purpose'[8] and therefore failed minimal scrutiny under equal protection doctrine.[9] The protection *Romer* provides against 'pro-discrimination' amendments is extremely important, because these amendments were threatening to proliferate and make state or local laws against sexual orientation discrimination impossible to enact (in the ordinary way) in many states, cities, and counties. But *Romer*'s protection could also prove to be minimal, in that it may be difficult to extend the US Supreme

---

[1] 132 L Ed 2d 487 (1995).   [2] Ibid. at 503.   [3] Ibid. at 499.
[4] Ibid. at 503.   [5] See infra p. 51, n. 226.
[6] 134 L Ed 2d 855 (1996). See also *Equality Foundation of Greater Cincinnati, Inc.* v. *City of Cincinnati*, 54 F 3d 261 (6th Cir 1995), vacated and remanded for further consideration in light of *Romer*, 135 L Ed 2d 1044 (1996).
[7] See infra pp. 56–60.   [8] 134 L Ed 2d at 868.   [9] See infra pp. 22, 78–83.

Court's reasoning to other kinds of public sector sexual orientation discrimination (e.g. exclusion from the military[10] and civil marriage[11]). Justice Kennedy, writing for the majority, described Amendment 2 as 'unprecedented' and saw 'its sheer breadth' as making it 'inexplicable by anything but animus toward the class that it affects'.[12] The novel and extreme[13] nature of Amendment 2 thus caused the Court to cite the well established but rarely invoked principle that 'a bare . . . desire to harm a politically unpopular group cannot constitute a legitimate governmental interest'.[14] A more traditional and less sweeping form of sexual orientation discrimination may not trigger the same reaction.

Can the Court's finding no rational basis for Amendment 2 in *Romer* be reconciled with its finding 'majority sentiments about the morality of homosexuality'[15] a rational basis for a criminal prohibition of same-sex oral or anal intercourse[16] in *Hardwick*? Justice Scalia's scathing dissent points out the *Romer*

---

[10] Challenges to President Clinton's version of the ban on gay, lesbian, and bisexual military personnel have begun to reach federal courts of appeals. See *Thomasson* v. *Perry*, 80 F 3d 915 (4th Cir 1996) (en banc, 9-4) (cert. petition filed) (ban does not violate First Amendment and has a rational basis); *Able* v. *US*, 880 F Supp 968 (EDNY 1995), vacated and remanded, 88 F 3d 1280 (2d Cir 1996). In *Able*, a unanimous Second Circuit panel held that the 'statements' branch of the ban (10 USCA s. 654(b)(2)) does not violate the First Amendment and that same-sex sexual activity can rationally be presumed from an 'I am gay/lesbian/bisexual' statement. However, it ordered the District Court to consider the constitutionality of the 'acts' branch of the ban (10 USCA s. 654(b)(1)), upon which the constitutionality of the 'statements' branch depends.

[11] Although the Hawaii Supreme Court's final decision in *Baehr* v. *Lewin* (not expected before late 1997) cannot be appealed to the US Supreme Court, refusals by other states to recognize any resulting Hawaii same-sex marriages could be, and would require an interpretation of the Full Faith and Credit Clause (US Constitution, Article IV). As of July 1996, 15 states had passed legislation seeking to prevent recognition, and the federal House of Representatives had passed the 'Defense of Marriage Act of 1996', purporting to remove any obligation on states to recognize, and defining marriage as opposite-sex only for the purposes of federal law. See [1996] *Lesbian/Gay Law Notes* 102. Two important contributions to the US same-sex marriage debate are William Eskridge, *The Case for Same-Sex Marriage: From Sexual Liberty to Civilized Commitment* (New York: The Free Press, 1996), and Andrew Sullivan, *Virtually Normal: An Argument About Homosexuality* (New York: Knopf, 1995). In *Shahar* v. *Bowers*, 70 F 3d 1218 (11th Cir 1995), vacated and rehearing en banc ordered, 78 F 3d 499 (11th Cir 1996) (en banc), the Eleventh Circuit panel held that a public employer's withdrawing a job offer because the plaintiff had entered into a religious (Reconstructionist Jewish) same-sex marriage burdened her federal constitutional right of intimate association and required strict scrutiny.

[12] 134 L Ed 2d at 865–6. The amendments in *Reitman* v. *Mulkey*, 387 US 369 (1967), and *Hunter* v. *Erickson*, 393 US 385 (1969), were comparable to Amendment 2, except that they were confined to discrimination in housing and did not expressly mention the targeted group (African-Americans).

[13] The *Hardwick* majority effectively told gay, lesbian, and bisexual persons seeking protection against discrimination to look, not to the Supreme Court, but to legislatures. Amendment 2 and others like it were designed to block access to state and local legislatures. This must have struck the *Romer* majority as going too far.

[14] *US Department of Agriculture* v. *Moreno*, 413 US 528 at 534 (1973).

[15] *Hardwick*, 478 US at 196.

[16] The Tennessee prohibition (see Appendix III) appears to have been judicially invalidated by the Tennessee Supreme Court. See *Campbell* v. *Sundquist*, 1996 Tenn App LEXIS 46 (Tenn Ct App), permission to appeal denied and publication recommended, [1996] *Lesbian/Gay Law Notes* 91 (Tenn 10 June 1996).

majority's failure to cite *Hardwick* or attempt a reconciliation.[17] I would agree with Justice Scalia that *Romer* and *Hardwick* are inconsistent, but would propose a different solution: the overruling of *Hardwick* and the extension of the right of privacy to decisions about sexual orientation or sexual activity. By relying on rational basis review, which can be invoked by any group (whether they be hippies or optometrists), and stressing the uniqueness of Amendment 2, the *Romer* majority could be said to have maintained the Court's record of providing no protection against sexual orientation discrimination *per se*.[18] Like First Amendment protection, the protection in *Romer* does not depend on there being anything 'special' about sexual orientation, or any feature it shares with race, religion or sex, that would warrant heightened protection beyond the First Amendment and the basic requirement of rationality. Indeed, the *Romer* majority's use of rational basis review avoided the larger issue raised by the case and addressed in this book: should discrimination based on sexual orientation be treated like discrimination based on race, religion or sex?[19]

In Europe, the European Court of Human Rights decided no cases of sexual orientation discrimination, but the European Commission of Human Rights decided two age of consent cases and one same-sex couple case, and received a military employment case.[20] In *H.F.* v. *Austria*, the Commission followed *Zukrigl* and again upheld Austria's unequal age of consent, but the facts made the case an extremely poor one in which to raise the issue. The sexual activity appeared to have been 'against the will' of the 15-year-old male, who was an employee of the applicant and under his authority.[21] By contrast, in *Sutherland* v. *UK*,[22] brought by a 17-year-old gay male challenging the UK's unequal age of consent, the Commission declared the application admissible, the first time since 1977 it has done so in a case of sexual orientation discrimination (not involving blanket criminalization of male-male sexual activity). It remains to be

---

[17] 134 L Ed 2d at 871–3. The majority's sole attempt to do so was its description of Amendment 2 as a 'status-based enactment'. Ibid. at 868.

[18] See infra pp. 87–8.

[19] Cf. *Nabozny* v. *Podlesny*, 1996 US App LEXIS 18866 (7th Cir) (public school officials' alleged failure to protect openly gay student who was assaulted and harassed by other students for years, if proved, would fail both heightened scrutiny, as sex discrimination, and rational basis review, as sexual orientation discrimination).

[20] The Court will soon decide the sado-masochistic sexual activity case of *Laskey, Jaggard, & Brown* v. *UK* (Nos. 21627/93, 21826/93, 21974/93) (Commission's report of 26 Oct. 1995 found no violation of Article 8, 'private life', by 11–7) (Court hearing on 21 Oct. 1996), and the female-to-male transsexual father case of *X, Y and Z* v. *UK* (No. 21830/93) (Commission's report of 27 June 1995 found a violation of Article 8, 'family life', by 13–5) (Court hearing on 27 Aug. 1996). In *X, Y and Z*, at paras 53–8, the Commission effectively distinguished the family in *Kerkhoven* v. *Netherlands* as lacking a person with the appearance of a man. See infra p. 111. In *Reiss* v. *Austria* (No. 23953/94) (6 Sept. 1995), unpublished, an 'obscenity' case very similar to *Scherer* v. *Switzerland*, the Commission declared the application inadmissible under Article 8, 'private life', but Article 10 had not been argued. See infra p. 115.

[21] (No. 22646/93) (26 June 1995), unpublished at p. 8.

[22] (No. 25186/94) (21 May 1996), unpublished.

seen whether the Commission will note the shift in 'European consensus' on the age of consent[23] and find a violation of Article 8 or 14. Whatever the outcome, the case is likely to be referred to the Court. In *Röösli* v. *Germany*,[24] where a same-sex partner was denied the right of an opposite-sex partner to succeed to the tenancy of his deceased male partner's apartment, the Commission declared the application inadmissible in a decision virtually identical to that in *Simpson* v. *UK*. The Commission said nothing about whether 'European consensus' on the treatment of same-sex couples had changed between 1986 and 1996. Finally, applications by Jeanette Smith, Duncan Lustig-Prean, Graeme Grady, and John Beckett will give the Commission the chance to revisit the UK's ban on gay, lesbian, and bisexual military personnel.[25]

As of 27 August 1996, the number of Council of Europe member states had risen to thirty-nine, with the admission of Albania, Macedonia, Moldova, Russia, and Ukraine. This means that the jurisdiction of the European Court of Human Rights will soon extend from Reykjavik to Istanbul to Vladivostok and cover a population of over 700,000,000. This will increase both the political difficulty of achieving a 'European consensus' on any particular issue, and the logistical difficulty of demonstrating that such a consensus exists. Surveying the laws of thirty-nine linguistically diverse countries is an arduous task even for the most enthusiastic comparative lawyer. Nonetheless, there is evidence of a continuing shift in 'European consensus' in a number of areas.[26] Iceland adopted a Scandinavian-style registered partnership law in June 1996, and Hungary granted same-sex couples the same rights as opposite-sex common-law couples in May 1996.[27] Finland, Slovenia, and Spain have enacted anti-discrimination legislation (see update to Appendix II below).

A potentially very important development affecting 'European consensus' could emanate from the European Court of Justice (ECJ) in Luxembourg, which will soon be asked to interpret European Community sex discrimination law as requiring all fifteen European Union member states to prohibit sexual orientation discrimination in employment. The argument that European Community sex discrimination law prohibits sexual orientation discrimination (which is essentially the same as the sex discrimination argument discussed in Chapter 8), has always been a possibility.[28] But its viability increased greatly on 30 April 1996 when the ECJ held, in *P.* v. *S. & Cornwall County Council*,[29] that the Equal

---

[23] See infra pp. 134–5.   [24] (No. 28318/95) (15 May 1996), unpublished.

[25] See infra pp. 109–10, 123–4. The applications arise out of *R.* v. *Ministry of Defence, ex parte Smith*, [1995] 4 All ER 427 (Div Ct), aff'd (1995), [1996] 1 All ER 257 (CA).

[26] It would appear that potential member Belarus decriminalized same-sex sexual activity in 1991, that Moldova did so in 1995, and that Macedonia has undertaken to do so by the end of 1996. See National Danish Organization for Gays and Lesbians, *Euro-Letter*, No. 34 (July 1995), No. 41 (May 1996), No. 43 (Aug. 1996).

[27] *Euro-Letter*, No. 42 (June 1996). See infra p. 112, n. 134; Council of Europe (Venice Commission), *Bulletin on Constitutional Case-Law* (1995, No. 1), pp. 43–4.

[28] See infra p. 128, n. 54.   [29] Case C-13/94, [1996] IRLR 347.

Treatment Directive's prohibition of 'discrimination on grounds of sex' applies to the dismissal of a transsexual person 'for a reason related to a gender re-assignment'. The first case to test the 'sexual orientation discrimination is sex discrimination' argument under EC law has been referred to the ECJ. *Grant* v. *South-West Trains Ltd*[30] concerns the denial of an employment benefit to the female partner of a female employee, where the female partner of a male employee (not married to his partner) would receive the benefit. A second case, a challenge by Terence Perkins to the UK's ban on gay, lesbian, and bisexual military personnel, could also be referred (by the Divisional Court) in early 1997.[31]

In Canada, no case of sexual orientation discrimination[32] has reached the Supreme Court since *Egan* v. *Canada*. The appeal to the Ontario Court of Appeal in *Layland* v. *Ontario*, a same-sex marriage case, was stayed indefinitely after *Egan*.[33] There was no appeal in *R.* v. *M. (C.)*,[34] in which the Ontario Court of Appeal used Section 15(1) of the Charter to strike down the Criminal Code's unequal age of consent to anal intercourse (18 vs. 14 for all other sexual activity). But leave to appeal has been sought in *Vriend* v. *Alberta*,[35] in which the Alberta Court of Appeal declined to follow *Haig* v. *Canada*[36] and held that the omission of 'sexual orientation' from Alberta's human rights (anti-discrimination) legislation does not violate Section 15(1). The Supreme Court may decide to resolve the conflict between *Vriend* and *Haig* and determine whether the Charter requires Alberta, Newfoundland, Prince Edward Island, and the Northwest Territories to amend their legislation. Apart from the problem of reliance on *Haig* since 1992, any decision in *Vriend* would not affect the Canadian Human Rights Act (CHRA), into which the federal Parliament finally inserted 'sexual orientation' in 1996 (see update to Appendix II below).

Lower courts and human rights tribunals are continuing to deal with the Supreme Court's ambiguous decision in *Egan* v. *Canada*: distinctions between same-sex couples and unmarried opposite-sex couples are 'discrimination' based on sexual orientation, contrary to Section 15(1), but can be justified under Section 1.[37] There seems to be no dispute that *Egan* resolved the 'discrimination' issue, both under Section 15(1) of the Charter and under human rights legislation

---

[30] (19 July 1996), Case No. 1784/96 (Southampton Industrial Tribunal).

[31] Sedley J. granted Perkins leave to seek judicial review on 3 July 1996.

[32] See the first two books on Canadian law on this topic: Donald Casswell, *Lesbians, Gay Men and Canadian Law* (Toronto: Emond Montgomery, 1996), and Yogis, Duplak & Trainor, *Sexual Orientation and Canadian Law: An Assessment of the Law Affecting Lesbian and Gay Persons* (Toronto: Emond Montgomery, 1996).

[33] *Xtra* (8 Dec. 1995) 1.

[34] (1995), 98 CCC (3d) 481 (Ont CA). One judge found (indirect) sexual orientation discrimination and two found age discrimination. See infra pp. 235–6.

[35] (1996), 132 DLR (4th) 595 (Alta CA).

[36] See infra pp. 223–4. *Haig* was followed in *Newfoundland (Human Rights Commission)* v. *Newfoundland (Minister of Employment and Labour Relations)* (1995), 127 DLR (4th) 694 (Nfld Sup Ct).

[37] See infra pp. 254–60. See also Robert Wintemute, 'Discrimination Against Same-Sex Couples: Sections 15(1) and 1 of the Charter: *Egan* v. *Canada*' (1995) 74 Can. Bar Rev. 682.

that includes 'sexual orientation'.[38] But courts and tribunals are reaching different conclusions as to whether *Egan* can be distinguished, and whether the discrimination can be justified under Section 1 of the Charter[39] or comparable provisions of human rights legislation.[40] In the area of freedom of expression, *Little Sisters Book and Art Emporium* v. *Canada (Minister of Justice)* held that repeated seizures by customs officials of books bound for a lesbian and gay bookstore violated Sections 2(b) and 15(1) of the Charter.[41]

At the global level, the United Nations Human Rights Committee has not yet had a chance to apply or extend *Toonen* v. *Australia*. But commentary on the implications of *Toonen* has begun to grow.[42] As for the 'global census' of constitutions and legislation in Appendix II, the inclusion of 'sexual orientation' in the equality provision of the final South African Constitution leads the list of additions:[43]

[38] See e.g. *Vogel* v. *Manitoba* (1995), 126 DLR (4th) 72 (Man CA) (case referred to adjudicator to determine existence of 'bona fide and reasonable cause', under Manitoba legislation, for denial of employment benefits to employee's same-sex partner). See also *Korn* v. *Potter* (1996), 134 DLR (4th) 437 (BCSC), aff'g (1995), 23 CHRR D/319 (BCCHR) (doctor's denial of donor insemination, a service, to lesbian couple violated British Columbia legislation); *Oliver* v. *Hamilton (City) (No. 2)* (1995), 24 CHRR D/298 (Ont HRC) (mayor's refusal to issue Lesbian and Gay Pride Week proclamation was denial of a service, contrary to Ontario legislation).

[39] See e.g. *Rosenberg* v. *Canada (Attorney General)* (1995), 127 DLR (4th) 738 (Ont Ct Gen Div) (challenge to opposite-sex definition of 'spouse' in federal Income Tax Act; *Egan* indistinguishable); *M.* v. *H.* (1996), 132 DLR (4th) 538 (Ont Ct Gen Div) (challenge to similar definition in Ontario legislation on support obligations; *Egan* distinguished because dispute between private parties, a divorcing female-female couple). See also *Re K. & B.* (1995), 125 DLR (4th) 653 (Ont Ct Prov Div) (striking down, pre-*Egan*, a similar definition in Ontario legislation that prevented lesbian co-parents from adopting their female partners' biological children). Cf. the new British Columbia Adoption Act, SBC 1995, c. 4, s. 5(1): 'A child may be placed for adoption with one adult or two adults jointly.'

[40] In *Moore* v. *Canada (Treasury Board)* (13 June 1996), [1996] CHRD No 8 (QUICKLAW) (Can HRC), the tribunal held that the denial of certain benefits to the same-sex partners of federal government employees violated the CHRA. At paras. 79–82, it distinguished *Egan* as a Charter case and as a case of 'discretionary social benefits'. With regard to 'earned' employment benefits, '[t]he government . . . can no more rely upon [Section 1] . . . than can a private employer who is federally regulated'.

[41] (1996), 131 DLR (4th) 486 (BCSC). See also *McAleer* v. *Canada (Human Rights Commission)* (1996), 132 DLR (4th) 672 (FCTD) (telephone message likely to expose gay, lesbian, and bisexual persons to hatred violated CHRA s. 13(1)).

[42] See Laurence Helfer and Alice Miller, 'Sexual Orientation and Human Rights: Toward a United States and Transnational Jurisprudence' (1996) 9 Harv. Hum. Rts. J. 61; Douglas Sanders, 'Getting Lesbian and Gay Issues on the International Human Rights Agenda' (1996) 18 Hum. Rts. Q. 67; Brenda Thornton, 'The New International Jurisprudence on the Right to Privacy: A Head-On Collision with *Bowers* v. *Hardwick*' (1995) 58 Albany L. Rev. 725; James Wilets, 'Using International Law to Vindicate the Civil Rights of Gays and Lesbians in United States Courts' (1995) 27 Colum. Hum. Rts. L. Rev. 33; Sarah Joseph, 'Gay Rights Under the ICCPR—Commentary on *Toonen* v. *Australia*' (1994) U. Tasmania L. Rev. 392; Wayne Morgan, 'Identifying Evil For What It Is: Tasmania, Sexual Perversity and the United Nations' (1994) 19 Melbourne U. L. Rev. 740; James Wilets, 'International Human Rights Law and Sexual Orientation' (1994) 18 Hastings Int'l & Comp. L. Rev. 1.

[43] Article 26(2) of the 19 June 1996 draft of Poland's new Constitution includes '*orientację seksualną*'. In Ireland, the *Report of the Constitution Review Group* (May 1996) recommends (at p. 230) the addition to Article 40.1 of the Constitution a list of prohibited grounds of discrimination,

Constitutions

South Africa—Constitution of the Republic of South Africa, 8 May 1996, Sections 9(3), 9(4) ('sexual orientation')

Legislation

Canada (federal level)—Canadian Human Rights Act, RSC 1985, c. H-6, ss. 2, 3(1), as amended by SC 1996, c. 14 ('sexual orientation')

Finland—Penal Code (as amended by Law 21.4.1995/578), c. 11, para. 9, c. 47, para. 3 (*'sukupuolinen suuntautuminen'* or 'sexual orientation')

New Zealand—New Zealand Bill of Rights Act 1990,[44] No. 109, s. 19, as amended by Human Rights Act 1993, No. 82, ss. 21(1)(m), 145, Second Schedule ('sexual orientation')

Slovenia—Penal Code (1 Jan. 1995), art. 141 (*'spolni usmerjenosti'* or 'sexual orientation')[45]

South Africa—Labour Relations Act, 1995, No. 66, s. 187(1)(f), Schedule 7, item 2(1)(a) ('sexual orientation')

Spain—Penal Code, Organic Law of 23 Nov. 1995, No. 10/1995, arts. 314, 511–12 (see also arts. 22(4), 510, 515(5)) (*'orientación sexual'*)

United States, Rhode Island—R.I. Gen. Laws (e.g.) ss. 11-24-2 to 11-24-2.2, 28-5-2 to 28-5-7.3, 28-5-41, 34-37-1 to 34-37-5.4 (added in 1995) ('sexual orientation')

Additional thanks are owed to Edwin Cameron in Johannesburg, Ronald Louw in Durban, Jamie Gardiner in Melbourne, Bruce MacDougall in Vancouver, Elizabeth Christopher in Bermuda, Pere Cruells in Barcelona, Rainer Hiltunen in Helsinki, and my colleague Birgit Friedl, who assisted with German materials. Finally, I would also like to dedicate this book to the memory of *mi querido amigo* Felix José Tovar of Judibana, Venezuela and New York City, and to his bereaved partner Brian McCarthy.

Robert Wintemute
School of Law, King's College, University of London
29 August 1996

---

including 'sexual orientation'. Denmark's legislation (see infra p. 266) was extended to private employment by the Law of 12 June 1996, nr. 459. See also Alon Harel, 'Gay Rights in Israel: A New Era?' (1996) 1 Int'l J. of Discrim. & the L. 261.

[44] I have not listed this Bill of Rights under 'Constitutions' because it does not give courts the power to invalidate a clearly inconsistent Act of Parliament. See 1990 Act, ss. 4, 6.

[45] See *Euro-Letter*, No. 42 (June 1996).

Preface

In this United Nations Year of Tolerance, today marks the fiftieth anniversary of the end of the horror of Nazi persecution in Europe, and the beginning of an international effort to achieve better respect for human rights. It is a fitting coincidence that I am writing the preface to a book about an aspect of human rights that remains controversial fifty years later.

This book is a revised and updated version of my University of Oxford D.Phil. thesis, which I began at Wolfson College and in the Faculty of Law in October 1987 and submitted in January 1993. It grew out of the *pro bono* work I did in New York in 1985 and 1986 for Lambda Legal Defense and Education Fund, Gay Men's Health Crisis, and Front Runners, and was indirectly inspired by three articles: Harvard Note (1985 US), Girard (1986 Eur), and Jefferson (1985 Can). Portions of Chapter 8 were first published in 'Sexual Orientation Discrimination as Sex Discrimination: Same-Sex Couples and the Charter in *Mossop*, *Egan* and *Layland*' (1994) 39 McGill Law Journal 429, 459–78.

Striving to keep up with developments relating to sexual orientation discrimination under the US Constitution *and* the European Convention *and* the Canadian Charter has made me feel at times like a circus performer trying to ride three galloping horses at once! I have attempted to 'state the law', based on developments of which I was aware and materials that were available to me, as of 31 December 1994. Selected developments in early 1995 have been incorporated where possible.

I would like to thank all those who assisted me in researching and writing this book. The greatest debt of gratitude is owed to my supervisor, Christopher McCrudden, who provided me with tremendous support, both academic and moral, and whose B.C.L. seminars on Comparative Anti-Discrimination Law helped me immensely. I am also very grateful to the Social Sciences and Humanities Research Council of Canada, without whose financial assistance the thesis would never have been undertaken, and to Barry Radick of Milbank, Tweed, Hadley & McCloy in New York, who stood behind my *pro bono* work, and supported me in many ways throughout my studies in Oxford. Thanks also to his current and former partners Stephen Blauner, Alexander Forger, Alan Kornberg, and Toni Lichstein.

Many people very kindly provided me with materials that were not available in the UK. I can only mention a few of them: the late Henry Haywood, Laurence Helfer, and Arthur Leonard (editor of the invaluable Lesbian/Gay Law Notes) in New York; Kees Waaldijk (whose help with Dutch legislation I particularly appreciated) in Maastricht; Steffen Jensen (co-editor of the extremely useful Euro-Letter) in Copenhagen; Ulrike Dreyer and Heike Niebergall in Passau;

Helmut Graupner in Vienna; László Rusvai in Budapest; Yizhar Tal in Tel Aviv; Andrew Fleming, Patricia Kosseim, and Michael McAuley in Montréal; Jean Gilbert, Philip MacAdam, and Svend Robinson in Ottawa; Monique Charlebois and Clayton Ruby in Toronto; Ken Steffenson in Winnipeg; Douglas Sanders in Vancouver; Joseph Arvay in Victoria; Juan Pablo Ordoñez in Bogotá; David Harrad and Toni Reis in Curitiba (Brazil). My colleagues Mads Andenæs and Leo Flynn assisted with Norwegian and Irish materials respectively.

Various people took the time to read and comment on the whole or parts of earlier drafts. For their very helpful comments I would like to thank Christopher McCrudden, my D.Phil. examiners Nicola Lacey and Colin Warbrick, my qualifying test examiners Eric Barendt and John Bell, and Nicholas Bamforth, Brian Bix, Donald Casswell, David Feldman, Laurence Helfer, Rosalyn Higgins, Peter Oliver, and Shauna Van Praagh. I am especially grateful to Laurence Helfer for our transatlantic correspondence about the European Convention and the International Covenant. Thanks to René Provost and Shauna Van Praagh for suggesting the title. I am indebted to John Whelan of Oxford University Press for his enthusiastic and unswerving support for this book, and to his colleagues Kristin Clayton and Nick Couldry for their work in editing and producing it. The friendship of Patricia Carnese, David Fagelson, and Felix Tovar has been a great help along the way. Finally, but most importantly, I would like to dedicate this book to my mother, my father, and my partner.

Robert Wintemute
School of Law, King's College, University of London
8 May 1995

Contents

Table of Treaties, Constitutions, Statutes, and Cases

I. UNITED STATES

A. Constitutions

1. Federal

2. State

B. Statutes

1. Federal

2. State

C. Cases

1. Federal Courts and Agencies

2. State Courts and Agencies

II. EUROPE

A. European Convention on Human Rights

1. Provisions

2. Cases

(a) European Court of Human Rights

B. Other Council of Europe Treaties

C. National Law of Council of Europe Member States

1. Constitutions

2. Statutes

(a) UK and Dependent Territories

3. Cases (European Community and National Law)

(a) UK

III. CANADA

A. Constitution

Table of Cases and Legislation

B. Statutes

1. Federal

2. Provincial and Territorial

C. Cases

I

Introduction

'I love you. What's wrong with that?' (Max speaking to Horst, who has just been shot dead by an SS guard at Dachau, in Act 2, Scene 5 of Martin Sherman's 1979 play *Bent*.)[1]

I. SEXUAL ORIENTATION AND HUMAN RIGHTS

What *is* wrong with two men or two women choosing to love each other, to express physically their love for each other, to live together, to raise children together? Is it not discrimination against gay, lesbian, and bisexual individuals because of their sexual orientation, rather than same-sex love, that is wrong? Should the right to be free from sexual orientation discrimination be recognized as a human right? Over the fifty years since the end of World War II in 1945, this question has been raised more and more frequently, in fora ranging from city councils to the United Nations, in an ever increasing number of countries (as diverse as Brazil, Iceland, Israel, Japan, New Zealand, Nicaragua, and South Africa), by representatives of the millions of gay, lesbian, and bisexual persons around the world[2] who are affected by this kind of discrimination. They are seeking to establish a general principle of human rights law: that discrimination based on a person's sexual orientation is prima facie wrongful and requires a strong justification.[3] The adoption of such a principle would place a heavy onus of justification on public and private actors practising such discrimination, requiring them to show in particular cases why it should exceptionally be permitted.

There are two main routes that can be taken in challenging sexual orientation discrimination and attempting to achieve recognition of a human right to be free from it. Perhaps the most obvious is the 'political route', which involves persuading legislators or governments to change the law, by repealing existing

---

[1] Sherman (1979 Other), 77–9. On Nazi persecution of gay and bisexual men, see e.g. Grau (1995 Other); Plant (1987 Other); Heger (1980 Other). Günter Grau discusses, at 86–130, the establishment of the *Reichszentrale zur Bekämpfung der Homosexualität und der Abtreibung* or Reich Office for the Combating of Homosexuality and Abortion (Grau's translation).

[2] If gay, lesbian, and bisexual persons form only one per cent of the world's population (which is the lower end of the typical one to ten per cent range of estimates), then there are over 50,000,000 gay, lesbian, and bisexual persons in the world, including children who will decide that they are gay, lesbian, or bisexual when they reach adolescence or adulthood. However, none of the three arguments considered in this book depends in any way on numbers. They can all be made whether there are 500,000,000 such persons in the world or 500.

[3] See also Heinze (1995 Other).

discriminatory legislation or by creating new legal protection against discrimination, such as by amending an existing national law or constitution or an international treaty. But marching on legislatures with banners and loudspeakers, or lobbying elected and appointed government officials behind the scenes, is not the only option. An alternative is walking into courthouses, armed with briefcases bulging with legal documents. This 'legal route' involves persuading national and international courts and human rights tribunals that a particular instance of sexual orientation discrimination violates *existing* human rights law, whether statutory, constitutional or international. To establish such a violation, the plaintiff must identify some general principle embodied in a particular human rights instrument (by which I mean a national statute or constitution or an international treaty), and argue that this principle applies to the particular instance of sexual orientation discrimination. (The 'political route' and the 'legal route' can, of course, be pursued simultaneously by a particular person or organization with regard to a particular issue.)[4]

In this book, I will focus on the 'legal route' to human rights protection, on its use under three human rights instruments, and on three of the most commonly used arguments for interpreting these instruments as prohibiting sexual orientation discrimination. I have chosen the legal route over the political one because, as a human rights lawyer, I am most interested in attempts to argue that an existing human rights principle applies to a case of sexual orientation discrimination and virtually compels a decision against the validity of the discrimination. Such arguments carry far more weight in the judicial arena, where decisions must be justified and consistency of treatment of similar cases is an important goal, than in the legislative arena, where the votes of legislators are not generally accompanied by written reasons and politically expedient compromises are more likely to prevail. The legal route is also particularly attractive to members of unpopular minority groups. Such groups will often be unable to influence the decisions of legislators, who may disregard arguments of principle and see support for the group as costing them more votes among the majority than the group can deliver. They may also feel free to found their decisions openly on prejudice or religious doctrines. This is especially true in the case of sexual orientation discrimination. Where a legislature fails to provide any relief (as in many states in the United States, or in Council of Europe countries such as the United Kingdom), gay, lesbian, and bisexual persons often turn to a national or international court or tribunal, where they hope that arguments of principle will be more likely to succeed.

---

[4] On the limitations of law reform, whichever route is pursued, see Bamforth (1996 Other). For an approach involving critical theory, see Stychin (1995 Other).

II. CHOICE OF HUMAN RIGHTS INSTRUMENTS

'Existing human rights law in every jurisdiction in the world' would clearly be an impossibly ambitious scope for this book. While attempting to mention important developments from as many countries as possible, I had to narrow the topic in two ways. First, I decided to focus on national constitutions and international human rights treaties, rather than on national legislation, because constitutions and treaties can be said to be a form of 'higher law' that stands above ordinary legislation. Where a national court or international tribunal has interpreted a constitution or treaty as prohibiting sexual orientation discrimination, a national legislature that is legally bound to comply with the decision (or effectively bound to comply because of its past practice of compliance or the threat of expulsion from an international organization) may find it difficult or impossible to have the constitution or treaty amended so as to override the decision. Where a national legislature disagrees with such an interpretation of its own legislation by a national court, it may more easily pass an amendment negating the interpretation, and only political rather than legal obstacles will prevent it from doing so.

Second, I had to choose from amongst the hundreds of national, federal, and state constitutions and international human rights treaties in the world. Why were the United States Constitution, the European Convention on Human Rights, and the Canadian Charter of Rights and Freedoms chosen, as opposed to other human rights instruments or only one of them? When I began my research in 1987, it was primarily in the United States, Canada, Western Europe, Australia, and New Zealand that the issue of prohibiting sexual orientation discrimination had been raised and received serious consideration. The prime candidates were thus the constitutions of the United States, Canada, and individual Western European countries, and the European Convention on Human Rights, there being then no comprehensive bill of rights in Australia or New Zealand.[5]

Of these, I chose the United States Constitution, not only because its Bill of Rights is one of the oldest and most influential in the world, but because by far the largest body of cases dealing with sexual orientation discrimination has been decided by US courts applying the federal constitution. (I will refer to developments under the constitutions of individual states of the USA where appropriate.)

---

[5] New Zealand has since adopted the New Zealand Bill of Rights Act 1990, No. 109. Legislation prohibiting discrimination based on sexual orientation (or a similar ground) has been enacted in 6 of the 8 Australian states and territories, and in New Zealand: see Appendix II. In New South Wales, the Anti-Discrimination Act 1977, No. 48, as amended by the Anti-Discrimination (Homosexual Vilification) Amendment Act 1993, No. 97, s. 3, Schedule 1, prohibits incitement of hatred on the ground of 'homosexuality'. At the federal level in Australia, the Human Rights and Equal Opportunity Commission Regulations, Statutory Rules 1989, No. 407 (21 Dec. 1989) permit the Commission to investigate complaints of 'sexual preference' discrimination in employment. Both Australia and New Zealand permit the same-sex partners of citizens or residents to immigrate. See Hart (1993 Other); and Stewart, B. (1993 Other).

I chose the European Convention on Human Rights, not only because it has the most effective enforcement mechanism of any international human rights treaty, but because the tribunals interpreting it have decided a significant number of cases of sexual orientation discrimination, and because its territorial application exceeds that of the constitution of any single European country. Indeed, it could be seen as the quasi-constitutional bill of rights of a nascent, quasi-federal Europe.[6] Finally, I chose the Canadian Charter of Rights and Freedoms (part of the Canadian Constitution),[7] not only because of my Canadian background, but also because it dates from as recently as 1982 (making it a relatively clean slate, open to new approaches), and because its text appears in many respects to be a hybrid of the US Constitution and the European Convention (making comparisons with those two human rights instruments particularly appropriate). Three human rights instruments were chosen rather than one, because comparing the success of different approaches to a single, novel question under different legal frameworks should help illuminate the relative strengths and weaknesses of these approaches. It is also interesting to compare the levels of protection provided by the three instruments against sexual orientation discrimination, and to attempt to explain any differences that might be found.

It must be acknowledged that the assumption underlying my initial choice of human rights instruments, that sexual orientation discrimination has not been addressed by legislatures or courts outside of the United States, Canada, Western Europe, Australia, and New Zealand, is no longer true. The spread of democracy and greater consciousness of human rights around the world since 1989 has been accompanied by a 'globalization' of the question of sexual orientation discrimination.[8] Several jurisdictions have adopted constitutions which include express prohibitions of discrimination based on sexual orientation: the Brazilian states of Mato Grosso and Sergipe in 1989,[9] the German *Länder* of Brandenburg in 1992

---

[6] See e.g. Eissen (1990 Eur), 138 (the Convention 's'analyse en un instrument international, certes, mais à contenu constitutionnel'; the Court is 'une sorte de juridiction quasi constitutionnelle au sens matériel—sinon formel—du terme'); Warbrick (1990 Eur), 1076, 1080; Warbrick (1989 Eur), 700, 702, 714, 722 ('limited analogy between the role . . . of the [US] Bill of Rights and the Convention'; 'proceedings before the Court increasingly resemble proceedings before a national constitutional tribunal'; the Court's interpretation of Art. 6, '[i]f pursued vigorously . . . will transform the Convention into a constitutional bill of rights'; 'a majority on the Court might want to . . . aspire to a supra-national or constitutional role'); Girard (1986 Eur), 6 ('[t]he Court, and to a lesser extent the Commission, are in a very real sense constitutional courts which apply a supra-national charter of rights to disputes between individuals and states'); Drzemczewski (1983 Eur), 33, 334 (the Convention is a 'novel form of common constitutional order' and a 'positive step towards the progressive creation of European Constitutional Law').

[7] See Appendix I for the full text of most of the provisions of the US Constitution, the European Convention, the Canadian Charter, and the International Covenant on Civil and Political Rights cited in this book.

[8] For information about specific countries, see Tielman and Hammelburg (1993 Other), 249–342; Amnesty International (1994 Other).

[9] See Appendix II. An attempt to add a similar provision to the federal constitution of Brazil in 1994 was unsuccessful: Dignidade, *News from Brazil* No. 2 (28 June 1994). At least 73 cities and towns in Brazil, including São Paulo, Rio de Janeiro, Salvador, and Brasilia, have laws prohibiting sexual orientation discrimination: see *The Washington Blade* (29 July 1994) 12.

and Thuringia in 1993,[10] and South Africa in 1993, which became the first country to include sexual orientation in the equality provision of its national constitution.[11] The phenomenon of legislation prohibiting sexual orientation discrimination in employment spread beyond North America, Western Europe, and Australasia to Israel in 1992.[12] And in 1994, courts in Colombia and Japan made decisions invalidating acts of sexual orientation discrimination. The Colombian Constitutional Court held that 'the condition of homosexual, by itself, cannot be a reason for exclusion from the armed forces [or the police]',[13] while the Tokyo District Court held that the Tokyo Board of Education's refusal to permit a gay and lesbian group to use a youth centre 'violated the spirit of human rights enshrined in the constitution'.[14]

By far the most important event in this recent 'globalization' was, however, the 31 March 1994 decision of the United Nations Human Rights Committee in *Toonen* v. *Australia*.[15] The Committee found that Tasmanian laws prohibiting all sexual activity between men violated the privacy provision (Article 17) of the International Covenant on Civil and Political Rights. I will analyse the decision and its implications at the end of Chapter 5. What is important to note here is that 128 countries had ratified the International Covenant as of 31 December 1994, including at least 82 in Asia, Africa, Latin America, and the Caribbean.[16] In all these countries, the potential now exists for gay, lesbian, and bisexual plaintiffs to invoke the International Covenant, as interpreted in *Toonen*, and argue before national legislatures or courts (or, in some cases, the UN Human Rights Committee) that particular kinds of sexual orientation discrimination are

[10] See Appendix II. The Constitutional Committee drafting Poland's new Constitution has proposed a prohibition of sexual orientation discrimination in Article 22(2). See *The Warsaw Voice* (23 April 1995) 18.

[11] See Constitution of the Republic of South Africa Act, No. 200 of 1993, s. 8(2). ('No person shall be unfairly discriminated against . . . on one or more of the following grounds in particular: race, gender, sex, . . . sexual orientation. . . .') Express inclusion prevailed over proposals that sexual orientation be implicitly included in 'natural characteristics', and occurred in spite of the continued criminalization of male-male anal intercourse. See Cameron (1993 Other), 453–4, 465–9. Express inclusion could theoretically be deleted from the final constitution to be adopted by 1996, which need only give 'due consideration to . . . the fundamental rights contained in [the interim] Constitution' and 'prohibit racial, gender and all other forms of discrimination': Constitution, ss. 71(1) and 73(1) and Schedule 4 (II, III).

[12] See Equal Opportunities in Employment Act 1988, s. 2(a), as amended by Israel Book of Laws, No. 1377 of 2 Jan. 1992. In *El Al Airlines Ltd.* v. *Jonathan Danilowitz* (30 Nov. 1994), No. HCJ 721/94, the Supreme Court of Israel interpreted this statute as requiring an airline to provide the same free flight benefits to same-sex and opposite-sex partners of its employees: see [1995] *Lesbian/Gay Law Notes* 7 (analysis by Alon Harel).

[13] See *J.* v. *Director de la Escuela de Carabineros* (7 March 1994), Sentencia No. T-097/94, Corte Constitucional de Colombia (Sala Tercera de Revisión), [1994] *Revista Mensual* 611, 623. At 621, the court implied that same-sex sexual activity outside of army or police premises was permitted, but seemed to exclude openly gay, lesbian, and bisexual soldiers and police officers from its decision by stating that '[t]he condition of homosexual must not be declared or manifested' because 'discretion and silence with regard to sexual preferences' can be required (author's translations).

[14] See 'Tokyo court backs rights for gays' *The Independent* (31 Mar. 1994) 19.

[15] (Commun. No. 488/1992) (31 March 1994) (50th Session), UN H.R. Committee Doc. No. CCPR/C/50/D/488/1992, 1 I.H.R.R. 97.

[16] United Nations (1995 Other).

contrary to international human rights law. If sexual orientation discrimination was ever a human rights issue only in 'Western' or 'Northern' countries, that is most certainly not the case any more.

'Globalization' has not, however, given me second thoughts about my choice of human rights instruments. Notwithstanding the importance of the International Covenant after *Toonen*, and the potential of other national constitutions or international human rights treaties, the largest bodies of sexual orientation discrimination case law (published in English or English and French) are those under the US Constitution, the European Convention, and (since 1988) the Canadian Charter. Although I am focusing on three human rights instruments to give this book a manageable scope, the arguments I will be discussing should not be seen as necessarily limited to these human rights instruments. They could be applied to similar provisions of other national constitutions, other international human rights treaties (such as the International Covenant or the American Convention on Human Rights) or national legislation (especially legislation prohibiting sex discrimination).

III. CONCEPTS TO BE USED

A. *Sexual Orientation*

It should now be clear that the scope of the book could be described, with greater precision but at the expense of brevity, as 'Sexual Orientation Discrimination and Constitutional and International Human Rights Law'. I must now define the concepts to be used in examining this topic. The first of these is 'sexual orientation'. This term describes a complex phenomenon and has several senses, making its meaning uncertain and creating confusion as to which principles of constitutional or international human rights law are implicated by sexual orientation discrimination. But there are two main senses that are, in my view, most relevant for legal analysis. Used in (a) the *first sense*, a person's *sexual orientation* indicates whether, in deciding with whom to engage in 'emotional-sexual conduct', they are emotionally or sexually attracted to persons of the opposite sex (i.e. they are 'heterosexual'), persons of both sexes (i.e. they are 'bisexual'), or persons of the same sex (i.e. they are 'gay', if they are male, or 'lesbian', if they are female). This sense is applied to a person's *attraction*, without regard to their actual conduct, and will be referred to as the 'direction of their emotional–sexual attraction',[17] whether they perceive their attraction as unchosen or not. I should note here that I will use 'gay or lesbian' rather than

---

[17] See *The Oxford English Dictionary*, 2nd ed., vol. X (Oxford: Clarendon Press, 1989), 930–1 (an 'orientation' means the 'condition of being oriented'; 'to orient' means 'to assign or give a specific direction or tendency to'). Cf. Harvard Survey (1989 US), 1568 ('sexual orientation classifications are based on the direction of an individual's sexual and affectional attractions').

'homosexual', which (in my opinion) is irrevocably tainted by years of use in a pejorative sense and means nothing more than 'same-sex' (as 'heterosexual' means 'other-sex').

By *'emotional-sexual conduct'*, I mean any kind of activity or relationship involving two (or more) persons that has, or could be perceived as having, both emotional and sexual aspects or a purely sexual aspect, including private sexual activity, public displays of affection, and the formation of 'couple relationships'. By *'couple relationship'*, I mean an emotional and (at least initially) sexual relationship between two (usually adult) persons, which is intended to continue indefinitely, usually but not always involves living together and financial inter-dependence, may or may not be monogamous, and may or may not involve the raising of children. 'Emotional–sexual conduct' is a broad concept intended to encompass and unite the entire sphere of conduct of a sexual, or emotional and sexual, nature, in which the sexes of the (two or more) participants may cause the conduct to be treated unequally. I use it both to test the breadth of potential human rights principles, and attempt to identify one that is equally broad,[18] and to indicate that this sphere of conduct includes much more than private sexual activity. Thus, sexual orientation also involves the expression of emotions and the formation of emotional relationships,[19] i.e. it is about love as well as sex.

Apart from this single, colloquial use of 'sex' as meaning 'sexual activity', I will always use 'sex' as meaning 'biological sex'. I prefer to use 'sex' rather than 'gender', for two reasons. First, both Article 14 of the European Convention and Section 15(1) of the Canadian Charter use 'sex'. Second, although 'gender' may be merely a synonym for 'biological sex' to avoid confusion with 'sex' as 'sexual activity', it often has the different meaning of socially imposed 'sex role'. I find the latter meaning problematic because sex discrimination usually involves a distinction that is ultimately based on 'biological sex' and not on a socially imposed 'sex role' , e.g. 'male-gendered' biological women are not exempted from an exclusion of biological women from military combat.[20] Rather than being the basis of a distinction, a socially imposed 'sex role' is more likely to be invoked by a discriminator as a justification for a distinction based on 'biological sex'.

Used in (b) the *second sense*, a person's *'sexual orientation'* indicates whether the emotional–sexual conduct in which they actually choose to engage is with persons of the opposite sex (i.e. they are 'heterosexual'), persons of both sexes

---

[18] I would consider a human rights principle that could apply to sexual orientation discrimination affecting any kind of emotional–sexual conduct as superior to one that cannot, because I prefer the global application of a single principle to the piecemeal application of a variety of principles.

[19] The debate regarding the validity of sexual orientation discrimination tends to focus obsessively on same-sex sexual activity and ignore the fact that gay, lesbian, and bisexual persons are human beings who fall in love with persons of their own sex, just as heterosexual persons do with persons of the opposite sex.

[20] In single-sex situations, where comparison with a person of the opposite biological sex is impossible, the concept of social 'sex role' or 'gender' is useful. See Ch. 8, Part II.E.

(i.e. they are 'bisexual'), or persons of the same sex (i.e. they are 'gay' or 'lesbian').[21] This sense is applied to a person's *conduct*, without regard to the direction of their attraction, and will be referred to as the 'direction of their emotional–sexual conduct'. With respect both to the direction of a person's attraction and the direction of their conduct, there are essentially four possibilities:[22] heterosexual, bisexual,[23] gay or lesbian, or asexual/celibate. But there is no necessary connection between the direction of a person's attraction and the direction of their conduct.[24] And, as will be seen below, neither the direction of a person's attraction nor the direction of their conduct tells one anything about the 'content' of the emotional–sexual conduct the person may engage in; these directions reveal only the sex (or sexes) of the persons to whom the person in question is attracted, or with whom that person actually engages in such conduct.

There are, of course, *additional senses* in which '*sexual orientation*' can be used. Any statement that a specific person is heterosexual, bisexual, gay, or lesbian could refer to (a) the direction of the person's attraction, (b) the direction of their conduct (taken as a whole), (c) the direction of a specific instance of their conduct, or (d) their 'identity' (i.e. whether they consider that the direction of their emotional–sexual attraction or conduct serves in part to define them both as a unique individual and as part of a group or community of similar individuals). The addition of (c) and (d) further complicates the analysis, because there is again no necessary consistency among the four senses. For example, a married man who has just engaged in sexual activity with another man, does so frequently, and is primarily attracted to men, but considers himself heterosexual and frequently engages in sexual activity with his wife, might be gay under (a) or (c), bisexual under (b), and heterosexual under (d). I have decided to focus

---

[21] '[S]exual orientation . . . means the direction of sexual feelings or *behavior* toward individuals of the opposite sex (heterosexuality), the same sex (homosexuality), or some combination of the two (bisexuality) . . . The direction of sexual feelings is . . . less susceptible to change than the direction of sexual behavior': Levay (1993 Other), 105 (emphasis added). 'Sexual orientation has been interpreted as including all tendencies or directions taken by one's sexuality including the *behaviour* generated by the tendency': Bergeron (1980 Can), C/18 (emphasis added). Many courts and commentators, particularly in the US, use sexual orientation only in the first sense of 'direction of emotional-sexual attraction', and would use 'sexual conduct (or activity or behaviour)' to cover the second sense of sexual orientation. But see N. J. Stat. Ann. s. 10:5–5. hh.–kk. which defines 'affectional or sexual orientation' as including 'affectional, emotional or physical attraction or *behavior* which is primarily directed towards persons of the [other/same/either] gender' (emphasis added).

[22] Alfred Kinsey concluded that sexual orientation is a continuum, that it is arbitrary to use two or three categories, and that a 'seven-point scale comes nearer to showing the many gradations that actually exist': see Kinsey (1948 Other), 639, 657.

[23] See Weinberg, Williams, and Pryor (1994 Other). Where the direction of a person's conduct is bisexual, the direction of individual instances of conduct (involving two persons) will be either opposite-sex or same-sex, with the direction of persons who engage in both at different times being bisexual. 'Polygamous' emotional–sexual conduct involving three or more persons all of the same sex, or with both sexes represented, does not raise an issue of sexual orientation discrimination if all such conduct is treated equally.

[24] Thus, I will not use the terms 'heterosexuality' or 'homosexuality', because they fail to distinguish between the two senses of sexual orientation as 'direction of emotional–sexual attraction' and 'direction of emotional–sexual conduct'.

on (a) (attraction), and (b) or (c) (conduct, either taken as a whole or specific instances of it), as the more significant aspects of sexual orientation for the purpose of determining whether a constitution or human rights treaty implicitly contains a prima facie prohibition of sexual orientation discrimination. This is because attraction may be unchosen and conduct is almost always chosen. Although (d) identity is also chosen, the law usually seeks to regulate the conduct underlying an identity, or through which the identity is expressed, rather than the identity itself.[25]

With regard to sense (c), it is important to note that each specific instance of emotional–sexual conduct (e.g. a sexual act or a couple relationship) can also be said to have a sexual orientation, in that (if it involves two persons) it will necessarily be either opposite-sex or same-sex. Its sexual orientation is determined solely by the sexes of the participants, without regard to their individual sexual orientations (as direction of attraction or of conduct as a whole) or identities. Thus, it is much easier to categorize a specific instance of conduct as opposite-sex or same-sex than to categorize a person as heterosexual, bisexual, gay, or lesbian (unless they have categorized themselves).[26] Although it is an awkward distinction to maintain when speaking rather than writing, I will use the words heterosexual, bisexual, gay, and lesbian to refer to the sexual orientations of persons, and opposite-sex (male–female) or same-sex (male–male or female– female) to refer to the sexual orientations of acts or relationships. While the sexual orientations of the persons engaging in an act or relationship will often be the same as that of the act or relationship, this will not always be the case. This is especially true of sexual activity, but may also be true of couple relationships. For example, it is hard to describe two bisexual women (or men) who are partners as a 'lesbian (or gay) couple'.

I have included senses (b) and (c) because it is essential that a fully developed concept of 'sexual orientation' includes both emotional–sexual attraction and actual emotional–sexual conduct resulting from emotional–sexual attraction. Such a broad concept of sexual orientation is similar to a concept of 'religion' that includes both religious beliefs and religious practices that are motivated by religious beliefs. It will be seen below that sexual orientation discrimination may be directed both at persons (because of their actual or presumed attraction or their actual or presumed conduct) and at conduct. If a concept of sexual orientation that excludes conduct is used, it may be difficult to provide comprehensive protection against sexual orientation discrimination.

---

[25] Many commentators would argue that 'identity' is the legally significant sense of 'sexual orientation': see e.g. Halley (1989 US). I find the concept too broad because I cannot see any way to limit a principle that 'discrimination affecting an important aspect of an individual's identity is *prima facie* wrongful'. If an individual can choose any identity, on what basis could protection be limited to certain 'legitimate' identities rather than all identities? I also find it too narrow because a person may experience discrimination based on a particular characteristic (e.g. sexual orientation), yet not see that characteristic as a part of their identity at all. See Harvard Note (1989 US), 621–3.

[26] See Boswell (1980 Other), 41–3, 58–9.

As for the conflicting answers that the four senses may yield in the case of a specific person, a court or tribunal can usually ignore the conflict.[27] This is because a discriminator will often have no knowledge of (a), (b), (c) or (d), and will base their decision whether or not to discriminate on (e) their perception of the person's sexual orientation (e.g. in a job interview). Thus, it makes no difference how a discriminator defines a person's sexual orientation, or whether their definition or perception is consistent with that person's self-identified sexual orientation. All that matters is that the discriminator has treated the person less favourably, because they consider the person to be of one sexual orientation, than if they had considered the person to be of another sexual orientation.

B. Sexual Orientation Discrimination

The second concept that needs to be clarified is that of 'sexual orientation discrimination'. The concept itself can easily be described by using the terminology associated with Great Britain's Sex Discrimination Act 1975 and Race Relations Act 1976 (section 1(1) of both Acts). One person may discriminate *directly* against another person either because of the sexual orientation (as direction of attraction or of conduct as a whole) of the other person, or because of the sexual orientation of a specific instance of emotional–sexual conduct in which the other person has engaged. This will involve treating the other person less favourably than persons of another sexual orientation, or than persons who have engaged in a specific instance of emotional–sexual conduct of another sexual orientation. One person may also discriminate *indirectly* against another person by applying a neutral requirement (other than being of a particular sexual orientation) with which a disproportionate number of persons of the other person's sexual orientation are unable to comply, and which cannot be justified.

I will focus primarily on examples of *direct discrimination* (disparate treatment in the US; express discrimination or denial of formal equality in Canada), rather than *indirect discrimination* ('disparate impact' in the US; 'adverse effect' discrimination or denial of substantive equality in Canada: hereinafter I will mainly use the terms 'direct' and 'indirect').[28] This is not because the concepts of indirect discrimination and substantive equality are less relevant to the gay, lesbian, and bisexual minority than to women and ethnic or religious minorities. Rather, it is because, unlike women and racial, ethnic, or religious minorities, whose main concern with regard to legislation and government policies (as opposed to employment and other decisions by individual government officials) tends to be indirect rather than direct discrimination (at least in the US, Canada,

---

[27] The conflict would only need to be resolved in cases of indirect (disparate impact or adverse effect) discrimination where a plaintiff had to show that they belonged to the disproportionately affected group.

[28] The absence of a common vocabulary for concepts of 'discrimination' makes it difficult to discuss them across several jurisdictions.

and Western Europe), the gay, lesbian, and bisexual minority still faces a tremendous amount of legislation that discriminates directly on the basis of sexual orientation (broadly defined as including direction of conduct), and many litigated cases of sexual orientation discrimination involve direct discrimination. Neutral rules that apply equally to all sexual orientations may well discriminate indirectly against (have a disproportionate impact on) gay, lesbian, and bisexual persons (e.g. the impact of a prohibition of opposite-sex and same-sex oral or anal intercourse). But challenges to indirect sexual orientation discrimination are likely to be taken more seriously once a prohibition of direct sexual orientation discrimination has been clearly established.

Sexual orientation discrimination must be distinguished from other interferences with 'sexuality' or 'sexual freedom'. The significance of defining sexual orientation as whether or not a person is heterosexual, bisexual, gay or lesbian, or whether a specific instance of emotional–sexual conduct is opposite-sex or same-sex, is that many general issues of 'sexuality' (i.e. a person's capacity to engage in emotional-sexual conduct and every aspect of their exercise of that capacity) or 'sexual freedom' may not involve any discrimination on the ground of sexual orientation. Thus, the law's treatment of such issues as paedophilia,[29] incest, prostitution, pornography, sado-masochism or polygamy may interfere with sexual freedom or constitute prima facie discrimination on other grounds (e.g. criminal prohibitions of paedophilia involve age discrimination but are easily justified by a child's inability to consent). But it does not raise an issue of sexual orientation discrimination, provided that all such conduct (or expression) is treated in the same way, whether it is opposite-sex or same-sex, or involves persons who are heterosexual, bisexual, gay or lesbian.

It is important to remember that sexual orientation (as I have defined it) is just one aspect (the direction, as between the sexes) of sexuality or sexual freedom.[30] As a result, sexual orientation discrimination may be prohibited without having to address every controversial aspect of sexual freedom, and without necessarily precluding legal regulation of aspects other than sexual orientation (e.g. the

---

[29] Advocates of discrimination against gay, lesbian, and bisexual persons often attempt to conflate same-sex sexual activity and adult-child sexual activity, which forces non-paedophile gay, lesbian, and bisexual persons (the vast majority) to distance themselves from all paedophile persons (heterosexual, bisexual, gay or lesbian). The consultative status of the International Lesbian and Gay Association (ILGA) at the United Nations Economic and Social Council was suspended on 16 September 1994, because it was alleged that one paedophile organization remained an ILGA member after the expulsion of three paedophile organizations (to preserve consultative status) in June 1994. See 'United Nations suspends international association' *Capital Gay* (23 Sept. 1994) 3. US legislation effectively requires the expulsion of such organizations from ILGA as a condition of US funding of the UN: see 22 USCA s. 287e (note, referring to Pub. L. 103–236, Title I, s. 102(g), 30 Apr. 1994) (US President must certify that no UN agency 'grants any official status . . . to any organization which promotes, condones, or seeks the legalization of pedophilia, or which includes as a . . . member any such organization').

[30] See Levay (1993 Other), 105 ('[o]ne way to categorize people's sexuality is along the dimension of sexual orientation') and 137 (['s]exual orientation and gender identity are just two aspects of human sexuality').

parties' ages or relatedness, consensual use of force, commercial sexual activity), each of which can be considered on its own merits. Similarly, sexual orientation discrimination does not include discrimination against transvestite or transsexual persons, because transvestism and transsexuality are not sexual orientations (as I have defined them). They involve choosing to dress in a way associated with the opposite sex, or choosing to change one's physical sex characteristics to those of the opposite sex and have the change legally recognized. But these choices are separate from the choice of the sex of the persons with whom one engages in emotional–sexual conduct.[31] Because these choices are separate, a transvestite or transsexual person may be heterosexual, bisexual, gay or lesbian (just as a paedophile or sado-masochist person may be heterosexual, bisexual, gay or lesbian).

Who is primarily affected by sexual orientation discrimination and in what areas of their lives are they affected? Clearly, such discrimination is aimed almost exclusively at gay, lesbian, and bisexual persons and same-sex emotional-sexual conduct (the only potential exceptions being isolated cases of discrimination against heterosexual persons by gay, lesbian, or bisexual employers or service providers in the private sector, or by any public or private sector 'affirmative action' programmes).[32] Nonetheless, I will use 'sexual orientation discrimination' as the relevant concept rather than 'gay, lesbian, and bisexual rights'. This is intended to suggest that prohibitions of such discrimination should be symmetrical, protecting not only gay, lesbian, and bisexual persons, but also

---

[31] I would argue that discrimination against transvestite or transsexual persons should be treated as a kind of sex discrimination or prohibited independently. Minneapolis, San Francisco, and Seattle have prohibited discrimination based on 'gender identity': see *The Washington Blade* (6 Jan. 1995) 25. See also *Underwood* v. *Archer Management Services Inc.*, 857 F Supp 96, 98 (DDC 1994) (dismissed transsexual woman could allege discrimination based on personal appearance, a prohibited ground in DC, but not sex or sexual orientation). The most common statutory definition of 'sexual orientation' is 'heterosexuality, bisexuality, or homosexuality': see Appendix II (Canada—Yukon Territory; New Zealand; US—Connecticut, DC, Hawaii, Massachusetts, New Jersey, Vermont, Wisconsin). Cf. Bergeron (1980 Can), C/18 ('sexual orientation', undefined in Québec, includes 'transsexuality'). 'Sexuality' is defined as including 'transsexuality' in South Australia and the Northern Territory, whereas 'sexuality' and 'transsexuality' are separate grounds in the Australian Capital Territory: see Appendix II. In Minnesota, 'sexual orientation' includes 'having . . . a self-image or identity not traditionally associated with one's biological maleness or femaleness': see Minn Stat Ann s. 363.01(45).

[32] The inclusion of gay, lesbian, and bisexual persons in such programmes is still relatively rare. See e.g. 'Diversity or Quotas? Northeastern U. [Boston] will accord gays and lesbians preferential treatment in hiring' *The Chronicle of Higher Education* (8 June 1994) A13. Some jurisdictions that prohibit sexual orientation discrimination in employment expressly exclude the possibility (e.g. California Labor Code, s. 1102.1(d)); others expressly permit it (e.g. Manitoba Human Rights Code, SM 1987–88, c. 45, s. 11). In addition to the general issue of the fairness of 'affirmative action' to non-beneficiaries, 'affirmative action' in the area of frequently invisible differences such as sexual orientation raises specific issues: how to determine (a) whether gay, lesbian, and bisexual persons are under-represented vis-à-vis their percentage in the local or national population; (b) who counts as a representative (only such persons who are open about their sexual orientation or any such person); and (c) what the sexual orientations of employees are (without invading their privacy). See Byrne (1993 US).

heterosexual persons. It is also intended to emphasize the importance of thinking of sexual orientation as a neutral, universal characteristic, with several different manifestations, rather than a phenomenon unique to gay, lesbian, and bisexual persons. Heterosexual persons need to be reminded that they too have a sexual orientation, and that theirs is not the only possibility. Just as there is more than one religion, political opinion, race or sex in the world, there is more than one sexual orientation.

The areas of the lives of gay, lesbian, and bisexual persons that are affected by sexual orientation discrimination are not confined to emotional–sexual conduct. Persons who desire to engage in, or actually engage in, same-sex emotional–sexual conduct will often be treated unequally in other areas of conduct (e.g. employment, civil marriage and associated rights, or parental rights). All such unequal treatment interferes with their choice of same-sex emotional–sexual conduct, but the degree of interference could be said to vary depending upon the kind of sanction used. Thus, sexual orientation discrimination could be divided into 'criminal law discrimination' (which seeks actively to prohibit, altogether or in certain circumstances, the choice of same-sex emotional–sexual conduct, or its depiction or discussion, through fines or imprisonment),[33] and 'all other discrimination' (which permits the choice but seeks to discourage it through other sanctions, such as failure to protect against violence or incitement to hatred, or denial of jobs, housing, public funding, benefits for a partner or custody of children). This division illustrates how the concept of 'sexual orientation discrimination' can cover, and unite under a common concept, apparently different kinds of discrimination. I prefer this unifying concept, and the subdivisions of 'criminal law discrimination' and 'all other discrimination', to the more common categorization of 'gay, lesbian, and bisexual rights' as 'privacy rights' and 'equality rights'.

Examples of 'criminal law discrimination' and 'all other discrimination' will be seen in the case law, legislation, and other decisions discussed throughout this book.[34] 'Criminal law discrimination' includes total prohibitions of sexual activity between men or between women, and discrimination as to the age of consent to such activity, the definition of when such activity is 'in private', and the severity of punishment when such activity is not 'in private'. It also extends to fines for public displays of same-sex affection and harsher application of 'obscenity' laws to gay, lesbian, and bisexual publications and other expression. 'All other discrimination' can be divided into 'other discrimination against gay, lesbian, and bisexual individuals or associations' (inadequate protection against violence or incitement to hatred, and discrimination in employment, housing, education or services), 'other discrimination against same-sex couples' (exclusion

[33] Anal intercourse was punishable by death in England, Wales, and Ireland until 1861, and in Scotland until 1889. See Crane (1982 Eur), 12.
[34] For a discussion of UK examples, see Wintemute (1994 Eur).

from marriage,[35] denial of the rights of married opposite-sex couples and of unmarried opposite-sex couples), and 'other discrimination against gay, lesbian, and bisexual parents' (discrimination in custody decisions or access to adoption, fostering, donor insemination or surrogate motherhood).

If one could establish that a particular constitution or human rights treaty implicitly contained a prima facie prohibition of sexual orientation discrimination, this general principle would apply to discrimination in all the many areas described above (at least to the extent that they involved a public sector actor). However, in each of these areas, the justifications that might be asserted for exceptionally permitting discrimination in that area would vary greatly (e.g. military employment versus child custody). Consideration of all these asserted justifications would go well beyond the scope of this book. Instead, this book will concern itself with attempting to establish a general principle of non-discrimination on the basis of sexual orientation in constitutional and international human rights law, capable of applying to every kind of sexual orientation discrimination, rather than with asserted justifications for specific exceptions to such a principle in relation to specific kinds of sexual orientation discrimination. Frequently raised justifications that might affect the choice of argument used to establish such a principle will, however, be considered in Chapter 9.

One final feature of sexual orientation discrimination is worth noting: the sexual orientation of gay, lesbian, and bisexual persons may often be 'invisible', thus allowing them to avoid many of the kinds of discrimination mentioned above. This is certainly true of their attraction and of their private sexual activity. And they may choose to refrain from '*public aspects of emotional-sexual conduct*' (e.g. public displays of affection, seeking legal or other public recognition of a couple relationship),[36] or from '*other public manifestations of sexual orientation*'[37] that would rebut the presumption that every person is heterosexual. These 'other manifestations' include any aspect of a person's appearance, manner or dress, or any statement (e.g. saying they are gay, lesbian or bisexual,[38] referring to a same-sex partner, or discussing a gay, lesbian or bisexual community event) or expressive act (e.g. displaying a picture of a same-sex

---

[35] All references to opposite-sex or same-sex marriage in this book are to civil marriage, not religious marriage. The freedom of religion provisions of human rights instruments would probably prevent legislatures from requiring religious institutions to marry same-sex couples. On evidence of early Christian liturgies for same-sex couples, see Boswell (1994 Other).

[36] US employers have dismissed, or withdrawn job offers from, persons who sought to marry a same-sex partner, civilly or religiously. See *McConnell* v. *Anderson*, 451 F 2d 193 (8th Cir 1971); *Singer* v. *US Civil Service Commission*, 530 F 2d 247 (9th Cir 1976); *Shahar* v. *Bowers*, 836 F Supp 859 (ND Ga 1993).

[37] 'Other public manifestations' are meant to cover conduct or statements that do not relate to another person who is physically present, and thus include ways in which an individual, rather than a couple, may be open about their sexual orientation. The same-sex couple examples straddle the two categories.

[38] Heterosexual persons never need to make such a statement because of the presumption that every person is heterosexual (which resembles the presumption, common in the US, Canada, and Europe, that every person is Christian).

partner or wearing a pink triangle)[39] that may be presumed to reveal (accurately or not) a person's sexual orientation (as direction of attraction or conduct). Most discrimination against them will be triggered by these 'public aspects' and 'other public manifestations', rather than their private sexual activity (the criminal law's interference with such activity being difficult to enforce).

What is remarkable about these 'public aspects' and 'other public manifestations' is how frequently heterosexual persons engage in them, and how such persons take their ability to do so, and therefore to be open about their sexual orientation, completely for granted. The inability of gay, lesbian, and bisexual persons to do so, and their feeling obliged to live their lives hidden 'in the closet' (e.g. never holding their partner's hand in public, or mentioning or introducing their partner to co-workers), constitutes a major cost of sexual orientation discrimination. Indeed, it renders such discrimination comparable to a form of 'apartheid', with the heterosexual majority enjoying the right to live openly, and the gay, lesbian, and bisexual minority denied that right. In short, they are neither to be seen nor heard. Full protection against sexual orientation discrimination would have to protect these 'public aspects' and 'other public manifestations'. Such protection could perhaps help break the vicious circle whereby fear of discrimination on the part of gay, lesbian, and bisexual persons prevents their being open with heterosexual persons, and thereby precludes the educative process that would increase understanding and reduce prejudice and discrimination.

C. Sexual Orientation Discrimination and Constitutional and International Human Rights Law

In asking how sexual orientation discrimination can be conceived of as an issue of constitutional and international human rights law, one is asking what the right to be free from such discrimination has in common with other human rights, and particularly with the rights to be free from other kinds of discrimination. Are there any general principles that can explain why certain kinds of discrimination are considered prima facie wrongful and such that they are permitted only in limited circumstances where they can be justified? Such a question arises whenever a court or a human rights tribunal must interpret a constitution or treaty's express open-ended guarantees of 'liberty', 'respect for private life', 'privacy', 'equality', or freedom from 'discrimination', in order to decide which kinds of discrimination the constitution or treaty permits and which it does not. Unlike a legislature, which is under no obligation to display any consistency in its decisions as to which grounds it includes in anti-discrimination legislation, and which is free to respond to political pressures on a purely *ad hoc* basis, a

---

[39] See *Boychuk* v. *H.J. Symons Holdings Ltd.*, [1977] IRLR 395 (EAT) (lesbian woman dismissed for wearing 'Lesbians Ignite' badge); *Xtra* (27 May 1994) 18 (gay and lesbian police officers in Toronto not permitted to wear pink triangles while on duty).

national court or international human rights tribunal should strive to provide a coherent, principled basis for finding that some grounds are prima facie prohibited and some are not.

When a court or tribunal is presented with a new ground, like sexual orientation, that is not expressly mentioned in a constitution or treaty, it needs to examine the traditionally prohibited grounds (e.g. race, religion, and sex) to determine what principles connect them, before it can apply those principles to the new case. The identification and justification of these principles (for one human rights instrument, let alone three) is a daunting and highly controversial task that lies outside the scope of this book. As a result, I have had to select the principles I consider appropriate from amongst the various candidates discussed in the case law or commentary dealing with the US Constitution, the European Convention, and the Canadian Charter.

The principles I have selected are: (1) governments should not make distinctions based on 'immutable statuses', such as race and sex, without a special justification; and (2) governments should not interfere with 'fundamental choices (or rights or freedoms)', such as religion, political opinion, and choices protected by the 'right of privacy' or the 'right to respect for private life', without a special justification. An additional principle, which either could be derived from principle (1) (if one accepted that sex is an immutable status) or could stand independently of principles (1) and (2) (if one did not accept principles (1) and (2)), is: (3) in particular, governments should not make distinctions based on sex, without a special justification. I realize that principles (1) and (2) (if not (3)) are controversial. Some readers may reject most of the arguments in the rest of this book, either because they reject these principles outright or because they feel that their selection must be justified at the outset. Although I believe the selection of these principles can be justified,[40] I could not do so with regard to all three human rights instruments without doubling the length of this book. Instead, I will ask readers to recognize principles (1) and (2) as amongst the leading candidates in human rights law, particularly US constitutional law. In Chapters 2 to 8, it will be seen that principle (1) is a criterion mentioned in 'suspect classifications' case law under the US Constitution (and could be argued under the European Convention and the Canadian Charter), principle (2) is an arguable generalization of 'right of privacy' case law under the US Constitution and of the express 'right to respect for private life' in Article 8 of the European Convention (and could be argued under the Canadian Charter), and principle (3) is found in 'suspect classifications' case law under the US Constitution and in the texts of both the European Convention and the Canadian Charter.

Applied to the phenomenon of sexual orientation, these three principles suggest

---

[40] I will attempt to do so, in the context of the Canadian Charter, in an article to be published in a Canadian law journal in 1996.

three arguments that a constitution or treaty contains a prima facie prohibition
of sexual orientation discrimination:

1. an *immutable status argument*: because many gay men and lesbian women
   believe that their sexual orientation (as direction of attraction) is unchosen,
   sexual orientation may be an 'immutable status' like race or sex.
2. a *fundamental choice argument*: because every person's sexual orientation
   (as direction of conduct) is chosen and is extremely important to their
   happiness, it may be a 'fundamental choice (or right or freedom)', like
   religion or political opinion, and come wholly or partly within a specific
   'fundamental right' such as freedom of expression, association or religion,[41] or a residual and more general 'right of privacy' or 'right to respect
   for private life'.
3. a *sex discrimination argument*: because the acceptability of the direction of
   a person's emotional-sexual attraction or conduct depends on their own
   sex, sexual orientation discrimination may be a kind of sex discrimination,
   like sexual harassment or pregnancy discrimination.

These three arguments (which are perhaps the most commonly used in challenges to sexual orientation discrimination brought under the US Constitution,
the European Convention, and the Canadian Charter) correspond to three different ways of looking at a person's choice of a particular instance of emotional–
sexual conduct, e.g. a man's choice of a couple relationship with another man.
An immutable status argument focuses not on the choice itself, but on the man's
reason for making the choice (e.g. his emotional–sexual attraction being partly
or exclusively to men), which arguably causes it not to be a choice for him. A
fundamental choice argument focuses not on the reason for the choice, but on
the choice itself and its importance to the man making it. A sex discrimination
argument focuses not on the reason for the choice, or the choice itself, but on
the basis on which the law determines who may make that choice without
risking criminal sanctions or the loss of various rights or benefits (i.e. a man
choosing a couple relationship with another man will not be permitted to marry
him; a woman choosing a couple relationship with a man will be permitted to
marry him).

Some readers may object that the names I give to these three arguments
('immutable status argument', 'fundamental choice argument', 'sex discrimination argument') do not correspond to the vocabulary used by courts or tribunals
under the US Constitution, the European Convention, and the Canadian Charter.
By using these names, I am attempting to describe categories of similar arguments that are used under these human rights instruments. Any argument that
emphasizes absence of choice with regard to sexual orientation, I would consider
an 'immutable status argument'. Any argument that emphasizes the importance

---

[41] See Mohr (1988 US), 189–91; Ryder (1990 Can), 80–81; Herman (1990 Can), 811 n. 88.

of, and the need to respect, choice, freedom, liberty or privacy in relation to sexual orientation, I would consider a 'fundamental choice argument'. Any argument that points out that the sex of the choosing person is the basis of almost all sexual orientation discrimination, I would consider a 'sex discrimination argument'. By giving similar arguments used under the different human rights instruments a common name, I am attempting to facilitate the comparison of these arguments and of the different instruments throughout the book, and especially in Chapter 9.

I will also occasionally classify arguments in a different way by referring to 'liberty' arguments and 'equality' arguments. A 'liberty' or 'pure liberty' argument is one which points to an interference with a protected freedom that could not be imposed on any person, and does not stress that the interference discriminates directly or indirectly against particular persons (in some cases, because any such discrimination may be difficult to establish). An 'equality' argument is either a 'discriminatory interference with liberty' argument (i.e. even if the interference with the protected freedom could be applied equally to all persons, this has not been done or an equally applied interference has an unequal impact) or a 'pure equality' argument (i.e. whether or not any protected freedom is affected, some right, interest or opportunity has been restricted on the basis of a prohibited ground of discrimination). A fundamental choice argument may be presented as a 'pure liberty' argument, a 'discriminatory interference with liberty' argument or a 'pure equality' argument, depending on whether the plaintiff wants to emphasize interference with a protected choice, discriminatory interference with a protected choice or use of a protected choice as a ground of discrimination in relation to a non-protected right, interest or opportunity. Immutable status and sex discrimination arguments may be presented as 'discriminatory interference with liberty' arguments or as 'pure equality' arguments, but not as 'pure liberty' arguments, there being no freedom to change an immutable status (including sex) which could be protected.

Finally, it should be noted that none of the three arguments is necessary where a national, federal or state constitution (such as those in South Africa and a number of Brazilian and German states)[42] or a national, federal, state or local statute expressly mentions 'sexual orientation'. But even though the initial hurdle of establishing the implicit inclusion of 'sexual orientation' is removed, there remains the problem of interpreting 'discrimination based on sexual orientation' and deciding exactly what it covers (e.g. discrimination against same-sex sexual activity or against same-sex couples). This problem is discussed throughout the book, but especially in Chapters 7 and 8.

---

[42] See Appendix II.

IV. STRUCTURE OF THE BOOK

I will devote two Chapters to each of the US Constitution (Chapters 2 and 3) and the European Convention (Chapters 4 and 5), and three chapters to the Canadian Charter (Chapters 6, 7, and 8). Chapter 2 will begin by examining the most commonly used kind of argument under the US Constitution (i.e. fundamental choice arguments). Chapter 3 will consider alternative immutable status and sex discrimination arguments, and assess the level of protection against sexual orientation discrimination provided by the US Constitution. Chapters 4 and 5 will follow the same format, with respect to the European Convention, as Chapters 2 and 3 with respect to the US Constitution, and Chapter 5 will close with an analysis of the UN Human Rights Committee's decision in *Toonen* v. *Australia*. Chapter 6 will examine the still very unsettled question of the criteria for identifying grounds of discrimination under Section 15(1) of the Canadian Charter, and the response of courts and commentators to date to the question of whether sexual orientation is an 'analogous ground'. Chapter 7 will consider, in a more general way than in Chapters 2 to 5, whether sexual orientation is an 'immutable status' or a 'fundamental choice' (assuming that those criteria could be adopted by the Canadian Supreme Court). Chapter 8 will undertake a detailed evaluation of a sex discrimination argument, in the context of the Canadian Charter, and assess the level of protection provided by the Charter. Finally, Chapter 9 will compare the merits of the three arguments and the levels of protection provided by the three human rights instruments. It will also consider whether one of the arguments is best overall, and whether there is any explanation for any differences in the levels of protection provided by the three instruments.[43]

---

[43] 'Ch. 2, note 1' refers the reader to a footnote in another chapter, 'note 1' to a footnote in the same chapter, and 'n.1' to a footnote within a cited publication.

The United States Constitution:
Fundamental Choice Arguments

I. INTRODUCTION

Before examining the ways in which gay, lesbian, and bisexual plaintiffs have argued for an interpretation of the US Constitution that would protect them against sexual orientation discrimination, it is appropriate to look back to the position from which they started. In 1960, so-called 'sodomy' laws prohibited all oral or anal intercourse, between men, between women, or between a man and a woman, in all 50 states and the District of Columbia.[1] (Laws of this type will hereinafter be referred to as 'oral or anal intercourse' laws. 'Sodomy', with its religious and highly judgmental connotation of an act that brought divine retribution in biblical times, could hardly be described as a neutral term.)[2] While this uniform, total prohibition of oral or anal intercourse (opposite-sex or same-sex) was similar to the laws in such common law jurisdictions as Canada, Australia, New Zealand, the UK, and Ireland (which generally prohibited all sexual activity between men, but not between women, and opposite-sex anal intercourse), it contrasted sharply with the position in the majority of Western European countries. By 1960 (indeed already by 1944), prohibitions of same-sex sexual activity (if they ever existed) had already disappeared in at least 12 of the 23 countries that would be members of the Council of Europe by 1989 (before its expansion to include Eastern Europe).[3] Thus, the whole of the US lay behind an 'iron curtain' of criminalization, with no state providing a counter-example of reform.

Although these oral or anal intercourse laws are rarely enforced, their exist-ence has been used by judges to justify many other kinds of sexual orientation discrimination,[4] such as in employment, services, or child custody,[5] and by

[1] See Rivera (1979 US), 949–51. The adoption by 8 states of prohibitions limited to same-sex oral or anal intercourse occurred only in the period from 1973 to 1989. See Hunter (1992 US), 538 n. 30. By 'oral or anal intercourse', I mean oral–genital contact or penile–anal intercourse.
[2] See e.g. *Commonwealth* v. *Wasson*, 842 SW 2d 487 at 511 (Ky 1992) (Wintersheimer J. dissenting) ('"sodomy" is derived from the biblical name of the city of Sodom which was destroyed by God for its perverse behavior').
[3] See Tatchell (1992 Eur), 139 (Belgium, Denmark, France, Iceland, Italy, Luxembourg, Nether-lands, Portugal, Spain, Sweden, Switzerland, Turkey).
[4] For surveys of such discrimination in the US, see Hunter, Michaelson, and Stoddard (1992 US); Harvard Survey (1989 US); and Rivera (1979 US), 1980–81 US, and 1985–86 US).
[5] See e.g. *Inman* v. *City of Miami*, 197 So 2d 50 (Fla Dist Ct App 1967) (holding constitutional an ordinance prohibiting a liquor licensee from knowingly employing 'a homosexual person', serv-ing liquor to such a person, or allowing such persons to congregate; its object was 'to prevent the

legislators to refuse to enact legislation prohibiting such discrimination. As a result, they have been the primary focus of persons challenging such discrimination in the US (as in other common law countries and in Council of Europe countries), their elimination being seen as essential to achieving progress in areas outside the criminal law. The process of legislative reform was perhaps initiated by the American Law Institute's tentative recommendation in 1955 that all private, consensual, adult sexual activity be decriminalized.[6] The first state to decriminalize oral or anal intercourse was Illinois in 1961, followed by Connecticut in 1969, and 20 states in the 1970s. After Wisconsin in 1983, the slow, difficult, state-by-state process of legislative reform ground to a halt, and no legislature repealed an oral or anal intercourse law until Nevada and the District of Columbia did so in 1993.[7] In an attempt to accelerate the process, gay, lesbian, and bisexual persons turned to the US Constitution. If the Supreme Court could be persuaded to interpret it as prohibiting the criminalization of oral or anal intercourse, it might be possible to have all remaining oral or anal intercourse laws struck down with a single constitutional blow. The remainder of this Chapter will consider how fundamental choice arguments have been used under the US Constitution, in challenging both oral or anal intercourse laws and other kinds of sexual orientation discrimination. Chapter 3 will examine use of immutable status and sex discrimination arguments, and assess the level of protection the US Constitution provides against sexual orientation discrimination.

II. USE OF FUNDAMENTAL CHOICE ARGUMENTS

In sexual orientation discrimination cases under the US Constitution, as under other human rights instruments, the first decision that faces a gay, lesbian or bisexual plaintiff is whether to frame the issue as one of 'liberty' (denial of a particular right to all persons) or one of 'equality' (discriminatory denial of a particular right to certain persons). If the plaintiff prefers or feels bound to invoke 'liberty', they will generally argue that the discrimination in question interferes with one of the express or implied 'fundamental rights' that the US Constitution guarantees to all persons in the US. Where a law affects a 'fundamental right', the Supreme Court will usually apply 'strict scrutiny' and require a showing that the law is 'necessary to promote a compelling government interest'.[8] If the plaintiff prefers or feels bound to invoke 'equality', they will turn instead to the doctrine of 'equal protection', under both the Fourteenth Amendment

congregation . . . of persons likely to prey upon members of the public by attempting to recruit other persons for [illegal] acts' of oral or anal intercourse); *Bottoms* v. *Bottoms*, 1995 Va. LEXIS 43 at *14 (illegality of female–female oral intercourse in Virginia is an 'important consideration in determining custody'; custody granted to child's grandmother rather than his lesbian mother).

[6] See Hunter, Michaelson, and Stoddard (1992 US), 128.

[7] See Rivera (1979 US); Hunter, Michaelson, and Stoddard (1992 US), 538–9; [1993] *Lesbian/Gay Law Notes* 18, 48, 75.

[8] See Nowak and Rotunda (1991 US), 370–1.

('[n]o State shall ... deny to any person ... the equal protection of the laws') and the Fifth Amendment.[9]

Equal protection doctrine consists of two branches ('fundamental rights' and 'suspect classifications') and three levels of scrutiny, depending on the type of right or interest that the law affects and on the classification that the law uses to identify the persons to whom it applies. If the right affected is 'fundamental' or the classification is 'suspect', the Supreme Court will apply 'strict scrutiny' and demand a showing that the law is 'necessary to promote a compelling government interest'. If the right or interest affected is 'important' or the classification is 'quasi-suspect', 'intermediate scrutiny' will be applied and the party defending the law will have to demonstrate that it is 'substantially related to an important government interest'. Finally, if the law affects no such right or interest and involves no such classification, 'minimal scrutiny' is employed, under which the law need only be 'rationally related to a legitimate state interest'.[10]

The fundamental choice arguments discussed in this Chapter include both (a) fundamental right arguments that are made in a pure 'liberty' form, primarily under the First Amendment or the doctrine of 'substantive due process' under the Fifth and Fourteenth Amendments; and (b) fundamental right arguments that are made in an 'equality' form under the 'fundamental rights' branch of equal protection doctrine under the Fifth and Fourteenth Amendments.[11] In either form, the argument that a particular fundamental right covers a particular instance of sexual orientation discrimination is essentially the same. Fundamental right arguments can be characterized as 'fundamental choice' arguments because the plaintiffs are claiming that a particular activity that is clearly chosen is conduct, expression, association or political activity of a kind that the US Constitution protects. They are not seeking (directly) to protect an unchosen status. The immutable status and sex discrimination arguments discussed in Chapter 3 are arguments made under the 'suspect classifications' branch of equal protection doctrine under the Fifth and Fourteenth Amendments. These arguments do not seek to protect a chosen activity, but rather an unchosen status.

Fundamental choice arguments are considered first because they have been the most frequently used by gay, lesbian, and bisexual plaintiffs relying on the US Constitution. The specific fundamental rights invoked have tended to be either (a) the 'right of privacy', a controversial implied fundamental right; or (b) other existing fundamental rights, including the First Amendment's express fundamental rights to freedom of speech and assembly and non-controversial

---

[9] The Fifth Amendment's Due Process Clause has been interpreted as containing an equal protection component that applies to the federal government. See *Bolling* v. *Sharpe*, 347 US 497 (1954).

[10] See generally Nowak and Rotunda (1991 US), 568–9, 574–6; *Cleburne* v. *Cleburne Living Center, Inc.*, 473 US 432 at 437, 440–2 (1985); Tribe (1988 US), 1439–43, 1610.

[11] On 'substantive due process' and 'equal protection', see generally Tribe (1988 US) chs. 8, 11, 15 and 16.

implied fundamental right to freedom of association, and an arguable implied fundamental 'right to participate equally in the political process'. Gay, lesbian, and bisexual plaintiffs have generally invoked the right of privacy where discrimination was based on their actual or presumed conduct (i.e. private same-sex sexual activity), and other existing fundamental rights where the discrimination affected some form of speech, assembly or association in a public setting (e.g. a gay, lesbian, and bisexual students' organization), or affected their ability to participate in the political process (i.e. to seek legislative protection against discrimination).

A. Use of the Right of Privacy

Until 1986, the 'right of privacy' was probably the most important of the fundamental choice arguments used by gay, lesbian, and bisexual plaintiffs. This is because many litigated cases of sexual orientation discrimination have challenged directly or indirectly the existence of oral or anal intercourse laws. Because these laws criminalize chosen conduct, rather than an unchosen status, gay, lesbian, and bisexual plaintiffs needed to argue that the US Constitution contains a fundamental right that is sufficiently broad to include this conduct. Because private sexual activity does not appear to be a traditionally protected form of expression or association, they needed to find a fundamental right outside the First Amendment. And because in most states these laws apply to all such intercourse, whether opposite-sex or same-sex, they often had to present their fundamental right argument in a 'pure liberty' (denial of the right to all persons) form, rather than in an 'equality' (discriminatory denial of the right to certain persons) form. They therefore generally turned to the Fifth and Fourteenth Amendments' prohibitions of deprivations of 'liberty . . . without due process of law' (i.e. to the doctrine of substantive due process), rather than to equal protection doctrine under those same amendments.[12] Since the 1960s, the US Supreme Court has used the doctrine of substantive due process to develop an implied fundamental right of privacy, shielding certain important decisions by individuals from government interference. In a series of four decisions from 1965 to 1977, the Court struck down laws prohibiting the use of contraceptives by married persons,[13] and their distribution to unmarried persons[14] or persons under 16,[15] as well as laws prohibiting the procuring of abortions.[16]

---

[12] Even where they did turn to equal protection doctrine before 1986, it was usually to the fundamental rights branch of that doctrine, rather than to its 'suspect classifications' branch.
[13] *Griswold* v. *Connecticut*, 381 US 479 (1965).
[14] *Eisenstadt* v. *Baird*, 405 US 438 (1972).
[15] *Carey* v. *Population Services International*, 431 US 678 (1977).
[16] *Roe* v. *Wade*, 410 US 113 (1973).

1. Extending the Right of Privacy

To gay, lesbian, and bisexual plaintiffs, it seemed a logical extension of the contraception and abortion decisions to hold that an individual's decision whether or not to engage in private, consensual, adult sexual activity (opposite-sex or same-sex) is protected by the right of privacy. Thus, a right of privacy argument seemed the most promising way of striking down oral or anal intercourse laws. Whether or not the Supreme Court would accept the argument would depend on whether its contraception and abortion decisions (as well as other decisions interpreted as implicating the right of privacy),[17] could be generalized to produce an implicit, residual right to make any 'fundamental' decision or choice not falling within an express constitutional guarantee (such as the First Amendment), or at least a right general enough to include decisions to engage in any kind of non-procreative sexual activity.

Two Supreme Court decisions in the 1960s gave little ground for optimism. In *Poe* v. *Ullman*,[18] the majority dismissed a challenge to the same law prohibiting use of contraceptives that was later struck down in *Griswold* v. *Connecticut*[19] (there having been no prosecution in *Poe*, as there was in *Griswold*). Justices Douglas and Harlan dissented in *Poe*, arguing that the law violated the plaintiffs' right of privacy. But Justice Harlan observed that 'laws forbidding adultery, fornication and homosexual practices . . . , confining sexuality to lawful marriage, form a pattern so deeply pressed into the substance of our social life that any Constitutional doctrine in this area must build upon that basis'.[20] As a result, '[t]he right of privacy . . . is not an absolute' and 'adultery, homosexuality, fornication and incest are [not] immune from criminal enquiry, however privately practiced'. Unlike sexual activity within opposite-sex marriage, '[a]dultery, homosexuality and the like are sexual intimacies which the State forbids altogether', 'which the law has always forbidden and which can have no claim to social protection'.[21] Indeed, Justice Harlan's distinction between opposite-sex marital 'intimacy' and 'extra-marital sexuality' was cited with approval by Justice Goldberg in *Griswold*, in asserting that the decision in *Griswold* 'in no way interferes with a State's proper regulation of sexual promiscuity or misconduct'.[22]

A similar abhorrence of same-sex sexual activity and persons engaging in it was displayed, two years after *Griswold*, in *Boutilier* v. *Immigration and Naturalization Service*.[23] There, a Canadian man living in the US admitted that he

[17] See *Moore* v. *City of East Cleveland*, 431 US 494 (1977) (grandparent-grandchild relationship); *Cleveland Board of Education* v. *LaFleur*, 414 US 632 (1974) (pregnant schoolteacher); *Stanley* v. *Georgia*, 394 US 557 (1969) ('obscene' material in home); *Loving* v. *Virginia*, 388 US 1 (1967) (marriage); *Skinner* v. *Oklahoma*, 316 US 535 (1942) (involuntary sterilization); *Pierce* v. *Society of Sisters*, 268 US 510 (1925) (parental control of child's education); *Meyer* v. *Nebraska*, 262 US 390 (1923) (same).
[18] 367 US 497 (1961).   [19] 381 US 479 (1965).   [20] Ibid. at 546.
[21] Ibid. at 552–3.   [22] 381 US 479 at 498–9 (concurring).   [23] 387 US 118 (1967).

was gay (i.e. he had engaged in sexual activity with other men three or four times per year, before and after his entry into the US) in response to government questions in connection with his application for US citizenship. The Court upheld a deportation order because, upon his entry into the US, he 'was a homosexual and therefore "afflicted with a psychopathic personality" and excludable under . . . the Immigration and Nationality Act of 1952'.[24] The majority found that 'Congress used the phrase "psychopathic personality" not in the clinical sense, but to effectuate its purpose to exclude from entry all homosexuals and other sex perverts'.[25] The 'alien' petitioner could not argue that the phrase was 'void for vagueness' because, at the time of his entry, 'he was already afflicted with homosexuality', and because he was not entitled to 'fair warning' of the consequences of his pre-entry conduct. 'Congress has plenary power to make rules for the admission of aliens and to exclude those who possess those characteristics which Congress has forbidden', such as Chinese persons[26] and 'homosexuals'.

In dissent, Justice Douglas, the author of the majority opinion in *Griswold*, argued that '[t]he term "psychopathic personality" is a treacherous one like "communist"' and 'is much too vague by constitutional standards for the imposition of penalties'.[27] Although '[t]he homosexual is one, who by some freak, is the product of an arrested development', many 'have risen high in our own public service . . . and have served with distinction. It is therefore not credible that Congress wanted to deport everyone . . . who was a sexual deviate, no matter how blameless his social conduct . . . nor how creative his work nor how valuable his contribution to society.'[28] To exclude every 'alien' who had ever engaged in same-sex sexual activity 'would be tantamount to saying that Sappho, Leonardo da Vinci, Michelangelo, Andre Gide, and perhaps even Shakespeare, were they to come to life again, would be deemed unfit to visit our shores'.[29] He concluded that Clive Boutilier was not 'afflicted' with psychopathic personality because his '[o]ccasional acts' were not a 'way of life',[30] but did not suggest that deportation might infringe his right of privacy.

In spite of these indications that the Supreme Court did not intend *Griswold* to protect extra-marital sexual activity, and especially not same-sex sexual activity, plaintiffs argued that an oral or anal intercourse law applying to married opposite-sex couples was contrary to *Griswold* and must be struck down, for the

[24] Ibid. at 118. The exclusion, which was supplemented in 1965 with 'or sexual deviation' (see Rivera (1979 US), 938), was only repealed in 1990. See Foss (1994 US).

[25] 387 US 118 at 122 (1967). An express exclusion of 'homosexuals or sex perverts' had been omitted: ibid. at 121.

[26] Ibid. at 123–4, citing *The Chinese Exclusion Case*, 130 US 581 (1889). Because of this plenary power, a Congressional decision to exclude same-sex partners of US citizens is subject only to 'limited judicial review', even if the US citizen's constitutionally protected rights are affected. See *Adams* v. *Howerton*, 673 F 2d 1036 at 1041–2 (9th Cir 1982).

[27] 387 US 118 at 125 (1967).

[28] Ibid. at 127, 129.   [29] Ibid. at 130.   [30] Ibid. at 133.

benefit of all choosing oral or anal intercourse. A three-judge federal district court accepted this argument in 1970 in *Buchanan* v. *Batchelor*, holding that the Texas oral or anal intercourse law 'is void on its face for unconstitutional overbreadth insofar as it reaches the private, consensual acts of married [opposite-sex] couples'.[31] The plaintiffs were two gay men (only one of whom had been prosecuted) and a married opposite-sex couple who feared prosecution.[32] On appeal, the Supreme Court declined to reach the merits and vacated the judgment on procedural grounds.[33] In 1974, the Texas legislature replaced the law with one applying only to same-sex oral or anal intercourse.[34]

Another three-judge federal district court reached the opposite conclusion in 1975 in *Doe* v. *Commonwealth's Attorney*.[35] The majority upheld Virginia's oral or anal intercourse law against a challenge by several gay men who feared prosecution, finding that Supreme Court precedents protect 'the privacy of the incidents of marriage, . . . the sanctity of the home, or . . . the nurture of family life',[36] and relying on the statements about 'homosexuality' in *Poe* and *Griswold* mentioned above.[37] Judge Merhige, in dissent, took a broader view of the privacy cases 'as standing for the principle that every individual has a right to be free from unwarranted governmental intrusion into [their] decisions on private matters of intimate concern' (i.e. 'of substantial importance to [their] well-being'), *Eisenstadt* v. *Baird*[38] having 'significantly diminished the importance of the marital-nonmarital distinction'.[39]

On appeal, the Supreme Court summarily affirmed the judgment without opinion,[40] creating doubt as to whether or not the Court had preferred the view of the district court's majority, or merely found that, not having been prosecuted, the plaintiffs lacked standing.[41] Two prior *per curiam* opinions, which upheld the 'crime against nature' (i.e. oral or anal intercourse) statutes of Tennessee[42] and Florida[43] against vagueness challenges, added to the uncertainty, as did a subsequent statement by the majority in *Carey* v. *Population Services International* that 'the Court has not definitively answered the difficult question whether . . . the Constitution prohibits state statutes regulating [private consensual sexual] behavior among adults'.[44]

By 1980, although no federal appellate court had accepted the right of privacy

[31] 308 F Supp 729 at 735 (ND Tex 1970).
[32] Ibid. at 730.   [33] 401 US 989 (1971).
[34] See *Baker* v. *Wade*, 553 F Supp 1121 at 1148–51 (ND Tex 1982).
[35] 403 F Supp 1199 (ED Va 1975).
[36] Ibid. at 1200.   [37] Ibid. at 1201–2.   [38] 405 US 438 (1972).
[39] 403 F Supp 1199 at 1203–4 (ED Va 1975).
[40] 425 US 901 (1976) (Justices Brennan, Marshall, and Stevens would have set the case for oral argument).
[41] See e.g. *Hardwick* v. *Bowers*, 760 F 2d 1202 at 1207–8 (11th Cir 1985); *People* v. *Onofre*, 415 NE 2d 936 at 943 (NY 1980).
[42] *Rose* v. *Locke*, 423 US 48 (1975) (Justices Brennan, Marshall and Stewart dissenting).
[43] *Wainwright* v. *Stone*, 414 US 21 (1973) .
[44] 431 US 678 at 688 n. 5, 702, 718 n. 2 (1977).

argument as invalidating a law prohibiting oral or anal intercourse (or other private, consensual, adult sexual activity), the highest courts of at least five states had done so (or had accepted a related argument as having the same result). In *Commonwealth* v. *Balthazar*, which involved non-consensual opposite-sex oral intercourse, the Massachusetts Supreme Judicial Court held (5–0) that, in light of the US Supreme Court's privacy decisions, the statute prohibiting 'unnatural and lascivious acts' 'must be construed to be inapplicable to private, consensual conduct of adults'.[45] Although the court reserved the question of the constitutionality of 'a statute which explicitly prohibits specific sexual conduct, even if consensual and private',[46] *Balthazar* is often treated as judicially invalidating a related Massachusetts statute prohibiting 'the abominable and detestable crime against nature' (i.e. anal intercourse).[47]

The legislative repeal of oral or anal intercourse laws in Iowa and New Jersey[48] followed the decisions of those states' supreme courts in *State* v. *Pilcher*[49] and *State* v. *Saunders*.[50] In *Pilcher*, which involved allegedly non-consensual opposite-sex oral intercourse, the Iowa Supreme Court held (5–4) that the oral or anal intercourse law 'cannot constitutionally be applied to alleged sodomitical acts performed in private between consenting adults of . . . opposite sex[es]', but expressly declined to reach 'the question of homosexuality'.[51] The majority found that, under *Griswold* and other cases, 'the right of privacy extends to sexual relations between husband and wife' and, under the rationale of *Eisenstadt*, 'between consenting adults of . . . opposite sex[es] not married to each other'.[52] The minority argued that *Griswold* protected only 'sexual conduct of spouses in their home', and that *Eisenstadt* 'forbids different treatment of non-spouses with respect to limiting procreation, but not with respect to other state-prohibited sexual activities'.[53]

In *Saunders*, the New Jersey Supreme Court held (4–3) that a statute prohibiting 'fornication' (i.e. vaginal intercourse between a man and an unmarried woman, which 'involves . . . a fundamental personal choice') 'infringes upon the right of privacy' under the US Constitution.[54] Taking a broad view of 'privacy' as relating to 'individual autonomy' and protecting 'the freedom of personal development', the majority concluded:

It would be rather anomalous if [the decision to bear children] could be constitutionally protected while the more fundamental decision as to whether to engage in the conduct which is a necessary prerequisite to child-bearing could be constitutionally prohibited. Surely, such a choice involves considerations which are at least as intimate and personal as those which are involved in choosing whether to use contraceptives.[55]

---

[45] 318 NE 2d 478 at 481 (Mass 1974).   [46] Ibid.
[47] See e.g. Harvard Survey (1989), 1519 n. 2. But see Halley (1993 US), 1774.
[48] See Rivera (1979), 951; Hunter, Michaelson, and Stoddard (1992 US), 165.
[49] 242 NW 2d 348 (Iowa 1976).   [50] 381 A 2d 333 (NJ 1977).
[51] 242 NW 2d 348 at 359–60 (Iowa 1976).   [52] Ibid. at 358–9.
[53] Ibid. at 362, 365.   [54] 381 A 2d 333 at 339 (NJ 1977).
[55] Ibid. at 339–40.

28   *United States Constitution*

The minority interpreted 'the federal right of privacy as encompassing . . . choices related to childrearing and childbearing', in light of *Griswold*, *Carey* and *Doe*.[56]

Finally, exceptions permitting oral or anal intercourse only by married opposite-sex couples were used to strike down the oral or anal intercourse laws of Pennsylvania and New York. In *Commonwealth* v. *Bonadio*, the Pennsylvania Supreme Court held (4–3) that a prohibition of 'deviate sexual intercourse' (oral or anal intercourse 'between human beings who are not husband and wife') violated the Equal Protection Clause of the US Constitution because, as in *Eisenstadt*, the distinction between married and unmarried persons had no rational basis.[57] This made it unnecessary to consider the right of privacy. The minority argued that the statute was constitutional as applied to the defendants, who included two women charged with engaging in sexual acts with (presumably male) members of the audience in a theatre that charged an admission fee.[58]

In *People* v. *Onofre*, the four defendants challenged convictions for consensual male–male or male–female oral or anal intercourse either at home (and discovered because photographs were taken) or in parked vehicles late at night.[59] The New York Court of Appeals held (5–2) that an oral or anal intercourse law exempting married persons violated 'the right to equal protection enjoyed by persons not married to each other', because (as in *Eisenstadt*) there was no 'rational relationship' between the protection of marriage and the challenged law.[60] The minority found one in that 'the institution of marriage is so important to our society that even offensive intimacies between married individuals should be tolerated'.[61]

On the right of privacy issue, the decision was closer (4–3). The majority defined the right of privacy as 'a right of independence in making certain kinds of important decisions'. This right is not confined to 'marital intimacy' and 'procreative choice', but also covers 'individual decisions as to indulgence in acts of sexual intimacy by unmarried persons and as to satisfaction of sexual desires by resort to material condemned as obscene . . . when done in a cloistered setting',[62] under *Eisenstadt* and *Stanley* v. *Georgia*.[63] 'No rational basis appears for excluding from the same protection decisions . . . to seek sexual gratification from . . . "deviant" conduct, so long as the decisions are voluntarily made by adults in a noncommercial, private setting.'[64] The minority declined to read the privacy cases as encompassing 'all types of consensual sexual behavior in private',[65] or establishing a 'right to unfettered sexual expression'.[66] Although the opinions mention only the US Constitution, the US Supreme Court denied a petition for certiorari.[67]

[56] Ibid. at 345, 347.   [57] 415 A 2d 47 at 51 (Pa 1980).   [58] Ibid. at 52.
[59] 415 NE 2d 936 at 937–8 (NY 1980). The majority found it unnecessary (at 938 n. 2) to consider the suggestion that the vehicles were 'in public'.
[60] Ibid. at 942–3.   [61] Ibid. at 950 n. 4.   [62] Ibid. at 939–40.
[63] Respectively, 405 US 438 (1972) and 394 US 557 (1969).
[64] 415 NE 2d 936 at 940–1 (NY 1980).   [65] Ibid. at 944.
[66] Ibid. at 946.   [67] 451 US 987 (1981).

Against this background of the uncertain significance of *Doe* and the success of litigants in state courts, gay, lesbian, and bisexual plaintiffs in the early 1980s continued to raise the right of privacy argument in federal court challenges to oral or anal intercourse laws and dismissals from the armed forces. This resulted in three conflicting decisions by federal courts of appeals: *Dronenburg* v. *Zech*,[68] *Hardwick* v. *Bowers*[69] and *Baker* v. *Wade*.[70] In *Dronenburg*, the D.C. Circuit upheld (3–0) the Navy's policy of dismissing all personnel who engage in same-sex sexual activity, concluding that there is 'no constitutional right to engage in homosexual conduct'. Judge Bork rejected the appellant's argument that the 'thread of principle' running through the privacy cases is that 'the government should not interfere with an individual's freedom to control intimate personal decisions regarding his or her own body', the US Supreme Court having expressly rejected such a broad description of the right of privacy in *Roe* v. *Wade*.[71] As for the Court's illustrations of the right of privacy (activities relating to marriage, procreation, contraception, family relationships, and child rearing and education), '[i]t need hardly be said that none of these covers a right of homosexual conduct'.[72] Is there 'a more general principle [less sweeping than the appellant's] that explains [the privacy] cases and is capable of extrapolation to new claims'? The only principle provided by the Court is that 'only rights that are "fundamental" or "implicit in the concept of ordered liberty" are included in the right of privacy'. 'Homosexual conduct' could not be so categorized unless 'any and all private sexual behavior' could be, which Judge Bork was unwilling to do.[73]

The Eleventh Circuit (2–1) reached the opposite conclusion in *Hardwick*.[74] Michael Hardwick challenged Georgia's oral or anal intercourse law after being arrested in his bedroom by a police officer while engaging in oral intercourse with another man, held in jail for 12 hours, and charged.[75] After a Muncipal Court hearing, the prosecution was later dropped.[76] The majority defined the right of privacy as protecting 'certain individual decisions critical to personal autonomy because those decisions are essentially private and beyond the legitimate reach of civilized society'.[77] Although Hardwick's sexual activity was 'not procreative', it involved 'important associational interests'. *Griswold* protected not only procreation but also 'intimate association', which could exist 'outside the traditional marital relationship' (as in *Eisenstadt*). 'For some, the sexual

---

[68] 741 F 2d 1388 (DC Cir 1984).   [69] 760 F 2d 1202 (11th Cir 1985).
[70] 769 F 2d 289 (5th Cir 1985) (*en banc*).
[71] 741 F 2d 1388 at 1391, 1395 (DC Cir 1984).   [72] Ibid. at 1395–6.
[73] Ibid. at 1396. See Ronald Dworkin's critique of Bork's reasoning: Dworkin (1984 US).
[74] 760 F 2d 1202 (11th Cir 1985). The dissenting judge held that *Doe* was a binding Supreme Court decision upholding oral and anal intercourse laws.
[75] See Rubenstein (1993 US), 125–31 ('Interview With Michael Hardwick'); Garrow (1994 US), 653–4; Goldstein (1988 US), 1073. The police had entered his home with a warrant to arrest him for a 'public drinking' fine he had already paid.
[76] 760 F 2d 1202 at 1204 (11th Cir 1985).   [77] Ibid. at 1211.

activity in question . . . serves the same purpose as the intimacy of marriage.'[78]
And, as in *Stanley*, 'the fact that the activity is carried out in seclusion bolsters
its significance'. Because Hardwick's activity was 'quintessentially private
and . . . at the heart of an intimate association beyond the proper reach of state
regulation', Georgia would have to prove at trial a 'compelling interest' in
regulating it.[79]

Finally, in *Baker*, the Fifth Circuit held (9–7, in an *en banc* decision) that
Doe was a binding authority precluding a federal right of privacy challenge to
the Texas same-sex oral or anal intercourse law.[80] The direct conflict between the
Eleventh Circuit in *Hardwick* and the Fifth Circuit in *Baker* (supported by the
D.C. Circuit in *Dronenburg*), regarding the applicability of the right of privacy
to same-sex oral or anal intercourse, provided the split in federal courts of
appeals decisions that is often a prerequisite for Supreme Court review. Nearly
25 years after Justice Harlan mentioned 'homosexuality' in *Poe* (1961), and
after declining opportunities to address the merits of the issue in *Buchanan*
(1971), *Doe* (1976), and *Onofre* (1981), the Supreme Court granted certiorari in
Hardwick.[81] Gay, lesbian, and bisexual persons in the US hoped that the Court
would affirm the Eleventh Circuit's decision by extending the right of privacy
to private, consensual, adult sexual activity, thus facilitating the striking down
of the oral or anal intercourse laws that remained (in 1986) in 24 or 25 states
and the District of Columbia.[82]

2. *Bowers* v. *Hardwick*

The Supreme Court announced its long-awaited decision in *Bowers* v. *Hardwick*
on 30 June 1986,[83] the day after Lesbian and Gay Pride parades and festivals
across the US, and four days before the celebration of the 100th anniversary of
the Statue of Liberty. The hopes of all those who supported an extension of the
right of privacy were dashed. The Court held, 5–4, reversing the Eleventh Circuit, that Georgia's oral or anal intercourse law does not 'violate[ ] the fundamental rights of homosexuals', because the US Constitution (specifically, the
Due Process Clause of the Fourteenth Amendment) does not confer 'a fundamental

---

[78] Ibid. at 1211–12.   [79] Ibid. at 1212–13.

[80] 769 F 2d 289 at 292 (5th Cir 1985). The minority dissented on procedural grounds.

[81] 474 US 943 (4 Nov. 1985). On the vote to grant review, see Garrow (1994 US), 656–7.

[82] See *Bowers* v. *Hardwick*, 478 US 186 at 193, 198 nn. 1–2, 210 n. 5 (1986) (totals of 24 and
25 states mentioned). The count was 24 states and D.C. with such laws, 26 states without, if one
excluded the Massachusetts law as judicially invalidated. If one included the Massachusetts law
because its judicial invalidation in *Balthazar* was not sufficiently certain (see note 45 and see Halley
(1993 US), 1774), the totals were 25 states and D.C. with such laws, 25 states without. The 25 states
without consisted of 23 where legislative reform had taken place, and 2 where judicial invalidation
by the state's highest court had clearly taken place (New York in *Onofre* and Pennsylvania in
Bonadio: see notes 41 and 57 respectively).

[83] 478 US 186 (1986). On 7 July 1986, the Court denied certiorari in *Baker* v. *Wade*, allowing
the Fifth Circuit's decision to stand: 478 US 1022 (Marshall J. dissented).

right on homosexuals to engage in sodomy', or contain 'a fundamental right to engage in homosexual sodomy', as part of the right of privacy or otherwise.[84] Because the law implicates no fundamental right, 'the presumed belief of a majority of the electorate in Georgia that homosexual sodomy is immoral and unacceptable' provides an adequate 'rational basis' for the law.[85] Chief Justice Burger, in his concurring opinion, added insult to injury by observing that '[h]omosexual sodomy was a capital crime under Roman law' (which permitted slavery), and citing Blackstone's description of consensual anal intercourse 'as an offense "of deeper malignity" than [vaginal] rape[!], a heinous act "the very mention of which is a disgrace to human nature", and "a crime not fit to be named".'[86]

Justice Powell cast the deciding vote, joining the four anti-extension justices (Burger, O'Connor, Rehnquist, and White) but expressing reservations, in his concurring opinion, that 'a prison sentence for such conduct . . . would create a serious Eighth Amendment issue [of infliction of a "cruel and unusual punishment"]'.[87] He had originally joined the four pro-extension justices, but changed his vote.[88] He later publicly stated that he 'probably made a mistake in [*Hardwick*]', and conceded in a telephone interview that *Hardwick* 'was inconsistent in a general way with *Roe*', and that on rereading the opinions in *Hardwick*, '[he] thought the dissent had the better of the arguments'.[89] The four dissenting, pro-extension justices (Blackmun, Brennan, Marshall, and Stevens) would have affirmed the Eleventh Circuit's finding that the law infringed the right of privacy and that Georgia must provide some special justification for it, greater than a rational basis.

In 1980, one commentator found that 38 of 41 articles surveyed 'took the view that the better, natural, principled reading of the privacy cases would bring the sexual relations of consenting adults within the protection of the constitutional right of privacy'.[90] It was not surprising then that the Supreme Court's contrary conclusion in *Hardwick* unleashed a flood of over 50 articles and notes in US legal journals,[91] many of them highly critical. The main objection to Justice White's majority opinion was his confining the right of privacy to specific

---

[84] 478 US 186 at 189–91 (1986). The Court's inconsistent language shows an interesting failure to distinguish between a right of particular persons ('homosexuals') and a right of any person to engage in particular conduct ('homosexual sodomy').

[85] Ibid. at 196.   [86] Ibid. at 197.

[87] Ibid. If convicted, Hardwick would have faced a minimum of one and a maximum of twenty years in prison: ibid. at 188 n. 1.

[88] See Garrow (1994 US), 658–61; Rubenstein (1993 US), 148–9. See also *Zablocki* v. *Redhail*, 434 US 374 at 399 (1978) (Powell J., concurring) ('State regulation [of marriage] has included bans on incest, bigamy and homosexuality').

[89] See 'Ex-Justice Says He May Have Been Wrong' *The National Law Journal* (5 Nov. 1990) 3; Rubenstein (1993 US), 149.

[90] Grey (1980 US), 99.

[91] For lists of some of these publications, see Bibliography (1994 US), 88–91; Garrow (1994 US), 902 n. 97.

32 United States Constitution

categories ('family, [opposite-sex] marriage, or procreation'),[92] and declining to
identify any principle that would explain the limitation of the right to those
categories. Thus, the decision has been described as 'a significant narrowing of
the Court's conception of the right of privacy',[93] 'one of the most transparently
unprincipled exercises of judicial power in recent years',[94] and 'judgment by
pigeonhole',[95] Justice White having 'neither sought nor found a unifying principle underlying his three categories'.[96] Indeed, one commentator concluded that
'[t]he utter lack of reasoning in the majority's opinion ... strongly suggests that
the explanation lies in the emotional response of five justices to ... the subject
of homosexuality' which, it seems, they 'simply do not like'.[97]

Is the majority's opinion in *Hardwick* based on principle or prejudice? Justice
White gave, expressly or impliedly, at least five reasons for dismissing Michael
Hardwick's constitutional claim. First, he found that 'none of the rights announced in [the privacy] cases bears any resemblance to the claimed constitutional right of homosexuals to engage in acts of sodomy', '[n]o connection
between family,[98] [opposite-sex] marriage, or procreation ... and homosexual
activity ... [having] been demonstrated'.[99] Second, he interpreted the decision in
Stanley v. *Georgia*, that 'possessing and reading obscene material in the privacy
of one's home' cannot be criminalized, as 'firmly grounded in the First Amendment' and therefore not capable of extension to non-expressive activities in the
home.[100] Third, there is no general principle underlying the privacy cases that
might apply to Hardwick's claim. Fourth, although the Court has used two tests
to determine whether a right (not falling within the right of privacy) is otherwise
a fundamental right, 'to claim that a right to engage in [oral or anal intercourse]
is "deeply rooted in this Nation's history and tradition" or "implicit in the
concept of ordered liberty" is, at best, facetious'. As for a 'more expansive' test,
protecting the Court from 'illegitimacy' demands 'a great resistance to expand[ing]
the substantive reach of [the Due Process] Clauses, particularly if it requires
redefining the category of rights deemed to be fundamental'.[101] Fifth, 'laws
representing essentially moral choices' are valid, if they do not affect a fundamental right.[102]

I will now consider each of these five reasons in turn, but will concentrate on
the first two (and mainly the first), because the latter three raise very broad
questions going well outside the scope of this Chapter. The first two, on the
other hand, concern the narrowest ground on which Hardwick's claim might

[92] 478 US 186 at 191 (1986). [93] Harvard Case (1986 US), 210.
[94] Richards (1986 US), 801. [95] Stoddard (1987 US), 653.
[96] Rubenfeld (1989 US), 748. [97] Stoddard (1987 US), 655.
[98] In deciding whether a deceased man's male partner was a 'family member' under a rent-
control law, the New York Court of Appeals concluded that 'a family includes two adult lifetime
partners whose relationship is long term and characterized by an emotional and financial commitment and interdependence'. See *Braschi* v. *Stahl Associates Co.*, 543 NE 2d 49 at 54 (NY 1989).
[99] 478 US 186 at 190–91 (1986). [100] Ibid. at 195.
[101] Ibid. at 194–5. [102] Ibid. at 196.

have been accepted (i.e. that the Supreme Court's precedents implicitly cover consensual, adult sexual activity in the home), and which would not have required the identification of a more general principle explaining what the right of privacy includes, or what rights are fundamental, or the invalidation of all laws that are based solely on 'morality'.

(a) Application of Griswold and Other Privacy Cases

Could Hardwick's claim be brought within the privacy cases, especially *Griswold*, *Eisenstadt*, and *Carey*? Laurence Tribe and Michael Dorf have observed that the level of generality at which the asserted right is described will often determine whether it falls within the right of privacy or is otherwise fundamental: the more general, the more likely it is to be included, and the more specific, the more likely it is to be excluded.[103] Thus, the majority in *Hardwick* effectively decided the case by framing the issue as 'whether the Federal Constitution confers a fundamental right upon homosexuals to engage in sodomy',[104] a formulation which Jed Rubenfeld describes as 'calculated to shock the judicial conscience'.[105] Their choice of words was such that they might as well have asked 'whether the Constitution confers a fundamental right on a despised minority to engage in a disgusting practice'. Apart from its tone, the statement narrowed the issue to same-sex oral or anal intercourse, even though the statute prohibited *all* oral or anal intercourse. As Justice Stevens stressed, both the statute and the majority's rationale for upholding it 'applie[d] equally to the prohibited conduct regardless of whether the parties who engage in it are married or unmarried, or are of the same or different sexes'.[106]

This narrowing of the issue was facilitated by the Eleventh Circuit's affirming the dismissal of the claim of Hardwick's co-plaintiffs, John and Mary Doe, a married opposite-sex couple who alleged that they desired to engage in oral or anal intercourse in their home, but were 'chilled and deterred' by the existence of the Georgia statute.[107] The Eleventh Circuit found that the Does had not alleged 'a serious risk of prosecution'.[108] Their inclusion was an essential part of an argument for extending the right of privacy to private sexual activity, that mirrored the extension of the right to use contraceptives (in *Griswold, Eisenstadt*, and *Carey*) from married opposite-sex couples to unmarried opposite-sex couples and to persons under 16. The first, critical step in the argument was that *Griswold* protected not only the right of married opposite-sex couples to use

---

[103] See Tribe and Dorf (1990 US).
[104] 478 US 186 at 190 (1986).   [105] Rubenfeld (1989 US), 747–8.
[106] 478 US 186 at 214 (1986). See also at 200 (Blackmun J.) ('the Court's almost obsessive focus on homosexual activity').
[107] Ibid. at 188 n. 2. A similar combination of plaintiffs was used in *Buchanan*: see note 31.
[108] 760 F 2d 1202 at 1206 (11th Cir 1985). Cf. *Roe* v. *Wade*, 410 US 113 at 127–9 (1973) (dismissal of complaint of the Does, a married opposite-sex couple who were forced to abstain from vaginal intercourse to avoid a pregnancy that could have endangered Mary Doe's health and could not legally have been terminated).

contraceptives, but also their right to engage in private sexual activity, including vaginal, oral, and anal intercourse. If this were true, then any limitations on the scope of this right (e.g. to married but not unmarried opposite-sex couples, or to opposite-sex but not same-sex couples) would have to be addressed and justified. Thus, the application of *Griswold* to marital opposite-sex oral or anal intercourse provided the 'connection' between same-sex oral or anal intercourse and the privacy cases, and the 'chink in the armour' of the argument that *Griswold* and *Eisenstadt* were only about 'contraception'.[109]

The dismissal of the Does' claim was virtually fatal to Hardwick's, because it allowed the majority to dodge the question of the scope of *Griswold*. Their narrowing of the issue was not unprecedented, in that the Court generally declines to permit 'facial' rather than 'as applied' challenges to statutes that do not affect First Amendment rights.[110] Indeed, in *Griswold*, the Court did so by considering the application of the statute only to married opposite-sex couples, whereas it applied to all persons engaging in vaginal intercourse. But even accepting that the issue was only whether the statute could constitutionally be applied to the specific act of oral intercourse between Michael Hardwick and his male friend, the majority should have adopted the two-stage analysis proposed by Justice Stevens. 'First, may a State totally prohibit [oral or anal intercourse] by means of a neutral law applying without exception to all persons subject to its jurisdiction [as Georgia had done]? If not, may the State save the statute by announcing that it will only enforce the law against homosexuals?'[111] In other words, the majority should have asked itself why, if some forms of oral or anal intercourse enjoy constitutional protection, Hardwick's did not.

So were *Griswold*, *Eisenstadt*, and *Carey* only about contraception or also about sexual activity? In *Eisenstadt*, the Court rested its decision on a very narrow (and tenuous) ground: whether or not *Griswold* protects distribution of contraceptives to married persons (as opposed to their use by married persons), the Fourteenth Amendment's Equal Protection Clause precludes a prohibition of distribution to unmarried persons, but not to married persons, there being no rational basis for such a distinction.[112] The Court concluded that the 'deterrence of premarital sex' was not the legislative aim of the prohibition, but did not suggest that such a goal presented a constitutional issue, and referred to 'the State['s] . . . regard[ing] the problems of extramarital and premarital sexual relations as "evils . . . of different dimensions".'[113] (Likewise in *Roe* v. *Wade*, the Court did not comment on Jane Roe's reference to 'personal, marital, familial,

---

[109] 478 US 186 at 190 (1986).
[110] See Tribe (1988 US), 1022–3.   [111] 478 US 186 at 216 (1986).
[112] 405 US 438 at 447 n. 7, 452–4 (1972). The vigorous rational basis review in *Eisenstadt*, which found it unnecessary to consider a 'morality' justification for a distinction between married and unmarried persons, bears no resemblance to the rational basis review in *Hardwick*. Subsequent decisions have treated *Eisenstadt* as a right of privacy case dealing with contraception. See *Carey*, 431 US 678 at 684–7 (1977); *Hardwick*, 478 US 186 at 190 (1986).
[113] 405 US 438 at 448 (1972).

and sexual privacy', or her assertion that 'discourag[ing] illicit sexual conduct ... is not a proper state purpose'.[114])

In *Carey*, the avoidance of the issue of sexual activity was even more striking. The majority described *Griswold* as 'protect[ing] individual decisions in matters of childbearing', and carefully limited its application of the 'compelling state interest' standard to regulations burdening decisions about 'prevent[ing] conception or terminat[ing] pregnancy', and not regulations 'implicat[ing] sexual freedom' or 'affect[ing] adult sexual relations'.[115] The plurality (on the question of the ban on distribution of contraceptives to persons under 16) assumed 'that the Constitution does not bar state regulation of the sexual behavior of minors', observing that the question with regard to adults remained open.[116]

Ironically, Justice Powell, in his concurring opinion in *Carey*, seemed to bring sexual activity expressly within the right of privacy, by referring to 'the "cluster of constitutionally protected choices" relating to sex and marriage', 'decisions concerning sex and procreation' (in connection with 'the privacy interests of married females between the ages of 14 and 16'), and 'constitutionally protected privacy decisions concerning sexual relations'.[117] His concern was that the majority opinion would impose a 'compelling state interest' standard whenever state regulation 'implicates sexual freedom' or 'affect[s] adult sexual relations'. In his view, that standard applied 'only when the state regulation entirely frustrates or heavily burdens the exercise of constitutional rights *in this area* [i.e. 'sexual freedom']'.[118] As for Justice Stevens in *Carey*, he found 'a significant state interest in discouraging sexual activity among unmarried persons under 16', but concluded that the ban on distributing contraceptives to them was ineffective. As for 'the important *symbolic* effect of communicating disapproval of sexual activity by minors', which made the statute 'a form of propaganda, rather than a regulation of behavior', 'an attempt to persuade by inflicting harm [unwanted pregnancy and venereal disease] on the listener is an unacceptable means of conveying a message that is otherwise legitimate'.[119]

Although the Court studiously avoided the issue of sexual activity in *Eisenstadt*, *Roe*, and *Carey*, it had already 'crossed the Rubicon' in *Griswold*. Justice Douglas's majority opinion described the ban on use of contraceptives as 'operat[ing] directly on *an intimate relation* of husband and wife' and 'having a maximum destructive impact upon' '*a relationship* lying within the zone of privacy'.[120] He

---

[114] 410 US 113 at 129, 148 (1973).   [115] 431 US 678 at 687, 688 n. 5 (1977).

[116] Ibid. at 694 n. 17.   [117] Ibid. at 706, 708, 711.

[118] Ibid. at 704–5 (emphasis added). Surely, the statute in *Hardwick* 'affect[ed] adult sexual relations' and 'entirely frustrat[ed] or heavily burden[ed]' Hardwick's right to make 'decisions concerning sexual relations'.

[119] Ibid. at 713–15. A similar argument might be made against oral or anal intercourse (or unequal age of consent) laws, which do not effectively deter the prohibited conduct and have a largely symbolic effect that inflicts harm (causing persons violating the law to avoid treatment for, or counselling regarding ways of preventing, sexually transmitted diseases, including AIDS).

[120] 381 US 479 at 482, 485 (1965) (emphasis added).

asked: 'Would we allow the police to search the marital *bedrooms* for telltale signs of the use of contraceptives? The very idea is repulsive to the notions of privacy surrounding the marriage *relationship*.'[121] Similarly, the concurring opinions refer to 'a particularly important and sensitive area of privacy—that of the marital *relation* and the marital *home*', and to 'the right ... to be free of regulation of the *intimacies* of the marriage *relationship*'.[122]

In view of these descriptions of the right at issue in *Griswold*, it is difficult to contend that *Griswold* was solely about the right of married opposite-sex couples to decide to use contraceptives to avoid procreating. Implicitly, it recognized that other decisions relating to 'the marriage relationship' are protected by the right of privacy, including decisions regarding sexual activity, such as the decision to engage in vaginal intercourse (whether or not contraceptives are used to avoid procreating). As Hardwick's counsel argued, '[i]t would surely trigger strict judicial scrutiny ... if a state were to ban [vaginal intercourse] between infertile [married opposite-sex] couples, or [between married] women past the age of menopause [and their husbands], even though such a ban could have no impact at all on [their] decisions whether or not to beget a child'.[123] And a 'search [of] the sacred precincts of marital bedrooms for telltale signs of [oral or anal intercourse]' would also be 'repulsive to the notions of privacy surrounding the marriage relationship'.[124]

It is interesting to note here that *Loving* v. *Virginia*, in which the Court struck down laws banning certain mixed-race marriages,[125] and which Justice White in *Hardwick* characterized as a right of privacy case dealing with marriage, began with just such a bedroom search. 'In the wee hours of one morning ... three law officers walked into [the] bedroom [of Mildred and Richard Loving, a mixed-race married opposite-sex couple] and shined a flashlight on the couple', asked Richard 'what [he was] doing in bed with this lady', and took them to jail.[126] This fact strengthens Justice Blackmun's observation in *Hardwick* that '[t]he parallel between *Loving* and this case is almost uncanny'.[127] Michael Hardwick asked the police officer, upon realizing that he and his friend were being watched, 'What are you doing in my bedroom?'[128] Yet the majority in *Hardwick* curtly dismissed the possibility of a 'connection between ... [opposite-sex] marriage ... and homosexual activity'.[129]

The application of *Griswold* to the sexual activity (with or without procreative

---

[121] Ibid. at 485–6 (emphasis added).   [122] Ibid. at 495, 503 (emphasis added).

[123] Brief for Respondent (Case No. 85-140) (31 Jan. 1986), at 12–13.

[124] See ibid. at 17 n. 28 (raising possibility of body cavity searches 'for "telltale" signs of oral or anal sexual contact').

[125] 388 US 1 at 4–5 (1967) (e.g. marriages between 'white' persons and persons with 'any Negro blood').

[126] 'A Marriage That Went Into Lawbooks' *International Herald Tribune* (16 June 1992) 18.

[127] 478 US 186 at 210 n. 5 (1986). See also ibid. at 216 n. 9 (mixed-race marriage 'was once treated as a crime similar to sodomy').

[128] Rubenstein (1993 US), 128.   [129] 478 US 186 at 191 (1986).

potential) of married opposite-sex couples provided the beginning of a 'connection'.[130] If the majority had conceded that marital opposite-sex oral or anal intercourse is protected by the right of privacy, as did counsel for Georgia in *Hardwick*,[131] they would then have had to consider what justification there could be for not extending that protection to oral or anal intercourse (opposite-sex or same-sex) between unmarried persons. Justice Stevens conducted just such an analysis. He began with the propositions that 'individual decisions by married persons, concerning the intimacies of their physical relationship, even when not intended to produce offspring, are . . . protected' under *Griswold*, and that 'this protection extends to intimate choices by unmarried . . . persons' under *Carey* and *Eisenstadt*. Because the right of privacy 'surely embraces the right to engage in non-reproductive, sexual conduct that others may consider offensive or immoral', 'a State may not prohibit sodomy within "the sacred precincts of marital bedrooms" [under *Griswold*] or . . . between unmarried heterosexual adults [under *Eisenstadt*]'.[132] Because the statute 'cannot be enforced as it is written', Georgia must meet 'the burden of justifying a selective application of the generally applicable law'.[133] At this last step, his analysis faltered, because he framed the issue, not as whether the right of privacy included same-sex oral or anal intercourse, but as whether a law that could not constitutionally be enforced against opposite-sex oral or anal intercourse could be 'selectively applied' to same-sex oral or anal intercourse.[134] Presumably, if the right of privacy did not extend to such intercourse, that would provide a justification for 'selective application'.

If the majority in *Hardwick* had chosen to expand their brief opinion, they might have explained why *Griswold* did not apply to marital opposite-sex sexual activity, and why the Eleventh Circuit in *Hardwick*, the district courts in *Buchanan* and *Baker*, and the state courts in *Balthazar*, *Pilcher*, *Saunders*, and *Onofre* were mistaken in their view that it did.[135] Or they could have conceded that *Griswold* did protect such activity, but that the courts in *Bonadio* and *Onofre* erred in finding no rational basis for a distinction between married and unmarried persons. Here, they could have pointed to the statements in the concurring opinions (but not in the majority opinion) in *Griswold* that the protection did not extend to 'adultery', 'fornication', 'homosexuality', and 'all forms of . . . illicit sexual relationships, be they premarital or extramarital'.[136] They could also have tried

---

[130] Cf. Hunter (1992 US), 536 (connection between 'procreation . . . and homosexual activity' in that oral intercourse has the same procreative potential as vaginal intercourse with contraceptives); Stoddard (1987 US), 653–4 (*Eisenstadt* and *Hardwick* involved same choice of sexual activity 'for purposes other than procreation'). But it is unlikely that many persons' primary purpose in choosing same-sex sexual activity is to avoid procreation.

[131] 478 US 186 at 218 n. 10 (1986).

[132] Ibid. at 216–18.   [133] Ibid. at 218, 220.

[134] Cf. *Yick Wo* v. *Hopkins*, 118 US 356 (1886) (discretionary denial of laundry licenses to Chinese applicants).

[135] See Stoddard (1987 US), 653.   [136] 381 US 479 at 498–9, 505 (1965).

to limit *Loving* to marriage by citing the Court's earlier, pre-*Griswold* decision in *McLaughlin* v. *Florida*. There, the Court struck down a law prohibiting 'negro'– 'white' unmarried opposite-sex couples from 'habitually liv[ing] and occupy[ing] in the nighttime the same room', but said it would have been valid had it applied to all unmarried opposite-sex couples, as 'express[ing] a general and strong state policy against promiscuous conduct' and 'protect[ing] the integrity of the marriage laws'.[137] Or they could have allowed protection of all opposite-sex oral or anal intercourse under *Eisenstadt*, but found (unlike the district court in *Baker*)[138] a rational basis for distinguishing same-sex oral or anal intercourse. The most frustrating aspect of the majority's opinion is that they saw no need to do any of this. Their simple assertion that '[n]o connection between . . . [opposite-sex] marriage . . . and homosexual activity . . . has been demonstrated' was enough.[139]

At this stage, two conclusions can be drawn regarding the failure of Michael Hardwick's claim, in spite of his 'perfect facts': an actual prosecution, eliminating standing problems; and an arrest in his bedroom, demonstrating as forcefully as possible the intrusiveness of the law. First, the Supreme Court's strict standing rules can have the effect of insulating a stigmatizing law from constitutional review. The dismissals of the Does' claim, and ultimately of Hardwick's, involved a Catch-22. Hardwick could not succeed without first establishing the Does' right of privacy under *Griswold*. But the Supreme Court would not consider the Does' right unless they had been threatened with prosecution (and thus had standing), which was extremely unlikely (and remains so for opposite-sex couples).[140] Second, the failure illustrates the difficulty of a member of an unpopular minority (gay, lesbian, and bisexual persons) basing their case on 'liberty', rather than 'equality', where the asserted aspect of protected 'liberty' (to engage in oral intercourse) has not been clearly recognized for members of the majority (heterosexual persons). A minority plaintiff is unlikely to succeed in establishing the new right, particularly where its non-recognition is of little practical importance to members of the majority (e.g. because of non-prosecution). Thus, Hardwick's attempt to establish a new right for the benefit of all was like a 15-year-old girl attempting to establish, before *Griswold*, a right of all persons to use contraceptives (especially if the ban on contraceptives had only been enforced against persons under 16). It is much easier for a member of a minority to argue that they should be extended a right already recognized for members

---

[137] 379 US 184 at 185, 196 (1964).
[138] 553 F Supp 1121 at 1143–4 (ND Tex 1982).　　　[139] 478 US 186 at 191 (1986).
[140] Charges of opposite-sex oral or anal intercourse are usually only brought in non-consensual situations (involving, e.g., vaginal, oral or anal rape), in case the jury has any doubt as to the absence of consent. See e.g. *Fry* v. *Patseavouras*, 1992 US App LEXIS 21048 (4th Cir) (10 year sentence for opposite-sex oral intercourse where jury acquitted on vaginal rape charge); *US* v. *Gates*, 40 Military Justice Reporter 354 (Ct Mil App 1994) (armed forces member acquitted of vaginal rape, convicted of opposite-sex oral intercourse that he alleged was private and consensual). See also Halley (1993 US), 1777–80. As a result, they may be poor vehicles for extending the right of privacy to opposite-sex sexual activity. But see, e.g., *Balthazar*, and *Pilcher* (cited in notes 45 and note 49 respectively).

of the majority (by invoking 'equality'), than to establish new rights in the abstract.

(b) Application of Stanley v. Georgia

Did *Stanley* v. *Georgia* apply to Hardwick's claim? The majority in *Hardwick* interpreted *Stanley* (which protected the right to read or view 'obscene' materials in one's home)[141] as 'firmly grounded in the First Amendment', whereas the right to engage in sexual activity in one's home had 'no similar support in the text of the Constitution'.[142] Justice Blackmun argued that *Stanley* also rested on the Fourth Amendment's guarantee of '[t]he right of the people to be secure in their . . . houses'.[143] And Richard Mohr has pointed out that, prior to *Hardwick*, the Court's privacy cases had cited *Stanley* as a privacy case.[144] An alternative interpretation of *Stanley* is that of the New York Court of Appeals in *Onofre*: 'the defendant's choice to seek sexual gratification by viewing [the 'obscene' material] and the effectuation of that choice within the bastion of his home, removed from the public eye, was held to be blanketed by the constitutional right of privacy'.[145] Thus, *Stanley* protected not just the individual's right to read or view a pornographic magazine or videotape in their home, it protected their right to engage in 'auto-sexual activity' (i.e. to masturbate) while doing so. As Richard Mohr puts it, '[p]ornography is protected because sex is protected; pornography affords one mode of conducting one's sex life by one's own lights'.[146] Indeed, if *Stanley* does not protect the activity for which pornography is often used (and, by extension, sexual activity in the home generally), it creates the anomaly that Michael Hardwick and his friend could not be prosecuted for viewing, in his bedroom, an 'obscene' videotape of two men engaging in oral intercourse, but could be prosecuted for doing so themselves.[147]

Even if the asserted protection of *Stanley* were limited to 'voluntary sexual conduct between consenting adults' (as opposed to other activities in the home), in the majority's view in *Hardwick*, 'it would be difficult, except by fiat, to limit the claimed right to homosexual conduct while leaving exposed to prosecution adultery, incest, and other sexual crimes even though they are committed in the home'. They were 'unwilling to start down that road'.[148] Justice Blackmun argued that 'a court could find simple, analytically sound distinctions between certain private, consensual sexual conduct . . . and adultery and incest', suggesting

---

[141] 394 US 557 at 559 (1969).
[142] 478 US 186 at 195 (1986).   [143] Ibid. at 207–8.
[144] See Mohr (1988 US), 132 n. 20. See e.g. *Roe*, 410 US 113 at 176 (1973).
[145] 415 NE 2d 936 at 940 (NY 1980).   [146] See Mohr (1988 US), 132.
[147] See Brief of Respondent (Case No. 85-140) (31 Jan. 1986), at 16; Tribe (1988 US), 1426; *Baker* v. *Wade*, 553 F Supp 1121 at 1141 (ND Tex 1982). Some would resolve this apparent inconsistency by allowing them to be prosecuted for both, others would allow prosecution for neither, and others might favour prosecution for use of pornography but not for sexual activity.
[148] 478 US 186 at 195–6 (1986).

that adultery is a breach of the marriage contract,[149] and that 'true consent to incestuous activity is sufficiently problematical that a blanket prohibition . . . is warranted'.[150] The majority's reluctance to protect same-sex sexual activity because of the need to make principled distinctions between it and other kinds or aspects of sexual activity amounts to an abdication of its responsibility for defining constitutional rights (i.e. 'we cannot recognize this new right because we would have to define its scope').[151] A way of avoiding this problem by limiting the scope of the right will be discussed, in the context of the Canadian Charter, in Chapter 7, Part II.

(c) Application of a General Privacy Principle

If Hardwick's claim did not fall within any of the existing categories of the right of privacy, or within *Stanley*, did it fall within a more general principle explaining what decisions the right of privacy protects? Justice Blackmun remarked on the majority's 'overall refusal to consider the broad principles that have informed our treatment of privacy in specific cases', the right being 'more than the mere aggregation of a number of entitlements to engage in specific behavior'.[152] Could any general principle be found in the Court's prior privacy decisions?

Griswold was said to 'concern[ ] a relationship lying within the zone of privacy created by several fundamental constitutional guarantees',[153] but the Court did not attempt to define that 'zone'. In *Eisenstadt*, the right of privacy was said to mean 'the right of the *individual*, married or single, to be free from unwarranted governmental intrusion into matters so fundamentally affecting a person as the decision whether to bear or beget a child'.[154] This formulation suggests that there may be other 'matters so fundamentally affecting a person', besides procreative decisions, and was supported by the citation of *Stanley*. But as Judge Bork pointed out in *Dronenburg*, *Eisenstadt* provided no criteria for deciding whether other 'personal decision[s]' 'so fundamentally affect[ ] a person'.[155]

In *Roe* v. *Wade*, the Court referred to 'a right of personal privacy, or a guarantee of certain areas or zones of privacy', and found it 'broad enough to encompass a woman's decision to terminate her pregnancy',[156] but did not attempt to define it any more precisely. In *Carey*, the right was said to include 'the interest in independence in making certain kinds of important decisions. While the outer limits of this aspect of privacy have not been marked by the Court, it

---

[149] It is hard to see why such a 'breach of contract' should constitute a criminal offence, as opposed to a ground for divorce. Laws against 'fornication' (generally, vaginal intercourse between unmarried persons) are equally hard to justify. See Harvard Note (1991 US), 1661 n. 9 and 1671 n. 83 (almost half the states and D.C. prohibit adultery; 13 states and D.C. prohibit 'fornication').
[150] 478 US 186 at 209 n. 4, 217 (1986).
[151] Cf., in the context of abortion, *Planned Parenthood* v. *Casey*, 120 L Ed 2d 674 at 730 (1992) ('[w]e accept our responsibility not to retreat from interpreting the full meaning of the [Constitution] in light of all our precedents').
[152] 478 US 186 at 206 (1986).   [153] 381 US 479 at 485 (1965) (emphasis in original).
[154] 405 US 438 at 453 (1972).   [155] 741 F 2d 1388 at 1393–4 (DC Cir 1984).
[156] 410 US 113 at 152–3 (1973).

is clear that *among* the decisions that an individual may make without unjustified government interference are personal decisions "relating to marriage, procreation, contraception, family relationships, and child rearing and education".'[157]
The *Hardwick* majority cited this list,[158] but treated it as exhaustive rather than
illustrative.

It is not surprising that the Court would be cautious about attempting to define
a general privacy principle, because it is extremely difficult to fashion one that
is sufficiently broad to cover the infinite variety of decisions to which it might
be applied, yet not hopelessly vague and malleable. This will be seen, in the
context of the Canadian Charter, in Chapter 7, Part II. I cannot consider here
what that principle ought to look like, but can only examine briefly the two
candidates that were competing in *Hardwick* (those of the majority and the
minority). Justice Blackmun's minority principle is not concisely stated in one
place, other than in his opening statement that the case is about 'the right to be
let alone', an unworkably broad formulation.[159] But his discussion of the privacy
cases suggests two other formulations. The more general is that decisions forming a 'central part of an individual's life', 'alter[ing] . . . dramatically an individual's self-definition', 'contribut[ing] . . . powerfully to the happiness of
individuals',[160] or 'touch[ing] the heart of what makes individuals what they
are'[161] are protected because the 'ability independently to define one's identity
. . . is central to any concept of liberty'. Decisions about 'sexual intimacy', 'a
sensitive, key relationship of human existence' through which 'individuals define themselves in a significant way', are included. The more specific formulation seems to be that decisions are protected if they relate to 'the fundamental
interest all individuals have in controlling the nature of their intimate associations with others'.[162]

The general formulation, 'decisions that are important to the definition of an
individual's identity', has been supported by a number of commentators.[163] But
this broad principle of 'personhood' has a number of problems, which Jed
Rubenfeld has cogently identified. For example, how are harmful or intolerant
identities to be excluded, or conflicts between individual and community identities to be resolved? He suggests that 'both sides of the *Hardwick* Court claimed
to be championing self-definition', one side for the individual, the other for the
legislating community.[164] And by asserting that protected conduct is 'essential to
an individual's identity', it assumes that the persons engaging in it are essentially different, thereby 'reintroducing . . . the very premise of the invidious uses

[157] 431 US 678 at 684–5 (1977) (emphasis added, citations omitted).
[158] 478 US 186 at 190 (1986).   [159] Ibid. at 199.
[160] Ibid. at 204–5.   [161] Ibid. at 211.   [162] Ibid. at 205–6.
[163] See e.g. Harvard Case (1986 US), 216–17: 'The essence of a privacy right that protects
personal decisions is its protection of the right of individuals to define their own identities . . . Because
private, consensual sexual conduct is integral to self-identity, [*Hardwick*] wrongly denies homosexuals the ability to define their own identity'.
[164] Rubenfeld (1989 US), 762.

of state power it seeks to overcome'. He sees the use of contraceptives and abortion as especially difficult to conceptualize as 'acts of self-definition'. In the latter case, women should have the right to choose abortion to 'avoid being forced into an identity', not to define their own identities.[165] Instead of 'personhood', he proposes an 'anti-totalitarian principle' as underlying the 'right of privacy', which focuses on the conduct a law coerces (e.g. pregnancy and motherhood or opposite-sex sexual activity), rather than the conduct it prohibits (e.g. abortion or same-sex sexual activity), and would invalidate laws 'involv[ing] the forced, affirmative occupation and direction of individuals' lives'. The 'right to be let alone' thus becomes 'the right not to have the course of one's life dictated by the state'.[166]

The more specific formulation of 'intimate association' was developed by Kenneth Karst from *Griswold*'s references to opposite-sex marriage as an 'intimate relation' and an 'association'.[167] The Court's pre-*Hardwick* decisions are said to have 'characterized the privacy right as a right of individuals in intimate association to decide important matters fundamentally affecting their lives and their relationships'.[168] The problem with 'intimate association' is that, although it certainly encompasses many important decisions about emotional–sexual conduct (especially couple relationships) that ought to fall within a right of privacy, it may be too narrow in some respects. Laurence Tribe and Michael Dorf have suggested that certain procreative choices not involving 'intimacy', e.g. surrogate motherhood, should not fall within a right of privacy.[169] And Richard Mohr has pointed out that many casual sexual encounters between men could not be described as 'intimate', if 'intimacy' means knowing the other person well, rather than merely physical intimacy. (The same is true of some male–female and female–female sexual encounters.) Should Michael Hardwick's ability to invoke a constitutional right of privacy depend on how long he had known his male friend?[170]

The *Carey* list of categories, cited in *Hardwick*, was also cited in a 1992 abortion decision, *Planned Parenthood* v. *Casey* (which upheld *Roe* v. *Wade* in a modified form), but the majority opinion did not use the word 'privacy', referring instead to 'a realm of personal liberty which the government may not enter', 'a person's most basic decisions about family and parenthood', and 'personal decisions relating to [the *Carey* list]'.[171] It then described 'these matters' as:

---

[165] Ibid. 777–82.
[166] Ibid., 783–4, 796, 806–7. Cf. Thomas (1992 US), 1435 (same-sex oral or anal intercourse laws legitimize violence against gay, lesbian, and bisexual persons and therefore violate the Eighth Amendment's prohibition of 'cruel and unusual punishments').
[167] Karst (1980 US).
[168] Harvard Case (1986 US), 216.
[169] Tribe and Dorf (1990 US), 1068, 1108.
[170] Mohr (1988 US), 67–8. But see Karst (1980 US), 633 ('[o]ne reason for extending constitutional protection to casual intimate associations is that they may ripen into durable intimate associations').
[171] 120 L Ed 2d 674 at 695–8 (1992).

involving the most intimate and personal choices a person may make in a lifetime, choices central to personal dignity and autonomy, [and] central to the liberty protected by the Fourteenth Amendment. At the heart of liberty is the right to define one's own concept of existence, of meaning, of the universe, and of the mystery of human life. Beliefs about these matters could not define the attributes of personhood were they formed under compulsion of the State.[172]

It is not clear whether the intriguing but cryptic references to 'defin[ition]' and 'personhood' in this passage are meant to propose a more general privacy principle. Nor is it clear why Justice O'Connor, one of the three authors of the majority opinion in *Planned Parenthood* (on reaffirming 'the essential holding of *Roe* v. *Wade*'),[173] and a member of the *Hardwick* majority, did not see Michael Hardwick as making an 'intimate and personal choice', 'central to personal dignity and autonomy', by which he 'defin[ed] [his] own concept of existence . . . and of the mystery of human life'. Justice Scalia, in dissent, pointed out her inconsistency, arguing that 'homosexual sodomy, polygamy, adult incest, and suicide . . . are equally "intimate" and "deeply personal" decisions involving "personal autonomy and bodily integrity", . . . [but] which can constitutionally be proscribed because it is our unquestionable constitutional tradition that they are proscribable'.[174]

Although the *Hardwick* majority did not expressly state any general principle defining the right of privacy, their implicit principle might be described as including 'decisions relating to family, opposite-sex marriage or procreation that have traditionally been recognized by the majority as fundamental'. Such a principle cannot rely on any constitutional text supporting the particular categories selected. Nor could the principle explain the decisions in *Roe*, *Griswold* and *Loving*, which set aside laws reflecting long-standing traditions condemning abortion, contraception, and mixed-race opposite-sex marriage. The best explanation of the majority's principle and its particular categories may be that it conforms to a certain conservative ideology. Anne Goldstein sees *Hardwick* as 'a battle between two incommensurable and incompatible systems of fundamental values: classical liberalism and classical conservatism', as in the Hart–Devlin debate.[175]

If this is true, *Roe* especially (if not *Griswold* or *Loving*)[176] does not fit the majority's principle. Daniel Conkle described *Hardwick* as the 'second death of

---

[172] Ibid. at 698.
[173] Ibid. at 693–4. An ironic connection between *Roe* v. *Wade* and *Hardwick* is the fact that the partner of Norma McCorvey (Jane Roe) since 1973 has been a woman, Connie Gonzalez. See *The Independent* (10 Aug. 1994) 17.
[174] Ibid. at 785.   [175] Goldstein (1988 US), 1092, 1099.
[176] In *Planned Parenthood*, Justice Blackmun suggested that, '[g]iven the Chief Justice's exclusive reliance on tradition, people using contraceptives seem the next likely candidate for his list of outcasts': 120 L Ed 2d 674 at 756 (1992). But it is unlikely, today, that any US legislature would enact a ban of contraceptives that would raise the issue of overruling *Griswold*. *Loving* can be explained as turning on race discrimination and the Equal Protection Clause.

substantive due process' because it was inconsistent and irreconcilable with *Roe*, and could lead to the overruling of *Roe*.[177] Similarly, Norman Vieira suggested that the majority's real target in *Hardwick* was *Roe* and the notion of a general right of privacy.[178] It should come as no surprise then that in *Planned Parenthood* (in which the opinions are so charged and caustic as to resemble a kind of 'judicial civil war'), four justices (including Chief Justice Rehnquist and Justice White from the *Hardwick* majority) state their belief 'that *Roe* was wrongly decided, and . . . should be overruled'.[179] Rehnquist C.J. argues that the pre-*Roe* cases 'do not endorse any all-encompassing "right of privacy"' and, in an analysis very similar to the *Hardwick* majority's, argues that 'the historical traditions of the American people [do not] support the view that the right to terminate one's pregnancy is fundamental'. He then cites the *Hardwick* majority's statement that '[t]he Court . . . comes nearest to illegitimacy when it deals with judge-made constitutional law having little or no cognizable roots in the language or design of the Constitution'.[180] But for one vote, abortion would have joined same-sex sexual activity outside the right of privacy. Whether or not judges should be discovering an implied right of privacy, or other implied fundamental rights, in the US Constitution is an extremely controversial issue. The difficulty faced by a gay, lesbian or bisexual plaintiff seeking to extend the right of privacy to their case is that they find themselves caught up in a raging battle as to whether such a right should exist at all.

(d) Application of Fundamental Right Tests

Even though the *Hardwick* majority found no 'connection' between same-sex oral intercourse and 'family, marriage, or procreation', and therefore that the right of privacy did not apply, it felt obliged to consider whether the right to engage in such intercourse was otherwise fundamental because it satisfied either the 'implicit in the concept of ordered liberty' test, or the 'deeply rooted in [the] Nation's history and tradition' test. If the asserted right had been defined more generally as 'the right of adults to respect for their private, consensual sexual activities', rather than as 'the right to engage in homosexual sodomy', Justice White might not have been able to dismiss so contemptuously as 'facetious' the argument that such a right is indeed 'implicit in the concept of ordered liberty', as necessary to preclude police invasions of bedrooms. While the argument that the asserted right is 'deeply rooted in . . . history and tradition' was harder to maintain, in view of the long history of legal interferences with sexual activity, this merely casts doubt on whether 'history and tradition' is the appropriate test. Moreover, even that test could be satisfied if the relevant historical period the Court examined had been 1961–1986, during which the majority of state oral or anal intercourse laws were repealed or invalidated.[181] As for a new and different

[177] See Conkle (1987 US), 237–41.   [178] See Vieira (1988 US), 1186.
[179] 120 L Ed 2d 674 at 757 (1992).   [180] Ibid. at 763–5.
[181] See Dubber (1990 Eur), 211–12.

test of what is 'fundamental', this involves essentially the same difficulties and controversy as a general principle explaining the right of privacy. In *Planned Parenthood*, the majority did not appear to use the term 'fundamental' (other than in a quotation), let alone attempt to redefine it, saying only that the 'boundaries [of substantive due process] are not susceptible of expression as a simple rule'.[182]

(e) 'Morality' as a 'Rational Basis'

Can the 'presumed belief of a majority of the electorate in Georgia that homosexual sodomy is immoral and unacceptable' be a sufficient 'rational basis' for a law that prohibits it? It is clear that such a view could not have served as a 'compelling state interest', had Hardwick succeeded with his right of privacy argument. The invocation of 'morality' in support of Virginia's prohibition of mixed-race marriage in *Loving* was implicitly rejected.[183] But one can also argue that such a view cannot be a rational basis because it is based either on religious beliefs or on prejudice against gay, lesbian, and bisexual persons. Georgia's counsel in *Hardwick* cited 'Leviticus, Romans, St. Thomas Aquinas, and sodomy's heretical status during the Middle Ages',[184] and Chief Justice Burger openly referred to 'Judeao-Christian moral and ethical standards' and 'millennia of moral teaching'.[185] But, as Justice Blackmun reminded the Court, '[t]he legitimacy of secular legislation depends ... on whether the State can advance some justification for its law beyond its conformity to religious doctrine'.[186]

Stripping away the religious beliefs supporting the electoral majority's disapproval, there remains nothing but a prejudice against persons engaging in the allegedly 'immoral' sexual activity, unless that majority could point to specific harmful consequences of the activity (none had yet been established in *Hardwick*).[187] The Supreme Court has held at least twice that, for the purposes of rational basis review, 'a bare [legislative] desire to harm a politically unpopular group cannot constitute a *legitimate* governmental interest'.[188] The Court's majority could have remanded Hardwick's claim to the district court and required Georgia to prove some rational basis other than the electoral majority's disapproval.[189] It is interesting to compare the fact that Justice O'Connor found majoritarian morality sufficient in *Hardwick* with her more recent statement in *Planned Parenthood*: 'Some of us as individuals find abortion offensive to our

---

[182] 120 L Ed 2d 674 at 697 (1992).

[183] 388 US 1 at 3 (1967) (quoting trial judge's statement that 'Almighty God created the races ... placed them on separate continents ... [and] did not intend for [them] to mix'). See also *Evans* v. *Romer*, 882 P 2d 1335 at 1347 (Colo 1994) (promoting public morality not a compelling governmental interest).

[184] 478 US 186 at 211 (1986). [185] Ibid. at 196–7.

[186] Ibid. at 211. [187] Ibid. at 209.

[188] See *US Department of Agriculture* v. *Moreno*, 413 US 528 at 534 (1973) ('hippies' living in communes); *Cleburne* v. *Cleburne Living Center, Inc.*, 473 US 432 at 447–8 (1985) ('mentally retarded' persons). See also Stoddard (1987 US), 656.

[189] See Ch. 3, Part I.D.

basic principles of morality, but that cannot control our decision. Our obligation
is to define the liberty of all, not to mandate our own moral code.'[190] She
allowed the moral code of Georgia's electoral majority to prevail in *Hardwick*,
even though the absence of any countervailing interest as substantial as the
protection of the foetus should have made it an easier case.[191]

3. Oral or Anal Intercourse Laws Post-*Hardwick*

In theory, *Hardwick* decided the narrow issue of whether the US Constitution
prevents state legislatures from enacting laws prohibiting same-sex oral or anal
intercourse, and did not 'require a judgment on whether [such] laws . . . are wise
or desirable'.[192] The front-page headline of *The New York Times* ('High Court,
5–4, Says States Have the Right to Outlaw Private Homosexual Acts')[193] was
technically correct. But the decision's real impact was better reflected by the
front-page headlines of two tabloids, the *New York Post* ('Top Court Hits Gay
Lifestyle') and the *Daily News* ('Top Court OKs Gay Sex Ban').[194] One comment, echoing the tabloid headlines, described *Hardwick* as 'an utter rejection
of the homosexual lifestyle', making judicial (as opposed to legislative) protection against sexual orientation discrimination unlikely 'in the near future'.[195] By
effectively 'blessing' oral or anal intercourse laws and the stigma they impose,
Hardwick has had a ripple effect extending well beyond the area of such laws,
as will be seen in the section on equal protection doctrine and use of an immutable status argument. For example, *Hardwick* has been cited as supporting
the constitutionality of a New Hampshire law prohibiting 'homosexuals' from
adopting or fostering children.[196]

   Hardwick has not, however, spelled the end of right of privacy challenges to
oral or anal intercourse laws. Instead, plaintiffs have moved to the state courts
and invoked express or implied rights of privacy in state constitutions.[197] In
Commonwealth v. *Wasson*, the Kentucky Supreme Court (the state's highest
court) struck down Kentucky's same-sex oral or anal intercourse law. It held
(4–3) that the 'Kentucky Constitution offer[s] greater protection of the right of
privacy', describing *Hardwick* as 'a misdirected application of the theory of
original intent', inconsistent with *Loving*.[198]

   In *State* v. *Morales*, the Texas Court of Appeals (an intermediate court) struck
down (3–0) the Texas same-sex oral or anal intercourse law, as a violation of the
implied right of privacy in the Texas Constitution, 'which accords individuals

---

[190] 120 L Ed 2d 674 at 697 (1992).
[191] See Conkle (1987 US), 230; Vieira (1988 US), 1185 (*Hardwick* was a stronger case than *Roe*).
[192] 478 US 186 at 190 (1986).   [193] (1 July 1986) A1.
[194] (1 July 1986) 1 (both).   [195] Harvard Case (1986 US), 220.
[196] See *Opinion of the Justices*, 530 A 2d 21 (NH 1987).
[197] See Harvard Survey (1989 US), 1534–6.
[198] 842 SW 2d 487 at 491, 497 (Ky 1992). See Harvard Case (1993 US), 1374–5 (state constitutions provide weaker protection).

greater safeguards than its federal counterpart'.[199] '[W]e can think of nothing
more fundamentally private and deserving of protection than sexual behaviour
between consenting adults in private. If [so] . . . it cannot be constitutional . . . to
prohibit lesbians and gay men from engaging in the same conduct in which
heterosexuals may legally engage.' The Court went on to reject a 'public morality' justification for the law, and noted that it is rarely enforced.[200] The Texas
Court of Appeals then applied *Morales* in *City of Dallas* v. *England*, where it
enjoined the Dallas Police Department from continuing their policy of denying
employment to applicants who admitted violating the same-sex oral or anal
intercourse law or 'being homosexual'.[201] However, the Texas Supreme Court
(the state's highest court for civil appeals) declined opportunities to strike down
the law when it reversed *Morales* (5–4) on jurisdictional grounds (there had
been no criminal prosecution and no threat of irreparable injury to property or
personal rights), and declined to review *England* on procedural grounds.[202] By
deciding not to address the merits of the state right of privacy argument in either
case, the Texas Supreme Court has left the status of the Texas same-sex oral or
anal intercourse law uncertain.[203] Thus, at the end of 1994, the total of states
with oral or anal intercourse laws stood at 22 or 23 with, and 27 or 28 and D.C.
without.[204]

4. Limitations of the Right of Privacy

What if Justice Powell had not changed his initial vote, and the Supreme Court
had extended the right of privacy to private, consensual sexual activity in
Hardwick? Would *Hardwick* have been a watershed decision, like *Brown* v.
Board of Education,[205] not only invalidating all remaining oral or anal intercourse laws, but establishing a general principle that could be applied to all
forms of public sector sexual orientation discrimination in the US? One could
argue that all discrimination against gay, lesbian, and bisexual persons or same-
sex emotional–sexual conduct burdens the exercise of a fundamental right to

[199] 826 SW 2d 201 at 204 (Tex Ct App 1992), rev'd, 869 SW 2d 941 (Tex 1994).

[200] Ibid. at 204–5. See also *Michigan Organization for Human Rights* v. *Kelley*, [1990] *Lesbian/
Gay Law Notes* 53 (Mich Cir Ct) (oral or anal intercourse law struck down by trial court; no appeal);
Campbell v. *Sundquist*, [1995] *Lesbian/Gay Law Notes* 1, 30 (Tenn Cir Ct) (same-sex oral or anal
intercourse law struck down by trial court).

[201] 846 SW 2d 957 at 958 (Tex Ct App 1993) (Mica England had admitted being lesbian when
asked at her interview).

[202] 869 SW 2d 941 at 942, 942 n. 5 (Tex 1994).

[203] See [1994] *Lesbian/Gay Law Notes* 13–14 (Arthur Leonard's analysis suggesting that the law
is unconstitutional under *England*, in which the jurisdictional requirements of *Morales* were satisfied
by the loss of employment).

[204] See Appendix III. The decision in *Wasson* and the repeals in Nevada and the District of
Columbia (note 7) have changed the pre-*Hardwick* totals (note 82). I have included Michigan and
Texas (see notes 199–203) in the 'with' total because those states' laws have not been struck down
by the highest courts of those states.

[205] 347 US 483 (1954).

engage in private same-sex sexual activity, and therefore attracts 'strict scrutiny'.[206] The dissenting opinion in *Onofre* warned that, '[i]f ... the freedom ... to engage in acts of consensual sodomy is truly a "fundamental right", ... the State cannot impose a burden upon the free exercise of that right by limiting ... access to government jobs', and cannot interfere with 'homosexual marriage'.[207]

But it is far from clear that a different result in *Hardwick* would have been so sweeping. Hardwick's counsel made several (perhaps strategically necessary) concessions in his brief. He said that Hardwick 'of course, claims no right whatever to have any homosexual relationship recognized as a marriage'.[208] Moreover, a decision for Hardwick would 'mandat[e] heightened scrutiny only of a *criminal* law', and would not 'cast doubt on any administrative programs that states might fashion to encourage traditional heterosexual unions', just as contraceptives and abortions could be discouraged by granting tax subsidies or denying public funds.[209] Justice Stevens also suggested that other types of sanction or interference might be permissible: 'Society has every right to encourage its individual members to follow particular traditions in expressing affection for one another and in gratifying their personal desires. ... And it may explain the relative advantages and disadvantages of different forms of intimate expression.'[210]

Even if a majority of five had been mustered in *Hardwick*, it is unlikely that it would have been maintained in cases involving non-criminal sanctions intended to discourage same-sex sexual activity. For evidence that some 'fundamental rights' are much less 'fundamental' than others, one need only look to the post-*Roe* abortion decisions. Although a government may not criminalize pre-viability abortions under *Roe* (as reaffirmed by *Planned Parenthood*), it may deny public funding to poor women seeking abortions (who would otherwise qualify for free medical care),[211] or to family planning clinics that 'provide counseling concerning', or 'encourage, promote or advocate', abortion;[212] it may prohibit the performance of abortions by public employees or in public facilities;[213] and it may require a 24-hour waiting period or parental consent.[214] Sanctions of these kinds would not be permitted if they were used to encourage particular political opinions or religious beliefs, rather than childbirth. Thus, a right of privacy seems to provide a minimal level of protection against interference

---

[206] See e.g. *Shapiro* v. *Thompson*, 394 US 618 at 638 (1969) ('fundamental right of interstate movement').

[207] 415 NE 2d 936 at 950 n. 3 (NY 1980).

[208] Brief for Respondent (Case No. 85-140) (31 Jan. 1986), at 23 n. 44.

[209] Ibid., 24.

[210] 478 US 186 at 217 (1986). He probably would not have made such a statement about religious beliefs, if by 'society' he meant government.

[211] See *Maher* v. *Roe*, 432 US 464 at 473–4 (1977); *Harris* v. *McRae*, 448 US 297 at 316–17 (1980).

[212] See *Rust* v. *Sullivan*, 500 US 173 (1991).

[213] See *Webster* v. *Reproductive Health Services*, 492 US 490 at 507–11 (1989).

[214] See *Planned Parenthood* v. *Casey*, 120 L Ed 2d 674 at 675.

with the choice of abortion, and may well have done so for the choice of same-sex sexual activity.

The right of privacy has an additional limitation. Although Justice Blackmun stressed that Hardwick's claim implicated both the decisional and spatial aspects of the right of privacy,[215] the heavy emphasis on the spatial aspect (the invasion of his bedroom) tends to limit the right's potential for application to the public aspects of emotional–sexual conduct, such as public 'solicitation' of sexual activity, public displays of affection, and legal recognition of couple relationships.[216] The analogy to *Stanley* v. *Georgia* is particularly dangerous. As one commentator has noted, it suggests that 'homosexuality, like obscenity, may be tolerated only if quarantined'.[217]

B. Use of Other Existing Fundamental Rights

Because of the controversy surrounding the right of privacy, gay, lesbian, and bisexual plaintiffs have often invoked other existing fundamental rights under the US Constitution: (1) the First Amendment's express fundamental rights to freedom of speech and assembly (from which the non-controversial implied fundamental right to freedom of association was derived); and (2) an implied fundamental 'right to participate equally in the political process'. The difference between these rights and the right of privacy is that they tend to provide protection against sexual orientation discrimination in spite of the fact that sexual orientation or sexual activity is an aspect of the case, rather than because there is something about sexual orientation or sexual activity that justifies constitutional protection. Instead, protection is provided because gay, lesbian, and bisexual persons are exercising a particular right which cannot be denied to any person (or any 'independently identifiable group') in the US, or because some aspect of same-sex emotional–sexual conduct overlaps with such a right.

1. First Amendment Rights

Gay, lesbian, and bisexual plaintiffs have successfully invoked the First Amendment freedoms of speech, assembly, and association[218] to protect traditional 'First Amendment activities' (e.g. gay, lesbian, and bisexual publications, parades, and student organizations). First Amendment freedoms have also been used to protect certain public aspects of same-sex emotional–sexual conduct

---

[215] 478 US 186 at 204 (1986).

[216] See Harvard Note (1985 US), 1288–92 (discussing 'the poverty of privacy').

[217] Ibid., 1291. See also Wilkinson & White (1977 US), 594 (under *Stanley* rationale, public could be protected from offence by 'permitting arrest even for mild public displays of homosexual affection').

[218] See *High Tech Gays* v. *Defense Industrial Security Clearance Office*, 668 F Supp 1361 at 1378 (ND Cal 1987), rev'd, 895 F 2d 563 at 580 (9th Cir 1990) ('use of mere membership in a "gay organization" to refuse to grant a [security] clearance violates plaintiffs' first amendment rights'; Ninth Circuit found membership not sole reason for refusal).

(e.g. same-sex dancing or publicly 'soliciting' private same-sex sexual activity). And these freedoms have been relied on as protecting public employees against dismissal for being open about their same-sex or bisexual sexual orientation, or publicly discussing same-sex emotional–sexual conduct and related legal issues. However, courts have rejected arguments that oral or anal intercourse laws violate the First Amendment's prohibition of 'an establishment of religion',[219] and arguments that denial of employment to a woman because she planned to marry another woman (partly for religious reasons) violated her First Amendment right to the 'free exercise' of her religion.[220] The particular relevance of expression in the context of sexual orientation and religion, although not in the context of race or sex, is that it often serves as the means by which members of the generally invisible gay, lesbian, and bisexual minority make themselves visible to the heterosexual majority. Even if First Amendment rights can provide only partial protection against sexual orientation discrimination, this partial protection is important if it amounts in effect to protection of a 'right to be visible'.

(a) Publications, Parades, and Student Organizations

Almost any publication dealing with or aimed at gay, lesbian or bisexual persons or same-sex sexual activity is open to the charge that it is 'offensive' and therefore 'obscene'. Gay, lesbian, and bisexual persons benefit from the fact that the US Supreme Court, in interpreting the First Amendment's guarantee of freedom of speech, has not equated 'offensiveness' and 'obscenity'. Thus, any gay, lesbian or bisexual publication that is not 'obscene' will enjoy nearly absolute protection against state-sponsored censorship. Indeed, of the very few cases in which the US Supreme Court could be said to have held against an instance of sexual orientation discrimination, the first two involved attempts by post office officials to prevent the mailing of magazines aimed at gay, lesbian, and bisexual persons.[221]

Similarly, gay, lesbian, and bisexual persons have secured protection for their own parades and demonstrations, and equal access to 'public forums' open to others.[222] For example, in *Olivieri* v. *Ward*, the Second Circuit confirmed that the presence of an organization of gay and lesbian Roman Catholics on the

---

[219] See *Hatheway* v. *Secretary of the Army*, 641 F 2d 1376 (9th Cir 1981); *Baker* v. *Wade*, 553 F Supp 1121 at 1145–6 (ND Tex 1982); *National Gay Task Force* v. *Board of Education*, 729 F 2d 1270 at 1273 (10th Cir 1984). But see Richards (1994 US), 521–2 ('discrimination on grounds of sexual preference is . . . a form of religious intolerance' which violates the First Amendment).

[220] See *Shahar* v. *Bowers*, 836 F Supp 859 at 866 (ND Ga 1993) (any indirect burden on her right was justified by the Georgia Department of Law's concerns about 'efficient operation').

[221] See *One, Inc.* v. *Olesen*, 355 US 371 (1958); *Manual Enterprises, Inc.* v. *Day*, 370 US 478 (1962). For detailed discussions of these cases and most of the US cases cited in Chapters 2 and 3, see Leonard (1993a US).

[222] See e.g. *Alaska Gay Coalition* v. *Sullivan*, 578 P 2d 951 (Alaska 1978) (government-published guide to services and organizations in Anchorage); *Toward a Gayer Bicentennial Committee* v. *Rhode Island Bicentennial Foundation*, 417 F Supp 632, 417 F Supp 642 (DRI 1976) (use of Old State House for meeting).

sidewalk in front of St. Patrick's Cathedral in New York 'is assured as an exercise of its members' constitutional rights'.[223] The neutrality of the First Amendment may, however, permit the organizers of other parades to exclude organizations of gay, lesbian, and bisexual persons, in spite of state or local laws prohibiting sexual orientation discrimination in 'public accommodations'. A federal district court upheld exclusion from the New York St. Patrick's Day parade under the First Amendment, because the parade was 'sponsored by a private organization'.[224] But the Massachusetts Supreme Judicial Court held that the Boston St. Patrick's Day/Evacuation Day parade is a 'public accommodation' from which a gay, lesbian, and bisexual organization cannot be excluded under a state anti-discrimination law, and is not used by its organizers 'for expressive purposes'. Thus, they could not 'cloak their discriminatory acts in the mantle of the First Amendment'.[225] The US Supreme Court has granted certiorari and will decide whether the Boston parade is expression protected by the First Amendment, and how any conflict between the Massachusetts law and the First Amendment should be resolved.[226]

Perhaps the greatest success in obtaining protection against sexual orientation discrimination under the US Constitution has been by gay, lesbian, and bisexual student organizations at public universities (especially in states that prohibit same-sex oral or anal intercourse).[227] Federal courts of appeals have required universities, in at least four cases, to grant official recognition to such organizations[228] and, in at least one case, to provide funding on the same basis as to

[223] 801 F 2d 602 at 606 (2nd Cir 1986). See also *Irish Lesbian & Gay Organization* v. *Bratton*, 1995 US Dist LEXIS 3094 at *11 (SDNY) (although plaintiff had no right to a parade permit for 17 March on Fifth Avenue, '[t]here is no question that ILGO has a First Amendment right to proclaim its pride in its Irish cultural history and in its homosexuality').

[224] See *New York County Board of Ancient Hibernians* v. *Dinkins*, 814 F Supp 358 (SDNY 1993). See also *Gay Veterans Association, Inc.* v. *American Legion*, 621 F Supp 1510 (SDNY 1985) (exclusion from privately sponsored Veterans Day parade permitted).

[225] See *Irish-American Gay, Lesbian and Bisexual Group of Boston* v. *City of Boston*, 636 NE 2d 1293 at 1300 (Mass 1994). See generally Yackle (1993 US). A federal district court has upheld exclusion from the 1995 parade, which will have the 'expressive purpose' of protesting (using black flags and armbands) against the court-ordered inclusion of this organization in the 1992, 1993, and 1994 parades. Inclusion was avoided in 1994 by cancelling the parade. See *South Boston Allied War Veterans Council* v. *City of Boston*, 875 F Supp 891 (D Mass 1995).

[226] *Hurley* v. *Irish-American Gay, Lesbian and Bisexual Group of Boston*, 130 L Ed 2d 621 (6 Jan. 1995) (No. 94–749). The case will not deal directly with the question of whether the US Constitution generally prohibits sexual orientation discrimination, but rather with the question of whether the First Amendment requires a narrow exception to legislation prohibiting such discrimination. If the Supreme Court were to hold that the organizers have a First Amendment right to discriminate on the basis of sexual orientation in the particular context of a parade, it would not be an 'anti-gay' decision, if the same rationale would apply to other kinds of discrimination by parade organizers (e.g. the hypothetical exclusion of organizations of 'Irish-American Protestants', 'Irish-American Jews', or 'Americans of Irish and African Ancestry'). Such a decision would thus not prevent the Court from later finding that the US Constitution generally prohibits sexual orientation discrimination.

[227] See Harvard Survey (1989 US), 1585–94.

[228] See e.g. *Gay Student Services* v. *Texas A & M University*, 737 F 2d 1317 (5th Cir 1984), cert. denied, 471 US 1001 (1985).

other student organizations.[229] They have rejected arguments that recognition
may be refused because the activities of such organizations are likely to lead to
violations of oral or anal intercourse laws. Although the Supreme Court denied
certiorari in *Gay Student Services* v. *Texas A & M University*,[230] it is not clear
whether it would uphold these decisions after *Hardwick*. In 1978, Justice
Rehnquist dissented from the denial of certiorari in one such case. He argued
that 'the question [was] whether a university can deny recognition to an organization the activities of which . . . will . . . lead directly to violations of a concededly
valid state criminal law'.[231] A decision of a federal court of appeals upholding
a denial of recognition or funding could take the issue to the Supreme Court. A
potential source of new litigation is a 1992 Alabama law that prohibits universities from using public funds or facilities to support 'any organization or group
that fosters or promotes a lifestyle or actions prohibited by the sodomy and
sexual misconduct laws'.[232]

(b) Public Aspects of Same-sex Emotional–sexual Conduct

Some courts have been willing to treat a public aspect of same-sex emotional–
sexual conduct as protected 'expressive conduct' of a political nature. *Gay Students Organization of the University of New Hampshire* v. *Bonner* invalidated
a refusal to permit the plaintiffs to hold dances (involving same-sex dancing) on
campus.[233] And *Fricke* v. *Lynch* upheld the First Amendment right of a male
high school student to take a male escort to his high school graduation dance.[234]
Freedom of speech has also been used to challenge laws prohibiting public
'solicitation' of private, same-sex sexual activity, or 'loitering' for that purpose.
In *People* v. *Uplinger*, the New York Court of Appeals struck down such a law
without mentioning freedom of speech, referring to the law as a 'companion
statute' to the statute struck down in *Onofre*, and seeing 'no basis on which the
State may continue to punish loitering' for a purpose that 'may not be deemed
criminal'.[235] The Supreme Court granted certiorari, but five justices (the *Hardwick*
minority plus Justice Powell) dismissed the writ as improvidently granted, with
four justices (the *Hardwick* majority less Justice Powell) dissenting.[236] In *State*
v. *Neal*, the Louisiana Supreme Court upheld against a First Amendment challenge a law prohibiting 'solicitation of a crime against nature' as applying to
speech 'directed to inciting or producing imminent lawless acts' (i.e. breaches
of Louisiana's oral or anal intercourse law).[237]

---

[229] See *Gay and Lesbian Students Association* v. *Gohn*, 850 F 2d 361 (8th Cir 1988).
[230] 471 US 1001 (1985).
[231] *Ratchford* v. *Gay Lib*, 434 US 1080 (1978), denying cert. in *Gay Lib* v. *University of Missouri*,
558 F 2d 848 (8th Cir 1977).
[232] See Alabama Code s. 16–1–28 (groups whose sole activity is 'political advocacy of a change
in [those] laws' are exempted).
[233] 509 F 2d 652 (1st Cir 1974).   [234] 491 F Supp 381 (DRI 1980).
[235] 447 NE 2d 62 (NY 1983).   [236] 467 US 246 (1984).
[237] 500 So 2d 374 at 377–8 (La 1987). See also Harvard Survey (1989 US), 1537–40.

(c) Public Employment

More problematic has been the use of freedom of speech (or association) to protect gay, lesbian, and bisexual persons against discrimination by public employers.[238] Such an argument seems to have greater strength where the discrimination is for public discussion of same-sex emotional–sexual conduct outside the workplace, than for being open to one's (actual or prospective) employer or co-workers about being gay, lesbian or bisexual. In *National Gay Task Force* v. *Board of Education*, the Tenth Circuit (2–1) struck down as contrary to the First Amendment an Oklahoma law providing for the dismissal of any teacher who engaged in 'advocating . . . encouraging or promoting public or private homosexual activity in a manner that creates a substantial risk that such conduct will come to the attention of school children or school employees'.[239] The majority interpreted the law as applying to '[a] teacher who went before the Oklahoma legislature or appeared on television to urge the repeal of the Oklahoma anti-sodomy statute'.[240] The dissenting judge saw it as prohibiting teachers from '*inciting* school children to participate in the abominable and detestable crime against nature'.[241] The Supreme Court granted certiorari and affirmed the judgment without opinion on a 4–4 vote, in which Justice Powell did not participate.[242] It is thus not clear whether the Supreme Court would uphold a similar law today. The right of a teacher to speak about gay, lesbian, and bisexual issues outside of school was also recognized in *Acanfora* v. *Board of Education*.[243] The Fourth Circuit held that a refusal to reinstate a gay teacher after his transfer to a non-teaching position was not justified by his participating in television, radio, and press interviews about being gay, because '[his] public statements were protected by the first amendment'.[244] However, the court upheld the transfer because he had failed to disclose his membership of a gay student organization in his application for a teaching position, in order to circumvent the school's policy of refusing to employ gay teachers, which his 'deception' precluded him from challenging![245]

A gay, lesbian or bisexual employee who accepts this implied invitation to be open may fare no better. In *Rowland* v. *Mad River Local School District*, a teacher told a secretary that she was bisexual and had a female lover, and told the assistant principal and several teachers that she was bisexual. Her statements led to her suspension and the non-renewal of her contract.[246] The Sixth Circuit (2–1) rejected her First Amendment claim on the ground that her speech was not on a 'matter of public concern', with the dissent arguing that, before her

---

[238] See Harvard Survey (1989), 1571–3, 1595–9.

[239] 729 F 2d 1270 at 1272 (1984).　　[240] Ibid. at 1274.　　[241] Ibid. at 1276.

[242] 470 US 903 (1985).　　[243] 491 F 2d 498 (4th Cir 1974).

[244] Ibid. at 501. See also *Van Ooteghem* v. *Gray*, 654 F 2d 304 (5th Cir 1981), cert. denied, 455 US 909 (1982); *Aumiller* v. *University of Delaware*, 434 F Supp 1273 (D Del 1977); Harvard Note (1985 US), 1293 n. 48.

[245] 491 F 2d 498 at 501, 504 (4th Cir 1974).

[246] 730 F 2d 444 at 446 (6th Cir 1984).

non-renewal, she had become 'a center of public controversy in the [local] community'.[247] Justices Brennan and Marshall dissented from the Supreme Court's denial of certiorari because the teacher's speech was 'no less deserving of constitutional attention than speech relating to [racial discrimination]' and was not disruptive.[248] In *Shahar* v. *Bowers*, the Georgia Department of Law withdrew an offer of employment as a lawyer from Robin Shahar after learning that she planned to marry another woman. A federal district court was willing to conclude that 'her relationship with her female partner constitute[d] a constitutionally-protected intimate [rather than expressive] association', but held that 'defendant's interests in the efficient operation of the Department outweigh[ed] plaintiff's interest in her intimate association with her female partner'. Her marriage might 'appear[ ] inconsistent with Department efforts in enforcing Georgia law' (which does not recognize same-sex marriages), and her openness about it showed a lack of 'discretion and good judgment'.[249]

Attempts to use freedom of speech or 'intimate association' to protect the right to be openly gay, lesbian or bisexual raise a number of difficulties.[250] First, it is currently unlikely that either speech or 'intimate association' (which is arguably a part of the right of privacy) could include private, same-sex sexual activity.[251] The Supreme Court has said that sexual activity between men in an adult bookstore 'manifests absolutely no element of protected expression' and has 'nothing to do with books or other expressive activity'.[252] And *Hardwick* would seem to preclude protection of same-sex sexual activity as an 'intimate association'. As a result, an employer can avoid any protection which an employee's statement about their sexual orientation (or an employee's 'intimate association') may have, by asserting that the dismissal is based on the employee's actual or presumed private sexual activity, or the possibility that they may engage in such activity in the future. 'Non-conforming lifestyles are not themselves protected . . . the state can legitimately outlaw gay conduct and discriminate on the basis of gay status as long as it gives the "concept" of homosexuality its due'.[253]

In *Ben-Shalom* v. *Marsh*, the Seventh Circuit rejected the First Amendment claim of an Army Reserve member who had been denied re-enlistment because

---

[247] Ibid. at 449, 452–3. See also *Woodward* v. *US*, 871 F 2d 1068 at 1071 n. 2 (Fed Cir 1989), cert. denied, 494 US 1003 (1990) (naval officer's statements that he was gay 'were made "for personal reasons and not to inform the public . . ." [so were] not entitled to First Amendment protection').

[248] 470 US 1009 (1985).

[249] 836 F Supp 859 at 863–5 (ND Ga 1993).

[250] See Harvard Note (1985 US), 1292–7.

[251] But see Cole and Eskridge (1994 US), 335 ('First Amendment strict scrutiny is required for both the [military's] "don't ask, don't tell" policy *and* for state and federal sodomy laws, on the ground that both laws regulate expressive conduct because of what the conduct expresses to others').

[252] *Arcara* v. *Cloud Books, Inc.*, 478 US 697 at 705, 707 (1986). Cf. *Barnes* v. *Glen Theatre, Inc.*, 501 US 560 (1991) ('non-obscene' nude dancing performed for entertainment is expression).

[253] Harvard Note (1985 US), 1294.

of her statement that she was lesbian, there being no proof that she had ever engaged in sexual activity with a woman.[254] The court held that the dismissal was not based on her 'speech *per se*': '[she] is free . . . to say anything she pleases *about* homosexuality and about the Army's policy . . . to advocate that the Army change its stance . . . to know and talk to homosexuals . . . [but] cannot . . . declare herself to *be* a homosexual'. This 'is . . . an act of identification' and 'it is the identity that makes her ineligible for military service, not the speaking of it aloud'.[255] Her 'admission that she is a homosexual . . . reasonably implies . . . a "desire" to commit homosexual acts', and 'the Army does not have to take the risk' that she might do so.[256] The district court had accepted her First Amendment claim, holding that 'desire' is not 'reliable evidence' of 'a propensity to engage in actual homosexual conduct'.[257] Similarly, in *Pruitt* v. *Cheney*, an Army Reserve member was discharged after revealing in a newspaper interview that she was lesbian, but without proof of any same-sex sexual activity. The Ninth Circuit rejected her First Amendment claim, holding that she 'was discharged not for the content of her speech, but for being a homosexual', i.e. a person who 'desires to engage' in 'homosexual acts'.[258] And in *Dahl* v. *Secretary of the US Navy*, the court declined to extend First Amendment protection to 'homosexual thoughts, feelings, emotions and desires', i.e. same-sex sexual orientation (as direction of attraction).[259]

Second, even if an employee's statement that they are gay, lesbian or bisexual (or an instance of public same-sex emotional–sexual conduct in which they have engaged) is held to be protected First Amendment expression, and the employer does not seek to base the discrimination on private conduct, that protection may be tenuous if it depends on the characterization of the statement or public conduct as 'political'. The element of political controversy has been emphasized in three cases in which an expression argument has succeeded. In *Bonner*, the court stressed the 'message' the plaintiffs sought to convey in holding dances,[260] while in *Fricke*, the court found that 'attending the dance with another young man would be a political statement'.[261] And in *Gay Law Students Association* v. *Pacific Telephone & Telegraph Co.*, the California Supreme Court held that an

---

[254] 881 F 2d 454 (7th Cir 1989), cert. denied, 494 US 1004 (1990).
[255] Ibid. at 462.   [256] Ibid. at 460–1.
[257] 703 F Supp 1372 at 1377 (ED Wis 1989). See also *Able* v. *US*, 1995 US Dist LEXIS 3928 at *23 (EDNY) ('under the First Amendment a mere statement of homosexual orientation is not sufficient proof of intent to commit acts as to justify . . . discharge').
[258] 963 F 2d 1160 at 1163 (9th Cir 1992), cert. denied, 121 L Ed 2d 581 (1992). See also *Schowengerdt* v. *US*, 944 F 2d 483 at 489 (9th Cir 1991) (plaintiff 'not discharged for writing about bisexuality but rather for *being* a bisexual, of which his . . . private correspondence was evidence'); *Steffan* v. *Perry*, 41 F 3d 677 at 692, 715 n. 20 (DC Cir 1994) (*en banc*) (majority says discharge of Naval Academy student for saying 'I am gay' not a First Amendment case because he had not expressed sympathy for gay, lesbian, and bisexual persons or opposed the Navy's policy; minority suggests First Amendment could have been argued); *Cammermeyer* v. *Aspin*, 850 F Supp 910 at 928–9 (WD Wash 1994).
[259] 830 F Supp 1319 at 1324, 1338 (ED Cal 1993).
[260] 509 F 2d 652 at 661 (1st Cir 1974).   [261] 491 F Supp 381 at 385 (DRI 1980).

employer's policy of discriminating against 'persons who identify themselves as homosexual, who defend homosexuality, or who are identified with activist homosexual organizations' was a 'policy . . . tending to control or direct the political activities . . . of employees', contrary to the California Labor Code.[262] If the protection depends on the political nature of the statement or public conduct, what happens when it ceases to be controversial, or when the affected individual does not intend the statement or conduct to be 'political'?[263] Gay, lesbian, and bisexual persons are seeking the right to be open about their sexual orientation in a casual way, and to take same-sex dates to social events (or to kiss or hold hands in public) for the inherent pleasure in doing so, rather than because such statements or conduct further a political cause.

2. The 'Right to Participate Equally in the Political Process'

In the US, gay, lesbian, and bisexual persons in many states can seek legislation prohibiting sexual orientation discrimination not only from the federal Congress or the state legislature, but also from their local (city or county) council. However, the decision of a state legislature or local council to adopt such legislation is not final. In many states, a group of citizens can require, after gathering a certain number of voters' signatures, that a state or local referendum be held on the question of whether the legislation should be repealed.[264] From 1974 to 1993, at least 21 referendums were held on the sole question of whether an existing law or executive order prohibiting sexual orientation discrimination should be repealed or retained. In 15 of these 21 cases, a majority voted to repeal the law or executive order.[265] The US Constitution clearly permits this kind of repeal by referendum, there being no right to have the law or executive order adopted.[266] But a gay, lesbian, and bisexual organization remains free to lobby the legislature

[262] 595 P 2d 592 at 611 (Cal 1979). The decision was codified in 1992. See Cal Labor Code s. 1102.1; Dickey (1993 US).

[263] See Harvard Survey (1989 US), 1587 ('speech by gay or lesbian students who do not wish to make political statements or thrust themselves into political controversy' unprotected).

[264] See e.g. Colorado Constitution, Article V, s. 1, Colo. Rev. Stat. ss. 1–40–101 to 1–40–119, considered in *Meyer* v. *Grant*, 486 US 414 (1988).

[265] See '19 Years of Ballot Battles' *The Washington Blade* (12 Nov. 1993) 24. Majorities voted for repeal in Boulder, CO (1974); Dade County, FL (1977); St. Paul, MN, Eugene, OR, Wichita, KS (1978); Duluth, MN (1984); Houston, TX (1985); Oregon (1988); Athens, OH, Irvine, CA, Tacoma, WA (1989); Wooster County, OH (1990); Concord, CA (1991); Tampa, FL (1992) (repeal judicially invalidated); Lewiston, ME (1993); and against repeal in Seattle, WA (1978); Austin, TX (1982); Davis, CA (1986); Denver, CO (1991); St. Paul, MN (1991); Portland, ME (1992). I am not aware of any country, other than the US, in which a law prohibiting sexual orientation discrimination has been repealed after the legislature had taken the (controversial) decision to enact it. In the US, all repeals had been effected by the electorate until the Cincinnati City Council became the first legislative body to repeal its own law. See *The Washington Blade* (10 March 1995) 23.

[266] See e.g. *Reitman* v. *Mulkey*, 387 US 369 at 376–7 (1967). The Ontario Court of Appeal has interpreted Section 15(1) of the Canadian Charter as requiring that anti-discrimination legislation include sexual orientation as a prohibited ground. See the discussion of *Haig* v. *Canada* in Chapter 8, Part III.

or government in question and request that the law or executive order be adopted again.

In 1992, 'pro-family' groups, often dominated by fundamentalist Christians, began proposing a new form of sexual orientation discrimination. Instead of using referendums merely to repeal laws prohibiting sexual orientation discrimination in public and private sector employment, housing, and services (which they have characterized as conferring 'special rights' on gay, lesbian, and bisexual persons),[267] they have initiated referendums on the question of whether a state constitution, or a city or county charter, should be amended so as to repeal any existing laws of that kind *and* prohibit their adoption by the state legislature or a local council in the future. Such an amendment to a state constitution or local charter has the effect of entrenching 'freedom to discriminate on the basis of sexual orientation (or only against gay, lesbian, and bisexual persons)' as a constitutional right (the antithesis of a constitutional provision that expressly or impliedly prohibits such discrimination).[268] 'Pro-discrimination' amendments of this kind were rejected by voters in Oregon in 1992[269] and 1994,[270] and in Idaho in 1994.[271] And a 1993 Oregon law invalidated similar amendments passed in at least 17 Oregon counties.[272] However, 'pro-discrimination' amendments were adopted by voters in Colorado in 1992, Cincinnati, Ohio in 1993, and Alachua County, Florida in 1994, and have had to be challenged in the courts.[273]

---

[267] See Schacter (1994 US), 293–4, 300–7. See also *Equality Foundation* (6th Cir), note 278 at *15, *20, *22 n. 8 (describing such laws as 'special protection [or preferential enactments] for homosexuals').

[268] In *Reitman*, 387 US 369 at 377 (1967), the US Supreme Court struck down an amendment to the California Constitution which had the effect of entrenching 'freedom to discriminate on any ground in the sale or lease of real property', and said: 'The right to discriminate, including the right to discriminate on racial grounds, was now embodied in the State's basic charter, immune from . . . regulation at any level of the state government. Those practicing racial discriminations . . . could now invoke express constitutional authority.'

[269] For the full text, see Schacter (1994 US), 289 n. 39 ('(3) State . . . and local governments . . . , including . . . the public schools, shall assist in setting a standard for Oregon's youth that recognizes homosexuality, pedophilia, sadism and masochism as abnormal, wrong, unnatural and perverse').

[270] For the full text, see *Mabon* v. *Keisling*, 856 P 2d 1023 at 1024 (Or 1993) ('(1) . . . minority status shall not apply to homosexuality . . . (2) Children . . . shall not be . . . taught . . . that homosexuality is the legal or social equivalent of race, color, religion, gender, age or national origin . . . nor shall public funds be expended in a manner that has the purpose or effect of promoting or expressing approval of homosexuality. (a) . . . [no] marital status or spousal benefits on the basis of homosexuality').

[271] For the full text, see *American Civil Liberties Union, Idaho Chapter* v. *Echohawk*, 857 P 2d 626 at 627–8 (Idaho 1993) ('. . . no minority status to persons who engage in homosexual behavior . . . Same-sex marriages and domestic partnerships . . . shall not be legally recognized . . . No . . . school . . . shall . . . promote, sanction, or endorse homosexuality as a healthy, approved or acceptable behavior . . . No [expenditure of public funds] . . . that has the purpose or effect of promoting, making acceptable, or expressing approval of homosexuality . . .').

[272] See the first article cited in note 265 (list of counties); Or. Rev. Stat. s. 659.165(1) ('[a] political subdivision of the state may not enact . . . any charter provision . . . granting special rights . . . or singl[ing] out citizens . . . on account of sexual orientation').

[273] For the 1994 results, see [1994] *Lesbian/Gay Law Notes* 139. Courts have been persuaded to keep some proposed amendments off the ballot, for technical and substantive reasons. See e.g.

This new form of sexual orientation discrimination (which threatens any state or local attempt to protect gay, lesbian, and bisexual persons against discrimination, in any state where a citizen-initiated 'pro-discrimination' amendment is possible) has forced gay, lesbian, and bisexual plaintiffs to search for a new source of protection in equal protection doctrine under the US Constitution. With a fundamental right of privacy argument (and possibly a suspect classification argument) foreclosed by *Hardwick*, a new fundamental right argument was needed that did not stress the basis upon which the amendments sought to restrict access to legislative bodies (sexual orientation), but rather the activity or opportunity which the amendments sought to restrict (access to legislative bodies). Gay, lesbian, and bisexual plaintiffs were able to find such an argument in a line of US Supreme Court cases, beginning with *Hunter* v. *Erickson*,[274] that dealt with provisions of state or local law withdrawing certain issues from the ordinary legislative process.

In *Evans* v. *Romer*, plaintiffs argued that these US Supreme Court cases had established, as an aspect of 'equal protection' doctrine, a 'fundamental right to participate equally in the political process', which was infringed by Amendment 2 to the Constitution of Colorado. Amendment 2, proposed by 'Colorado for Family Values' and supported by fifty-three per cent of voters in 1992, provides as follows:

Neither the State of Colorado, through any of its branches or departments, nor any of its agencies, political subdivisions, municipalities or school districts, shall enact, adopt or enforce any statute, regulation, ordinance or policy whereby homosexual, lesbian or bisexual orientation, conduct, practices or relationships shall constitute or otherwise be the basis of or entitle any person or class of persons to have or claim any minority status, quota preferences, protected status or claim of discrimination.[275]

The Colorado Supreme Court agreed (6–1) that 'the Equal Protection Clause ... protects the fundamental right to participate equally in the political process, and that any ... state constitutional amendment which infringes on this right by

Citizens for Responsible Behavior v. *Superior Court*, 2 Cal Rptr 2d 648 at 663 (Ct App 1991) (ordinance would have provided that '[t]he City of Riverside does not recognize homosexuality or bisexuality as fundamental human rights requiring special protection', repealed an existing prohibition of sexual orientation discrimination, and required that any future prohibition be enacted by a majority of voters).

[274] 393 US 385 (1969) (invalidating city charter amendment which required legislation prohibiting race or religion discrimination in housing to be approved by the electorate). See also *James* v. *Valtierra*, 402 US 137 (1971) (upholding state constitutional amendment which required majority approval for construction of low-rent housing projects); *Gordon* v. *Lance*, 403 US 1 (1971) (upholding state constitutional and statutory requirements that a 60% majority of electorate approve the incurring of bonded indebtedness); *Washington* v. *Seattle School District*, 458 US 457 (1982) (invalidating state statute which prohibited school boards from using mandatory bussing to achieve racial integration).

[275] *Evans* v. *Romer*, 854 P 2d 1270 at 1272 (Colo 1993). Amendment 2 would be s. 30b of Article II (Bill of Rights) of the Colorado Constitution. On 'pro-discrimination' amendments, see e.g. Adams (1994 US), Burke (1993 US), Goldberg (1994 US), Harvard Note (1993 US), Niblock (1993 US), Richards (1994 US).

"fencing out" an independently identifiable class of persons must be subject to strict judicial scrutiny'.[276] After considering and rejecting various 'compelling state interests' raised as justifications, the Court permanently enjoined the enforcement of Amendment 2.[277] In *Equality Foundation of Greater Cincinnati, Inc.* v. *City of Cincinnati*, a federal district court struck down a similar amendment to a city charter (proposed by 'Equal Rights Not Special Rights') on several grounds, including violation of plaintiffs' 'fundamental right to equal participation in the political process'.[278]

This 'right to equal participation' argument faces two difficulties. First, it can be argued, as Justice Erickson did in dissent in *Evans* v. *Romer*, that the US Supreme Court has never 'explicitly identified the fundamental right that the [*Evans*] majority extrapolates from the [*Hunter* line of cases]'.[279] These cases can be explained as turning on whether or not the challenged measure explicitly or implicitly used a suspect classification (race).[280] Second, even if the US Supreme Court meant to identify a new fundamental right in the *Hunter* line of cases, extending beyond 'suspect classes',[281] it made clear its intention not to extend this right to any 'identifiable group' which was prevented from obtaining passage of legislation it desired by a state constitutional or local charter amendment. If the right had such a scope, no such amendment could ever withdraw a subject from a legislative body and require a referendum on it.[282] Instead, the Court seems to have limited the right to 'independently identifiable groups'.[283] This raises the question of what criteria can be used to distinguish 'identifiable groups' from 'independently identifiable groups', and how these criteria differ (if at all) from those used to identify 'suspect classes'.

In *Equality Foundation*, Judge Spiegel suggested that an 'identifiable group' is one 'whose sole identifying characteristic is [its] support for a single issue',

[276] Ibid. at 1282 (upholding preliminary injunction).
[277] *Evans* v. *Romer*, 882 P 2d 1335 (Colo 1994) (upholding permanent injunction).
[278] 860 F Supp 417 at 430–4 (SD Ohio 1994), rev'd, 1995 US App LEXIS 10462 (6th Cir). Judge Spiegel also found, at 444–7, violations of plaintiffs' First Amendment rights to freedom of speech and association and 'to petition the Government for redress of grievances'. These arguments (which the Sixth Circuit rejected, at *21–*22) seem to differ from the 'right to equal participation' argument only in relying on express (or less controversial implied) First Amendment rights, and in stressing the chilling effect of the 'pro-discrimination' amendment's removal of protection against discrimination on the plaintiffs' political advocacy. It is not clear how this chilling effect differs from that caused by the repeal of an anti-discrimination law, or the absence of any such law, both constitutionally valid situations. See note 266 and accompanying text.
[279] 854 P 2d 1270 at 1294 (Colo 1993).
[280] Ibid. at 1282 n. 21, 1300. See also *Equality Foundation* (6th Cir), note 278 at *15–*21 (the district court 'erroneously fashioned this innovative right from [the *Hunter* line of cases]').
[281] Ibid. at 1283–4.
[282] See *James* v. *Valtierra*, 402 US 137 at 142 (1971) ('a State would not be able to require referendums on any subject unless referendums were required on all, because they would always disadvantage some group').
[283] See *Gordon* v. *Lance*, 403 US 1 at 5 (1971) ('no independently identifiable group . . . favors bonded indebtedness over other forms of financing'). The Court also referred to the absence of discrimination against a 'discrete and insular minority' (at 5) or 'any identifiable class' (at 7).

whereas an 'independently identifiable group' has a 'defining characteristic' (e.g. race, sex, sexual orientation) that 'transcends the mere support for a single political issue'.[284] In other words, if the group were to obtain the legislation they desire (and which the amendment blocks), would they still have anything in common? The answer might be yes with regard to gay, lesbian, and bisexual persons considered in *Evans* and *Equality Foundation*, and no with regard to 'persons favouring bonded indebtedness' considered in *Gordon* v. *Lance*.[285] But why was the answer no with respect to 'persons on low incomes' in *James* v. *Valtierra*?[286] And would the answer clearly be no in the case of a Roman Catholic organization challenging a state constitutional amendment guaranteeing a woman's right to choose an abortion (passed because of a hypothetical reversal of *Roe* v. *Wade*) or a rifle club challenging a state constitutional ban on private gun ownership? Indeed, could 'Colorado for Family Values' use the 'right to equal participation' to challenge an 'anti-discrimination' amendment to the Colorado Constitution that repealed Amendment 2 and substituted a prohibition of sexual orientation discrimination by the state and local governments?

The US Supreme Court has agreed to hear the State of Colorado's appeal in *Evans*.[287] It will thus have the opportunity to decide whether or not an implied fundamental 'right to participate equally in the political process' exists under the US Constitution, and whether or not 'pro-discrimination' amendments aimed at gay, lesbian, and bisexual persons infringe it. It is not clear what the Court will decide. It could agree with the majority's reasoning in *Evans*, and develop workable criteria for identifying 'independently identifiable groups' that are less demanding than those for 'suspect classes'. Or it could decide that no workable criteria are possible and confine the *Hunter* line of cases to 'suspect or quasi-suspect classes'(or classes exercising other fundamental rights). If so, in view of *Hardwick*, this would require gay, lesbian, and bisexual plaintiffs challenging 'pro-discrimination' amendments to argue that sexual orientation is a 'suspect or quasi-suspect classification'. In *Equality Foundation*, this argument was accepted by the district court, was rejected by the Sixth Circuit, and may ultimately be presented to the US Supreme Court.[288] Chapter 3 will address its merits.

---

[284] 860 F Supp 417 at 434 n. 12 (SD Ohio 1994). See also *Evans*, 854 P 2d 1270 at 1282 (Colo 1993) (group must not be 'created by the statute itself').

[285] 403 US 1 (1971). But see *Equality Foundation* (6th Cir), note 278 at *13, *21 ('persons having a homosexual "orientation" simply do not . . . comprise an identifiable class'). Cf. Harvard Note (1993 US), 1918 (toxic polluters not an 'independently identifiable group').

[286] 402 US 137 (1971).

[287] *Romer* v. *Evans*, 130 L Ed 2d 1061 (21 Feb. 1995) (No. 94-1039).

[288] In *Equality Foundation*, 860 F Supp 417 at 440, 449 (SD Ohio 1994), Judge Spiegel also struck down the amendment on the ground that gay, lesbian, and bisexual persons are a 'quasi-suspect class' (argument rejected by 6th Cir, see note 278 at *15). If the US Supreme Court were to reject all arguments for invalidating 'pro-discrimination' state constitutional amendments under the US Constitution, only federal legislation (or a federal constitutional amendment) could override such amendments, under the Supremacy Clause (US Constitution, Article VI). State legislation (or a state constitutional amendment) could override local amendments, as in Oregon (see note 272).

3

The United States Constitution: Immutable Status and Sex Discrimination Arguments

I. USE OF AN IMMUTABLE STATUS ARGUMENT

In the aftermath of *Hardwick*, gay, lesbian, and bisexual plaintiffs have looked for alternatives to a right of privacy argument under the US Constitution. In addition to invoking state rights of privacy, federal First Amendment rights, and an arguable federal 'right to participate equally in the political process', they have turned to the suspect classifications branch of federal equal protection doctrine. (*Hardwick* limits use of the fundamental rights branch of that doctrine to fundamental rights other than the right of privacy, such as freedom of speech.)[1] In arguing that sexual orientation is a 'suspect' or 'quasi-suspect' classification, they propose an analogy between sexual orientation discrimination and race or sex discrimination, rather than between same-sex sexual activity and contraception or abortion. Unlike the seemingly limited protection offered by the right of privacy or the First Amendment, the suspect classification argument is seen as capable of protecting both public and private same-sex emotional–sexual conduct, and potentially encompassing all aspects of public sector discrimination against gay, lesbian, and bisexual persons, especially in employment, housing, and services, and with respect to the rights of couples and parents.[2] A Supreme Court decision that sexual orientation constitutes a suspect classification might thus serve as the *Brown* v. *Board of Education* that gay, lesbian, and bisexual persons in the US have been seeking.

A. Criteria for Identifying Suspect Classifications

The Supreme Court has referred to various criteria in the course of deciding whether particular classifications warrant suspect status. Race, national origin, and (in some cases) 'alienage' (i.e. not being a US citizen) have been held to

[1] See Ch. 2, Part II.B. Cf. *High Tech Gays* v. *Defense Industrial Security Clearance Office*, 668 F Supp 1361 at 1370–2 (ND Cal 1987) (finding a 'fundamental right' to engage in any same-sex or opposite-sex sexual activity other than oral or anal intercourse); *Cammermeyer* v. *Aspin*, 850 F Supp 910 at 927 (WD Wash 1994) (court 'need not decide whether plaintiff has a fundamental right to be a homosexual').

[2] See Harvard Note (1985 US), 1297 ('an equal protection analysis seeks to unify the private and the political by protecting gay personhood as a whole').

be suspect;[3] in addition, sex,[4] the marital status of a child's parents,[5] and the legality of a child's immigration status[6] have been treated as quasi-suspect. Classifications that have been deemed not to merit strict or intermediate scrutiny include a person's wealth or income,[7] age,[8] mental disability,[9] the legality of an adult's immigration status,[10] and being closely related to another person.[11]

What do the suspect and quasi-suspect classifications have in common that separates them from the rejected classifications? The consensus in both the Supreme Court's decisions and in commentary[12] seems to be that some or all of the following requirements will be satisfied by the individuals disfavoured by a suspect classification:

(1) they have suffered a history of intentional unequal treatment;[13]

(2) the classification imposes on them a stigma that brands them as inferior;[14]

(3) they have been the object of widespread prejudice and hostility;[15]

(4) the unequal treatment they have suffered has often resulted from stereo-typed assumptions about their abilities;[16]

(5) they constitute a 'discrete and insular minority' whose political participation has been seriously curtailed because of prejudice;[17]

(6) the basis of the classification is an immutable (and often highly visible) personal characteristic that each such individual possesses;[18]

---

[3] See *Loving* v. *Virginia*, 388 US 1 at 11 (1967) (race); *Korematsu* v. *US*, 323 US 214 at 216 (1944) (national origin); *Graham* v. *Richardson*, 403 US 365 at 371–2 (1971) (alienage).

[4] *Mississippi University for Women* v. *Hogan*, 458 US 718 at 723–4, 724 n. 9 (1982) (O'Connor J.) (unnecessary to decide whether sex is suspect because discrimination in question could not withstand intermediate scrutiny); *J.E.B.* v. *Alabama ex rel. T.B.*, 128 L Ed 2d 89 at 102 n. 6 (1994) (same). Cf. *Frontiero* v. *Richardson*, 411 US 677 at 688 (1973) (plurality of 4) (sex is suspect): Justice Powell (at 691–2) declined to provide the fifth vote partly because of the ongoing Equal Rights Amendment ratification process.

[5] *Mills* v. *Habluetzel*, 456 US 91 at 97–9 (1982).

[6] *Plyler* v. *Doe*, 457 US 216 at 224 (1982) (4–4 affirmance).

[7] *San Antonio Independent School District* v. *Rodriguez*, 411 US 1 at 27–28 (1973).

[8] *Massachusetts Board of Retirement* v. *Murgia*, 427 US 307 at 313–14 (1973).

[9] *Cleburne* v. *Cleburne Living Center, Inc.*, 473 US 432 at 442 (1985).

[10] *Plyler* v. *Doe*, 457 US 216 at 219 n. 19 (1982).

[11] *Lyng* v. *Castello*, 477 US 635 at 638 (1986).

[12] See e.g. Harvard Note (1985 US), 1290–91; Miller (1984 US), 812; Friedman (1979 US), 556–8; Penn Note (1979 US), 202–3; Karst (1977 US), 23–6.

[13] See *Lyng*, 477 US at 638; *Cleburne*, 473 US 432 at 441 (1985); *Murgia*, 427 US 307 at 313 (1973); *Rodriguez*, 411 US 1 at 28 (1973); *Frontiero*, 411 US 677 at 684–5 (1973) (plurality).

[14] See e.g. *Regents of the University of California* v. *Bakke*, 438 US 265 at 357–62 (1978) (Brennan J.). See also Karst (1977 US), 23–4; Harvard Survey (1969 US), 1127. But see *Bakke* at 294 n. 34 (Powell J.) ('[t]he Equal Protection Clause is not framed in terms of "stigma"').

[15] See *Cleburne*, 473 US 432 at 440, 442–3 (1985); *Plyler*, 457 US 216 at 216 n. 14 (1982); *Rodriguez*, 411 US 1 at 105 (1973) (Marshall J., dissenting).

[16] See e.g. *Hogan*, 458 US 718 at 725 (1982); *Murgia*, 427 US 307 at 313 (1973).

[17] See *United States* v. *Carolene Products*, 304 US 144 at 152 n. 4 (1938). See also *Lyng*, 477 US 635 at 638 (1986); *Cleburne*, 473 US 432 at 445 (1985); *Plyler*, 457 US 216 at 216 n. 14 (1982); *Murgia*, 427 US 307 at 313 (1973); *Rodriguez*, 411 US 1 at 28 (1973); *Frontiero*, 411 US 677 at 686 n. 17 (1973); *Graham*, 403 US 365 at 372 (1971). Cf. *Bakke*, 438 US 265 at 290 (1978).

[18] See e.g. *Lyng*, 477 US 635 at 638 (1986) ('obvious, immutable, or distinguishing characteristics that define them as a discrete group'); *Plyler*, 457 US 216 at 216 n. 14, 220 (1982) ('groups

(7) the characteristic is irrelevant to their ability to perform in or contribute to society (and to any legitimate public purpose).[19]

The Supreme Court has never clearly defined the distinction between suspect and quasi-suspect classifications, but it would seem that the same requirements must be fulfilled, except to lesser degrees.[20] Thus, while a suspect classification deals with a trait that is 'constitutionally an irrelevance'[21] (i.e. almost never relevant, except in compelling circumstances), a quasi-suspect classification is generally irrelevant, but may occasionally be relevant to a legitimate public purpose.[22]

In its various suspect classification decisions, the Supreme Court has referred to different combinations of these requirements, but has never provided a coherent theory explaining their purpose and relative importance.[23] Thus, it is not clear whether they are all essential or whether certain combinations are sufficient. Each writer seeking to apply them to a new classification is left to supply his or her own framework. In determining whether these requirements are met with respect to sexual orientation or gay, lesbian, and bisexual persons, I will group the requirements according to the purposes they appear to serve.[24] The first four criteria (i.e. history of unequal treatment, stigma, prejudice, and stereotyping) seem to identify potential suspect classifications that have inflicted harm of a degree and kind sufficient to warrant strict judicial scrutiny. The fifth criterion (i.e. lack of political power) seems to screen out classifications disfavouring individuals who have the political power to obtain redress from the legislative and executive branches. Taken together, the first five criteria would

disfavoured by virtue of circumstances beyond their control'); *Parham* v. *Hughes*, 441 US 347 at 351 (1979) (plurality) ('classes based on certain . . . immutable human attributes', such as race, national origin, alienage, 'illegitimacy', sex); *Mathews* v. *Lucas*, 427 US 495 at 505–6 (1976) ('illegitimacy . . . is, like race or national origin, a characteristic determined by causes not within the control of the illegitimate individual'; '[it] does not carry an obvious badge, as race or sex do'); *Frontiero*, 411 US 677 at 686 (1973) ('high visibility of the sex characteristic'; 'sex, like race and national origin, is an immutable characteristic determined solely by the accident of birth'). See also Harvard Survey (1969 US), at 1126–7. In *Cleburne*, 473 US 432 at 442 n. 10 (1985) the Supreme Court cited John Ely's rejection of immutability as a criterion (see Ely (1980 US), 150) in holding that 'mentally retarded' persons are not a quasi-suspect class. Janet Halley argues that immutability is at most a factor and not a requirement: see Halley (1994 US), 507–10. Visibility must also be a factor, not a requirement, because otherwise national origin, alienage, and the marital or immigration status of a child's parents would not fit. But see *Equality Foundation* (6th Cir), Ch. 2, note 278 at *13 ('[b]ecause homosexuals generally are not identifiable "on sight" unless they elect to be so identifiable by conduct (such as public displays of . . . affection or self-proclamation . . .), they cannot constitute a suspect [or quasi-suspect] class').

[19] See *Cleburne*, 473 US 432 at 442 (1985); *Mathews*, 427 US 495 at 505 (1976); *Frontiero*, 411 US 677 at 686 (1973). See also Harvard Survey (1969 US), 1126–7.

[20] See e.g. *Mathews*, ibid. at 505–6. See also Harvard Note (1985 US), 1287 n. 14; Penn Note (1979 US), 208–9.

[21] *Edwards* v. *California*, 314 US 160 at 184–5 (1941).

[22] See e.g. *Cleburne*, 473 US 432 at 453–4 (1985) (Stevens J., concurring); *Plyler*, 457 US 216 at 220–4 (1982); *Hogan*, 458 US 718 at 726–8 (1982).

[23] See Harvard Note (1985 US), 1298.

[24] Some of the criteria, such as history of unequal treatment and prejudice or stigma, prejudice and stereotypes, or immutability and irrelevance, are frequently lumped together.

appear to designate candidates for suspect classification status that have caused a sufficient degree of particular kinds of harm to individuals sufficiently deprived of access to political remedies. With respect to these candidates, the judiciary feels entitled to intervene in the political process. The sixth and seventh criteria address the difficult substantive question of whether the harm is of a kind that can rarely, if ever, be justified, thus warranting a judicial presumption against the validity of the classification causing the harm.[25]

B. Is Sexual Orientation a Suspect Classification?

One could spend a great deal of time analysing the Supreme Court's criteria and suggesting others, or applying them to the case of sexual orientation. Space limitations prevent me from doing so here. Instead, I will take the criteria as they are and focus on the areas of controversy when they are applied to sexual orientation.[26] There is little doubt (and several courts have found) that sexual orientation satisfies the first four criteria, because the history of intentional unequal treatment[27] of, and imposition of stigma[28] on, gay, lesbian, and bisexual persons, as well as the prejudice and hostility against them,[29] and stereotyped assumptions about them,[30] are relatively easy to demonstrate. Thus, the use of sexual orientation as a classification has inflicted harm sufficient to warrant strict judicial scrutiny. The areas of controversy lie in the fifth, sixth, and seventh criteria: whether gay, lesbian, and bisexual persons have sufficient 'political power' to achieve legislative protection against the harm done by the classification; and whether the harm is justifiable, either because sexual orientation (as direction of attraction) is not 'immutable' or because the lack of constitutional protection for

[25] One could argue, as I will (very briefly) in Ch. 6 in relation to the Canadian Charter, that none of the seven criteria should be necessary apart from the sixth (immutability). Cf. Nowak (1974 US), 1082 (all classifications based on personal characteristics or statuses should be subject to intermediate review).

[26] For more detailed discussions, see e.g. Roberts (1993 US); Strasser (1991b US); Hayes (1990 US); Harvard Survey (1989 US), 1564–71; Harvard Note (1985 US); Miller (1984 US); Penn Note (1979 US); Friedman (1979 US); Michigan Note (1974 US); Chaitin and Lefcourt (1973 US); Barnett (1973 US), 263.

[27] See Ch. 2, note 3. See also *High Tech Gays* v. *Defense Industrial Security Clearance Office*, 895 F 2d 563 at 573 (9th Cir 1990); *Ben-Shalom* v. *Marsh*, 881 F 2d 454 at 465 (7th Cir 1989); *Watkins* v. *US Army*, 875 F 2d 699 at 724 (9th Cir 1989) (Norris J., concurring); *Equality Foundation*, 860 F Supp 417 at 436–7 (SD Ohio 1994); *Jantz* v. *Muci*, 759 F Supp. 1543 at 1549 (D Kan 1991), rev'd on other grounds, 976 F 2d 623 (10th Cir 1992).

[28] The fact that a legal distinction confirms or compounds an existing social stigma is probably only essential in cases of 'separate but equal treatment', such as *Brown* v. *Board of Education*. See Ely (1980 US), 150; Brest (1976 US), 9–10. Evidence of the enormous social stigma attached to being gay, lesbian, or bisexual can be seen in the extraordinary lengths that many such persons (e.g. actors) go to conceal their sexual orientation from employers, neighbours, family, friends, or fans.

[29] See *Rowland* v. *Mad River Local School District*, 470 US 1009 at 1014 (1985) (Brennan J., dissenting); *Watkins*, 875 F 2d 699 at 724–5 (9th Cir 1989) (Norris J., concurring); *High Tech Gays*, 668 F Supp 1361 at 1369 (ND Cal 1987).

[30] See *Watkins*, ibid. at 725; *Equality Foundation*, 860 F Supp 417 at 436–7 (SD Ohio 1994); *Jantz*, 759 F Supp 1543 at 1548–9 (D Kan 1991); *High Tech Gays*, ibid. at 1369.

same-sex sexual activity means that sexual orientation (as direction of attraction) is not 'irrelevant'. Although I will consider whether sexual orientation is a 'suspect classification', rather than whether gay, lesbian, and bisexual persons are a 'suspect class', both terms are used in US cases and commentary.[31] The question of whether grounds of discrimination should be viewed as symmetrical (all uses of the ground are prima facie prohibited) or asymmetrical (only uses disfavouring members of certain 'disadvantaged groups' are prima facie prohibited) will be raised briefly, in the context of the Canadian Charter, in Chapter 6.

1. Lack of Political Power

This criterion is derived from the famous footnote in which Justice Stone suggested that 'prejudice against discrete and insular minorities may . . . curtail the operation of those political processes ordinarily to be relied upon to protect minorities, and . . . call for a correspondingly more searching judicial inquiry'.[32] It is not clear whether the key element in this formulation is the existence of prejudice against the minority,[33] the minority's being 'discrete and insular',[34] or the minority's consequent inability to influence the political process. Gay, lesbian, and bisexual persons certainly face widespread prejudice, and some courts have been willing to describe them as 'discrete and insular'.[35] But controversy has arisen regarding what is probably the substance of the criterion, i.e. lack of political power.[36] While several courts have concluded that the criterion is easily satisfied,[37] others have asserted that 'homosexuals are not without political power' and 'have the ability to and do "attract the attention of the lawmakers"'.[38]

---

[31] See e.g. *Watkins*, ibid. at 728 ('homosexuals constitute a suspect class'); *Jantz*, ibid. at 1551 ('a governmental classification based on an individual's sexual orientation is inherently suspect'); *Ben-Shalom*, 703 F Supp 1372 at 1378 (ED Wis 1989) (both used). See also Harvard Note (1985 US); Miller (1984 US).

[32] *Carolene Products*, 304 US 144 at 152 n. 4 (1938).

[33] See Ackerman (1985 US), 731–40; Ely (1980 US), 153–4, 162–4.

[34] The Supreme Court has occasionally used this term to characterize a 'suspect class'. See e.g. *Murgia*, 427 US 307 at 313 (1973); *Graham*, 403 US 365 at 372 (1971).

[35] See *Ben-Shalom*, 703 F Supp 1372 at 1380 (ED Wis 1989); *High Tech Gays*, 668 F Supp 1361 at 1361 (ND Cal 1987); *Adolph Coors Co.* v. *Wallace*, 570 F Supp 202 at 209 n. 24 (ND Cal 1983). See also Tribe (1988 US), 1427. Cf. Ackerman (1985 US), 729 ('anonymous' and 'somewhat insular').

[36] In *Lyng*, 477 US 635 (1986), the Supreme Court requires a showing that a class is 'a minority or politically powerless', perhaps suggesting that the lack of political power of numerical minorities is presumed.

[37] See *Rowland*, 470 US 1009 at 1014 (1985) (Brennan J., dissenting); *High Tech Gays* v. *Defense Industrial Security Clearance Office*, 909 F 2d 375 at 377–8 (9th Cir 1990) (Canby J., dissenting from denial of rehearing *en banc*); *Watkins*, 875 F 2d 699 at 726–7 (9th Cir 1989) (Norris J.); *Jantz*, 759 F Supp 1543 at 1550–51 (D Kan 1991); *Ben-Shalom*, 703 F Supp 1372 at 1380 (ED Wis 1989); *High Tech Gays*, 668 F Supp 1361 at 1380 (ND Cal 1987).

[38] *High Tech Gays*, 895 F 2d 563 at 574 (9th Cir 1990). See also *Ben-Shalom*, 881 F 2d 454 at 466 (7th Cir 1989); *Dahl*, 830 F Supp 1319 at 1324, 1325 n. 9 (ED Cal 1993) ('[t]he recent Congressional and executive dialogue concerning homosexuals' ability to serve in the military

If the courts that have found 'political power' are correct, then the slightest degree of success in achieving legislative protection disqualifies a minority from seeking constitutional protection through recognition of a suspect classification. These courts' conclusions are based on the existence of some state or local legislation prohibiting sexual orientation discrimination, the fact that a few (now three) of the 435 members of the House of Representatives are openly gay men, the participation of mayors in gay and lesbian pride parades, and the influence of gay, lesbian, and bisexual groups on the HIV/AIDS policies of governments.[39] Although eight states, the District of Columbia, and over seventy cities and counties now prohibit sexual orientation discrimination in, for example, public and private employment,[40] the federal Congress, forty-two states, and hundreds or thousands of cities and counties have yet to enact similar legislation.

This surprising controversy over the significance of anti-discrimination legislation can also be found in conflicting statements by the Supreme Court. In *Frontiero* v. *Richardson*, Justice Brennan viewed the fact that federal civil rights legislation already prohibited sex discrimination as supporting the argument for treating sex as suspect.[41] However, in *Cleburne* v. *Cleburne Living Center, Inc.*, Justice White referred to federal legislation protecting persons with disabilities as 'negat[ing] any claim that the mentally retarded are politically powerless in the sense that they have no ability to attract the attention of lawmakers', and therefore precluding their designation as a quasi-suspect class.[42]

In *Equality Foundation*, Judge Spiegel argued that the status of a class as 'suspect' or 'quasi-suspect' should not depend on a political power test, pointing to the fact that men do not satisfy the test but are clearly a 'quasi-suspect' class, and to the threat such a test represents for the protected status of women and racial minorities.[43] If this standard (existence of anti-discrimination legislation and the other 'indicia of influence' cited above) were applied to women or racial minorities, neither would qualify as lacking political power and neither race nor sex would be suspect or quasi-suspect.[44] Even if 'political powerlessness' is relevant, Judge Spiegel was able to conclude that gay, lesbian, and bisexual persons, 'while not a wholly politically powerless group, do suffer significant political impediments'.[45] He cited the difficulty they face in forming political

demonstrates that . . . homosexuals have a significant ability to attract Congress' attention'); *Steffan* v. *Cheney*, 780 F Supp 1 at 7–9 (DDC 1991) (*Steffan I*); *State* v. *Walsh*, 713 SW 2d 508 at 511 (Mo 1986) ('[h]omosexuals . . . have never been denied the ability to engage in "political give and take" . . . Are we to say that drug addicts and pedophiliacs are a powerless class because the democratic process has refused to sanction [their] activity . . . ?').

[39] See ibid. (evidence of 'political power' mentioned in the decisions just cited).
[40] See Appendix II.   [41] 411 US 677 at 687–8 (1973).
[42] 473 US 432 at 445–6 (1985). Cf. at 465–7 (Marshall J., dissenting).
[43] 860 F Supp 417 at 437 n. 17 (SD Ohio 1994).
[44] See *High Tech Gays*, 909 F 2d 375 at 378 (9th Cir 1990) (Canby J.) (federal law and laws of 48 states prohibit race discrimination); *Watkins*, 875 F 2d 699 at 727 n. 30 (9th Cir 1989); *Jantz*, 759 F Supp 1543 at 1550 (D Kan 1991).
[45] 860 F Supp 417 at 437 (SD Ohio 1994).

coalitions, the tenuousness of their political gains (repeal of legal protection against discrimination has been sought in 38 of 125 jurisdictions where it has been obtained and has succeeded in 34 cases), and their virtual absence from 'the Nation's decisionmaking councils', like women at the time of *Frontiero* (73 of 497,155 elected officials in the US were openly gay, lesbian or bisexual in June 1994).[46]

2. Immutability

The Supreme Court's frequent references to immutability as a criterion for identifying suspect classifications,[47] and the importance placed on this criterion by courts that have considered the case of sexual orientation, permit the argument that sexual orientation is a suspect classification to be characterized as an immutable status argument. The scientific debate over the immutability of sexual orientation (as direction of attraction) and the effectiveness of an immutable status argument in challenging sexual orientation discrimination will be considered, in the context of the Canadian Charter, in Chapter 7, Part I. Here, I will confine myself to the responses of US courts to the argument that sexual orientation is a suspect classification because it is immutable.

US courts have considered the sufficiency of scientific proof of the immutability of sexual orientation, and whether the relevant legal criterion is or should be immutability or 'importance to identity', but have mainly differed over whether the relevant phenomenon is the direction of emotional–sexual attraction or the direction of emotional–sexual conduct. In *Watkins* v. *US Army*, Judge Norris (referring to direction of emotional–sexual attraction) concluded that 'immutable' for equal protection purposes means 'effectively immutable' (change 'would involve great difficulty'). Thus, sexual orientation is immutable because 'we have little control over our sexual orientation and . . . , once acquired, [it] is largely impervious to change'. The 'possibility of . . . a difficult and traumatic change' ('through extensive therapy, neurosurgery or shock treatment') does not make it 'mutable'.[48] 'Scientific proof aside', he empathized with gay, lesbian, and bisexual persons by asking 'whether heterosexuals feel capable of changing *their* sexual orientation', and how they would react to discrimination against persons desiring or engaging in opposite-sex sexual activity.[49] He

---

[46] Ibid. at 427, 438–9.   [47] See note 18.

[48] 875 F 2d 699 at 726 (9th Cir 1989). See also *High Tech Gays*, 909 F 2d 375 at 375 (9th Cir 1990) (no change 'without immense difficulty'); *Jantz*, 759 F Supp 1543 at 1547 (D Kan 1991) (according to 'overwhelming weight of currently available scientific information', 'sexual orientation . . . is generally not subject to conscious change').

[49] *Watkins*, ibid. See also Henderson (1987 US), 1577 (discussing role of empathy in *Brown* v. *Board of Education* and *Roe* and describing *Hardwick* as 'an example of the complete failure of empathy in a legal decision'). *Brown* was argued by a visibly African-American lawyer, Thurgood Marshall, *Roe* by a visibly female lawyer, Sarah Weddington, but *Hardwick* by a law professor, Laurence Tribe, whom the Court would probably have presumed to be heterosexual.

also suggested that 'immutability' could instead describe 'those traits [including sexual orientation] that are so central to a person's identity that it would be abhorrent for government to penalize a person for refusing to change them, regardless of how easy that change might be physically'.[50] In *Equality Founda-tion*, Judge Spiegel held that sexual orientation (as direction of attraction) is 'beyond the control of the individual', exists 'independently of any conduct that the individual . . . may choose to engage in', and is 'unamenable to techniques designed to change it', which 'are considered unethical'.[51]

The courts that have declined to find sexual orientation immutable have failed to make a distinction between direction of emotional–sexual attraction and di-rection of emotional–sexual conduct. In *High Tech Gays* v. *Defense Industrial Security Clearance Office*, the Ninth Circuit held that '[h]omosexuality is not an immutable characteristic; it is behavioral and hence is fundamentally different from race, gender, or alienage' because '[t]he behavior or conduct of . . . already recognized [suspect] classes is irrelevant to their identification'.[52] This charac-terization of sexual orientation as 'behavioral' was also adopted by the district court in *Steffan* v. *Cheney (Steffan I)*.[53] There, the court found that sexual ori-entation is 'sometimes' chosen and thus closer to the chosen (and therefore non-suspect) immigration status of adult 'illegal aliens', which *Plyler* v. *Doe* distinguished from the unchosen (and therefore quasi-suspect) immigration sta-tus of their children.[54] Judge Canby responded to the 'behavioral' characteriza-tion in *High Tech Gays* by arguing that '[o]ne can make "behavioral" classes out of persons who go to church on Saturday, persons who speak Spanish, or per-sons who walk with crutches. The question is, what causes the behavior?'[55] The capacity of an immutable status to protect chosen behaviour or conduct will be considered, in the context of the Canadian Charter, in Chapter 7, Part I.

3. Irrelevance

Those courts that have accepted the distinction between emotional–sexual attrac-tion and emotional–sexual conduct have had no trouble in concluding that sexual orientation (as direction of attraction) is rarely, if ever, relevant to legitimate government purposes. Several judges have agreed that '[s]exual orientation plainly has no relevance to a person's "ability to perform or contribute to society".' Thus, the controversial issue in applying the irrelevance criterion is the link

---

[50] *Watkins*, ibid. See also *Jantz*, 759 F Supp 1543 at 1548 (D Kan 1991).

[51] 860 F Supp 417 at 437 (SD Ohio 1994).

[52] 895 F 2d 563 at 573 (9th Cir 1990), citing *Woodward* v. *US* 871 F 2d 1068 at 1076 (Fed Cir 1989).

[53] 780 F Supp 1 at 6–7 (DDC 1991). Gasch J. seems to have been discussing direction of emotional–sexual attraction because he found that same-sex sexual orientation is 'neither conclu-sively mutable nor immutable since the scientific community is still quite at sea on the causes of homosexuality'.

[54] 457 US 216 at 219 n. 19, 224 (1982).	[55] 909 F 2d 375 at 377 (9th Cir 1990).

between same-sex emotional–sexual attraction and same-sex emotional–sexual conduct (especially private, same-sex sexual activity). The argument, if one accepts the attraction–conduct distinction, is that the attraction may be immutable but the conduct to which it gives rise is 'immoral' or illegal and therefore makes the attraction 'relevant'. If one rejects that distinction, the argument is simply that same-sex emotional–sexual conduct is chosen (so not immutable) and 'immoral' or illegal (so not irrelevant).[56]

The argument that the immutability and irrelevance criteria together preclude constitutional protection against sexual orientation discrimination, because such protection would directly or indirectly apply to mutable and relevant conduct, is best put by advocates of that position. In a 1978 memorandum opposing a proposal to prohibit employers who discriminate against gay, lesbian, and bisexual persons from interviewing students at Yale Law School, Robert Bork wrote:

Contrary to the assertions made, homosexuality is obviously not an unchangeable condition like race or gender. Individual choice plays a role in homosexuality; it does not in race or gender; and societies can have very small or very great amounts of homosexual behavior, depending upon the degrees of moral disapproval or tolerance shown. *It is a mere play on words to say that homosexuality refers to status rather than conduct. The status is defined . . . by involvement in the behavior.* That behavior . . . is criminal in many States.[57]

Similarly, Linda Chavez, a former staff director of the US Commission on Civil Rights during the Reagan Administration, commented on the 1987 National March on Washington for Lesbian and Gay Rights:

If homosexuality is simply a behavior one chooses like whether to drink alcohol or smoke, then it seems pretty clear that it does not deserve protected status. Society interferes with the rights of persons to engage in a whole gamut of behaviors and regulates where and when they may engage lawfully in those acts. Just because homosexuality involves private sexual acts does not confer special rights on that behavior. Surely no one would argue for non-discrimination laws to protect persons who engage in pedophilia or incest even though the inclination to commit such acts may not be within the total control of the individual.

There is a compelling argument against extending civil-rights protection to sexual orientation on the basis that *it would be homosexual activity, not homosexual persons, that would be protected* by such laws. The distinction is a difficult one to articulate, I grant you, but it is real nonetheless. It has to do with whether society has the right to make judgments about which behaviors it approves or disapproves, not whether or not we have the right to approve or disapprove of certain kinds of people.[58]

[56] Michael Perry has argued that sexual orientation cannot be suspect because same-sex sexual activity is chosen and therefore 'morally relevant', but that such activity should be protected by the right of privacy. See Perry (1979 US), 1067.

[57] A copy of the memorandum (dated 27 April 1978 and circulated to the faculty of the Yale Law School) was obtained from Lambda Legal Defense, New York (emphasis added).

[58] *The Native* (9 Nov. 1987) 4 (quoting from 'Civil-rights laws shouldn't cover sexual orientation', Commentary, *Chicago Sun-Times* (15 Oct. 1987)).

These comments highlight the difference between the proponents of protection, who focus on unchosen and immutable attraction and disregard the link to conduct, and the opponents of protection, who focus on chosen or mutable conduct and disregard or discount attraction. Can the attraction–conduct distinction be maintained in view of *Hardwick*'s rejection of constitutional protection for same-sex oral or anal intercourse?

C. Does Hardwick *Mean That Sexual Orientation Cannot Be Suspect?*

It is clear that the Supreme Court did not expressly resolve the question of treating sexual orientation as a suspect classification in *Hardwick*. The majority rested their decision on the Fourteenth Amendment's Due Process Clause, noting that Hardwick had not relied on that Amendment's Equal Protection Clause in defending the Eleventh Circuit's judgment.[59] Justice Blackmun did not reach the equal protection issue himself, finding the right of privacy applicable, but argued that the majority ought to have considered it.[60]

Several courts have held, however, that the Supreme Court's holding in *Hardwick* implicitly resolved the issue. One of the first to do so[61] was the D.C. Circuit in *Padula* v. *Webster*, where it found that *Hardwick* forecloses the suspect classification argument:

It would be quite anomalous ... to declare status defined by conduct that states may constitutionally criminalize as deserving of strict scrutiny ... If the Court was unwilling to object to state laws that criminalize the behavior that defines the class, it is hardly open to a lower court to conclude that state sponsored discrimination against the class is invidious ... there can hardly be any more palpable discrimination ... than making the conduct that defines the class criminal.[62]

This reasoning has been adopted in panel decisions of four other circuit courts of appeals, one of which concluded that, '[a]fter *Hardwick*, it cannot be logically asserted that discrimination against homosexuals is constitutionally infirm'.[63]

In *Watkins* v. *US Army*, the most rigorous judicial examination of the issue

[59] 478 US 186 at 196 n. 8 (1986). See also *Doe* v. *Casey*, 796 F 2d 1508 at 1522 (DC Cir 1986) ('[a]lthough homosexual *conduct* is not constitutionally protected', '[the Court] did not reach the difficult issue of whether ... the federal government can discriminate against individuals merely because of sexual *orientation*').
[60] *Hardwick*, ibid. at 202, and 202 n. 2 (stating that '[h]omosexual orientation may well form part of the very fiber of an individual's personality', but referring to a discriminatory enforcement argument as avoiding 'the more controversial question whether homosexuals are a suspect class').
[61] See also *Walsh*, 713 SW 2d 508 at 511 (Mo 1986). ('If homosexual conduct is properly forbidden, any social stigma attaching to those who violate this proscription cannot be constitutionally suspect').
[62] 822 F 2d 97 at 103 (DC Cir 1987).
[63] See *Woodward*, 871 F 2d 1068 at 1076 (Fed Cir 1989); *High Tech Gays*, 895 F 2d 563 at 571 (9th Cir 1990); *Ben-Shalom*, 881 F 2d 454 at 464–5 (7th Cir 1989) (conclusion necessary to avoid 'an unjustified and indefensible inconsistency'); *Equality Foundation* (6th Cir.), Ch. 2, note 278 at *15.

to date, a panel of the Ninth Circuit rejected *Padula* in holding (2–1) that 'homosexuals constitute a suspect class'.[64] After a rehearing *en banc*, the full court withdrew the opinion of Judge Norris (joined by Judge Canby) and affirmed their decision requiring the Army to re-enlist Perry Watkins, a gay soldier, on the non-constitutional ground of equitable estoppel, 9 of 11 judges finding it unnecessary to discuss his equal protection claim.[65] But Judge Norris's reasoning and conclusion were preserved in an expanded form in his concurring opinion (supported by Judge Canby).[66]

Judge Norris argued that the class in *Hardwick* was 'those who engage in homosexual sodomy', whereas the class in *Watkins* was 'those with a homosexual orientation', and that *Hardwick* was a 'conduct' case, whereas *Watkins* was an 'orientation' case (using 'orientation' in the narrow sense of 'attraction'). *Hardwick* did not decide that the right of privacy protects opposite-sex oral or anal intercourse, and therefore by implication that 'the government may discriminate against homosexuals without violating equal protection'. Even if *Hardwick* had found such protection, any distinction made under the Due Process Clause would have no relevance under the Equal Protection Clause.[67] He relied on Cass Sunstein's argument that substantive due process 'looks backwards' and 'protect[s] traditional practices against short-run departures', whereas equal protection 'looks forward' and 'protect[s] disadvantaged groups from discriminatory practices, however . . . longstanding'.[68] Putting *Hardwick* aside, Judge Norris rejected the Army's argument that 'homosexuals, like burglars, cannot form a suspect class because they are criminals', i.e. they engage in criminal acts of oral or anal intercourse. Same-sex sexual orientation (as direction of attraction) 'has never been criminalized', and the Army excludes persons engaging in 'many forms of homosexual conduct other than sodomy such as kissing, hand-holding, caressing, and hand-genital contact'.[69]

The best argument against Judge Norris's attraction–conduct distinction is that of Judge Reinhardt, the dissenting member of the original three-judge panel in *Watkins*. He made it clear that, but for *Hardwick* and other binding precedents, he would have joined the majority, and that he believed that 'the Supreme Court egregiously misinterpreted the Constitution in *Hardwick*',[70] which he compared to the upholding of racial segregation in *Plessy* v. *Ferguson*.[71] The

---

[64] 847 F 2d 1329 at 1349 (9th Cir 1988).   [65] 875 F 2d 699 at 711 (9th Cir 1989).
[66] Ibid. at 728.   [67] Ibid. at 716–18.   [68] Sunstein (1988 US), 1163.
[69] *Watkins*, ibid. at 725. Judge Norris's distinction between attraction (or 'orientation' or 'status') and conduct has been adopted by several other judges. See *High Tech Gays*, 909 F 2d 375 at 380 (9th Cir 1990) (Canby J., dissenting); *Equality Foundation*, 860 F Supp 417 at 440 (SD Ohio 1994) ('sexual orientation . . . exists independently of any conduct'); *Jantz*, 759 F Supp 1543 at 1546–7 (D Kan 1991); *Ben-Shalom*, 703 F Supp 1372 at 1378–9 (ED Wis 1989). See also *Baker* v. *Wade*, 774 F 2d 1285 at 1287 (5th Cir 1985) (rejecting argument that 'homosexual persons are denied equal treatment' by a same-sex oral or anal intercourse law, because '[t]he statute is directed at certain conduct, not at a class of people').
[70] 847 F 2d 1329 at 1353, 1356, 1358 (9th Cir 1988).
[71] 163 US 537 (1896).

majority in *Hardwick* 'carefully crafted its opinion to proscribe and condemn only *homosexual* sodomy', so as to be able to recognize in a future case (as Judge Reinhardt was willing to do) that the right of privacy protects opposite-sex sexual activity (including oral or anal intercourse).[72] Even if *Hardwick* was 'about "sodomy"' rather than 'about "homosexuality"',[73] gay, lesbian, and bi-sexual persons could not be a suspect class. Their 'defining characteristic is their desire, predisposition or propensity to engage in conduct that the Supreme Court has held to be constitutionally unprotected', whereas '[w]ith other groups, such as blacks or women, there is no connection between particular conduct and the definition of the group'. 'Sodomy is . . . basic to homosexuality', because oral intercourse 'is the primary form of sexual activity among homosexuals', whereas vaginal intercourse 'is the primary form . . . among heterosexuals'.[74] The attrac-tion–conduct distinction is no answer because 'the class [of] those who have a "homosexual orientation" . . . will consist principally of active, practicing homo-sexuals. . . . [T]he small number . . . who are . . . celibate is irrelevant. . . . [D]efined by status or by conduct, [the group's] composition is essentially the same.'[75]

So who is right: Judge Norris or Judge Reinhardt? Judge Norris is correct in that a valid distinction can be made between attraction and conduct, even though it may well seem a strained, 'nicet[y] of the class definition'.[76] His distinction is a valiant attempt to make the best of a bad situation and provide the most protection possible in the face of *Hardwick*, rather than reluctantly accept, as Judge Reinhardt does, that no constitutional protection can be provided until *Hardwick* is overruled. While one can sympathize with Judge Reinhardt's view that '[t]o pretend that homosexuality or heterosexuality is unrelated to sexual conduct borders on the absurd',[77] and find unrealistic the protest that 'not one shred of evidence has been presented . . . to show that homosexuals as a group share a compelling desire to commit [oral or anal intercourse]',[78] Judge Norris's distinction merely takes advantage of the different meanings that 'sexual ori-entation' can have. When an employer dismisses a gay, lesbian or bisexual employee, it is not clear whether the dismissal is based on the direction of their attraction, of their conduct as a whole, or of a specific instance of their conduct.[79] Judge Norris's distinction works because the employer will often be relying only on a statement revealing attraction, and will have no evidence of the employee's conduct as a whole, or of specific instances of conduct. Although

---

[72] *Watkins*, ibid. at 1354–6.

[73] Ibid. at 1354. See Hunter (1992 US), 543–5 ('homosexuality' interpretation more common).

[74] *Watkins*, ibid. at 1356–7.

[75] Ibid. at 1360–1. See also *Equality Foundation* (6th Cir.), Ch. 2, note 278 at *14 ('orientation' class and 'conduct' class ('virtually impossible to distinguish').

[76] Ibid.   [77] *Watkins*, ibid. at 1361 n. 19.

[78] *Ben-Shalom*, 703 F Supp 1372 at 1379 (ED Wis 1989). Cf. *High Tech Gays*, 909 F 2d 375 at 380 (9th Cir 1990) (Canby J., dissenting) ('I will be the first to admit that homosexuals . . . frequently engage in sodomy, as do heterosexuals').

[79] See Ch. 1, Part III.A.

there may be a considerable overlap between the class of gay, lesbian, and bisexual persons and the class of persons who engage in same-sex oral or anal intercourse, the two are not identical and membership of the former is not conclusive evidence of membership of the latter. If federal and state constitutions were interpreted as permitting states to criminalize the speaking of Spanish in public and in private, and a state had done so, a person's being of Hispanic ethnic origin would not be conclusive evidence that they had violated the 'anti-Spanish' law.

What is more problematic is Judge Reinhardt's telling objection that 'the "protection" of homosexual rights provided by the majority . . . is hollow indeed', and that they are denied 'the right to engage in their most fundamental form of sexual activity'.[80] What kind of protection is provided by Judge Norris's compromise: 'sexual orientation (as direction of attraction) is suspect; sexual orientation (as direction of conduct) is not'? Two levels of protection are possible, depending on whether or not the Supreme Court would extend the right of privacy to opposite-sex oral or anal intercourse.

The *first level of protection* assumes (a) that the Supreme Court would *not* extend the right of privacy to opposite-sex oral or anal intercourse, and (b) that an employer does not dismiss heterosexual persons who engage in such intercourse. With regard to (a), the Supreme Court could confine *Griswold, Eisenstadt,* and *Carey* to contraception, or could protect only vaginal intercourse (marital or non-marital) or only marital opposite-sex sexual activity (including oral and anal intercourse) but not non-marital opposite-sex sexual activity.[81] Such a restrictive interpretation of the right of privacy would certainly be consistent with the *Hardwick* majority's resistance to expanding the scope of fundamental rights.[82]

If the Supreme Court were to limit the right of privacy in this way, recognition of sexual orientation (as direction of attraction) as a suspect classification would provide substantial protection without the contradiction Judge Reinhardt sees. This is because a public employer could not (absent a compelling government interest) dismiss a gay, lesbian or bisexual employee, even with proof or their acknowledgment that they had engaged in same-sex oral or anal intercourse, if the employer did not also dismiss heterosexual employees who had

[80] 847 F 2d 1329 at 1358 (9th Cir 1988).

[81] Justice Stevens stressed in *Hardwick* that the majority's 'tradition' argument and historical evidence applied equally to opposite-sex oral or anal intercourse. See 478 US 186 at 214 n. 2 (1986). See also *Watkins,* 875 F 2d 699 at 717–18 (9th Cir 1989) (Norris J.). A number of courts have held that the rationale of *Hardwick* applies to opposite-sex oral intercourse, in upholding convictions for such activity between unmarried persons. See e.g. *Fry* and *Gates,* cited in Ch. 2, n. 140. Cf. *Moseley* v. *Esposito,* [1989] *Lesbian/Gay Law Notes* 52 (Ga Super Ct 1989) (application of Georgia's oral or anal intercourse law to consensual, marital opposite-sex oral intercourse violated the US Constitution). James Moseley had served 18 months in jail for engaging in oral intercourse with his wife. See *International Herald Tribune* (1 Sept. 1989) 3. On *Moseley* and other prosecutions for opposite-sex oral or anal intercourse, see Halley (1993 US), 1777–80.

[82] 478 US 186 at 195 (1986).

engaged in opposite-sex oral or anal intercourse with a person other than their legal spouse (or even with their legal spouse, depending on the scope of the right of privacy). As Cass Sunstein argues, 'it is always immaterial to an equal protection challenge that members of the victimized group are engaging in conduct that could be prohibited on a general basis'.[83] An example cited by Judge Canby illustrates this point: 'a city would trigger [strict] scrutiny if it jailed all blacks convicted of speeding, while it only fined whites . . . even though the city is free to criminalize speeding'.[84] Discrimination against mixed-race (but not same-race) unmarried opposite-sex couples was struck down in *McLaughlin* v. *Florida*, even though the Supreme Court appeared to be willing to permit a state to criminalize all cohabitation by unmarried opposite-sex couples.[85] Thus, the first level of protection would permit a person to be openly gay, lesbian or bisexual and to acknowledge (where necessary or appropriate) that they engage in private, same-sex sexual activity (including oral or anal intercourse). Apart from any risk of prosecution that such acknowledgment would entail, this level would approach the protection that an extension of the right of privacy to same-sex sexual activity in *Hardwick* might have provided.

The *second (lower) level of protection* assumes either (a) that the Supreme Court *would* extend the right of privacy to opposite-sex oral or anal intercourse,[86] or (b) that an employer does dismiss heterosexual employees who engage in such intercourse. With regard to (a), the majority's narrowing of the issue in *Hardwick* certainly left the Court free to do so, and it declined a subsequent opportunity to overturn *Post* v. *State*, a pre-*Hardwick* Oklahoma decision applying the federal right of privacy to opposite-sex oral or anal intercourse.[87] If the Supreme Court ultimately agreed with *Post*, the protection offered by Judge Norris's distinction would be diminished in a significant respect, because a gay, lesbian or bisexual person could never acknowledge having engaged in same-sex oral or anal intercourse (as the Hispanic person in my example above could never admit to speaking Spanish at home). The protection would thus be limited to persons who: (i) are celibate, (ii) engage only in opposite-sex sexual activity falling within the right of privacy, (iii) engage only in same-sex sexual activity other than oral or anal intercourse,[88] or (iv) engage in same-sex oral or anal

[83] Sunstein (1988 US), 1167.

[84] *High Tech Gays*, 909 F 2d 375 at 379 (9th Cir 1990) (dissenting). See also *Watkins*, 875 F 2d 699 at 719 (9th Cir 1989) (Norris J.) (zoning ordinance aimed at African-American extended families could be challenged on equal protection grounds even if right of privacy did not cover extended families).

[85] 379 US 184 (1964).

[86] For arguments that such activity is protected post-*Hardwick*, see *Watkins*, 847 F 2d 1329 at 1354–56 (9th Cir 1988) (Reinhardt J., dissenting); Pearl (1988 US).

[87] 715 P 2d 1105 at 1109 (Okla Crim App 26 Feb. 1986) ('question of homosexuality' not reached), cert. denied, 479 US 890 (14 Oct. 1986). See also *Schochet* v. *State*, 580 A 2d 176 (Md 1990) (Maryland's oral or anal intercourse law interpreted as not applying to private, consensual opposite-sex sexual activity). But see note 81.

[88] Two judges have stressed this possibility, which will often be the case among men who practise 'safer sex' to avoid HIV transmission. See *Watkins*, 875 F 2d 699 at 725 (9th Cir 1989); *High Tech Gays*, 668 F Supp 1361 at 1371–2 (ND Cal 1987).

intercourse, of which there is no proof and about which they are not asked, or which they are willing to deny if asked.

Refusing to answer the question would not seem to be an option. Several courts have interpreted *Hardwick* as permitting public employers or officials to ask, through questionnaires or polygraph tests, whether a person has engaged in same-sex sexual activity.[89] These courts seemed to treat all same-sex sexual activity in the same way, with no distinction between oral or anal intercourse and other sexual activity, and one could argue that the Supreme Court would extend *Hardwick* to all such activity if it were faced with an appropriate prohibition. The Missouri Supreme Court upheld Missouri's unusual prohibition of same-sex manual-genital contact in *State* v. *Walsh*, citing *Hardwick*.[90] If the Supreme Court were to extend *Hardwick* in this way, the distinction between (iii) and (iv) above would disappear. But the remaining, thin shell of protection would still be of considerable practical importance.

Under this second level of protection, gay, lesbian, and bisexual persons could be open about their sexual orientation (as direction of attraction), and perhaps about some aspects of same-sex emotional–sexual conduct (e.g. having a couple relationship with a same-sex partner), but could not acknowledge that they engaged in private same-sex sexual activity. This would not present a problem in many public employment situations, because there would be no proof of such activity, the employee would not need to mention it, and the employer would not ask about it. However, if the employer did ask about it, the employee would have to be willing to lie to enjoy protection.[91] It might seem repugnant that they should have to lie, and anomalous that they should be protected against discrimination based on their attraction to particular conduct but not against discrimination based on their engaging in such conduct.[92] But a very similar legal situation prevails in such jurisdictions as Baltimore, Detroit, and New Orleans, which prohibit sexual orientation discrimination in employment but have no power to repeal an oral or anal intercourse law enacted by the state legislature.[93] And an even more anomalous situation prevails in Minnesota, where the state legislature passed a law prohibiting sexual orientation discrimination which expressly states that it does not alter Minnesota's (same-sex and opposite-sex) oral or anal intercourse law.[94]

[89] See *Stuart* v. *State*, 597 A 2d 1076 (NH 1991) (question permitted of prospective adoptive or foster parents); *Walls* v. *City of St Petersburg*, 895 F 2d 188 at 193 (4th Cir 1990) (policewoman discharged for refusing to answer such a question); *Truesdale* v. *University of North Carolina*, 371 SE 2d 503 at 509 (NC Ct App 1988) (polygraph test question of job applicant permissible). See also the hiring policy considered in *City of Dallas* v. *England*, 846 SW 2d 957 at 958 (Tex Ct App 1993).
[90] 713 SW 2d 508 (Mo 1986).
[91] Judge Reinhardt saw Perry Watkins' admission that he had engaged in sexual activity with other men, together with the likelihood that he would do so in the future, as fatal to his claim. See *Watkins*, 847 F 2d 1329 at 1361–2 (9th Cir 1988).
[92] A similar distinction could be made between being a woman and having an abortion, or between being attracted to stealing or to sexual activity with children, and actually stealing or engaging in such activity. Discrimination based solely on the status or attraction could be prohibited, whether or not the conduct could be prohibited.
[93] See Appendices II and III.   [94] See Minn Stat Ann ss. 363.20, 609.293.

The most important feature of this second level of protection is that, even if same-sex sexual activity could not be acknowledged, such activity could not be presumed from a statement that a person is gay, lesbian, or bisexual. Such a statement could only be treated as a disclosure of sexual orientation (as direction of attraction). A presumption that such a statement indicates past or potential future same-sex sexual activity would be over-inclusive because it would en- compass persons who said they were gay, lesbian or bisexual but were in fact celibate. Such over-inclusiveness would not survive strict scrutiny if sexual orientation (as direction of attraction) were a suspect classification. As will be seen below, this second level of protection would be extremely useful in the armed forces. The first level might not apply in the armed forces, because even if *Hardwick* means that the right of privacy does not extend to opposite-sex oral or anal intercourse,[95] it could be that the armed forces are consistent in discharg- ing all persons known to have engaged in oral or anal intercourse, opposite-sex or same-sex, thereby violating article 125 of the Uniform Code of Military Justice.[96]

Would the Supreme Court be willing to declare that sexual orientation is a suspect classification, without overruling *Hardwick*? Its decisions in other sexual orientation discrimination cases provide few indications of its potential response to this equal protection question. In *Webster* v. *Doe*, the Court declined to consider (at that stage of the litigation) an argument, relying on *Hardwick*, that 'a general CIA policy against employing homosexuals' is not a 'colorable con- stitutional claim'.[97] In *Rowland*, which raised both First Amendment and equal protection claims, only Justices Brennan and Marshall were willing to grant certiorari.[98] And in *San Francisco Arts & Athletics, Inc.* v. *US Olympic Commit- tee*, four out of nine justices were willing to find government action in the Committee's refusal to permit a sports festival to be called the Gay Olympics, and would have remanded the case to the trial court to consider the equal protection claim, but expressed no view on the appropriate level of scrutiny.[99]

But a clearer indication of how the Court might respond was given the year before *Hardwick* in *Cleburne*. There, the Court declined (6–3) to hold that 'mentally retarded' persons are a quasi-suspect class, because 'it would be dif- ficult to find a principled way to distinguish . . . other groups who have perhaps immutable disabilities . . . and who can claim some degree of [public] prejudice . . . [such as] the aging, the disabled, the mentally ill, and the infirm'.[100] (One

[95] See note 81.

[96] 10 USCA s. 925. See e.g. *US* v. *Gates*, 40 Military Justice Reporter 354 at 354 n. 1, 355 n. 4 (Ct. Mil. App. 1994) (but the prosecution seems to have occurred only because the woman involved alleged that the opposite-sex oral intercourse was non-consensual).

[97] 486 US 592 at 604 n. 8 (1988).

[98] 470 US 1009 (1985).   [99] 483 US 522 (1987).

[100] 473 US 432 at 445–6 (1985) ('[w]e are reluctant to set out on that course, and we decline to do so'). Cf. Americans With Disabilities Act, 42 USCA s. 12101(a)(7) (1990 Congressional deter- mination that 'individuals with disabilities' satisfy the Court's criteria for 'suspectness').

solution would have been to declare that classifications based on any kind of mental or physical disability or on age are quasi-suspect. These grounds are included alongside race and sex in Section 15(1) of the Canadian Charter.) This reluctance to expand the scope of suspect and quasi-suspect classifications,[101] because of the need either to make principled distinctions among new candidates or to include all those that qualify, is strikingly similar to Justice White's reluctance in *Hardwick* to expand the scope of the right of privacy and other fundamental rights, or to distinguish amongst kinds of sexual activity.[102] The Court's desire to halt the expansion of judicial review of government action may thus have frozen the list of suspect and quasi-suspect classifications in *Cleburne* in 1985, and the list of right of privacy categories in *Hardwick* in 1986.[103]

Most commentators, both before[104] and after[105] *Hardwick*, have concluded that sexual orientation should be treated as suspect or quasi-suspect. However, most courts, both before[106] and after[107] *Hardwick*, have reached the opposite conclusion, with the five post-*Hardwick*, non-vacated federal appellate court decisions carrying particular weight. Only two federal appellate court judges (in concurring, dissenting or vacated majority opinions) and four federal district court judges (all of whom have been reversed) have accepted the argument.[108] In view of these lower court decisions, *Cleburne*, and the 'anti-homosexual thrust of

---

[101] See *Steffan I*, 780 F Supp 1 at 9–10 (DDC 1991) (relying on Justice White's reasoning in concluding that sexual orientation is not a suspect classification).

[102] See *Hardwick*, 478 US 186 at 195–6 (1986) ('[w]e are unwilling to start down that road').

[103] Judge Norris argues that concerns about substantive due process should not apply to the suspect classifications branch of equal protection, which does not interfere with the electoral majority's substantive value choices, and cites John Ely's view that sexual orientation should be suspect even though the right of privacy should not exist at all. See *Watkins*, 875 F 2d 699 at 720, and 720 n. 21 (9th Cir 1989), Ely (1980 US), 162–4, 247 n. 52, 255 n. 92.

[104] See Ely, ibid.; Tribe (1978 US), 944 n. 17. See also Harvard Note (1985 US), 1287 n. 14, 1304–5; Miller (1984 US), 809–11; Penn Note (1979 US), 209; Friedman (1979 US), 558; Wilkinson (1975 US), 982; Michigan Note (1974 US), 1627; Chaitin and Lefcourt (1973 US), 53–4; Barnett (1973 US), 263. Cf. Perry (1979 US), 1067.

[105] See e.g. Roberts (1993 US); Strasser (1991b US); Hayes (1990 US); Harvard Survey (1989 US), 1570.

[106] See *Baker* v. *Wade*, 769 F 2d 289 at 292 (5th Cir 1985), and 553 F Supp 1121 at 1144 n. 58 (ND Tex 1982); *National Gay Task Force*, 729 F 2d 1270 at 1273 (10th Cir 1984); *Childers* v. *Dallas Police Dept.*, 513 F Supp 134 at 147 n. 22 (ND Tex 1981); *Singer* v. *Hara*, 522 P 2d 1187 at 1196 (Wash Ct App 1974). These courts relied on the absence of precedent or the fact that sex is not suspect. No court conducted any significant analysis of the question before *Watkins*, 847 F 2d 1329 (9th Cir 1988).

[107] See *Equality Foundation* (6th Cir), Ch. 2, note 278; *High Tech Gays*, 895 F 2d 563 (9th Cir 1990); *Ben-Shalom*, 881 F 2d 454 (7th Cir 1989); *Woodward*, 871 F 2d 1068 (Fed Cir 1989); *Padula*, 822 F 2d 97 (DC Cir 1987); *Dahl*, 830 F Supp 1319 at 1324 (ED Cal 1993); *Steffan I*, 780 F Supp 1 (DDC 1991); *Opinion of the Justices*, 530 A 2d 21 at 24 (NH 1987) (no analysis or authority); *Walsh*, 713 SW 2d 508 at 510–11 (Mo 1986).

[108] See *Watkins*, 875 F 2d 699 at 728 (9th Cir 1989), and 847 F 2d 1329 at 1349 (9th Cir 1988); *High Tech Gays*, 909 F 2d 375 at 376 (9th Cir 1990); *Equality Foundation*, 860 F Supp 417 at 440 (SD Ohio 1994); *Jantz*, 759 F Supp 1543 at 1551 (D Kan 1991); *Ben-Shalom*, 703 F Supp 1372 at 1380 (ED Wis 1989); *High Tech Gays*, 668 F Supp 1361 at 1368 (ND Cal 1987).

Hardwick',[109] it is difficult not to agree with Laurence Tribe that it is unlikely that the Court will declare sexual orientation to be suspect or quasi-suspect 'in the near future'.[110] But if a majority did wish to 'make amends' for *Hardwick*, while refraining from overruling it, Judge Norris has shown them a way to do so.

Several courts have suggested that sexual orientation could at most be declared quasi-suspect, because it could not rank higher than sex in the hierarchy of equal protection doctrine.[111] It can be argued that sexual orientation is as rarely relevant to government purposes as race, and should therefore be suspect. The apparent inconsistency with the treatment of sex could be resolved by elevating sex to full suspect status.[112]

D. Rational Basis Review as an Alternative

If neither the right of privacy nor the First Amendment nor any other fundamental right applies, and sexual orientation is not a suspect or quasi-suspect classification, a gay, lesbian or bisexual plaintiff has only one remaining argument under equal protection doctrine: that a law or policy does not serve a legitimate government interest or is not rationally related to any such interest. 'Rational basis review' is an 'equality' argument, because it invokes the requirement of equal protection doctrine that every classification or distinction made by government action have some rational basis. However, it is not an immutable status argument, because it is available with regard to any kind of classification, affecting any kind of group, whether or not the classification involves an immutable status (or satisfies any of the suspect classification criteria discussed above). Because right of privacy, First Amendment, and suspect classification arguments have been rejected, plaintiffs now frequently argue that rational basis review is sufficient to invalidate sexual orientation discrimination, especially the exclusion of gay, lesbian, and bisexual persons from the armed forces.

Several courts have used rational basis review to find the military's policy of excluding openly gay, lesbian, and bisexual personnel unconstitutional. In *Steffan* v. *Aspin* (*Steffan II*), a three-judge panel of the D.C. Circuit ordered (3–0) the reinstatement of Joseph Steffan, a Naval Academy student who had effectively been discharged after answering 'Yes' to the question 'Are you a

---

[109] *Watkins*, 847 F 2d 1329 at 1355 (9th Cir 1988).

[110] See Tribe (1988 US), 1616 n. 47.

[111] See *National Gay Task Force*, 729 F 2d 1270 at 1273 (10th Cir 1984); *Baker* v. *Wade*, 553 F Supp 1121 at 1144 n. 58 (ND Tex 1982); *Equality Foundation*, 860 F Supp 417 at 440 (SD Ohio 1994); *High Tech Gays*, 668 F Supp 1361 at 1369 (ND Cal 1987) ('standard of review [for sexual orientation] analogous to the standard . . . afforded classifications based on gender'); *Dean* v. *District of Columbia*, 653 A 2d 307 at 363 n. 3 (DC 1995) ('no warrant . . . for placing homosexuality in a status calling for greater scrutiny [than for sex]').

[112] See note 4.

homosexual?'.[113] Its reasoning involved two main steps. First, it held that, although the military has a legitimate interest in preventing (illegal) same-sex oral or anal intercourse by members of the armed forces, it is not rational to presume that a person who says they are gay, lesbian or bisexual will engage in such conduct.[114] (It follows that it is not rational to presume that they will engage in sexual activity likely to transmit HIV, or that they will actually invade the privacy of heterosexual persons, i.e. through actual 'staring in the showers'.)[115] Second, the panel found that preventing an adverse effect on morale, discipline, and recruitment, and fear of invasion of privacy (i.e. fear of 'staring in the showers'), are not legitimate government interests because they involve catering to the prejudices of heterosexual members of the armed forces or the general public.[116] The Supreme Court has held in *Moreno, Cleburne,* and *Palmore* v. *Sidoti* that government cannot give effect to private prejudices against a particular group, whether strict scrutiny or rational basis review is being applied.[117]

The reasoning of the *Steffan II* panel and of other courts achieves the second level of protection discussed above (openly gay, lesbian, and bisexual persons permitted if they do not acknowledge engaging in same-sex sexual activity), but does so through rational basis review, without declaring sexual orientation a suspect classification.[118] In *Meinhold* v. *US Department of Defense,* the Ninth Circuit achieved the same level of protection when it enjoined the discharge from the Navy of Keith Meinhold, who had said on television 'Yes, I am in fact gay'. Rather than strike down the military's regulations using rational basis review, the court held the regulations constitutional because they 'can reasonably be construed to reach only statements that show a concrete, fixed, or expressed desire to commit homosexual acts despite their being prohibited'.[119]

Other courts, however, have reached the opposite conclusion: that the military can rationally presume past, current or potential future same-sex sexual activity on the part of a person who says they are gay, lesbian or bisexual, and that this is a sufficient justification for the military's policy. In *Ben-Shalom,* the Seventh Circuit treated Miriam Ben-Shalom's acknowledgment that she was lesbian 'as reliable evidence of a desire and propensity to engage in homosexual conduct',

---

[113] 8 F 3d 57 (DC Cir 1993), vacated and district court's judgment aff'd, 41 F 3d 677 (DC Cir 1994) (*en banc*). See also *Dahl,* 830 F Supp 1319 (ED Cal 1993); *Cammermeyer,* 850 F Supp 910 (WD Wash 1994).

[114] *Steffan II,* ibid. at 64–7.

[115] Ibid. at 69. The panel also dismissed a 'preventing blackmail' rationale because the exclusionary policy serves to increase, rather than decrease, the risk of blackmail. Ibid. at 70.

[116] Ibid. at 67–9. See also *Pruitt,* 963 F 2d 1160 at 1165–6 (9th Cir 1992) (Army cannot rely on 'prejudice of others against homosexuals' as a rational basis).

[117] See Ch. 2, note 188; *Palmore* v. *Sidoti,* 466 US 429 (1984).

[118] The *Steffan II* panel did not find it necessary to decide whether sexual orientation is suspect: 8 F 3d 57 at 63 (DC Cir 1993).

[119] 34 F 3d 1469 at 1479 (9th Cir 1994). Cf. *Philips* v. *Perry,* 1995 US Dist LEXIS 4906 (WD Wash) (Navy may discharge member who has engaged in same-sex sexual activity and says he will continue to do so).

and therefore as 'compelling evidence that [she] has in the past and is likely to again engage in such conduct', which she had not expressly denied.[120] In *Steffan* v. *Perry* (*Steffan III*), the D.C. Circuit, sitting *en banc*, reversed (7–3) the panel's decision in *Steffan II* and upheld the discharge of Joseph Steffan. While the minority largely adopted the reasoning in *Steffan II*, the majority rejected it, preferring the reasoning of Judge Reinhardt in *Watkins*. They held that, even though there are exceptions, 'the class of self-described homosexuals is sufficiently close to the class of those who engage or intend to engage in homosexual conduct for the military's policy to survive rational basis review'.[121] Supreme Court decisions holding that a 'status' cannot be punished and that illegal conduct cannot be presumed were limited to the context of criminal prosecutions, and did not extend to employment decisions.[122] Nor did Steffan have standing to assert the rights of a 'celibate homosexual' because he had not alleged that 'he had not engaged in or intended to engage in homosexual conduct'.[123]

It is hard not to agree with the majority in *Steffan III* that the connection between a person's statement that they are gay, lesbian, or bisexual and their engaging in same-sex sexual activity is sufficiently close for rational basis review (even though it would not be for strict or intermediate scrutiny). The main weakness in their conclusion is the fact that the military does not discharge all openly heterosexual persons, because they are presumed to be likely to engage in prohibited opposite-sex sexual activity (oral or anal intercourse), but only heterosexual persons actually found to have engaged in such activity.[124] The *Steffan III* majority's response was that heterosexual persons have a 'permissible outlet' (vaginal intercourse), and less temptation because quarters are segregated by sex (not sexual orientation, which would be troubling and would not reduce mutual attraction).[125] The former assumption seems irrational, in view of the popularity of oral intercourse amongst heterosexual persons. The latter assumption would seem to be of marginal significance, given the extensive opportunities for opposite-sex oral or anal intercourse outside of quarters. An extension of the right of privacy by the Supreme Court to opposite-sex (but not same-sex) oral or anal intercourse might make the distinction rational (and invalidate the prohibition of such intercourse by members of the armed forces), but has yet to occur.

By permitting openness about attraction to support a presumption of past,

[120] 881 F 2d 454 at 464 (7th Cir 1989).

[121] *Steffan* v. *Perry*, 41 F 3d 677 at 686–7, 689–90 (DC Cir 1994) (*en banc*).

[122] Ibid. at 687–8, 691.   [123] Ibid. at 697–8.

[124] See *Steffan III*, ibid. at 712 (dissent); *Dahl*, 830 F Supp 1319 at 1335 n. 17 (ED Cal 1993). The *Dahl* court's analogy of a policy of excluding members of ethnic minorities for a 'propensity' to engage in theft, but excluding members of the ethnic majority only for actual theft, is weakened by the fact that race is a suspect classification. See also *Meinhold*, 34 F 3d 1469 at 1478 (9th Cir 1994) (serious question whether rational to presume violation of regulations by one class of persons defined by 'sexual preference' but not by another).

[125] See *Steffan III*, ibid. at 692.

current or future conduct, the *Ben-Shalom* and *Steffan III* courts effectively demolish the attraction–conduct distinction for the purposes of rational basis review (even though it might be valid, for the purposes of strict or intermediate scrutiny, if sexual orientation were suspect or quasi-suspect). They thereby reduce the level of protection provided from the second level to a *third* (*lower*) *level of protection*: openly gay, lesbian, and bisexual persons are permitted only if they are willing to rebut a presumption of conduct by affirmatively asserting their celibacy (i.e. denying that they have ever engaged, or ever intend to engage, in same-sex sexual activity). Silence or lack of evidence regarding such activity will not be sufficient. It is not clear whether courts will accept this hypothetical 'celibacy' defence, which appears to have been successfully invoked in a number of cases.[126]

The ban on gay, lesbian, and bisexual members of the armed forces was codified in a federal statute in 1993.[127] This version casts doubt on the existence of a 'celibacy' defence. It provides that '[a] member of the armed forces shall be separated . . . [if] the member has stated that he or she is homosexual or bisexual . . . unless . . . the member has demonstrated that he or she is not a person who engages in, attempts to engage in, has a propensity to engage in, or intends to engage in homosexual acts'. In *Able* v. *US*, a pending challenge to this latest version of the ban, the district court observed that the statute does not 'suggest how one who is born with an innate tendency, an "orientation" or a "propensity", to commit a homosexual act can prove that he or she does not have such an orientation or propensity', and described the defence as offering 'at best a hypothetical chance to escape separation'.[128] If the statute is interpreted as precluding a 'celibacy' defence, and the exclusion of open but celibate gay, lesbian or bisexual persons is upheld as having a rational basis (e.g. the military cannot take the risk that they may change their minds about celibacy), then protection against sexual orientation discrimination under equal protection doctrine will have been reduced from the third level, i.e none for those unwilling

---

[126] See *Able* v. *US*, 1995 US Dist LEXIS 3928 at *22 (EDNY) (government cites three cases in which Navy members 'escape[d] discharge by stating that [they] had not engaged and did not intend to engage in "homosexual acts"'). Cf. 'Navy tribunal recommends Lesbian not be ousted' *The Washington Blade* (9 Dec. 1994) 25, 'Landmark Case' *The Washington Blade* (16 Dec. 1994) 39 (Zoe Dunning said publicly she is lesbian but rebutted the presumption of conduct without swearing that she would remain celibate); 'No Rebuttable Presumption' *The Washington Blade* (2 Sept. 1994) 27 (discharge of Rich Richenberg recommended for saying he is gay, even though he promised he would abstain from same-sex sexual activity).

[127] 10 USCA s. 654(b). It is ironic that President Clinton, who promised to sign an executive order lifting the ban, ended up signing an essentially unchanged version of the ban into law, thereby signing away the power of any future president to lift the ban (by executive order). The 'statements' branch of the ban (s. 654(b)(2)) was held invalid under the First Amendment and the fundamental rights branch of equal protection doctrine in *Able* v. *US*, 1995 US Dist LEXIS 3928 at *35–*37; see text accompanying Chapter 2, notes 250–59.

[128] Ibid. at *20, *23.

to lie, to a *fourth* (*and lowest*) *level of protection*, i.e none.[129] An openly gay, lesbian or bisexual person may be dismissed (by the military or another public employer), regardless of whether they have ever engaged in same-sex sexual activity or intend to do so. Without any constitutional protection, they must therefore remain firmly in the closet.

Outside the context of military employment, rational basis review has occasionally provided protection. In 1969, in *Norton* v. *Macy*, the D.C. Circuit held that due process required the federal civil service to 'demonstrate some "rational basis" for its conclusion that a discharge [for off-duty same-sex sexual activity] "will promote the efficiency of the service".'[130] In applying this standard, the court rejected the argument that attaching the label 'immoral' to the employee's conduct was sufficient.

A pronouncement of 'immorality' tends to discourage careful analysis because it unavoidably connotes a violation of divine, Olympian, or otherwise universal standards of rectitude. However, the Civil Service Commission has neither the expertise nor the requisite annointment to make or enforce absolute moral judgments . . . [I]t may be doubted whether there are in the entire Civil Service many persons so saintly as never to have done any act which is disapproved by the 'prevailing mores of our society'. . . . [T]he notion that it could be an appropriate function of the federal bureaucracy to enforce the majority's conventional codes of conduct in the private lives of its employees is at war with elementary concepts of liberty, privacy, and diversity. . . . [T]he sufficiency of the charges against the appellant must be evaluated in terms of the effects on the service of what . . . he has done.[131]

This decision led to the adoption of new civil service regulations providing that 'a person is [not] unsuitable for Federal employment merely because [he/she] is a homosexual or has engaged in homosexual acts'.[132] But the rational basis protection in *Norton* was limited by the court's emphasis that Clifford Norton had not 'openly flaunt[ed] or carelessly display[ed] his unorthodox sexual conduct

---

[129] The differences between the four potential levels of protection under *Hardwick* could be summed up as: (1) lying about same-sex sexual activity not required to avoid dismissal, even if asked (but might be desirable to avoid prosecution, which *Hardwick* permits, by an entity other than one's employer); (2) lying only required if asked; (3) lying required to rebut presumption; (4) lying makes no difference. If *Hardwick* were overruled, prosecution would be unconstitutional and lying would not be required. See *Able*, ibid. at *32 (ban 'offers powerful inducements to homosexuals to lie').

[130] 417 F 2d 1161 at 1164–5 (DC Cir 1969). See also *Opinion of the Justices*, 530 A 2d 21 at 25 (NH 1987) (no 'rational basis' for excluding 'homosexuals' from operating child care agencies); *Doe* v. *Sparks*, 733 F Supp 227 at 234–5 (WD Pa 1990) (no 'rational basis' for prison's 'prohibition of visitation between homosexual inmates and their non-inmate boy/girlfriends'); *Equality Foundation*, 860 F Supp 417 at 443–4 (SD Ohio 1994) (no 'rational basis' for 'pro-discrimination' amendment); *Citizens for Responsible Behavior* v. *Superior Court*, 2 Cal Rptr 2d 648 at 665–9 (Ct App 1991) (same). But see *Equality Foundation* (6th Cir), Ch. 2, note 278 at *24–*26 ('rational bases' for 'pro-discrimination' amendment included 'enhanced associational liberty', 'reduced governmental regulation', 'cost savings', and 'reflect[ing] the majority's moral views').

[131] *Norton*, ibid. at 1165–6.

[132] See *Singer* v. *US Civil Service Commission*, 530 F 2d 247 at 254 n. 14 (9th Cir 1976). See also Harvard Survey (1989 US), 1559 n. 29.

in public'.[133] In *Singer* v. *US Civil Service Commission*, the Ninth Circuit upheld the dismissal of John Singer, a civil servant who had 'openly and publicly flaunt[ed] his homosexual way of life' by, *inter alia*, 'kissing a male in [a] company cafeteria', 'admitt[ing] being "gay"' in his federal office, applying for a license to marry another man, being the subject of television and newspaper publicity (some of which mentioned his employer), and being active with the Seattle Gay Alliance.[134]

Which version of rational basis review would the Supreme Court apply today? Would it follow the reasoning of *Norton* or *Steffan II*, or that of *Ben-Shalom* and *Steffan III*? Although the Supreme Court held in *Moreno* and *Cleburne* that catering to hostility towards a particular group is not a legitimate government interest for the purposes of rational basis review,[135] *Hardwick* found that 'majority sentiments about the morality of homosexuality' are sufficient.[136] It therefore seems unlikely that the Supreme Court would uphold the *Norton* or *Steffan II* versions of rational basis review.[137] Instead, it would probably follow *Steffan III* and hold that a statement that a person is gay, lesbian or bisexual permits a presumption that they engage in same-sex sexual activity, of which the majority is free to express its 'moral disapproval' by imposing criminal penalties or lesser sanctions, such as employment discrimination. Thus, discrimination against gay, lesbian, and bisexual persons would be upheld by recharacterizing hostility or prejudice against them as 'moral disapproval', or by accepting a stereotyped generalization about such persons as a sufficient rational basis.

II. USE OF A SEX DISCRIMINATION ARGUMENT

A sex discrimination argument has been the least frequently used in sexual orientation discrimination cases under the US Constitution. This is probably because, until *Hardwick*, it had been believed that a right of privacy argument would prevail and, since *Hardwick*, a suspect classification argument has been used whenever possible. A growing realization that *Hardwick* may be interpreted as foreclosing a suspect classification argument seems to have led commentators to reconsider a sex discrimination argument, as an additional alternative to the right of privacy.[138] This argument does not require the recognition of any

---

[133] 417 F 2d 1161 at 1167 (DC Cir 1969).   [134] 530 F 2d 247 at 249, 255 (9th Cir 1976).
[135] See Chapter 2, note 188.   [136] 478 US 186 at 196 (1986).
[137] In *Heller* v. *Doe*, 125 L Ed 2d 257 at 270–71, 279 (1993), the Court stressed again that rational basis review is deferential to governments, by requiring the plaintiff '"to negative every conceivable basis which might support [the legislation]" ... whether or not the basis has a foundation in the record', and stating that a 'plausible' or 'arguable' rationale is sufficient.
[138] For the most thorough analysis of the argument to date, see Koppelman (1994 US). See also Sunstein (1994 US); Eskridge (1993 US), 1504–10; Trosino (1993 US); Fajer (1992 US), 617–50; Strasser (1991a US); Harvard Survey (1989 US), 1526–8, 1578–80, 1641; Harvard Note (1989 US); Koppelman (1988 US); Law (1988 US); Chang (1987 US), 826, 868–9.

new fundamental right or suspect classification, but rather attempts to use, in sexual orientation discrimination cases, an existing quasi-suspect classification (i.e. sex).[139] Could it establish the general principle of non-discrimination (on the ground of sexual orientation) that right of privacy and suspect classification arguments have so far failed to provide?

The main use of a sex discrimination argument in the US has been under federal and state legislation prohibiting sex discrimination in employment. Under such legislation (unlike equal protection doctrine with its potentially open-ended list of suspect and quasi-suspect classifications), courts generally have no power to recognize new prohibited grounds of discrimination. As a result, gay, lesbian, and bisexual plaintiffs seeking to invoke the legislation have had to argue that discrimination based on their sexual orientation is in fact discrimination based on their sex. Until 1993, this argument had been uniformly rejected, both under Title VII of the federal Civil Rights Act of 1964,[140] and under state legislation.[141] In 1993, however, a California Court of Appeal held, in *Engel* v. *Worthington*, that a publisher's refusal to include a photograph of a same-sex couple in a high school reunion memory book was sex discrimination contrary to section 51 of the California Civil Code.[142]

Several courts have extended the rejection of a sex discrimination argument to claims by gay men, or men perceived to be gay, that verbal and physical anti-gay harassment by their (presumably heterosexual) male co-workers constituted 'hostile environment' sexual harassment contrary to Title VII.[143] These courts reached this conclusion despite prior decisions that sexual advances made by a male supervisor towards a male employee constitute 'quid pro quo' sexual harassment contrary to Title VII.[144] The fact that the latter interpretation would often protect heterosexual men sexually harassed by a gay or bisexual male

---

[139] See note 4.

[140] 42 USCA s. 2000e-2(a). See *Williamson* v. *A.G. Edwards & Sons, Inc.*, 876 F 2d 69 (8th Cir 1989); *Blum* v. *Gulf Oil Corporation*, 597 F 2d 936 (5th Cir 1979); *DeSantis* v. *Pacific Telephone & Telegraph Co.*, 608 F 2d 327 (9th Cir 1979); *Smith* v. *Liberty Mutual Insurance Co.*, 569 F 2d 325 (5th Cir 1978). See also Equal Employment Opportunity Commission, Decision No. 76–67, 2 Empl. Prac. Dec. (CCH) para. 6493 (1976), and Decision No. 76–75, 19 Fair Empl. Prac. Cases (BNA) 1823 (1975). See also Sinisalco (1976 US), 503–6. But see Capers (1991 US) (sexual orientation discrimination is sex discrimination contrary to Title VII).

[141] See *Phillips* v. *Wisconsin Personnel Commission*, 482 NW 2d 121 at 127–28 (Wis Ct App 1992); *Macauley* v. *Massachusetts Commission Against Discrimination*, 397 NE 2d 670 (Mass 1979); *Gay Law Students Association* v. *Pacific Telephone & Telegraph Co.*, 595 P 2d 592 at 611–12 (Cal 1979).

[142] 23 Cal Rptr 2d 329 (Ct App 1993).

[143] See *Dillon* v. *Frank*, 58 Empl. Prac. Dec. (CCH) para. 41332 (6th Cir 1992); *Vandeventer* v. *Wabash National Corp.*, 867 F Supp 790 (ND Ind 1994); *Carreno* v. *Local Union No. 226*, 54 Fair Empl. Prac. Cases (BNA) 81 (D Kan. 1990); *Goluszek* v. *Smith*, 697 F Supp 1452 (ND Ill. 1988). See also *Polly* v. *Houston Lighting & Power Co.*, 825 F Supp 135 at 137–8 (SD Tex 1993) (even if a Title VII claim of male–male sexual harassment is possible, male plaintiff failed to show that harassment would not have occurred 'but for' his sex). See generally Marcosson (1992).

[144] See *Joyner* v. *AAA Cooper Transportation*, 597 F Supp 537 (MD Ala 1983); *Wright* v. *Methodist Youth Services, Inc.*, 511 F Supp 307 (ND Ill 1981).

supervisor might explain the different results. The Michigan Court of Appeals seems to have applied this distinction, under state legislation prohibiting sex discrimination, to an employee who was perceived to be gay. The court dismissed his complaint of harassment resulting from 'his co-workers' perceptions of his sexual orientation', but allowed him to proceed with his complaint of 'specific homosexual advances directed to him by his supervisor'.[145] In *Garcia* v. *Elf Atochem North America*, the Fifth Circuit rejected this distinction, holding that '[sexual] harassment by a male supervisor against a male subordinate does not state a [Title VII] claim'.[146] Since *Garcia*, district courts have split on whether Title VII permits claims for male–male or female–female sexual harassment involving sexual advances by supervisors or co-workers.[147]

Under the federal and state constitutions, a sex discrimination argument has rarely been used and, until 1993, had never been accepted. This is partly because an argument that a law discriminates directly on the basis of sex is usually not available in challenges to oral or anal intercourse laws, most of which apply to all persons regardless of sex (as did the Georgia law in *Hardwick*). But there are six states that prohibit only same-sex oral or anal intercourse.[148] A sex discrimination argument has been made in challenges to two of these laws. In *Baker* v. *Wade*, the district court struck down the Texas law on right of privacy and rational basis grounds, finding it unnecessary to consider the plaintiff's sex discrimination argument.[149] The Fifth Circuit reversed without considering the argument,[150] and the Supreme Court denied a petition for certiorari that expressly made the argument.[151] In *State* v. *Walsh*, the Missouri Supreme Court upheld Missouri's same-sex oral or anal intercourse law against a sex discrimination challenge under the US Constitution.[152] Litigants may also have been discouraged by the failure of the argument in a same-sex marriage case in 1974. In *Singer* v. *Hara*, the Washington Court of Appeals upheld a refusal to issue a marriage licence to John Singer and Paul Barwick, rejecting a sex discrimination argument both under the federal Fourteenth Amendment and the Washington Constitution's Equal Rights Amendment.[153]

[145] See *Barbour* v. *Department of Social Services*, 497 NW 2d 216 at 218 (Mich Ct App 1993).
[146] 28 F 3d 446 at 451–2 (5th Cir 1994).
[147] Claims dismissed in e.g. *Myers* v. *City of El Paso*, 874 F Supp 1546 (WD Tex 1995) (female–female); *Hopkins* v. *Baltimore Gas & Electric Corp.*, 871 F Supp 822 (D Md 1994) (male–male). Claims permitted to proceed in e.g. *McCoy* v. *Johnson Controls World Services, Inc.*, 878 F Supp 229 (SD Ga 1995) (female–female); *Prescott* v. *Independent Life & Accident Ins. Co.*, 878 F Supp 1545 (MD Ala. 1995) (male–male).
[148] See Appendix III; Hunter (1992 US), 538; Harvard Survey (1989), 1526–8.
[149] 553 F Supp 1121 at 1144 (ND Tex 1982).   [150] 769 F 2d 289 at 292 (5th Cir 1985).
[151] 478 US 1022 (1986). See Petition for Certiorari (Case No. 85-1225) (18 Jan. 1986), at 26–7.
[152] 713 SW 2d 508 at 510 (Mo 1986).
[153] 522 P 2d 1187 at 1190 (Wash Ct App 1974). See also *Baker* v. *Nelson*, 191 NW 2d 185 at 187 (Minn 1971), appeal dismissed, 409 US 810 (1972) ('clear distinction between a marital distinction based merely upon race and one based upon the fundamental difference in sex'). See also *Opinion of the Justices*, 530 A 2d 21 at 24 (NH 1987) ('sexual preference is not a matter necessarily tied to gender, but to inclination, whatever the source thereof').

In 1993, however, the viability of a sex discrimination argument increased dramatically when the Hawaii Supreme Court, in *Baehr* v. *Lewin*, became possibly the first court in the world to accept it. Presented with a case very similar to *Singer* v. *Hara* (a challenge to the exclusion of same-sex couples from the right to marry under a state constitution that expressly prohibits sex discrimination), the court held that this exclusion is prima facie sex discrimination and can only be justified by a compelling state interest.[154] The case has been remanded to a lower court to determine whether such a compelling state interest exists. If the State of Hawaii ultimately fails to establish one, and the Hawaii Constitution is not amended, same-sex couples will be permitted to marry in Hawaii. Not only would this bring an end, in Hawaii, to one of the most symbolically harmful forms of sexual orientation discrimination, it could lead to greater use of a sex discrimination argument by gay, lesbian, and bisexual plaintiffs under federal and state constitutions and legislation. As with the suspect classification argument, the US Supreme Court has yet to hear oral argument on the merits of a sex discrimination argument under the US Constitution. In view of *Baehr* v. *Lewin* and its own recent statement that 'gender-based classifications require "an exceedingly persuasive justification" in order to survive constitutional scrutiny', the Court should at least find it difficult to dismiss the argument out of hand.[155]

The preceding discussion is only a brief outline of the cases in which a sex discrimination argument has been used in the US, and shows the total lack of success until *Baehr* v. *Lewin* and *Engel* v. *Worthington*. Because the US, European Convention, and Canadian decisions that have rejected this argument have given substantially similar reasons, I will leave the detailed analysis of these reasons, and the reasoning of the Supreme Court of Hawaii in *Baehr* v. *Lewin*, to the discussion of a sex discrimination argument under the Canadian Charter in Chapter 8.

III. ASSESSMENT OF PROTECTION UNDER THE UNITED STATES CONSTITUTION

When surveying the progress that gay, lesbian, and bisexual persons in the US have made in obtaining federal constitutional protection, it is not hard to understand why they approach the US Supreme Court with trepidation. Although it might not now accept, as readily as it did in *Boutilier* in 1967,[156] that they are 'afflicted with psychopathic personality', it may still be unwilling to take seriously an argument that the right of two men or two women to decide to engage in private sexual activity with each other is 'fundamental', having described such an argument in *Hardwick* in 1986 as 'at best, facetious',[157] i.e. a joke. If

---

[154] 852 P 2d 44 at 67 (Haw 1993). See the discussion of *Baehr* in Chapter 8, Part II.F.
[155] See *J.E.B.* v. *Alabama ex rel. T.B.*, 128 L Ed 2d 89 at 102 (1994).
[156] 387 US 118 (1967).   [157] 478 US 186 at 194 (1986).

this is the case, the Court might not permit the use of a First Amendment or suspect classification argument to circumvent *Hardwick*, by protecting the disclosure of attraction as speech, or the attraction itself as a suspect classification, even though the conduct to which it may give rise is not protected. It could well follow *Ben-Shalom*[158] and *Steffan III*[159] in treating the statement 'I am gay/lesbian/bisexual' as raising a presumption of 'conduct', rather than constituting 'speech' or the disclosure of an immutable attraction or 'status', and treat the illegality or 'immorality' of that conduct as a sufficient rational basis for discrimination.

It is less clear whether the Court will uphold the 'right to participate equally in the political process' identified in *Evans* v. *Romer* and *Equality Foundation*, or would accept a federal equivalent of the sex discrimination argument that succeeded in *Baehr* v. *Lewin*. The *Evans* right would provide important protection against a very serious form of sexual orientation discrimination, which threatens to spread across the US. But it would be difficult to apply outside the context of 'pro-discrimination' amendments, e.g. to public employment discrimination.[160] The acceptance of a sex discrimination argument, however, could provide a general principle that would apply to most forms of sexual orientation discrimination.

If the US Supreme Court were ultimately to reject suspect classification, rational basis, and sex discrimination arguments, the US Constitution could only be described as offering no protection against sexual orientation discrimination *per se*. To the extent that gay, lesbian, and bisexual persons enjoyed federal constitutional rights, it would be because they were persons and in spite of the fact that they were gay, lesbian or bisexual or engaged in same-sex emotional–sexual conduct.[161] This would be especially true under the First Amendment. Lower court decisions have protected them when engaging in traditional First Amendment activities (e.g. publishing 'non-obscene' books, forming associations, holding meetings, parades or demonstrations), but this is only because of the nearly absolute content-neutrality of the First Amendment, and not because of any special respect owed to a person's sexual orientation. (Nor has much of this protection been confirmed by a majority opinion of the Supreme Court.) While this First Amendment protection is itself of fundamental importance, and allows gay, lesbian, and bisexual persons to campaign for legislative protection against discrimination, it does put them on the same level as the Nazis marching in Skokie,[162] or racists burning a cross inside the fenced yard of an

[158] 881 F 2d 454 at 460–61, 464 (7th Cir 1989).
[159] 41 F 3d 677 at 686–7 (DC Cir 1994).
[160] An attempt to do so was rejected in *Dahl*, 830 F Supp 1319 at 1324–5 (ED Cal 1993).
[161] The 'equal participation' right in *Evans* and *Equality Foundation*, if upheld by the US Supreme Court, would at least give gay, lesbian, and bisexual persons some minimal protection as an 'independently identifiable group', if not as a 'suspect or quasi-suspect class'.
[162] See *Collin* v. *Smith*, 578 F 2d 1197 (7th Cir), cert. denied, 439 US 916 (1978).

African-American family's home.[163] Their right to talk about same-sex emotional–sexual conduct is protected, no matter how 'immoral', 'abhorrent', or
'offensive' their speech about such conduct may be, but they cannot actually
engage in the conduct without facing constitutionally permissible discrimination. The conduct is thus put on a par with the violence or discrimination that
Nazis and racists may be permitted to advocate, but not to practise. This level
of protection is about as low as one could imagine (short of no protection at all,
as in a state with no freedom of expression).

If the Supreme Court ultimately provides only this minimal level of protection, *Hardwick* will probably be the main reason. But *Hardwick* is also a potential reason for reducing this level of protection even further. *Hardwick* began by
eliminating a right of privacy argument and holding that particular conduct
(same-sex oral or anal intercourse, or potentially all same-sex sexual activity) is
not constitutionally protected. The lack of protection for this conduct has been
used to deny suspect classification status to sexual orientation (as direction of
attraction) because of the connection between attraction and conduct, to reject
the argument that saying 'I am gay/lesbian/bisexual' is protected speech (instead it is merely evidence of unprotected conduct), and to uphold the rationality
of discrimination based on sexual orientation (as direction of attraction) on the
ground that unprotected conduct can be presumed from the disclosure of the
attraction. If unprotected conduct can be presumed from an attraction, then even
the minimal First Amendment protection discussed above could be curtailed.
Could participation in the activities of a gay, lesbian, and bisexual students'
organization,[164] or attending a gay, lesbian, and bisexual pride parade, permit a
rational presumption of unprotected conduct? If so, perhaps some sanction against
the participants (e.g. expulsion from a public university or dismissal from public
employment), other than suppression of the expressive activity (a meeting or
parade), could be applied. The sanction would not be based on the expressive
activity but on the presumed conduct, of which the expressive activity was
merely evidence.

So long as *Hardwick* stands, analysis of sexual orientation discrimination
issues under the US Constitution is doomed to incoherence. This is because it
forces gay, lesbian, and bisexual plaintiffs to make a distinction between attraction and conduct, and then deny the connection between attraction and conduct.

---

[163] See *R.A.V.* v. *City of St. Paul*, 120 L Ed 2d 305 (1992).

[164] The *Steffan III* majority's 'presumption of conduct' could reverse the protection such organizations have enjoyed. See *Steffan III*, note 121 at 686–7, 714–15; Chapter 2, Part II.B.1. The 'right
to equal participation' in *Evans* and *Equality Foundation* would seem to be safe from *Hardwick*.
'Pro-discrimination' amendments are aimed at gay, lesbian, and bisexual persons as a group rather
than specific individuals, and would thus be hard to link to the presumed conduct of specific
individuals. But could they be seen as a very indirect means of discouraging same-sex oral or anal
intercourse? *Evans* rejected the argument that Amendment 2 could validly prohibit protection against
discrimination based on 'homosexual . . . conduct, practices or relationships'. See *Evans*, 882 P 2d
1335 at 1349–50 (Colo 1994).

This denial is completely unrealistic. The simple truth is that for most gay, lesbian, and bisexual persons, an important part of being gay, lesbian, or bisexual is engaging in same-sex sexual activity (including oral or anal intercourse).[165] Without protection of this conduct, full and coherent protection against sexual orientation discrimination is impossible. The problem can be illustrated by the analogies that are used to demonstrate the distinction between attraction and conduct, and by the breadth of the argument (under rational basis review) that conduct cannot be inferred from attraction. Same-sex or bisexual sexual orientation (as direction of attraction) is analogized to membership of a racial minority or the Communist Party, while same-sex sexual activity is analogized to speeding, theft, or conspiring to overthrow the government (activities which are not, and never could be, afforded constitutional protection).[166] Similarly, the plaintiff's (rational basis) argument in *Steffan III*, that same-sex sexual activity cannot be presumed from the statement 'I am gay', would apply to other statements on which employment decisions were based, whether the statement was 'I am Jewish', 'I am a paedophile', 'I am an arsonist', or 'I am a racist'. What plaintiffs should and could be arguing, were it not for *Hardwick*, is that same-sex sexual activity is protected, unlike speeding, theft, or conspiring to overthrow the government, and that the statement 'I am gay' is protected because the attraction (or status) and conduct which it reveals are both protected. This is what puts it in the same category as 'I am Jewish', and distinguishes it from 'I am a paedophile', 'I am an arsonist', and 'I am a racist'.

The incoherence of the attraction–conduct distinction is most evident in the question of permitting gay, lesbian, and bisexual persons to serve in the military.[167] It is difficult to understand how a proposal to permit gay, lesbian, and bisexual persons to serve, as long as they never reveal their sexual orientation (as direction of attraction) and never engage in same-sex sexual activity, could be described as 'lifting the ban'. Imagine the replacement of a ban on Jews in the military with a new policy of permitting Jews to serve, provided that they never engaged in any Jewish religious practices (e.g. attending a synagogue or observing a Jewish holiday) and did not tell anyone that they were Jewish, unless they were then willing to deny that they had ever, or would ever, engage in any Jewish religious practices. Would anyone describe this new policy as 'lifting the ban' on Jews in the military? A real 'lifting' of the ban would

---

[165] See Cain (1993 US), 1641 ('there is a certain degree of absurdity to making legal arguments in favor of gay and lesbian rights that ignore [sexual activity]').

[166] See *Steffan II*, 8 F 3d 57 at 66–7 (DC Cir 1993) (overthrowing government); *High Tech Gays*, 909 F 2d 375 at 379 (9th Cir 1990) (speeding); *Dahl*, 830 F Supp 1319 at 1335 n. 17 (ED Cal 1993) (theft). See also *Cammermeyer*, 850 F Supp 910 at 919 n. 13 (WD Wash 1994) (alcohol and drug abuse).

[167] See Karst (1991 US) (discussing the military's exclusion or segregation of women, men of African origin, and gay, lesbian, and bisexual persons). He notes (558–9) that 'the exclusion of gay men and lesbians from the armed forces . . . has been the single most important governmental action in maintaining public attitudes that stigmatize homosexual orientation'.

require, at a minimum, that openly gay, lesbian, and bisexual persons be permitted to serve, even if they could not acknowledge engaging in private same-sex sexual activity (the second level of protection above). But to remove the ban completely, the prohibition of all oral or anal intercourse by members of the armed forces would have to be repealed (something which *Hardwick* might effectively have done) and replaced by a prohibition of any sexual activity in certain circumstances (e.g. on duty, in barracks, on a ship).

The potentially minimal level of federal constitutional protection does not mean that gay, lesbian, and bisexual persons in the US are defenceless in the face of discrimination. In more and more cases, they can turn to federal civil service regulations, state constitutions, state or local legislation or executive orders,[168] or to state common law contract and tort remedies.[169] But will the US Supreme Court ever overrule *Hardwick*? It has changed its mind in the past, and has done so in as little as three years,[170] or as long as fifty-eight.[171] Gay, lesbian, and bisexual persons in the US have been waiting for a change of mind for nearly ten years. Perhaps *Hardwick* will soon have aged sufficiently to permit the US Supreme Court to recognize that it made a mistake.

[168] See Leonard (1993b US); Appendix II. An ominous development for such legislation and orders is the adoption of 'pro-discrimination' amendments such as Colorado's. See Chapter 2, note 275 and accompanying text.

[169] See e.g. *Collins* v. *Shell Oil Co.*, 56 Fair Empl. Prac. Cases (BNA) 440 at 441, 443 (Cal Super Ct 1991) (awarding US$5.3 million in contract and tort damages to manager dismissed after 19 years 'solely because he was a sexually active homosexual'). See also Harvard Survey (1989 US), 1575–8.

[170] See *Hardwick*, 478 US 186 at 213–14 (1986) (Blackmun J., dissenting) (reversal in flag salute cases).

[171] Compare *Plessy* v. *Ferguson*, 163 US 537 (1896) with *Brown* v. *Board of Education*, 347 US 483 (1954).

4

The European Convention on Human Rights:
Fundamental Choice Arguments

I. INTRODUCTION

Turning from the US Constitution to the European Convention on Human Rights, one is immediately confronted by the striking differences between the texts of the two instruments. These differences present both a major advantage and a major disadvantage for a gay, lesbian or bisexual person seeking to argue that a particular instance of sexual orientation discrimination violates the Convention. The advantage is the clear textual basis for 'right of privacy' arguments in the express guarantees of the 'right to respect for . . . private and family life' in Article 8, and the 'right to marry and to found a family' in Article 12. This strengthens the use of fundamental choice arguments under the Convention by precluding the controversy over the legitimacy of judicial discovery of such rights in the text of the US Constitution.

The disadvantage lies in the limited scope of Article 14, which prohibits discrimination only in '[t]he enjoyment of the rights and freedoms set forth in [the] Convention'. As will be seen in Chapter 5, this limitation has the effect of confining the Convention's equivalent of US equal protection doctrine to a 'fundamental rights' branch, and removing from it any potential 'suspect classifications' branch. Article 14 will apply to any discrimination that 'falls within the ambit of' one of the substantive rights or freedoms guaranteed by the Convention or the Protocols to it.[1] But there is no kind of discrimination (not even race or sex discrimination) that Article 14 prohibits regardless of what right or freedom is affected. Thus, immutable status and sex discrimination arguments are insufficient on their own, because Article 14 'has no independent existence'[2] and cannot be violated on its own, but only in conjunction with another provision of the Convention or Protocols. These arguments can only supplement a fundamental choice argument, where a right or freedom guaranteed by another Article can be shown to have been restricted in a discriminatory manner.

This Chapter will begin with a brief overview of the cases in which the European Court of Human Rights (the 'Court') and the European Commission of Human Rights (the 'Commission') have addressed issues of sexual orientation discrimination. In the remainder of Chapter 4, I will consider the ways in

---

[1] *Abdulaziz* v. *UK* (1985), Ser. A, No. 94, at para. 71.
[2] Ibid. See also Helfer (1991 Eur), 169 n. 61.

which applicants under the Convention have used fundamental choice arguments, relying on Article 8 and other Articles. In Chapter 5, I will examine the
extent to which they have used immutable status and sex discrimination arguments under Article 14. I will also attempt to determine what obstacles there
may be to the success of these three kinds of arguments under the Convention,
and assess the level of protection the Convention provides against sexual orientation discrimination. I will close Chapter 5 with a brief examination of the
protection which the United Nations Human Rights Committee began to provide
in 1994, under another international human rights treaty, the International Covenant on Civil and Political Rights.

II. CONVENTION CASES DEALING WITH SEXUAL ORIENTATION DISCRIMINATION

The issue of sexual orientation discrimination was raised by applicants to the
Commission very early in the history of the Convention. These applicants were
men who had been imprisoned (or subjected to other sanctions) in Germany or
Austria for consensual sexual activity with other men (or, presumably, with
adolescent males over 14 who were old enough to consent to opposite-sex sexual
activity). They argued that the prohibition of all sexual activity between men
(but not between women) violated their rights under Articles 8 and 14. In a
series of at least nine decisions from 1955 to 1967, the Commission found all
these applications inadmissible as 'manifestly ill-founded' under Article 27(2).[3]
In most of these cases, it tersely stated its conclusion in exactly the same way:
'the Convention allows a High Contracting Party to punish homosexuality since
the right to respect for private life may, in a democratic society, be subject to
interference as provided for by the law of that Party for the protection of health
or morals (Article 8(2) of the Convention)'.[4]

  The Commission's interpretation of the Convention, which had been criticized,[5] began to change in 1977–78, when it declared two applications admissible: the first attacking the discriminatory age of consent for male–male sexual
activity in England and Wales (21, versus 16 for male–female or female–female

---

[3] See *X* v. *Germany* (No. 104/55) (1955), 1 Y.B. 228; *X* v. *Germany* (No. 167/56) (1956), 1 Y.B.
235; *X* v. *Germany* (No. 261/57) (1957), 1 Y.B. 255; *X* v. *Germany* (No. 530/59) (1960), 3 Y.B.
184; *X* v. *Germany* (No. 600/59) (2 Apr. 1960), unpublished; *X* v. *Germany* (No. 704/60) (1960),
3 Coll. Dec.; *X* v. *Austria* (No. 1138/61) (1963), 11 Coll. Dec. 9; *X* v. *Germany* (No. 1307/61)
(1962), 5 Y.B. 230; *X* v. *Germany* (No. 2566/65) (1967), 22 Coll. Dec. 35.
[4] *X* v. *Germany* (No. 530/59) (1960), 3 Y.B. 184 at 194.
[5] See e.g. Vincineau (1979 Eur); Castberg (1974 Eur), 145 ('[s]ooner or later punishment for
homosexual relations will presumably be held contrary to . . . Art. 8'); Pinto (1965 Eur), 102–104
(Commission's interpretation ignores the concepts of 'democratic society' and 'necessity' in Article
8(2)).

sexual activity),[6] and the second challenging the total prohibition of sexual activity between men in Northern Ireland.[7] In the first case, the Commission ultimately found no violation,[8] but in the second, brought by Jeffrey Dudgeon, it found in 1980 that 'the legal prohibition of private homosexual acts between consenting adults over 21 years of age breaches the applicant's right to respect for private life under Article 8'.[9] The Court agreed with the Commission's opinion in 1981, concluding that the law could not be justified under Article 8(2) as 'necessary in a democratic society' for the protection of 'morals' or 'the rights and freedoms of others'. The Court relied on the absence of such a law 'in the great majority of the member States of the Council of Europe' and the non-enforcement of the law with respect to men over 21 in Northern Ireland.[10] It reached the same conclusion in 1988 and 1993, in similar cases brought by David Norris against the Republic of Ireland,[11] and by Alecos Modinos against Cyprus.[12]

After an inauspicious beginning in the 1950s and 60s, the Court and Commission's recent treatment of the crudest form of sexual orientation discrimination (criminal prohibition of same-sex sexual activity) provides a startling contrast with that of the US Supreme Court in *Hardwick*.[13] *Dudgeon, Norris*, and *Modinos* may ultimately lead to the elimination of laws prohibiting same-sex sexual activity in the member states of the Council of Europe. The *Dudgeon* case spurred the substantial decriminalization of sexual activity between men in several jurisdictions that are part of the United Kingdom, or are dependent territories to which the UK has extended the Convention under Article 63. The reforms contained in the Sexual Offences Act 1967, which applied only in England and Wales, were extended to Scotland in 1980 (perhaps partly as a result of the Commission's 1978 declaration of admissibility in *Dudgeon*), and to Northern Ireland in 1982 (in compliance with the Court's judgment in *Dudgeon*).[14] After the judgment in *Dudgeon*, a kind of 'domino effect' occurred in UK dependent

[6] *X* v. *UK* (No. 7215/75) (1977), 11 D.R. 36. The Commission did not refer to its prior decisions, but observed (at 43) that 'it should ... tak[e] into account the development of moral opinion in recent years concerning State interference with the private, consensual sexual lives of adults'.

[7] *Dudgeon* v. *UK* (No. 7525/76) (1978), 11 D.R. 117.

[8] *X* v. *UK* (No. 7215/75) (1978), 19 D.R. 66.

[9] *Dudgeon* v. *UK* (No. 7525/76) (1980), Ser. B, No. 40, p. 11, at p. 41.

[10] *Dudgeon* v. *UK* (1981), Ser. A, No. 45, at pp. 23–4.

[11] *Norris* v. *Ireland* (1988), Ser. A, No. 142, at pp. 20–21. In the Commission, see No. 10581/83 (1985), 44 D.R. 132 (dec. on adm.); (1987), Ser. A, No. 142, at p. 27 (report). See also *Norris* v. *Attorney-General*, [1984] Irish Rep 36 (Sup Ct); Norris (1993 Eur); Gearty (1983 Eur), 272–3; Connelly (1982 Eur).

[12] *Modinos* v. *Cyprus* (1993), Ser. A, No. 259, at paras. 23–6. In the Commission, see No. 15070/89 (1990), 67 D.R. 295 (dec. on adm.); (1991), Ser. A, No. 259, at pp. 23–7 (report).

[13] See 478 US 186 (1986). *Dudgeon* and *Norris* have attracted the attention of writers in the US. See e.g. Ermanski (1992 Eur); Glendon (1991 Eur), 146–59; Helfer (1991 Eur); Helfer (1990 Eur); Dubber (1990 Eur); Kane (1988 Eur); Kimble (1988 Eur); Self (1988 Eur), 426–31; Blackburn (1982 Eur).

[14] See Criminal Justice (Scotland) Act 1980, s. 80; Homosexual Offences (Northern Ireland) Order 1982, N.I. Statutes, SI 1982/1536 (N.I. 19).

territories. To avoid proceedings in Strasbourg, legislation was amended in Guernsey in 1983, Jersey in 1990, the Isle of Man in 1992, Gibraltar in 1993, and Bermuda in 1994.[15] Ireland took nearly five years to comply with *Norris*, but finally did so in 1993.[16] Cyprus will probably comply with *Modinos* in 1995,[17] two years after the Court's judgment. This would mark the eradication of laws prohibiting same-sex sexual activity within the 23 member states that had joined the Council of Europe by 1989.

Since 1989, the Council of Europe has expanded into Eastern Europe and will continue to do so. Until 1993, it seemed possible that compliance with *Dudgeon* would become an effective prerequisite for Council of Europe membership, either because the Council of Europe would insist on it[18] or because applicants for membership would comply in advance to avoid being found in violation by the Court. This would have made future recourse to the Court and Commission (regarding the single issue of criminalization) unnecessary. Of the ten Eastern European countries (as of 10 February 1995) that have joined since 1989, Hungary, the Czech Republic, Slovakia, Poland, Bulgaria, and Slovenia had already decriminalized long before they applied for membership (indeed before *Dudgeon*).[19] Estonia (1992), Latvia (1992), and Lithuania (1993) did so before, or shortly after, their membership applications were granted.[20] But Romania had not done so when it was admitted in October 1993. The Parliamentary Assembly of the Council of Europe recommended its admission on the understanding that 'Romania will shortly change its legislation in such a way that . . . Article 200 of the Penal Code will no longer consider as a criminal offence homosexual acts perpetrated in private between consenting adults'.[21] By the end of 1994, the Romanian parliament had yet to amend Article 200, which applies to private sexual activity between men and between women.[22] The law may therefore have to be challenged in Strasbourg. Of the European states that have yet to join the

---

[15] See Sexual Offences (Bailiwick of Guernsey) Law, 1983; Sexual Offences (Jersey) Law 1990; in the Isle of Man, Sexual Offences Act 1992; in Gibraltar, Criminal Offences (Amendment) Ordinance, 1993; and in Bermuda, Criminal Code Amendment Act 1994.

[16] Criminal Law (Sexual Offences) Act, 1993, No. 20, ss. 2–4 (in force on 7 July 1993).

[17] Legislation setting an age of consent to male–male sexual activity of 18 has been approved by the Cyprus Council of Ministers. See 'Cyprus gives in to Europe' *Gay Times* (March 1995) 28.

[18] But note Liechtenstein's 1982, post-*Dudgeon* reservation, under Article 64, in respect of its laws prohibiting sexual activity between men or between women (only amended in 1989): see October 1990 edition of the Convention (published by the Secretariat to the Commission), 27; Waaldijk (1991 Eur), 16.

[19] See Tatchell (1992), 139.

[20] See 'Third republic makes gay sex legal' *Capital Gay* (1 May 1992) 4 (Latvia and Estonia); Duda (1995 Eur), 15 (Lithuania).

[21] See Opinion No. 176, para. 7 (28 September 1993).

[22] See *Capital Gay* (10 Feb. 1995) 21. On 15 July 1994 (in the case of Bozdog, et al.), the Romanian Constitutional Court held that Article 200 is unconstitutional as applied to consensual, adult, same-sex sexual acts which were 'not committed in public or did not produce public scandal': see National Danish Organization for Gays and Lesbians, *Euro-Letter No. 27* (22 Aug. 1994), 5–7.

Council of Europe, Croatia and Montenegro changed their laws in 1977, while the prospect of membership may have induced recent reforms in Albania (1995), Russia (1993), Serbia (1994), and Ukraine (1991).[23] Total prohibitions remain in place in such potential future members as Armenia, Azerbaijan, Belarus, Bosnia-Herzegovina, Georgia, Macedonia, and Moldova.[24]

The possibility that the Court and Commission's decisions in *Dudgeon, Norris,* and *Modinos* could ultimately result in a continent of Europe free of laws forbidding same-sex sexual activity certainly suggests that the Convention has had an important impact in the area of sexual orientation discrimination. This impact seems particularly significant when compared with that of the US Constitution which, as interpreted in *Hardwick*, permits the maintenance of such laws by nearly half the states in the US. However, criminalization is but one aspect of sexual orientation discrimination, and the Court and Commission's record cannot be properly assessed without examining their decisions dealing with other aspects of the phenomenon. Such an examination reveals that *Dudgeon* has not served as a watershed decision, establishing a general principle that would permit the invalidation of all sexual orientation discrimination by Council of Europe member states, as did *Brown* v. *Board of Education*[25] in relation to public sector racial segregation in the US (and as *Hardwick* might have done in relation to public sector sexual orientation discrimination, had the minority's view prevailed).[26] Rather, its impact has been confined to the single issue of criminalization.

In at least sixteen cases dealing with other aspects of sexual orientation discrimination, the Commission has found no violation of the Convention, in all but one case dismissing the applications as 'manifestly ill-founded'. In the area of criminal law, six cases have upheld (under Articles 8 and 14) a higher age of consent for male–male sexual activity than male–female or female–female, with one of those (*Johnson* v. *UK*) finding that a prohibition of sexual activity between men 'when more than two persons take part or are present' did not violate Articles 8 and 14.[27] The Commission has also upheld (under Articles 7, 9, 10, and 14) the conviction of the publishers of *Gay News* for 'blasphemous libel',[28] and (under Articles 8 and 14) the criminalization of same-sex but not opposite-

[23] See Duda (1995 Eur), 12, 14–15; Tatchell (1992 Eur), 139.

[24] See National Danish Organization for Gays and Lesbians, *Euro-Letter No. 31* (Feb. 1995), 3; Tatchell (1992 Eur), 139. See also Parliamentary Assembly (1992 Eur) at 231, 233 (former Soviet republics in Central Asia not likely to become members); Parl. Ass. Recommendation 1247 (4 Oct. 1994), para. 2 (membership 'open only to states whose national territory lies wholly or partly in [geographical] Europe').

[25] 347 US 483 (1954).   [26] But see Ch. 2, Part II.C.

[27] See *Zukrigl* v. *Austria* (No. 17279/90) (13 May 1992), unpublished; *Johnson* v. *UK* (No. 10389/83) (1986), 47 D.R. 72; *Desmond* v. *UK* (No. 9721/82) (7 May 1984), unpublished; *X* v. *Belgium* (No. 9484/81) (1 Mar. 1982), unpublished; *X* v. *UK* (No. 7215/75) (1978), 19 D.R. 66; *X* v. *Germany* (No. 5935/72) (1975), 3 D.R. 46.

[28] See *Gay News Ltd.* v. *UK* (No. 8710/79) (1982), 28 D.R. 77, arising from [1979] AC 617.

sex prostitution.[29] In the area of employment discrimination,[30] the Commission has found justified (under Article 10) the dismissal of a lesbian Belgian teacher who said on television that she thought her sexual orientation had cost her the headship of a school mainly for girls, and (under Articles 8 and 14) the discharge of a gay British soldier over 21 who had engaged in sexual activity with a 20-year-old male soldier (junior in rank) and a male civilian over 21.[31]

In the area of discrimination against same-sex couples, five cases have found no violation (of Articles 8, 12 or 14) where same-sex couples are not treated like married or unmarried opposite-sex couples for the purposes of public housing[32] or immigration.[33] The Commission has concluded that the relationship of a same-sex couple does not fall within the scope of the right to respect for 'family life' under Article 8, or give rise to a right to 'marry and found a family' under Article 12; that neither the eviction of one partner from public housing after the death of the other, nor the deportation of one partner, interferes with 'private life'; and that differences in the treatment of same-sex and opposite-sex couples are 'objectively and reasonably justified' and therefore not 'discrimination' under Article 14.

Finally, in its first decision dealing with discrimination against gay, lesbian, and bisexual parents, the Commission has upheld (under Articles 8 and 14) the denial by Dutch courts of a lesbian woman's request that parental authority over her female partner's child by donor insemination be vested in both partners (which would have been possible in the case of an unmarried opposite-sex couple). The Commission found no discrimination, noting that, 'as regards parental authority over a child, a homosexual couple cannot be equated to a man and woman living together'.[34]

Clearly, the results obtained by Convention applicants challenging sexual orientation discrimination have been mixed. What arguments have they used and to what extent have these arguments been successful? What obstacles stand

---

[29] See *F* v. *Switzerland* (No. 11680/85) (1988), 55 D.R. 178. See also Delmas-Marty (1992 Eur), 253–4. Same-sex prostitution has since been legalized in Switzerland: see Tatchell (1992 Eur), 134.

[30] In *Boitteloup* v. *France* (No. 12545/86) (1988), 58 D.R. 127, 133–5, the applicant, an officer in the state security police, was dismissed for living with a transvestite man who engaged in prostitution. The applicant argued that he had been 'penalised for homosexuality', in violation of his Article 8(1) right to respect for his private life, but the Commission found any interference with his right justified under Article 8(2). If the applicant would also have been dismissed had he been living with a woman who engaged in prostitution, this was not a case of sexual orientation discrimination, but one of interference with sexual freedom.

[31] See *Morissens* v. *Belgium* (No. 11389/85) (1988), 56 D.R. 127; *Bruce* v. *UK* (No. 9237/81) (1983), 34 D.R. 68.

[32] See *Simpson* v. *UK* (No. 11716/85) (1986), 47 D.R. 274, arising from [1986] 2 Fam LR 91 (CA).

[33] See *B* v. *UK* (No. 16106/90) (1990), 64 D.R. 278, arising from [1989] Imm App Rep 595 (QB); *C.* and *L.M.* v. *UK* (No. 14753/89) (9 Oct. 1989), unpublished; *W.J. and D.P.* v. *UK* (No. 12513/86) (1986), 11 E.H.R.R. 49; *X* and *Y* v. *UK* (No. 9369/81) (1983), 32 D.R. 220, 5 E.H.R.R. 601.

[34] See *Kerkhoven* v. *The Netherlands* (No. 15666/89) (19 May 1992), unpublished.

in the way of further acceptance of these arguments by the Court and the Commission?[35]

III. USE OF FUNDAMENTAL CHOICE ARGUMENTS

As was suggested above, the limited scope of Article 14 effectively makes a fundamental choice argument of some kind mandatory under the Convention. A challenged case of sexual orientation discrimination must be brought within one of the substantive rights or freedoms in Articles 2 to 12 of the Convention, or in Protocols 1, 4, 6, and 7, either alone or in conjunction with Article 14. This Part will consider the Articles that have been invoked in sexual orientation discrimination cases. Chapter 5 will examine the possibility of supplementing these Articles with Article 14.

A. Article 8

For a gay, lesbian or bisexual applicant, the prime candidate amongst the array of rights or freedoms in the Convention and Protocols has always been 'the right to respect for . . . private and family life' in Article 8(1). This is because sexual orientation discrimination will usually involve some kind of interference with the choice of same-sex emotional–sexual conduct, whether it consists of private same-sex sexual activity, a same-sex couple relationship or the relationship between a same-sex couple and children. Such activity and relationships argu-ably fall within the scope of 'private and family life'. Until the 1980s, applicants focused on the 'private life' branch of Article 8(1), probably because they were all challenging total prohibitions of private, consensual sexual activity between men or discriminatory ages of consent to such activity. However, applicants in recent cases of discrimination against same-sex couples have relied on the 'fam-ily life' branch of Article 8(1).

It should be noted here that, of all the Convention rights and freedoms, Article 8 (especially its 'private life' component) is perhaps the most likely to serve as a residual guarantee of 'liberty', similar to that provided by the doctrine of 'substantive due process' under the Fifth and Fourteenth Amendments to the US Constitution, and (potentially) by Section 7 of the Canadian Charter. Article 5(1)'s 'right to liberty', the provision that corresponds textually to the US and Canadian provisions, has been interpreted as 'referring only to physical liberty' and meaning 'freedom from arrest and detention', as opposed to a more general freedom to make certain fundamental decisions.[36]

---

[35] The absence of any right to 'appeal' to the Court from a declaration of 'inadmissibility' by the Commission makes it unclear whether the Court would agree with the Commission's decisions on issues other than criminalization.

[36] See e.g. *Adler and Bivas* v. *Germany* (Nos. 5573/72, 5670/72), [1977] Y.B. 102, at 146. See generally van Dijk and van Hoof (1990 Eur), 251–71.

1. Private Life

Establishing a violation of 'the right to respect for . . . private . . . life' is, in most cases, a three-stage process. It must be shown: (1) that Article 8(1) applies, i.e. the challenged law or decision affects a freedom or activity that falls within the scope of 'private life'; (2) that there has been, contrary to the opening phrase of Article 8(2), an 'interference by a public authority with [the applicant's private life]'; and (3) that there exists no justification for the interference under Article 8(2).[37] Where an applicant challenges, not an active 'interference by a public authority with [the applicant's private life]', but a public authority's passive omission or failure to take certain steps to ensure 'respect' for their private life, the Court and Commission seem to combine the second and third stages. The question becomes whether or not 'respect' for private life, in the circumstances, entails not only the 'negative obligation' to refrain from active interference, but also certain 'positive obligations' requiring the public authority to act. If so, it would seem that breach of a 'positive obligation' under Article 8(1) cannot be justified under Article 8(2).[38] Most cases of sexual orientation discrimination challenged under the Convention are clear instances of 'interference' (or 'discrimination' under Article 14), so there is usually no need to establish the existence of 'positive obligations'.

(a) Scope of 'Private Life'

The first stage, scope of 'private life', has rarely presented a difficulty in a sexual orientation discrimination case. Even in the 1950s and 1960s, the Commission in consistently finding Article 8(2) justifications for total prohibitions of sexual activity between men assumed that such activity fell within 'private life'.[39] This assumption was confirmed in a 1975 age of consent decision in which the Commission observed that '[a] person's sexual life is undoubtedly part of his private life of which it constitutes an important aspect'.[40] And in *Dudgeon*, the Commission's view that 'private, consensual [sexual] acts . . . clearly fall within the sphere of private life'[41] was endorsed by the Court ('the applicant's . . . private life . . . includes his sexual life'; '[t]he present case concerns a most intimate aspect of private life').[42] The majority of the Court apparently rejected Judge Walsh's argument, in dissent, that an *ejusdem generis* interpretation of 'private and family life' would confine it to 'activities . . . akin to those pursued in the privacy of family life', and that '[n]o such claim can be made for homosexual

[37] See e.g. Drzemczewski (1985 Eur), 5; Evrigenis (1982 Eur), 124.
[38] See e.g. Forder (1990 Eur); Loucaides (1990 Eur), 181; Connelly (1986 Eur), 572–3; Duffy (1982 Eur), 199–200; Evrigenis (1982 Eur), 136–7.
[39] See note 3. See also Kane (1988 Eur), 451.
[40] *X* v. *Germany* (No. 5935/72) (1975), 3 D.R. 46 at 54.
[41] (No. 7525/76) (1980), Ser. B, No. 40, p. 11, at p. 34.
[42] (1981), Ser. A, No. 45, at pp. 18, 21.

practices'.[43] The Commission has also said that 'the choice of affirming and assuming one's sexual identity . . . comes under the protection of Article [8(1)]',[44] and that 'the relationship of a homosexual couple constitutes a matter affecting their private life'.[45]

Two reasons might explain the almost uniform success of applicants at this stage. First, under the Court and Commission's interpretation of Article 8, the main 'screening function' (i.e. the separation of the small number of violations from the much larger number of non-violations) is performed by Article 8(2) (i.e. the third stage of the process, although the second stage also plays a role). Thus, a broad interpretation is given to 'private life' and, in many cases, to 'interference' with private life, often making it easy to establish an interference with an Article 8(1) right and move to Article 8(2). For example, interferences with private life have been found where a government prohibited a hotelkeeper from keeping spirits in his home, or required the completion of a census form, the production of a list of private expenditure to a tax authority, the wearing of a prison uniform or the cutting of a soldier's hair.[46] However, the Court and Commission also tend to give a broad interpretation to the Article 8(2) justifications, thus making it easy for a respondent government to establish one (as in all the examples just mentioned). From the point of view of the applicant, Article 8(1) (the first and second stages) can be a low hurdle,[47] and Article 8(2) (the third stage) a much higher one.

This approach to the definition of a right and the justification of restrictions on the right differs greatly from that of the US Supreme Court (seen in Chapter 2) and that of the Canadian Supreme Court (to be seen in Chapter 6). These courts generally give narrow definitions both to the scope of the right and to the permissible justifications, with the net effect being that the primary 'screening function' is performed by the scope of the right. Once a plaintiff has surmounted that initial, higher hurdle, by bringing their case within the scope of the right, a defendant government will have great difficulty in establishing a justification for restricting the right and keeping the plaintiff from 'sailing over' the second,

---

[43] Ibid., at p. 47. This argument is similar to one accepted by the majority in *Hardwick*, 478 US 186 at 191 (1986). See Warbrick (1989 Eur), 721.

[44] *F.* v. *Switzerland* (No. 11680/85) (1988), 55 D.R. 178 at 180.

[45] *Kerkhoven* v. *The Netherlands* (No. 15666/89) (19 May 1992). See also *X* and *Y* v. *UK* (No. 9369/81) (1983), 32 D.R. 220; *C. and L.M.* v. *UK* (No. 14753/89) (9 Oct. 1989).

[46] See *DeKlerck* v. *Belgium* (No. 8307/78) (1980), 21 D.R. 116 (keeping spirits); *X* v. *UK* (No. 9702/82) (1982), 30 D.R. 239 (census); *X* v. *Belgium* (No. 9804/82) (1982), 31 D.R. 231 (tax deduction); *X* v. *UK* (No. 8231/78) (1982), 28 D.R. 5 at 28–30 (prison uniform); *Sutter* v. *Switzerland* (8209/78) (1979), 16 D.R. 166 (hair). See generally Loucaides (1990 Eur); Doswald-Beck (1983 Eur), 287–301; Duffy (1982 Eur), 192–94.

[47] But some matters have been held not to belong to the sphere of, not to affect, or not to be solely a matter of, 'private life'. See e.g. *F.* v. *Switzerland* (No. 11680/85) (1988), 55 D.R. 178 (prostitution); *X* v. *Belgium* (No. 8707/79) (1979), 18 D.R. 255 (compulsory seat belts); *Brüggemann* v. *Germany* (No. 6959/75) (1977), 10 D.R. 100 (abortion); *X* v. *Iceland* (No. 6285/74) (1976), 5 D.R. 86 (keeping a dog).

lower hurdle. In *Hardwick*, the plaintiff failed to establish that same-sex oral or anal intercourse came within the fundamental 'right of privacy', but would have placed a very heavy onus on the State of Georgia to establish a justification, had he succeeded.[48] As a result, coming within 'private life' under Article 8(1) is not a victory akin to establishing the application of a 'right of privacy' under the US Constitution. Indeed, a fundamental choice argument under Article 8 of the Convention cannot be said to have succeeded unless all three stages (scope, interference, and absence of justification) have been passed.

The second possible reason for success at the scope of 'private life' stage is the nature of the cases in which 'private life' has been argued. All have involved either private, same-sex sexual activity or same-sex couple relationships. The spatially private nature of such sexual activity, and of much of the interaction of a same-sex couple (e.g. in their home), may have made it conceptually easy to bring these cases within 'private life'. There appear to be only two cases in which claims of sexual orientation discrimination under Article 8 failed at the scope of 'private life' stage. In *F.* v. *Switzerland*, which dealt with criminalization of same-sex prostitution, the Commission held that 'prostitution ... do[es] not belong to the sphere of private life'. It is difficult to see why the presence of remuneration or advertising precludes the need to justify an interference with private sexual activity under Article 8(2).[49]

In *Dudgeon*, the applicant had also complained of 'the existence in Northern Ireland of the common law offences of conspiracy to corrupt public morals and conspiracy to outrage public decency', suggesting that 'they make advocacy of changes in homosexual laws potentially criminal, that explicit association in groups, clubs or societies by homosexual persons could be indictable and that counselling activities ... are of uncertain legal status.' In response to the government's argument that these activities do not fall within the scope of Article 8(1), the Commission said that 'the applicant has not shown how the existence of these offences, which appear by their very nature to concern *public activity*, could be said to have affected his private life'.[50] This limitation on the scope of 'private life' will be considered below.

(b) 'Interference' with Private Life

If 'private life' has not posed a significant barrier, what about 'interference'? In the criminalization and age of consent cases, 'interference' has been found in all but one case, in spite of some hesitation where no prosecution had taken place. The existence of an 'interference' with the applicant's private life has never been questioned where he had actually been prosecuted, convicted, and imprisoned

---

[48] Cf. Dubber (1990 Eur), 201–2.
[49] (No. 11680/85) (1988), 55 D.R. 178 at 181.
[50] (No. 7525/76) (1978), 11 D.R. 117 at 130 (emphasis added).

for sexual activity with another man.[51] The same has been true where the applicant's prison sentence was set aside, suspended, or cancelled, but other sanctions had been imposed (i.e. photographing, fingerprinting, and expulsion from the legal profession,[52] a fine and loss of certain rights,[53] or dishonourable discharge from the armed forces[54]).

Dudgeon was the first sexual orientation discrimination case under the Convention that did not involve a criminal prosecution,[55] but it did involve steps preliminary to a prosecution. Following the execution of a warrant to search the applicant's home for drugs, some of his personal papers were seized and he was asked to go to a police station where he was questioned about his sexual life for four and a half hours. He was not prosecuted and his papers were returned.[56] The Commission found that the mere existence of the laws prohibiting sexual activity between men meant that, under Article 25, he could 'claim[ ] to be the victim of a violation', and that the laws had 'concrete effects' (i.e. causing fear and distress, even though the risk of prosecution was not great) which amounted to 'interference' with his private life. It had stressed that a penal law may have 'effects amounting to interference', even where enforcement is unlikely, because it deters the proscribed conduct and 'stigmatises [it] as unlawful and undesirable'.[57] The Court agreed that 'the maintenance in force of the impugned legislation constitutes a continuing interference with the applicant's . . . private life', requiring him to refrain from 'sexual acts to which he is disposed' or commit a crime. It noted the absence of a 'stated policy on the part of the authorities not to enforce the law' and 'the possibility of a private prosecution'.[58] Three of the four dissenting judges (out of nineteen judges in all) denied that Dudgeon had been the 'victim' of a violation, as required by Article 25.[59]

In *Norris*, the element of steps preliminary to a prosecution was missing. Did this make a difference? Unlike the UK government in *Dudgeon*,[60] the Irish government contended both that Norris could not claim to be a 'victim' of a violation, as required by Article 25, and that there had been no 'interference' with his private life. The Court rejected both arguments, treating the case as

---

[51] See *X* v. *UK* (No. 7215/75) (1978), 19 D.R. 66; *X* v. *Germany* (1975) (No. 5935/72) (1975), 3 D.R. 46; *X* v. *Germany* (No. 2566/65) (1967), 22 Coll. Dec. 35; *X* v. *Austria* (No. 1138/61) (1963), 11 Coll. Dec. 9; *X* v. *Germany* (No. 704/60) (1960), 3 Coll. Dec.; *X* v. *Germany* (No. 530/59) (1960), 3 Y.B. 184; *X* v. *Germany* (No. 261/57) (1957), 1 Y.B. 255; *X* v. *Germany* (No. 167/56) (1956), 1 Y.B. 235; *X* v. *Germany* (No. 104/55) (1955), 1 Y.B. 228.
[52] *X* v. *Germany* (No. 1307/61) (1962), 5 Y.B. 230.
[53] *X* v. *Belgium* (No. 9484/81) (1 Mar. 1982).
[54] *Bruce* v. *UK* (No. 9237/81) (1983), 34 D.R. 68.
[55] See Dubber (1990 Eur), 196 n. 44 ('neither Dudgeon nor Norris would have been held to have standing by a US court'). The same is true of Modinos.
[56] (1981), Ser. A., No. 45, at pp. 15–16.
[57] (1980), Ser. B, No. 40, p. 11 at pp. 33–6.   [58] (1981), Ser. A., No. 45, at p. 18.
[59] Ibid. at pp. 33–5 (Judge Matscher), p. 38 (Judge Pinheiro Farinha), pp. 39–40 (Judge Walsh).
[60] Ibid. at p. 18.

indistinguishable from *Dudgeon*, in which the finding of an 'interference' did not depend on the fact that a police investigation had taken place.[61] However, six of the fourteen judges dissented on the 'victim' point, arguing that the absence of police action distinguished the case from *Dudgeon*, and that fear of prosecution was not enough. They may have been using Article 25 as a device to disagree with the extension of *Dudgeon* to the Republic of Ireland, without having to question the authority of *Dudgeon*, which they expressly denied they were doing.[62]

In *Modinos*, the Attorney-General of Cyprus had adopted a policy of not prosecuting. But eight out of nine judges still found an 'interference' because the law remained on the statute book, the Attorney-General's policy could change, and a police investigation or a private prosecution could still occur.[63] The Cypriot judge dissented on the ground that the challenged law was no longer part of the law of Cyprus.[64]

In most other criminalization or age of consent cases where the applicant has not been prosecuted, the Commission has easily dismissed Article 25 or lack of 'interference' arguments.[65] However, in *Johnson* v. *UK*, it found no 'interference' with the applicant's Article 8(1) right to respect for his private life and for his home. The police raided a party he was giving at 2:00 a.m., arrested him and 37 guests, took him to a police station, questioned him about 'his homosexuality', and detained him until 11:30 a.m. No one was prosecuted, but press publicity caused distress and may have caused the applicant to lose an offer of permanent employment.[66] He complained that the provisions of English law prohibiting sexual activity between men where one is under 21, or 'where more than two persons take part or are present',[67] interfered with his private life and his home, and that the raid 'illustrate[d] the potential threat to which he [was] vulnerable'.[68]

The Commission found that neither provision 'continuously and directly affect[ed] his private life', and therefore that there was no 'interference', because he did not contend that 'he has, has had or wishes to have homosexual relations with a male under 21', or that 'he is disposed to the commission of homosexual acts when more than two persons take part or are present'.[69] It thus seemed to impose a requirement that the applicant have engaged, or be interested in engaging in, the particular activity affected by the law for there to be an 'interference'. This is certainly consistent with its findings of 'interference' in the total prohibition cases, *Dudgeon*, *Norris*, and *Modinos*, and two age of consent cases where there had been no prosecution or other police action but the

---

[61] (1988) Ser. A, No. 142, at pp. 15–18.　　　[62] Ibid. at pp. 24–5.
[63] (1993), Ser. A., No. 259, at paras. 12, 20–24.　　　[64] Ibid. at p. 22.
[65] See *Zukrigl* v. *Austria* (No. 17279/90) (13 May 1992); *Desmond* v. *UK* (No. 9721/82) (7 May 1984). In *B.* v. *UK*, 64 D.R. 278 at 283, it was assumed that deportation of a gay man to a country with a total prohibition (Cyprus) might be an 'interference' with private life.
[66] (1986), 47 D.R. 72 at 73.
[67] Sexual Offences Act 1956, ss. 12 and 13, read with Sexual Offences Act 1967, s. 1.
[68] (1986), 47 D.R. 72 at 75.　　　[69] Ibid. at 76.

applicant was himself under 21 (*Desmond*), or desired sexual relations with a particular under age male (*Zukrigl*).[70]

But surely the requirement should be (i) 'a continuing interest in the prohibited activity' *or* (ii) 'having been affected by enforcement of the prohibition' *or* (iii) 'reasonably fearing being affected by future enforcement of the prohibition'. Although (i) did not apply in *Johnson*, (ii) and (iii) did. In rejecting (ii), the Commission declined to treat the raid itself as an interference because the application had been submitted five days after the expiration of the six-month deadline under Article 26.[71] The Commission did not consider (iii). Yet the whole point of the applicant's complaint was that, as a gay man, he was exposed to the risk of a raid whenever the police suspected that illegal activities were taking place in his home (no warrant being necessary in relation to the age of consent), whether or not such activities ever took place or he had any interest in them.[72] This strained interpretation of 'interference' was not necessary because the Commission could have found a justification under Article 8(2), as it was able to do under Article 14.[73]

In cases not involving a total or partial (limited as to age or number of participants) criminal prohibition of same-sex sexual activity, the need for an 'interference' with private life has posed a major stumbling block for applicants. These cases have involved discrimination against same-sex couples, as compared with married and unmarried opposite-sex couples, where the sanction imposed is not a criminal penalty but the denial of a particular benefit (i.e. the right to succeed as tenant of public housing, to immigrate or to have parental authority over a child). In *Simpson* v. *UK*, the Commission held that the eviction of a lesbian woman from public housing after the death of her partner did not 'interfere' with her private life 'in respect of that partner' because the partner was dead and she was living alone.[74] In *Kerkhoven* v. *The Netherlands*, the Commission found no 'interference' where a lesbian woman was refused parental authority over her female partner's son by donor insemination.[75]

Moreover, in four cases where same-sex partners of British citizens were attempting to immigrate, the Commission has found that the partners' relationship fell within their 'private life',[76] but that a deportation order requiring the non-British (and non-EU) partner to leave the UK did not 'interfere' with their private life.[77] In *X and Y* v. *UK*, which concerned a British-Malaysian male–

[70] See note 27.   [71] *Johnson* (1986), 47 D.R. at 75.
[72] See van Dijk (1993 Eur), 189 ('[t]he actual activities or inclinations of the person concerned seem totally irrelevant for the existence of an interference').
[73] *Johnson* (1986), 47 D.R. at 77–8.
[74] (1986), 47 D.R. 274 at 278. Presumably, this means that a government cannot 'interfere' with a relationship that has ended through the death of one partner.
[75] (No. 15666/89) (19 May 1992).   [76] See note 33.
[77] The Commission's treatment of same-sex couples can be contrasted with the Court's finding violations of Article 8 where the deported person's ties to the country fell within 'family life'. See e.g. *Beldjoudi* v. *France* (1992), Ser. A, No. 234A; *Moustaquim* v. *Belgium* (1991), Ser. A, No. 193; *Berrehab* v. *The Netherlands* (1988), Ser. A, No. 138. See also Storey (1990 Eur); Duffy (1982 Eur).

male couple, the Commission found that, because they were 'professionally mobile' (the British partner having worked in other parts of the world and the Malaysian partner having left employment in Malaysia), 'it has not been shown that the applicants could not live together elsewhere than the United Kingdom, or that their link with the United Kingdom is an essential element of their relationship'.[78] In *W.J. and D.P.* v. *UK*, where the applicants were a British-New Zealand male–male couple, the Commission stated that the disruption of a person's private life inherent in deportation 'cannot, in principle, be regarded as an interference . . . unless . . . there are exceptional circumstances'. None were present in that case because the New Zealand partner entered into the relationship knowing that 'his immigration status was unsettled', he had no other ties with the UK, and the impossibility of living together in New Zealand or elsewhere had not been shown. 'At no time [had] the applicants been prevented from developing their relationship.'[79] Similarly, in *C. and L.M.* v. *UK*, involving a British-Australian female–female couple and the Australian partner's daughter by donor insemination, the Commission found no 'exceptional circumstances' to justify a finding of 'interference', 'given the State's right to impose immigration controls and limits'.[80] Finally, in *B.* v. *UK*, the deportation of a gay Cypriot man with a male British partner did not constitute an 'interference', especially because 'the applicant formed his relationship . . . at a time when he was aware that he had no right to remain in the UK'.[81]

The Commission's reluctance to find an 'interference' in these cases could be explained by characterizing them as cases in which any lack of 'respect for . . . private life' lay, not in an active 'interference', but in the breach of 'positive obligations' to act imposed upon a government by Article 8(1). Because the applicants' claims could be seen as 'positive' claims of entitlement to certain benefits (subsidized public housing, permanent resident status,[82] parental authority) that are politically of a highly sensitive nature, the Commission declined to find such rights (and corresponding government obligations) in Article 8(1). However, the difficulty presented by a 'positive obligation' case can be avoided by characterizing it as a 'discrimination' case under Article 14, for a government's obligation to refrain from discriminating in respect of whatever benefits it confers (whether or not the Convention 'positively obliges' it to confer them) is a 'negative obligation'. Such an obligation can much more easily

---

[78] (1983), 32 D.R. 220. There was no 'interference' in spite of the Malaysian man's arrest, conviction, and fine for overstaying (p. 3, unpublished part). Nor did the Commission consider the applicants' complaints (p. 4, unpublished part) that the British man could not obtain permanent residence or employment in Malaysia, and that sexual activity between men is illegal in Malaysia. See van Dijk (1993 Eur), 191.

[79] (No. 12513/86) (11 Sept. 1986), 11 E.H.R.R. 49. See van Dijk (1993 Eur), 191–2 (the British man had been told that he would not be admitted to New Zealand to work).

[80] (No. 14753/89) (9 Oct. 1989).   [81] (1990), 64 D.R. 278.

[82] See *Abdulaziz* v. *UK* (1985), Ser. A, No. 94, at paras. 66–9 (no 'lack of respect' for family life in deporting husband of woman resident in UK).

be imposed on a government because it will always have two options in deciding how to discharge it: it can end the discrimination by extending the benefit to
those denied it, or by removing it from those receiving it. As the Court said in
Abdulaziz v. *UK*, '[t]he notion of discrimination within the meaning of Article 14
includes . . . cases where a person or group is treated, without proper justification, less favourably than another, even though the more favourable treatment is
not called for by the Convention'.[83] The Commission's treatment of the applicants' Article 14 arguments will be considered in Chapter 5.[84]

(c) 'Justification' for the Interference

As mentioned above, where the lack of 'respect for . . . private life' consists of
an active 'interference', rather than a passive breach of a 'positive obligation',
there will be a violation of Article 8 unless there exists a 'justification' for the
interference under Article 8(2). Such a 'justification' is present where the interference (1) is 'in accordance with the law', (2) pursues one or more of the eight
'legitimate aims' listed in Article 8(2), and (3) is 'necessary in a democratic
society' for the achievement of that aim or aims.[85] The first requirement has
rarely been an issue in a case of sexual orientation discrimination because, in
most such cases, the discrimination the government seeks to justify is found in
a statute or regulations.[86] The second requirement is also easy to satisfy because
the aims are so broad that a government can almost always bring the interference
within at least one of them. While the early cases cited 'protection of health or
morals', since the 1970s the Court and Commission have categorized asserted
justifications mainly as 'protection of morals' or 'protection of the rights and
freedoms of others'.[87]

The controversial requirement in sexual orientation discrimination cases
(argued under Article 8) has thus been the third, the 'necessity in a democratic
society' of the interference with private life. The Court has interpreted this
requirement as meaning that there must be a 'pressing social need' for the
interference, and that the interference must be 'proportionate to the legitimate
aim pursued'.[88] In applying these two criteria, the Court often refers to the
nebulous doctrine of the government's 'margin of appreciation',[89] under which
the government makes 'the initial assessment of the pressing social need' (and

---

[83] Ibid. at para. 82.
[84] Cf. Girard (1986 Eur), 24 (the 'restrictions . . . in *Dudgeon* were aptly suited for a privacy–type
analysis . . . discrimination in employment or housing or custody may not be, and will require a
direct confrontation with Article 14').
[85] *Dudgeon* v. *UK* (1981), Ser. A, No. 45, at para. 43.
[86] The issue was discussed in two Article 10 cases where the 'law' consisted of a common law
criminal offence (*Gay News Ltd.*—see note 28) or provincial teaching staff regulations (*Morissens*—
see note 31).
[87] See e.g. *X* v. *Germany* (No. 530/59) (1960), 3 Y.B. 184 at 194; *Dudgeon* (1981), Ser. A., No.
45, at paras. 45–7; *Norris*, (1988), Ser. A, No. 142, at p. 18.
[88] See e.g. *Dudgeon*, ibid. at paras. 51–3.
[89] See e.g. Yourow (1987 Eur); O'Donnell (1982 Eur).

presumably of proportionality), but the Court reviews that assessment and makes the final evaluation as to whether the reasons purporting to justify the interference are 'relevant and sufficient'.[90] The scope of the 'margin of appreciation' varies with the legitimate aim pursued, being 'more extensive where the protection of morals is in issue', but also varies with 'the nature of the activities involved'.[91] Thus, in *Dudgeon*, which 'concern[ed] a most intimate aspect of private life', the Court held that 'there must exist particularly serious reasons before interferences . . . can be legitimate' under Article 8(2).[92] It reaffirmed this view in *Norris*, rejecting the Irish government's argument that 'necessity in a democratic society' should be given a much wider interpretation in the area of 'protection of morals' which would essentially have allowed governments an unfettered discretion.[93]

Applying these criteria in *Dudgeon*, the Court concluded that the main reason given by the UK government to justify the interference ('a substantial body of opinion in Northern Ireland was opposed [on moral grounds] to a change in the law') was relevant but not sufficient to justify 'the maintenance in force of the impugned legislation in so far as it has the general effect of criminalising private homosexual relations between adult males capable of valid consent'.[94] Because 'the great majority of the member States of the Council of Europe' no longer prohibited sexual activity between men, and Northern Ireland itself no longer enforced the law against sexual activity between consenting men over 21, there was no 'pressing social need' to criminalize such activity, the 'risk of harm to vulnerable sections of society' or 'effects on the public' not providing a sufficient justification.[95] Further, the absolute prohibition of such activity was 'disproportionate to the aims sought to be achieved', in that the justification for retaining the law (protecting the feelings of those who consider such activity 'immoral') was 'outweighed by [the law's] detrimental effects . . . on the life of a person of homosexual orientation like the applicant'.[96] The dissenting views of Judges Zekia and Walsh (essentially that the moral convictions of the majority in Northern Ireland were a sufficient justification) did not prevail.[97] The Court reached the same conclusion in *Norris*[98] and in *Modinos*, where the government of Cyprus did not attempt to argue any justification under Article 8(2).[99]

While finding no justification for a total prohibition of sexual activity between men, the Court in *Dudgeon* did make it clear that 'some degree of regulation of male homosexual conduct, as indeed of other forms of sexual conduct, . . . can

---

[90] See *Dudgeon* (1981), Ser. A, No. 45, at paras. 52, 54, 59.
[91] Ibid. at para. 52.   [92] Ibid.
[93] (1988) Ser. A, No. 142, at pp. 19–20.
[94] *Dudgeon*, ibid. at paras. 57, 59, 61. The Court did not acknowledge the departure from the Commission's view stated in its early decisions (see notes 3 and 4) that the 'punishment of homosexuality' was justified under Article 8(2) for the 'protection of health or morals'.
[95] *Dudgeon*, ibid. at para. 60.   [96] Ibid. at paras. 60–61.
[97] Ibid. at pp. 29–31, 40–47. Compare the discussion of *Hardwick* in Chapter 2, Part II.A.2.(e).
[98] (1988), Ser. A, No. 142, at pp. 20–21.   [99] (1993), Ser. A, No. 259, at para. 25.

be justified as "necessary in a democratic society" [quote from Convention]', both ' "to preserve public order and decency" ' and (even in the case of consensual, private sexual activity) to prevent ' "exploitation and corruption of . . . those who are specially vulnerable [e.g.] because they are young" [quotes from Wolfenden Report]'. It described such legislation as 'protect[ing] particular sections of society as well as the moral ethos of society as a whole'.[100] But it declined to affirm the Commission's conclusion that an age of consent of 21 would be justified, holding that 'it falls in the first instance to the national authorities . . . to fix the age under which young people should have the protection of the criminal law'.[101]

Although the Court has yet to consider a case in which a government has set an age of consent for sexual activity between men, and decide whether the age is justified under Article 8(2), the Commission has heard six cases in which the applicant challenged such an age.[102] In all but one (*Johnson*), it has found a justication for the age.[103] In the first case, *X* v. *Germany* (1975), the applicant, a man over 21 who had engaged in sexual activity with adolescent males under 16, challenged an age of 21. The Commission observed that the purpose of the law was 'to prevent homosexual acts with adults having an unfortunate influence on the development of heterosexual tendencies in minors', especially because, on account of 'the social reprobation with which homosexuality is still frequently regarded', 'a minor . . . might . . . be cut off from society and seriously affected in his psychological development'.[104] It then concluded that, because opinions as to an appropriate upper age for protection varied, 'the age may be fixed within a reasonable margin and vary depending on the attitude of society', that an age of 21, 'although relatively high', did not go beyond this 'reasonable margin', and that the interference was justified under Article 8(2) for the 'protection of the rights of others'.[105]

In *X* v. *UK*, the applicant, a man over 21 who had engaged in sexual activity with a man aged 18, challenged an age of 21. The Commission declared the application admissible to decide 'whether eighteen year olds ought to be considered as "young people" in need of protection'.[106] In its report, it found that the UK age 'must be examined on its own merits and in the context of the society for which it is considered appropriate', regardless of the fact that 'the majority of European states have an age . . . [of] eighteen or below'.[107] Nor was the

---

[100] (1981), Ser. A, No. 45, at para. 49.   [101] Ibid. at para. 62.

[102] See cases cited in note 27. In two other cases where no age of consent had been set (in Northern Ireland and in the UK armed forces), the Commission nonetheless reaffirmed its view that a prohibition of sexual activity with a male under 21 is justified for the 'protection of the rights of others' or the 'protection of morals'. See *Dudgeon* (1980), Ser. B, No. 40, p. 11 at pp. 36–38; *Bruce* v. *UK* (1983), 34 D.R. 68 at 72.

[103] In *Johnson* v. *UK* (1986), 47 D.R. 72, no 'interference' with the applicant's private life was found. See also Helfer (1990 Eur), 1075–86.

[104] (1975), 3 D.R. 46 at 54.   [105] Ibid. at 55.

[106] (1977), 11 D.R. 36 at 43.   [107] *X* v. *UK* (1978), 19 D.R. 66 at 77.

domestic inconsistency with the age of 18 for voting and contracts decisive, in
view of the UK Parliament's adoption of the Wolfenden Committee's recommendation of 21,[108] the rejection of a private member's bill, and ongoing government studies of the issue. Because there was a 'realistic basis' for the
government's opinion that 'young men [18 to 21] . . . who are involved in homosexual relationships would be subject to substantial social pressures which could
be harmful to their psychological development', the Commission found the interference justified for the 'protection of the rights of others'.[109] In a separate
opinion, Mr. Opsahl noted 'the much more significant interference with
the rights of an applicant below [the age of consent] who is denied . . . the right
to have any [sexual] relations [with men] at all'.[110]

In *Desmond* v. *UK*, a 17-year-old male applicant responded to Mr. Opsahl's
observation by challenging the age of 21 and its total prohibition of sexual
activity between him and another man. He argued that the Commission, in *X* v.
Germany (1975) and *X* v. *UK* (decided before the Court's judgment in *Dudgeon*), had failed to find the 'particularly serious reasons' that *Dudgeon* demands
to justify an interference with sexual life, and had not examined the evidence
supporting the existence of a 'pressing social need', or the proportionality of the
measure. He also cited research suggesting that a high age of consent does not
provide 'young homosexuals . . . with social protection . . . [but] damages their
personalities', and opinions of experts favouring an age of 16 or 18.[111] However,
the Commission attached no significance to the applicant's being under 21 and
cited its conclusion in *X* v. *UK*, noting that 'the State is entitled to assert its
power of appreciation in a difficult and sensitive area of the criminal law, in
striking the appropriate balance between the competing interests involved'.[112]

In a 1992 decision on this issue, *Zukrigl* v. *Austria*, the Commission held to
its conclusion in *X* v. *UK* in 1978. A male applicant over 21, who had desired
to engage in sexual activity with a particular adolescent male under 18, challenged the Austrian age of 18. Again, in spite of the applicant's submitting
'extensive documents . . . [showing] that attitudes in general may have evolved
since 1978', the Commission found 'nothing in the present case to distinguish
it from [*X* v. *UK*], save that the Austrian legislation is less restrictive'[113] (i.e. the
age of consent is 18, rather than 21, and the offence may only be committed by
a man over 19, rather than a male of any age).

These decisions show the great, and perhaps understandable, reluctance of the
Commission to intervene in the setting of an age of consent to sexual activity,
especially between men. Instead of examining carefully the evidence supporting

[108] The Committee recommended the 'legal age of contractual responsibility', which was 21 in
1957 and 1967, but was lowered to 18 by the Family Law Reform Act 1969, s. 1(1). See Home
Office (UK) (1957 Eur), p. 27, para. 71; Wintemute (1994 Eur), 517–18.
[109] *X* v. *UK*, ibid. at 77–78. *X* v. *Belgium* (see note 27) upheld an age of 18, citing *X* v. *Germany*
(1975) (see note 27) and *X* v. *UK* and giving no new reasons.
[110] *X* v. *UK*, ibid. at 81.   [111] (No. 9721/82) (7 May 1984), unpublished, at 3–4, 6.
[112] Ibid. at 7–8.   [113] (No. 17279/90) (13 May 1992), unpublished at 8.

the 'justifications', and insisting that 'particularly serious reasons' be given, it seems to prefer to allow governments an effectively unfettered discretion (under Article 8(2)) as to which age they select.[114] However, as in the case of discrimination against same-sex couples, the difficulty of the issue is reduced considerably if it is treated as one of 'discrimination' under Article 14. Rather than attempt to decide in the abstract what age of consent violates Article 8, the Commission could compare the age of consent for sexual activity between men with that for sexual activity between a man and a woman or between women. In fact, it has had to do so, because the applicants in all six age of consent cases have also complained of violations of Article 14 combined with Article 8. The Commission's treatment of their claims will be considered in Chapter 5.

Outside the criminalization and age of consent cases, the Commission has usually found no 'interference' with private life, and thus has not had to determine whether a 'justification' existed (e.g. the six cases of discrimination against same-sex couples).[115] But in three cases it has had to do so. In *Bruce* v. *UK*, the applicant, a male UK soldier, challenged the former total prohibition of sexual activity between men (and between women) in the UK armed forces, even when off duty and off base.[116] He had engaged in sexual activity with a male soldier junior in rank and with a civilian, and was court-martialled and dishonourably discharged (a nine month prison sentence having been cancelled). Because there was a clear 'interference' with his private life, under *Dudgeon* the Commission had to consider the question of 'justification'. It accepted that 'homosexual conduct by members of the armed forces may pose a particular risk to order within the forces which would not arise in civilian life', and accepted the Ministry of Defence's assertions that a prohibition is needed (1) to exclude 'the potentially disruptive influence of homosexual practices' in the 'closed communities' in which members often lived, 'sometimes under stress, and without contacts with the opposite sex', (2) to prevent abuse of authority over junior members, and (3) to avoid the security risk inherent in blackmail of members engaging in same-sex sexual activity. 'Stricter rules over homosexual conduct in the military sphere than would be justifiable in the civilian sphere' could therefore be justified for the 'prevention of disorder'.[117] The Commission does not appear to have considered the proportionality of a total ban to the Ministry of Defence's aims (when sexual activity on duty or on base or with a junior member

[114] Although an age above 21 might be seen as stepping outside their 'margin of appreciation', that is by no means certain.

[115] See notes 32–34.

[116] (1983), 34 D.R. 68. See Sexual Offences Act 1967, s. 1(5); Army Act 1955, s. 66; Air Force Act 1955, s. 66; Naval Discipline Act 1957, s. 37. Section 1(5) of the 1967 Act and equivalent provisions for Scotland and Northern Ireland were repealed by ss. 146(1)–(2) and 147(2) of the Criminal Justice and Public Order Act 1994, but ss. 146(4) and 147(3) expressly preserve the power of the armed forces to dismiss gay, lesbian, and bisexual personnel.

[117] *Bruce* ibid. at 69–70, 72. See also van Dijk & van Hoof (1990 Eur), 375 ('the real risk to order . . . is not created by homosexual conduct . . . but rather by the discriminatory attitude towards it . . . against which the Convention . . . ought to protect the individual').

could be banned), or that it is the risk of court-martial and dismissal that creates the security risk used to justify the ban.

As for the other two cases, in *B.* v. *UK*, the Commission held that, even if deportation of the applicant (a gay man) to the northern part of Cyprus (where sexual activity between men is prohibited) were an 'interference' with his private life, it was 'justified ... for the prevention of disorder ... as a legitimate measure of immigration control'. The possibility of 'hostility and social ostracism because of his homosexuality' did not 'outweigh valid considerations relating to ... immigration controls', especially because the risk of prosecution was not high.[118] And in *Simpson* v. *UK*, the Commission found that any 'interference' with the applicant's 'home' resulting from her eviction from her deceased partner's house was 'necessary for the protection of the contractual rights of the landlord'.[119]

2. Family Life

The applicants in four of the six cases of discrimination against same-sex couples argued that there had been an interference with their 'family life', contrary to Article 8.[120] However, the Commission has given a much narrower interpretation to the scope of 'family life' than to the scope of 'private life', and has refused to accept that the relationship of a same-sex couple (with or without children) could constitute 'family life'. In *X and Y* v. *UK*, the Commission baldly stated its conclusion that, '[d]espite the modern evolution of attitudes towards homosexuality, ... the applicants' relationship does not fall within the scope of the right to respect for family life ensured by Article 8':[121] it has never given any reasons for this conclusion, merely repeating it in three other cases, while clarifying 'the applicants' relationship' as meaning 'a stable homosexual relationship between two men [or two women]'.[122] In *WJ and DP* v. *UK*, it asserted that '*[t]he Court* and the Commission have previously held that

---

[118] (1990), 64 D.R. 278 at 283.

[119] (1986), 47 D.R. 274 at 278. The real issue in the case was not an 'interference' with her 'home', but the discriminatory non-recognition that her relationship with her partner entitled her to remain in the house.

[120] See notes 32–34. In *B.* v. *UK* (1990), 64 D.R. 278 at 281, the applicant argued only 'private life' but referred 'to the nature of his relationship with Mr. R. which is closely akin to family life and the existence of a home established by them'. In *W.J.* and *D.P.* v. *UK* (No. 12513/86) (1986), 11 E.H.R.R. 49, the applicants also argued 'private life' but described themselves as 'living quietly together as a family unit' (unpublished part) and contended that 'their stable relationship is comparable with family life and merits similar protection' (at 50).

[121] (No. 9369/81) (1983), 32 D.R. 220 at 221. Cf. the Great Britain Local Government Act 1988, s. 28(1) ('[a] local authority shall not ... promote the teaching ... of the acceptability of homosexuality as a pretended family relationship').

[122] See *Simpson* v. *UK* (1986), 47 D.R. at 277–8; *C. and L.M.* v. *UK* (No. 14753/89) (9 Oct. 1989); *Kerkhoven* (No. 15666/89) (19 May 1992). See also van Dijk and van Hoof (1990 Eur), 379 (noting that the Commission indicates no criterion for its decision in *X and Y*; '[t]he difference with an unmarried couple is not evident, while there seems to be a clear similarity of interests').

homosexual relationships do not fall within the ambit of family life, but rather fall within the notion of private life',[123] citing paragraph 41 of the Court's judgment in *Dudgeon*. With all due respect, the Court's finding there of an 'interference with the applicant's . . . private life (which includes his sexual life)' can hardly be interpreted as excluding the relationship of a same-sex couple from 'family life'. The Commission's interpretation assumes that 'private life' and 'family life' are mutually exclusive and never overlap. And in any case, neither an argument of interference with 'family life' nor a specific, stable same-sex couple relationship was before the Court in *Dudgeon*, which dealt with a prohibition of sexual activity between men in any context (including contexts outside couple relationships that clearly would not fall within 'family life').

The Commission's resistance to recognizing that same-sex couples have a 'family life' weakened slightly in *Kerkhoven* v. *The Netherlands*.[124] This is only the second case involving a same-sex couple with a child,[125] and is the first case dealing with discrimination against same-sex couples with regard to parental rights. The presence of a child seems to have made it more difficult for the Commission to dismiss the possibility of 'family life'. It acknowledged that Article 8 protects 'the "legitimate" as well as the "illegitimate" family', which the applicants (a female–female couple and the child by donor insemination of one partner) certainly resembled (cf. an unmarried male–female couple with a child by donor insemination). And after repeating its conclusion that same-sex couples do not come within 'family life', it felt obliged to go beyond the scope issue for the first time and consider whether there had been any 'interference' with, or 'lack of respect' for, the applicants' 'family life'. It noted that 'the relevant legislation does not prevent the three applicants from living together as a family' (i.e. if they have a 'family life', there is no active 'interference' with it).[126] And, in spite of the problems that lack of parental authority would cause should the biological mother die or the couple's relationship end, 'the Commission [was] of the opinion that the . . . positive obligations of a State under Article 8 do not go so far as to require that a woman . . . living together with the mother of a child and the child . . . should be entitled to get parental rights over the child'.[127]

---

[123] (No. 12513/86) (1986), 11 E.H.R.R. 49 at 50.

[124] (No. 15666/89) (19 May 1992).

[125] See also *C. and L.M.* v. *UK* (No. 14753/89) (9 Oct. 1989).

[126] Never having found an 'interference' with 'family life', the Commission has not had to consider the existence of a 'justification' under Article 8(2).

[127] *Kerkhoven*, ibid. at 3. Cf. *X, Y & Z* v. *UK* (No. 21830/93) (28 Nov.–9 Dec. 1994 session), unpublished (application under Articles 8 and 14 declared admissible where female-to-male transsexual person was refused recognition as the father of his female partner's child by donor insemination). In *X* v. *The Netherlands* (No. 16944/90) (8 Feb. 1993), unpublished, noted in ([1993] *Medical Law Review* 404—commentary by Andrew Grubb), the Commission seems to have provided some, perhaps unintended, respect to families consisting of a female–female couple and their children. It held that a sperm donor who had agreed that the child would be raised by a female–female couple could be denied access to the child. He has no 'family life' with the child under Article 8, and cannot compare himself under Article 14 to a genetic father who is married to a child's mother.

B. Article 12

Article 12 guarantees to '[m]en and women of marriageable age' both the 'right to marry' and the 'right . . . to found a family'. No same-sex couple has yet asserted before the Commission or the Court that a refusal to permit them to marry violates Article 12. But it seems unlikely that the Commission would find a violation in view of the Court's interpretation of Article 12 in *Cossey* v. *UK*, where a (chromosomally male) transsexual woman had been prevented from marrying a man. The Court noted that Article 12 'referred to the traditional marriage between persons of opposite biological sex', and that its wording 'made it clear that its main concern was to protect marriage as the basis of the family'.[128] Even though some member states permit transsexual persons to marry, 'the developments . . . cannot be said to evidence any general abandonment of the traditional concept of marriage'; thus 'the Court does not consider that it is open to it to take a new approach to the interpretation of Article 12'.[129]

Judge Martens, in dissent, argued that prohibiting a transsexual woman from marrying a man violates Article 12 (to which there should be 'a more functional approach . . . tak[ing] into consideration the factual conditions of modern life'), because neither 'ability to procreate'[130] nor 'capacity for [vaginal] intercourse' is essential for marriage. Yet he did not seem willing to apply his reasoning to same-sex marriage, for he said that 'Article 12, by speaking of 'men' and 'women', clearly indicates that marriage is the union of two persons of opposite sex'.[131] Three weeks after *Cossey*, the Netherlands Supreme Court considered the case of two women who had attempted to marry each other.[132] It found no violation of Articles 8, 12, and 14 of the Convention, relying on the European Court's interpretation of Article 12 in *Rees* v. *UK*.[133] The German Federal Constitutional Court also cited *Rees* in rejecting a challenge to the exclusion of same-sex couples from marriage.[134] Neither the Dutch case nor the German case was subsequently taken to Strasbourg.

---

[128] (1990), Ser. A, No. 184, at para. 43, citing *Rees* v. *UK* (1986), Ser. A, No. 106, paras. 49–50. See van Dijk (1993 Eur), 198 ('[i]f . . . the concept of family is not necessarily linked with that of marriage, why should the opposite be the case?').

[129] *Cossey*, ibid. at para. 46.

[130] Cf. *Rees* v. *UK* (No. 9532/81) (1984), Ser. A, No. 106, pp. 28–9 (opinion of 5 of 15 Commission members) ('a Contracting State must be permitted to exclude from marriage persons whose sexual category itself implies a physical incapacity to procreate . . . in relation to the sexual category of the other spouse (in the case of individuals of the same sex)').

[131] *Cossey*, ibid. at paras. 4.4.3–4.5.2.

[132] *Hoge Raad der Nederlanden* (19 Oct. 1990), RvdW 1990, nr. 176, [1992] *Nederlandse Jurisprudentie*, No. 129.

[133] (1986), Ser. A, No. 106. See Waaldijk (1991 Eur), 32–3.

[134] *Herr S & Herr W*, No. 1 BvR 640/93, *Bundesverfassungsgericht* (4 Oct. 1993), [1993] *Neue Juristische Wochenschrift* 3058 ('marriage' in Article 6(1) of the German *Basic Law* interpreted as meaning 'opposite-sex marriage'). The French *Cour de cassation* has denied claims of same-sex couples to the same benefits as unmarried opposite-sex couples. See Cass. soc., 11 July 1989, Bull. civ. 1989.V.311, No. 514; Cass. soc., 11 July 1989, Bull. civ. 1989.V.312, No. 515. The Hungarian Constitutional Court held on 7 March 1995, in ordering the revision of a law on common-law

In *C. and L.M.* v. *UK*, the applicants (a British-Australian female–female couple and the Australian partner's daughter, 'who it [was] hoped [would] be brought up in the 'de facto' family unit of [the two women]') argued that the deportation of the Australian partner and her daughter would interfere with 'the Article 12 right of [the two women] to found a family, such right not being dependent on the right to marry which they are unable to do under national law'. The Commission, relying on *Rees*, held that 'the [Australian partner's] relationship with her lesbian cohabitee does not give rise to a right to marry and found a family within the meaning of Article 12'.[135] This interpretation (same-sex couples have no right 'to found a family') is consistent with the Commission's view that same-sex couples do not have a 'family life', 'family' being a concept confined to opposite-sex couples.

C. Other Articles of the Convention and Protocols

A survey of the rights and freedoms guaranteed by the Convention and the Protocols suggests that many of them are 'procedural' in nature, in that they permit interference with a particular activity provided that certain sanctions are not imposed (Articles 2, 3, and 4; Protocol 4, Article 1; Protocol 6, Article 1), or that certain procedural guarantees are respected (Articles 5, 6, and 7; Protocol 4, Article 1; Protocol 7, Articles 1–4). The rights and freedoms that might be characterized as 'substantive', in that they protect particular activities or interests, regardless of what sanction is imposed or procedure used, are Articles 8– 12, Article 14 (in its supplementary role), Protocol 1 (Articles 1, 2, and possibly 3), Protocol 4 (Articles 2–3), and Protocol 7 (Article 5). Articles 8 (except for 'home' and 'correspondence') and 12 have been considered above, and Article 14 will be considered in Chapter 5. Provisions protecting more specific activities or interests, such as Article 8 ('home' and 'correspondence'), Protocol 1 (Articles 1 on 'possessions' and 2 on 'education'), Protocol 4 (Articles 2–3 on mobility rights), and Protocol 7 (Article 5 on sex equality relating to marriage) can be invoked by gay, lesbian or bisexual applicants where such activities or interests are affected.[136] The remainder of this Part will examine the other more general 'substantive' rights (Articles 9–11), and the single 'procedural right' that has been given a 'substantive' effect in a case of race discrimination (Article 3).

---

opposite-sex marriage (Ptk 578/G), that '[i]t is arbitrary and contrary to human dignity . . . that the law withholds recognition from couples living in an economic and emotional union simply because they are same-sex', but that '[t]he constitution . . . defines [civil marriage] as a union between a man and a woman', and 'there is no reason to change the law on (civil) marriages'. See 'Hungary High Court Gives Blessing to Gay Couples', *Reuter News Service—CIS and Eastern Europe* (8 March 1995). See generally Waaldijk (1993 Eur), 91–101.

[135] (No. 14753/89) (9 Oct. 1989).

[136] See e.g. *Simpson* v. *UK* (1986), 47 D.R. 274 ('home' and 'possessions'); *X* v. *UK* (No. 7308/75) (1978), 16 D.R. 32 ('correspondence', but see note 142).

1. Article 9

In *Gay News Ltd.* v. *UK*, the Commission upheld the conviction of the publisher and editor of *Gay News* for 'blasphemous libel'.[137] They had published a poem describing the sexual fantasies of a male Roman soldier about Jesus Christ.[138] They argued that the prosecution was an unjustified interference with their 'right to freedom of thought . . . and religion' under Article 9. The Commission found either that 'publication of the poem . . . [did not] constitute[ ] the exercise of a religious or other belief', or that any 'interference' with their Article 9 rights 'would have been justified under Article 9(2) on the same grounds as . . . under Article 10(2)'.[139] Although it might be invoked in cases of expression relating to religious matters, Article 9 would not apply to most cases of sexual orientation discrimination. It could perhaps be used defensively to counter justifications (e.g. 'protection of morals') under Article 8(2) (or other limitation clauses or Article 14) that involve the imposition of religious beliefs on the gay, lesbian, and bisexual minority.[140]

2. Articles 10 and 11

Cases where a gay, lesbian or bisexual applicant claims an interference with their freedom of expression or association could be divided into 'pure' freedom of expression or association cases ('pure liberty' cases), and cases where the interference with freedom of expression or association involves sexual orientation discrimination ('discriminatory interference with liberty' cases). It is often difficult to classify a particular case, because it is not clear whether expression or association, relating to gay, lesbian or bisexual persons or same-sex emotional–sexual conduct, received the treatment that comparable expression or association relating to heterosexual persons or opposite-sex emotional–sexual conduct would have received. One example of a 'pure liberty' case might be *Hauer* v. *Austria*,[141] where the police removed the applicants' banner ('Thousands of homosexual victims of concentration camps wait for their rehabilitation'), which they had displayed during a solemn ceremony to unveil a memorial against war and fascism. The police seemed to object, not to the banner's message or its holders, but to the disruption of the ceremony, because they also removed a banner with a different message ('The Führer left, the "Aryanisers" stayed'). If so, this was not a case of sexual orientation discrimination, but of 'pure' freedom of expression.

The same difficulty of classification arises in 'obscenity' cases. It is not always

---

[137] (No. 8710/79) (1982), 28 D.R. 77.
[138] See *Whitehouse* v. *Lemon*, [1979] AC 617 at 632 (HL); Crane (1982 Eur), 93.
[139] *Gay News Ltd*, ibid. at para. 13 (unpublished part).
[140] Cf. *Johnston* v. *Ireland* (1986), Ser. A, No. 112, at paras. 62–3 (rejecting an Article 9 challenge to the non-availability of divorce in Ireland).
[141] (No. 18116/91) (13 Oct. 1993), unpublished.

clear whether a description or depiction of opposite-sex sexual activity would have been treated as harshly as a depiction of same-sex sexual activity. If the treatment would not have been as harsh, the case is one of '(directly) discriminatory interference with liberty', whereas if the treatment would have been the same, the case is one of 'pure liberty' (or at most of '(indirectly) discriminatory interference with liberty'). An example of a 'pure liberty' case in the area of obscenity might be *Scherer* v. *Switzerland*, where the applicant ran a sex shop for gay and bisexual men and showed pornographic video films at the back of the shop.[142] The Commission concluded (12–5) that his conviction for 'publishing obscene material' interfered with his Article 10(1) right to freedom of expression, and could not be justified under Article 10(2) for the 'protection of morals' because no unwilling adults and no minors would be confronted with the film.[143] The Court declined an opportunity to uphold the Commission's opinion and clarify the Convention's protection of 'obscene' expression. Instead, it struck the case from its list, because the applicant had died and changes in Swiss legislation had probably legalized the showing of a film like the one in question.[144]

At least four cases decided by the Commission under Article 10 could, however, be considered 'discriminatory interference with liberty' cases, because the interference with freedom of expression arguably involved (direct) sexual orientation discrimination. In each, the Commission rejected the Article 10 argument. In *X* v. *UK*, an age of consent case, the applicant's Article 10 complaint that his imprisonment for sexual activity with a man aged 18 'denied his right to express feelings of love for other men' was initially declared admissible.[145] However, in its report, the Commission found no 'interference' with the applicant's Article 10 right, '[i]n so far as [he] complains that he cannot engage in a sexual relationship as a result of imprisonment'. The Commission considered that 'the concept of 'expression' in Article 10 concerns mainly the expression of opinion and the receiving and imparting of information and ideas', and 'does not encompass any notion of the physical expression of feelings'.[146]

---

[142] (1994), Ser. A, No. 287. In the Commission, see No. 17116/90 (11 May 1992), unpublished (decision on admissibility); (1993), Ser. A, No. 287, pp. 16–27 (report). The sexual orientation of the acts depicted in the film did not appear to be relevant. The Court (at para. 7) and the Commission (at para. 17, unpublished part) both described them as 'sexual acts'. See also *X* v. *UK* (No. 7308/75) (1978), 16 D.R. 32 at 35 (no violation of Article 8 or 10 where seized pornographic magazines depicted 'adult persons engaged in homosexual acts with adolescents'; no sexual orientation discrimination if same sanction would have been applied to a depiction of comparable opposite-sex sexual activity).

[143] *Scherer*, ibid. at paras. 59–67 (report) (noting, at para. 62, that 'the nature of the . . . shop was not discernible from the street'). The Commission, at para. 59, distinguished *Müller* v. *Switzerland* (1988), Ser. A, No. 133 as involving 'obscene material . . . displayed to the general public'. The paintings in *Müller* were displayed at an exhibition that was open to persons of any age, and depicted sexual activity between men and between men and animals (see *Müller*, paras. 16, 36).

[144] *Scherer*, ibid. at paras. 31–32 (Court). The new legislation (see para. 24) seems to permit pornographic films to be shown on closed premises to persons over 16 warned of the nature of the film, if sexual acts with children, animals, human excrement or acts of violence are not shown.

[145] (1977), 11 D.R. 36 at 45.   [146] (1978), 19 D.R. 66 at 80.

In *Gay News Ltd.* v. *UK*, the Commission held that the undoubted interference with the applicants' freedom of expression was justified under Article 10(2) for the 'protection of the rights of others', i.e. 'the right of [the person bringing the private prosecution] not to be offended in [her] religious feelings by publications'. Because such feelings 'may deserve protection against indecent attacks on the matters held sacred . . . , then it can . . . be considered as necessary in a democratic society to stipulate that such attacks, if they attain a certain level of severity, shall constitute a criminal offence triable at the request of the offended person'. It was not 'disproportionate to the aim pursued that the offence [was] one of strict liability incurred irrespective of the intention to blaspheme . . . the intended audience . . . and the possible avoidability of the publication'.[147] In treating *Gay News* as a 'discriminatory interference with liberty' case, I am assuming that the use of the obsolete offence of 'blasphemous libel' would not have succeeded if the poem had concerned a woman's sexual fantasies about Jesus Christ.[147a] If this is true, it can be argued that the application of 'blasphemous libel' in *Gay News* constituted sexual orientation discrimination. If a poem describing opposite-sex sexual activity would also have led to a successful prosecution, then a 'pure liberty' challenge under Article 10 to the offence of 'blasphemous libel' would probably fail. In *Otto-Preminger-Institut* v. *Austria*, the Court (by 6–3) seems to have upheld blasphemy laws. It found no violation of Article 10 where a film was seized, and could not be shown in a cinema, because it was considered offensive to the 87% Roman Catholic majority of the Tyrol.[148]

In *Morissens* v. *Belgium*, a teacher was dismissed after appearing on a television programme about 'homosexual women' and describing the effects of being lesbian on her career. In particular, she said that she was expecting to take up the post of head teacher of a school, but was not appointed. Her referees were told that 'it was unthinkable that a homosexual woman should be put in charge of a school with 1,000 girls'. With regard to the two male head teachers who were appointed, she said: 'I don't know whether that doesn't make the risk all the greater'.[149] The Commission found that she was dismissed because 'she had publicly undermined the authority and reputation of her hierarchical superiors', not 'because of her homosexuality'. It then held that the interference with her right to freedom of expression was justified under Article 10(2) for the 'protection of the reputation and rights of others', i.e. the school and the two head teachers, in view of the 'harmful repercussions of her statements' on their reputations.[150] Putting aside her ill-considered remark about the male head teachers, it would seem that, even if the applicant had not been denied the post or

---

[147] (1982), 28 D.R. 77 at 83.

[147a] Cf. Ken Russell's 1971 film 'The Devils'; the video in *Wingrove* v. *UK* (No. 17419/90) (10 Jan. 1995), unpublished (report). In *Wingrove*, unlike *Gay News*, the Commission found a violation of Art 10 and has referred the case to the Court.

[148] (1994), Ser. A, No. 295-A, paras. 52–6. The Commission had found (9–5) a violation of Article 10: (No. 13470/87) (1993), Ser. A, No. 295-A, pp. 26–33.

[149] (1988), 56 D.R. 127 at 132–3.   [150] Ibid. at 136–7.

dismissed because of her sexual orientation,[151] she may have been dismissed for publicly accusing the school of sexual orientation discrimination. In Great Britain, under section 4 of the Sex Discrimination Act 1975 or section 2 of the Race Relations Act 1976, such a dismissal would have constituted illegal 'victimization' if the applicant's allegation had been of sex or race discrimination and had been made in good faith.

Finally, in *Dudgeon*, the Commission considered *ex officio* whether the applicant's complaint regarding the existence of the common law offences of 'conspiracy to corrupt public morals' and 'conspiracy to outrage public decency' violated Articles 10 or 11. It found 'no indication that the scope of these offences . . . could render illegal advocacy of changes in homosexual laws', or that their mere existence could restrict the applicant's freedom of association (despite the applicant's assertion that they might render illegal 'explicit association' in groups, clubs or societies by homosexuals' or counselling activities).[152] Presumably, the Commission might take a different view were these offences actually used to prosecute a gay, lesbian, and bisexual organization (e.g. a students' society).

These four cases suggest that Articles 10 or 11 may be relevant where a particular instance of sexual orientation discrimination is directed at expression or associational rights.[153] However, many cases of sexual orientation discrimination will fall outside Articles 10 and 11, especially if they involve sexual activity (as in *X* v. *UK*), but also if they involve other instances of emotional–sexual conduct (e.g. public displays of affection or formation of couple relationships) that may involve no attempt to communicate any idea and may go beyond mere 'association'.

3. Article 3

The other Convention right worth noting is Article 3. Its prohibition of 'inhuman or degrading treatment or punishment' was unsuccessfully invoked by at least two applicants in early criminalization cases.[154] After *Dudgeon*, it might be used in two ways. First, an applicant could argue that sexual orientation discrimination

---

[151] See van Dijk (1993 Eur), 200 ('the Commission should have investigated . . . to what extent homosexuality had played a role in the decision . . . to fire her').

[152] (1978), 11 D.R. 117 at 130–31.

[153] The potential for violations of Articles 10 and 11 is not insignificant, because Austria, Finland, Great Britain, and the Isle of Man have (infrequently enforced) laws prohibiting the 'promotion of homosexuality'. See Ch. 7, note 86; Helfer (1991 Eur), 181–3; Tatchell (1992 Eur), 99, 102, 109–10. Further, in Turkey in 1989, a newspaper was charged with 'spreading homosexual information': see Tatchell (1992 Eur), 135. Also, the Finnish law has been used to justify censorship of radio and television programmes dealing with gay, lesbian, and bisexual issues: see Ch. 5, notes 159–61 and accompanying text.

[154] See *X* v. *Germany* (No. 530/59) (1960), 3 Y.B. 184 at 190; *X* v. *Germany* (No. 1307/61) (1962), 5 Y.B. 230 at 234.

118   *European Convention on Human Rights*

constitutes 'inhuman or degrading treatment'.[155] In *East African Asians* v. *UK*, the Commission held that the application of a racially discriminatory UK immigration law, in the special circumstances of the case, amounted to 'degrading treatment', and violated Article 3.[156] However, this interpretation may have been a device to avoid the deficiencies of Article 14, which does not apply to most race discrimination because there is no Convention right to 'freedom of race'. The availability of Article 8 might preclude the extension of this interpretation to sexual orientation discrimination. Second, the deportation of a gay, lesbian or bisexual person from a Council of Europe member state to a country such as Iran, where anal intercourse between men and a fourth offence of 'lesbianism' are punishable by death,[157] might raise an issue under Article 3 (or 8) similar to that in *Soering* v. *UK*.[158]

---

[155] See Kane (1988 Eur), 479–80; van Dijk (1993 Eur), 201.

[156] See (1970), 13 Y.B. 928 at 994 (dec. on adm.); (1973), 78-A D.R. 5 at p. 62 (report) (published in 1994) ('discrimination based on race could, in certain circumstances, of itself amount to degrading treatment'). Cf. *Hector* v. *UK* (No. 14818/89) (1990), *The Guardian* (20 April 1990) 39 (refusal of private club to permit man of Afro-Caribbean origin to enter to collect money for charity because of his colour 'did not attain such a level of severity as to make it treatment proscribed by Article 3').

[157] See the Islamic Penal Law approved by the Islamic Consultancy Parliament on 30 July 1991, Chapter 1, Articles 110, 131. See also 'More than 90 people face death sentence in Iran' *Gay Times* (Oct. 1992) 27 (discussing asylum applications of gay and lesbian Iranians in Sweden and Denmark).

[158] (1989), Ser. A, No. 161 (extradition from UK to US would violate Article 3 because of 'death row phenomenon'). See also van Dijk (1993 Eur), 202–3. The issue could arise under Article 3 or Article 8, as in *B.* v. *UK* (see note 33). There, any 'interference' with the applicant's Article 8(1) right was held justified under Article 8(2), in view of the low risk of prosecution. The death penalty in Iran (as opposed to a maximum of 5 years' imprisonment in Cyprus: *Modinos*, see note 12) might lead to a different result.

5

The European Convention on Human Rights: Immutable Status and Sex Discrimination Arguments

I. USE OF AN IMMUTABLE STATUS OR SEX DISCRIMINATION ARGUMENT UNDER ARTICLE 14

A. Relevance of Article 14

As was mentioned at the beginning of Chapter 4, an immutable status or sex discrimination argument under Article 14 can only supplement a fundamental choice argument under one of the other Articles discussed above. Because it 'has no independent existence', the question arises whether Article 14 has any relevance in sexual orientation discrimination cases or whether it is effectively redundant. The Court has certainly shown its reluctance to consider Article 14 in conjunction with another Article, if it has already found a violation of the other Article. In *Airey* v. *Ireland*, the Court held that an examination of Article 14 is required only 'if a clear inequality of treatment in the enjoyment of the right in question is a fundamental aspect of the case'.[1] This test was not satisfied in *Dudgeon*, where the applicant had claimed a violation of Article 14 in conjunction with Article 8, in that sexual activity between men over 21 was legal in other parts of the UK, and the age of consent to male–female or female–female sexual activity was 17 in Northern Ireland. The Court held that it was not necessary to consider Article 14, because finding a violation of Article 8 would eliminate the discrimination as between parts of the UK, and the discrimination regarding the age of consent would present an Article 14 issue only after Northern Ireland had set an age of consent to sexual activity between men.[2] Five judges (out of nineteen) thought that Article 14 ought to have been examined.[3]

It has been argued in the US that equal protection doctrine should not concern itself with 'fundamental rights', and that issues of discrimination in respect of such rights should be addressed only under the substantive provisions that guarantee them.[4] Under the Convention, however, the Court has said that Article 14

---

[1] (1979), Ser. A, No. 32, para. 30.   [2] (1981), Ser. A, No. 45, at pp. 25–26.
[3] Ibid. at pp. 27, 32, 35–7. See also Mr. Polak's separate opinion in the Commission, (1980), Ser. B, No. 40 at p. 44; van Dijk and van Hoof (1990 Eur), 537–8 (suggesting that Article 14 should be considered).
[4] See Perry (1979 US), 1074–83.

implicitly 'form[s] an integral part of each of the provisions laying down rights and freedoms'.[5] When should it be used? It may well be that the Court is justified, for reasons of judicial economy, in declining to consider Article 14 where a violation of another Article, taken alone, has been found. This will be the case where, as in *Dudgeon*, the particular interference with the right (criminalization of private same-sex sexual activity) is clearly not justified, without having to compare the treatment of the applicant with the treatment of other persons. However, there will be cases where the existence of an 'interference', or a 'justification' for it, will not be obvious if the treatment of the applicant is viewed in isolation, without comparing it with that of other persons. Examples where such comparison is necessary were seen in Chapter 4 in the cases dealing with same-sex couples and with the age of consent. In such cases, the violation of a Convention right may only become clear when the difference in treatment is examined. The treatment may not violate the Convention right on its own, because it could justifiably be imposed on all persons. But the fact that it has been imposed only on certain persons means that it violates Article 14 in conjunction with the Convention right.[6]

It is worth noting again an important consequence of the limited scope of Article 14. Because Article 14 only applies to the enjoyment of Convention rights and freedoms, there are no special kinds of discrimination (corresponding to 'suspect or quasi-suspect classifications' in the US, or 'enumerated and analogous grounds' in Canada) that violate the Convention whether or not another Convention right or freedom is affected. As a result, most race or sex discrimination (e.g. in public employment or education) falls outside the Convention, there being no Convention rights to 'freedom of race' or 'freedom of (biological) sex'. A desire to avoid this limitation of the Convention may have motivated the arguably strained interpretation of Article 3 in *East African Asians* v. *UK*.[7] This limitation is less significant in sexual orientation discrimination cases, because of the potential applicability of Articles 8 and 12. However, if such a case falls outside of e.g. 'private life' in Article 8, Article 14 cannot be invoked. This occurred in *F.* v. *Switzerland*: because the Commission held that prostitution is not part of 'private life' and that Article 8 did not apply, Article 14 could not

---

[5] See *Marckx* v. *Belgium* (1979), Ser. A, No. 31, para. 32.

[6] See *Belgian Linguistic Case* (1965), Ser. B, No. 3, at p. 306 (Commission's report) ('different measures taken by a State in respect of different parts of its . . . population [may] entail no breach of . . . the right in question, but . . . differentiation [may] entail[ ] a violation if the State's conduct is judged from the point of view of Article 14'). The Court and Commission's reluctance to consider Article 14 is somewhat surprising, in that the Article 14 issue (can the difference in treatment be justified?) may often be easier than the issue under the other Convention article (can the treatment justifiably be imposed on all persons?). In two recent cases, the Court has proceeded directly to Article 14 (and found a violation), rather than consider the applicant's argument that Article 8 had been violated on its own: see *Burghartz* v. *Switzerland* (1994), Ser. A, No. 280–B, at para. 21; *Hoffmann* v. *Austria* (1993), Ser. A, No. 255–C, at para. 30. See also *Karlheinz Schmidt* v. *Germany* (1994), Ser. A, No. 291–B, at para. 23 (violation of Article 14 in conjunction with Article 4(3)(d); applicant did not rely on Article 4(2), which had probably not been violated on its own).

[7] See references cited in Ch. 4, note 156.

be invoked to challenge the clear sexual orientation discrimination involved in the criminalization of same-sex but not opposite-sex prostitution.[8]

B. Application of Article 14 to Sexual Orientation Discrimination

In one of its first decisions, the *Belgian Linguistic Case*,[9] the Court established a three-part test for a finding of 'discrimination' contrary to Article 14, in conjunction with another Article. In the Court's most recent formulations of the test, these three parts seem to be: (1) there is a difference in treatment among 'persons in similar situations'; *and* (2) there is no 'objective and reasonable justification' for the difference in treatment because it does not pursue a 'legitimate aim'; *or* (3) there is no 'objective and reasonable justification' for the difference in treatment because there is no 'reasonable relationship of proportionality between the means employed and the [legitimate] aim sought to be realised'.[10] How have these criteria been applied in cases of sexual orientation discrimination? Establishing a difference in treatment among 'persons in similar situations' has rarely proved difficult but, in at least twenty cases in which the Commission has considered Article 14, it has found an 'objective and reasonable justification' for the difference in treatment, i.e. a 'legitimate aim' and a 'reasonable relationship of proportionality'. These cases consist of five early criminalization cases,[11] the six age of consent cases,[12] *Dudgeon* in the Commission regarding the age of consent,[13] the six same-sex couple cases,[14] *Bruce* v. *UK*,[15] and *Gay News Ltd.* v. *UK*.[16]

In both the age of consent cases and the same-sex couple cases, the Commission has reached a conclusion in the first or second case and then repeated it in each subsequent case. In *X* v. *Germany* (1975), the Commission concluded, based on certain pre-1975 German studies, that there exists 'a specific social danger in the case of masculine homosexual[s] . . . result[ing] from the fact that [they] often constitute a distinct socio-cultural group with a clear tendency to proselytise adolescents and that the social isolation in which it involves the latter is particularly marked'. The need for 'social protection' against this 'danger' was therefore an 'objective and reasonable justification' for a difference between

---

[8] (No. 11680/85) (1988), 55 D.R. 178, at p. 5 (unpublished part); and text accompanying Ch. 4, note 49. It follows from *F* v. *Switzerland* that a prohibition of all prostitution, or of opposite-sex but not same-sex prostitution, could not be challenged under the Convention.

[9] (1968), Ser. A, No. 6, para. 10.

[10] See e.g. *Karlheinz Schmidt* v. *Germany* (1994), Ser. A., No. 291–B, at para. 24; *Hoffmann* v. *Austria* (1993), Ser. A, No. 255–C, at paras. 31, 33.

[11] *X* v. *Germany* (No. 104/55) (1955), 1 Y.B. 228 at 229; *X* v. *Germany* (No. 167/56) 1 Y.B. 235 at 236; *X* v. *Germany* (No. 261/57) (1957) 1 Y.B. 255 at 257; *X* v. *Germany* (No. 600/59) (2 Apr. 1960), unpublished; *X* v. *Germany* (No. 1307/61) (1962), 5 Y.B. 230 at 234.

[12] See the cases cited in Ch. 4, note 27.

[13] (1980), Ser. B, No. 40, at pp. 41–3. See also, in the Court, the dissenting opinion of Judge Matscher ((1981), Ser. A, No. 45, at pp. 35–7), who was willing to uphold certain differences of treatment under Article 14.

[14] See the cases cited in Ch. 4, notes 32–34.   [15] (1983), 34 D.R. 68 at 72.

[16] (No. 8710/79) (1982), 28 D.R. 77 at para. 14 (unpublished part).

the male–male age of consent (21) and the female–female age (14), and criminal sanctions were not disproportionate.[17] This conclusion was extended in *X* v. *UK*, for the reasons given in assessing the justification under Article 8(2), to a difference between the male–male (21) and male–female (16) ages of consent.[18] The two cases have been cited, and no additional reasons provided, in the four other age of consent cases,[19] and in the Commission's report in *Dudgeon*.[20] The only new development mentioned was the 1984 recommendation of the Criminal Law Revision Committee (UK)[21] that the female–female age of consent remain at 16 because: 'homosexual relationships tended to arise later in life among women . . . there was no comparable group of 16 to 18 year old girls whose sexual orientation had not yet become fixed and who were consequently in need of protection[22] . . . and . . . adolescent girls did not seem especially attractive to older women . . . , there being greater emphasis in male homosexual culture on this age group'.[23]

A similar pattern can be seen in the same-sex couple cases. In *X and Y* v. *UK*, the Commission initially took the view that the relationship of a male–male couple, not constituting 'family life', could not be compared with that of a male–female couple (i.e. the difference in treatment was not among 'persons in similar situations'). Because 'the only comparable group [was] that of lesbians', who would receive the same treatment, there was no difference in treatment.[24]

---

[17] (1975), 3 D.R. 46 at 56. See also Tatchell (1992 Eur), 112.

[18] (1978), 19 D.R. 66 at 79–80. See van Dijk (1993 Eur), 195 ('the Commission did not discuss at all the . . . question whether social pressure was caused by the homosexual relationships themselves or by the biased attitude of society towards homosexuality').

[19] Cited in Ch. 4, note 27.   [20] (1980), Ser. B, No. 40 at p. 42.

[21] (1984 Eur), 86. See also Policy Advisory Committee on Sexual Offences (UK) (1981 Eur), 17, 27 (8 votes for a male–male age of 18, 5 for 16, 2 for 16 except where older man in position of authority); van Dijk (1993 Eur) (noting, 195 n. 47, a Council of Europe study finding 'no scientific justification for a difference in the age of consent' and suggesting, 196, that 'national reports drafted in the country against which the complaint has been lodged would seem to be not the most convincing basis for an international assessment').

[22] The opinion of the British Medical Association on this point, which influenced the 1981 and 1984 reports (ibid.), has changed. See British Medical Association (1994 Eur), 7–8 (finding that 'adult sexual orientation is usually established before the age of puberty in both boys and girls' and recommending that 'the age of consent for homosexual men should be set at 16 [the male–female and female–female age] because the present law may inhibit efforts to improve the sexual health of young homosexual and bisexual men'). The B.M.A.'s recommendation was rejected by the UK Parliament in 1994, when it voted against an equal age of consent of 16 (17 in Northern Ireland) and in favour of lowering the male–male age throughout the UK from 21 to 18. See Criminal Justice and Public Order Act 1994, s. 145; *Hansard*, H.C. Deb., Vol. 238, 74–123 (21 Feb. 1994).

[23] *Johnson* v. *UK* (1986), 47 D.R. 72 at 77. *Johnson* also upheld (at 78) the application of a requirement that not 'more than two persons take part or are present' to male–male sexual activity, but not to male–female or female–female, because 'heterosexuality and lesbianism do not give rise to comparable social problems'. The 'need to protect the individual, particularly the young and vulnerable' justified the difference.

[24] (No. 9369/81) (1983), 5 E.H.R.R. 601 at 602. The Commission even doubted that the proposed deportation of the Malaysian man could 'be described as a measure of discrimination', because it was not 'based on the fact of the applicants' homosexual relationship'. But surely it was based on the non-recognition of that relationship as equivalent to one between a British man and a non-EU woman.

In *Simpson* v. *UK*, the Commission (in considering Article 14 in conjunction with 'respect for ... home' in Article 8) permitted the applicant to compare herself to a woman with a deceased male partner, and therefore found a difference in treatment (presumably among 'persons in similar situations').[25] However, it also found an 'objective and reasonable justification' in the legitimate aim of 'protect[ing] the family'. '[I]t was justified to protect families but not to give protection to other stable relationships ... [because] the family (to which the relationship of heterosexual unmarried couples living together as husband and wife can be assimilated) merits special protection in society.'[26] The conclusion in *Simpson* has been cited in *W.J. and D.P.* v. *UK*, in *C. and L.M.* v. *UK* ('priority to ... traditional established families, rather than other established relationships' justified), and in *B.* v. *UK* ('difference in treatment pursues the legitimate aim of protecting family based relationships (including relationships existing outside marriage) in a manner proportionate to the achievement of that aim').[27] In *Kerkhoven* v. *The Netherlands*, the applicants complained of discrimination compared with opposite-sex couples and of discrimination against their child on the basis of 'his birth and status in comparison with legitimate children'. The Commission responded that, 'as regards parental authority over a child, a homosexual couple cannot be equated to a man and a woman living together', giving no reason for its conclusion.[28]

Finally, in *Bruce* v. *UK* (one of only two public employment cases, *Morissens* v. *Belgium* being the other, and the only one in which Article 14 was raised), the applicant argued that he had 'suffered discrimination by virtue of being a homosexual' and that 'members of racial, religious or national minorities are not excluded from the armed forces and, under Article 14, the same should apply to homosexuals'.[29] He thus compared himself with ethnic minority soldiers but not (expressly) with heterosexual soldiers. The Commission held that the 'measures in question [court-martial and dismissal] were in pursuit of a legitimate aim, ... the protection of morals and prevention of disorder in the armed services, and were not ... disproportionate'.[30] It did not ask itself 'why comparable risks [to order] would not be created by heterosexual relationships within the forces or during

[25] (1986), 47 D.R. 274 at 279 ('[t]he Commission accepts that the treatment accorded to the applicant was different from the treatment she would have received if the partners had been of different sexes').

[26] Ibid. It would appear that proportionality does not have to be shown where an applicant challenges their exclusion from a law that would benefit them, rather than the application to them of a law that burdens. Ibid. at 279–80. Similarly, in *W.J. and D.P.* v. *UK* (No. 12513/86) (1986), 11 E.H.R.R. 49 at 51, 'no issue of proportionality [arose]' in relation to the applicants' exclusion from the 'family life provisions' of the Immigration Rules. The Commission went on to find that the deportation of the New Zealand man (who lacked a work permit) was proportionate to the legitimate aim of protecting 'the economic well-being of the country'. This added nothing to the Commission's reasoning because the whole point of the applicants' argument was that a New Zealand woman (without a work permit) in a relationship with a British man would have been permitted to stay.

[27] See Ch. 4, note 33.   [28] (No. 15666/89) (19 May 1992), unpublished.

[29] (No. 9237/81) (1983), 34 D.R. 68 at p. 6 (unpublished part).

[30] Ibid. at p. 10.

military service'.[31] And in *Gay News Ltd.* v. *UK*, the applicants alleged discrimination, *inter alia*, 'because of their opinion about the relationship between Christian and homosexual love'. However, the Commission denied that 'they were singled out . . . on account of their homosexual views', asserting that '[n]othing suggests that [the poem] would not have been restricted in exactly the same way if it had been published by persons without homosexual tendencies'.[32] The Commission did not ask itself whether the prosecution would have been brought or succeeded had the poem dealt with sexual fantasies involving opposite-sex sexual activity.

C. Does It Matter on What Ground the Discrimination Is Based?

The preceding Part has shown the complete failure of Article 14 arguments in cases of sexual orientation discrimination. The Commission's findings of 'objective and reasonable justifications' in every case could be criticized (e.g. its acceptance of the 'seduction of youth' stereotype, and the existence of social discrimination against gay and bisexual men, as justifications for a higher age of consent),[33] but that would exceed the limits of this Chapter. Instead, I will consider the question of whether a less deferential test than that in the *Belgian Linguistic Case*, which resembles 'rational basis review' in US equal protection doctrine,[34] should be applied to cases of sexual orientation discrimination. This raises the further question of whether or not the nature of the particular ground on which the challenged discrimination is based makes any difference under Article 14.

There are frequent indications in the decisions of the Court and Commission that the nature of the ground is of no importance whatsoever. *All* conceivable grounds of discrimination are included in Article 14's reference to 'discrimination on any ground' and residual category of 'other status', and are subjected to the same, deferential *Belgian Linguistic* test. There are thus no higher levels of scrutiny applicable to certain grounds. The net effect resembles US equal protection doctrine, shorn of the 'suspect classifications' branch and with a 'rational

---

[31] van Dijk (1993 Eur), 195.

[32] (No. 8710/79) (1982), 28 D.R. 77, at pp. 6, 18–19 (unpublished part).

[33] See e.g. the excellent analysis of the age of consent issue in Helfer (1990 Eur), 1075–1100. See also van Dijk and van Hoof (1990 Eur), 543–4 ('as far as the protection of vulnerable groups—in particular the young—is concerned, homosexual, lesbian, as well as heterosexual relationships have to be . . . treated equally').

[34] Laurence Helfer, (1990 Eur) at 1062, 1067, found no case in which the Court found a violation of Article 14 under the *Belgian Linguistic* test (other than the *Belgian Linguistic Case* itself), but three cases in which the Court found violations after applying a more stringent test. Cf. *Darby* v. *Sweden* (1990), Ser. A, No. 187, at paras. 33–4 (distinction between residents and non-residents in respect of exemption from 'church tax' violated Art. 14 taken together with Prot. 1, Art. 1, but government conceded distinction had no 'legitimate aim'). See also note 44 (distinctions based on sex violated Art. 14); and *Hoffmann*, note 46 (distinction based on religion violated Art. 14).

basis' test (rather than 'strict scrutiny') applied to the 'fundamental rights' branch. Support for this interpretation may be found in the statements of the Court that the list of grounds in Article 14 includes any 'personal characteristic ("status") by which persons or groups of persons are distinguishable from each other',[35] and that '[t]here is no call to determine on what ground [a] difference [of treatment is] based, the list . . . not being exhaustive'.[36]

The non-importance of the nature of the ground is reflected in the terms used by applicants and the Commission. In nine out of twenty sexual orientation discrimination cases under Article 14,[37] neither the applicant nor the Commission clearly defines a specific ground on which the discrimination is based. Instead, they merely state that another group of persons receives different treatment, without attempting to define the difference between that group and the applicant's group. In eight cases, the applicant or the Commission refers expressly to the ground as 'sex',[38] in two cases, to 'sexual preference',[39] and in *Gay News Ltd.*, to 'opinion'.[40] In *X* v. *UK*, the applicant did not clearly define a ground, but referred to 'sexual orientation' in several places and argued 'that it was anomalous for the Government to seek . . . to eliminate discrimination on grounds of sex and race . . . yet maintain a discriminatory regime as regards sexual orientation'.[41]

Because all grounds seem to be included and receive the same deferential review, there does not seem to be any need to define a theory or principle that would explain what grounds should be subjected to a stricter standard of review, as is the case with 'suspect or quasi-suspect classifications' in the US and 'enumerated and analogous grounds' in Canada. 'Sexual orientation' is automatically included in Article 14, but differences in treatment based on that ground always seem to have an 'objective and reasonable justification'.[42]

---

[35] *Kjeldsen* v. *Denmark* (1976), Ser. A, No. 23, para. 56.

[36] *Rasmussen* v. *Denmark* (1984), Ser. A, No. 87, para. 34.

[37] *X* v. *Germany* (No. 1307/61), cited in Ch. 4, note 3; *X* v. *UK*, *X* v. *Belgium*, *Desmond, Johnson, Zukrigl*, cited in Ch. 4, note 27; *W.J. and D.P.* v. *UK*, *B.* v. *UK*, cited in Ch. 4, note 33; *Kerkhoven*, cited in Ch. 4, note 34. See also *F* v. *Switzerland*, cited in Ch. 4, note 29.

[38] *X* v. *Germany* (Nos. 104/55, 167/56, 261/57 and 600/59), cited in Ch. 4, note 3; *X* v. *Germany* (1975), cited in Ch. 4, note 27; *Dudgeon*, cited in Ch. 4, note 9; *X and Y* v. *UK*, cited in Ch. 4, note 33; *Simpson*, cited in Ch. 4, note 32.

[39] *C. and L.M.* v. *UK*, cited in Ch. 4, note 33 and in *Bruce*, cited in Ch. 4, note 31. In the latter, at pp. 6–7 (unpublished part), the applicant describes the discrimination as 'by virtue of being a homosexual', but later refers to a proposed amendment to Article 14 adding 'sexual preference'. See notes 123–25 below and accompanying text.

[40] (No. 8710/79) (1982), 28 D.R. 77, at p. 6 (unpublished part).

[41] (No. 7215/75) (1978), 19 D.R. 66, at paras. 42–3, 77, 82 (unpublished part).

[42] Cf. *Dudgeon* (1980), Ser. B, No. 40, at p. 44 (separate opinion of Mr. Polak) (prohibition of sexual activity between men over 21 also violates Article 14, because '[t]he enumeration of the forbidden grounds of discrimination in Article 14 is clearly not an exhaustive one', '[t]he prohibition . . . stigmatises homosexuality', and 'the State discriminates strongly against this group of the population'; '[t]his . . . amounts to a clear inequality of treatment . . . which is a fundamental aspect of this case').

D. Would an Immutable Status or Sex Discrimination
Argument Make a Difference?

Despite the indications that 'all grounds are equal', the Court has also suggested on several occasions that differences of treatment based on certain grounds are more difficult to justify. Laurence Helfer has argued that the Court does in fact apply a form of 'heightened scrutiny' under Article 14, and cites as examples *Abdulaziz* v. *UK* and *Inze* v. *Austria*.[43] In *Abdulaziz*, the Court held that, because 'the advancement of the equality of the sexes is today a major goal in the member States of the Council of Europe, . . . *very weighty reasons* would have to be advanced before a difference of treatment on the ground of sex could be regarded as compatible with the Convention'.[44] And in *Inze*, it made an identical statement with respect to 'the ground of birth out of wedlock', having noted that '[t]he question of equality between children born in and children born out of wedlock . . . is today given importance in the member States of the Council of Europe'.[45] What would explain the use of a different test in cases of 'sex' and of 'birth out of wedlock'?[46] Is there something about the nature of these grounds? Or is it, as Helfer argues and as these statements suggest, a matter of the degree of 'European consensus' that exists with respect to the particular way in which the ground has been used as a basis for discrimination? If the former is the case, both an immutable status argument and a sex discrimination argument might be possible under Article 14.

An immutable status argument could result from an attempt to define (as with 'suspect or quasi-suspect classifications' in the US, and 'enumerated and analogous grounds' in Canada) what 'sex', 'birth out of wedlock', and any other candidates for 'heightened scrutiny' (e.g. sexual orientation) have in common. One relevant criterion could be 'immutability'. If it were adopted, it would then be necessary to determine whether sexual orientation is immutable and what consequences that would have for Convention protection against sexual orientation discrimination.

[43] See Helfer (1990 Eur), 1067–75.

[44] (1985), Ser. A, No. 94 at para. 78 (emphasis added). See generally Buquicchio-de Boer (1985 Eur). In several recent cases, the Court has repeated this 'very weighty reasons' requirement in finding that a distinction based on sex violated Article 14. See *Karlheinz Schmidt* (1994), Ser. A, No. 291–B, at paras. 24–9 (obligation to make financial contribution to fire service imposed only on men); *Burghartz* (1994), Ser. A, No. 280–B, at paras. 27–9 (women permitted to put own surname before family name, where family name is husband's surname; men not permitted to do so where family name is wife's surname); *Schuler-Zgraggen* v. *Switzerland* (1993), Ser. A, No. 263, at paras. 64–7 (Swiss court assumed that 'married women give up their jobs when their first child is born').

[45] (1987), Ser. A, No. 126, para. 41.

[46] See also *Jersild* v. *Denmark* (1994), Ser. A, No. 298, para. 30 ('[t]he Court . . . is particularly conscious of the vital importance of combating racial discrimination in all its forms and manifestations'); *East African Asians* v. *UK* (1973), 78-A D.R. 5 at 62 ('a special importance should be attached to discrimination based on race [which] . . . might, in certain circumstances, constitute a special form of affront to human dignity'); *Hoffmann* (1993), Ser. A, No. 225–C, at para. 36 ('a distinction based essentially on a difference in religion alone is not acceptable').

The concept of 'immutability' does not appear to have figured prominently in decisions of the Court and Commission. In *B*. v. *France*, a transsexual woman, relying on current research suggesting a pre-natal or early post-natal cause for transsexualism, argued that '[t]here might thus be a physical, not merely psychological, explanation of the phenomenon, which would mean that there could be no excuse for refusing to take it into account in law'.[47] In sexual orientation discrimination cases, there have also been references to 'immutability' by the applicant, the Court or the Commission, but it is not clear what influence (if any) the concept has had on decisions of the Court and Commission. It may have affected the findings that the applicant was a 'victim' under Article 25, and had suffered an 'interference' with his Article 8(1) right, in the three criminalization cases where there had been no prosecution.

In *Dudgeon*, the applicant said that he had been 'consciously homosexual from the age of 14', and the Court referred to 'sexual acts to which he is disposed by reason of his homosexual tendencies'.[48] In *Norris*, the applicant described himself as 'irreversibly homosexual',[49] and in *Modinos*, the applicant's 'homosexual tendencies [had] not been contested'.[50] As for 'justification', in the same three cases, the justifications for retaining the law were seen as 'outweighed by the detrimental effects [it] . . . can have on the life of *a person of homosexual orientation* like the applicant'.[51] However, in *X* v. *Germany* (1975), the purpose of a higher age of consent was described as being 'to prevent homosexual acts with adults having an unfortunate influence on the development of heterosexual tendencies in minors'.[52] This concern about the 'mutability' of sexual orientation in minors (as opposed to the adult applicants in the criminalization cases) may have affected the Commission's conclusion that a higher age of consent is justified.

[47] (1992), Ser. A, No. 232–C, at para. 46.
[48] (1981), Ser. A, No. 45 at paras. 32, 41.   [49] (1988), Ser. A, No. 142, at p. 8.
[50] (1990), 67 D.R. 295 at 299. See also *X* v. *Germany* (No. 530/59) (1960), 3 Y.B. 184 at 188 (applicant's 'innate propensity towards [homosexuality]'); *X* v. *Germany* (No. 600/59) (2 Apr. 1960), unpublished (applicant argues that 'homosexuals should not be blamed for their inclinations which are the result of an inherent physical condition'); *X* v. *Germany* (No. 704/60) (1960), 3 Coll. Dec. at 4–5 (applicant is 'constitutionally a homosexual'; argues that 'homosexuality is an inherent factor in the personality of certain individuals for which they cannot be blamed or punished').
[51] See *Dudgeon* (1981), Ser. A, No. 45 at para. 60; *Norris* (1988), Ser. A, No. 142 at para. 46; *Modinos* (1991), Ser. A, No. 259, at p. 27 (report). See also the dissenting opinions in *Dudgeon*, ibid., of Judges Zekia, p. 30 ('[i]f a homosexual claims to be a sufferer because of physiological, psychological or other reasons'), and Walsh, p. 43 ('[a] distinction must be drawn between homosexuals who are such because of some kind of innate instinct or pathological constitution judged to be incurable and those whose tendency comes from a lack of normal sexual development . . . but whose tendency is not incurable'; 'the case for the applicant was argued on the basis of a male person who is by nature homosexually predisposed or orientated'); and Dudgeon's submission to the Commission, concerning Article 8(2), that research 'had shown that sexual orientation was firmly established early in life' ((1980), Ser. B, No. 40 at p. 24); *X* v. *UK* (No. 7215/75) (1978), 19 D.R. 66, at paras. 43, 54 (unpublished part) ('homosexuality is a natural phenomenon' and '[not] a changeable condition').
[52] (1975), 3 D.R. 46 at 54. See also text accompanying notes 17 to 23 above.

Finally, it is worth noting an attempt by the UK government to argue that a prohibition of sexual activity between men does not involve any discrimination, because it applies to all men, regardless of sexual orientation (as direction of attraction). In *Dudgeon*, the UK government asserted before the Commission that 'the difference in treatment between homosexuals and heterosexuals . . . was not a difference capable of raising an issue under Article 14'; '[t]he mere fact that the provisions were framed by reference to particular conduct could not of itself give rise to an issue . . . of discrimination against those with a particular disposition towards [that] conduct'.[53] The government's analysis takes a narrow view of sexual orientation (as limited to direction of attraction) so as to preclude a claim of direct discrimination, but ignores the disproportionate effect of the prohibition on gay and bisexual men and a consequent claim of indirect discrimination.

A sex discrimination argument would be possible under Article 14 because, as will be argued in Chapter 8, almost all sexual orientation discrimination can be viewed as a kind of sex discrimination.[54] If differences in treatment based on sex require 'very weighty reasons' to be justified, but differences based on sexual orientation require something less, it may be worth advancing sex discrimination arguments under Article 14, in conjunction with Articles 8 and 12. Sex discrimination has in fact been expressly argued by applicants to the Commission at least eight times and has always been held to be justified. In four early criminalization cases (in which it was relevant that Germany did not prohibit sexual activity between women), the Commission found that 'Article 14 . . . , insofar as it mentions discrimination on the grounds of sex, does not prevent a High Contracting Party from making a distinction between the sexes in the measures which it takes for the protection of health and morals in accordance with [Art. 8(2)]'.[55] Again in *X* v. *Germany* (1975), the applicant expressly complained of 'discrimination founded on sex' in that the high age of consent did not apply to sexual activity between women.[56] In *Dudgeon*, the applicant alleged discrimination 'on sexual grounds', in that both male–female and female–female sexual activity were legal.[57] And in *X and Y* v. *UK*, the applicants' complaint of 'discrimination . . . on the basis of their sex' was rejected because no comparison with an opposite-sex couple was possible, and the immigration law treated female–female couples in the same way.[58] These 7 cases were all decided before

---

[53] (1980), Ser. B, No. 40, at p. 31, para. 78.

[54] Whether or not a sex discrimination argument is accepted under the Convention, gay, lesbian, and bisexual persons in Council of Europe countries could use it under any sex discrimination provisions of their national constitution or legislation, or (if applicable) under European Community sex equality law. On the argument that European Community sex equality law prohibits sexual orientation discrimination, see Waaldijk and Clapham (1993 Eur), 21, 31–2, 61–2, 216–17, 357; Wintemute (1994 Eur), 528–9.

[55] See *X* v. *Germany* (Nos. 104/55, 167/56, 261/57, 600/59), cited in Ch. 4, note 3.

[56] (1975), 3 D.R. 46 at 55.   [57] (1980), Ser. B, No. 40, at p. 41.

[58] (No. 9369/81) (1983), 5 E.H.R.R. 601 at 602.

Abdulaziz. The eighth case, *Simpson* v. *UK*, was decided later, but *Abdulaziz* and its 'very weighty reasons' requirement were not mentioned, even though the applicant clearly argued that 'she [had] been evicted from her home for no other reason than that she was of the wrong sex'.[59]

It is interesting to compare *Abdulaziz*, and its treatment of sex discrimination in immigration, with the four Commission decisions on discrimination against same-sex couples in immigration.[60] In *Abudulaziz*, the three applicants were women who were not permitted to sponsor the immigration of their legal spouses, whereas men in their position would have been permitted to do so. The Court held that this difference in treatment based on sex violated Article 14.[61] In the same-sex couple cases, three British men (and one woman) were denied permission to sponsor a non-EU male (female) partner for immigration, whereas a British woman (man) would have been permitted to sponsor a non-EU male (female) partner. The UK government might argue that the British woman (man) would have to marry her (his) non-EU male (female) partner, which a man (woman) could not do. The applicant could respond in three ways. First, the immigration rules provide for the discretionary admission of a partner of the opposite sex 'living in an established relationship outside marriage' with a UK national.[62] Second, sex discrimination cannot be said not to exist, or be justified, by referring to a criterion that itself discriminates on the basis of sex.[63]

The third possible response would be to attack the sex discrimination inherent in the criterion of 'being married', in that no Council of Europe member state permits a man to marry a man (as a woman may do), or a woman to marry a woman (as a man may do), as opposed to permitting the registration of same-sex partnerships. An applicant could invoke Article 12 ('the right to marry') in conjunction with Article 14 (sex discrimination). Nothing in the texts of Articles 12 and 14 would seem to preclude such an argument, in that Article 12 refers to 'men' and 'women' but does not say that they must marry each other, assuming that 'national laws governing the exercise of [the] right' cannot include sex discrimination. The Court's interpretation of Article 12 as confined to 'traditional [opposite-sex] marriage'[64] suggests that it would be unlikely to accept such an argument. However, it recently dismissed tradition as a justification for a sex distinction relating to the legal surnames of a married opposite-sex couple, stating that 'the Convention must be interpreted in the light of present-day conditions, especially the importance of the principle of non-discrimination'.[65]

---

[59] (1986), 47 D.R. 274 at 277.
[60] See cases cited in Ch. 4, note 33.   [61] (1985), Ser. A, No. 94, at paras. 74–83.
[62] See *B.* v. *UK* (1990), 64 D.R. 278 at 283. See also Macdonald and Blake (1991 Eur), 256–7; Stonewall Immigration Group briefing paper, *United Kingdom Immigration Law and Rules and Same-Sex Couples* (April 1994).
[63] Cf. *James* v. *Eastleigh Borough Council*, [1990] 2 AC 751 (HL) (under the Sex Discrimination Act 1975).
[64] Ch. 4, Part III.B.
[65] See *Burghartz* v. *Switzerland* (1994), Ser. A. No. 280–B, at para. 28.

II. OBSTACLES TO THE SUCCESS OF THE THREE ARGUMENTS

A. *Did* Dudgeon *Establish a General Non-discrimination Principle?*

One view of *Dudgeon* is that it implicitly recognized, or laid the foundation for the express recognition of, a general principle that all sexual orientation discrimination violates the Convention, in the absence of 'particularly serious reasons' justifying it. Philip Girard, a Canadian commentator, read *Dudgeon* as 'effectively saying that categorizations based on sexual orientation *are* suspect, and will be reviewed using a standard of at least intermediate and possibly strict scrutiny'.[66] If this view is correct, it is only the Commission's failure to perceive the generality of *Dudgeon*, and to take the decision to its logical conclusion, that has prevented the Commission from finding that kinds of sexual orientation discrimination other than criminalization violate the Convention. To give effect to this general principle, the Commission would have to alter its interpretation of the Convention in at least four ways.

First, it would have to recognize that 'private life' does not necessarily have 'spatial' limits,[67] and that sanctions relating to activities that take place in 'public' locations (e.g. expression of affection,[68] employment,[69] association, and even sexual activity where the sanction is imposed in a discriminatory manner[70]) can affect 'private life' by interfering with a person's choice of sexual orientation (as direction of conduct). This broader view of 'private life' is consistent with a number of statements by the Commission and the Court which suggest that 'private life' may protect certain decisions or choices, wherever they are carried out. In *Brüggemann* v. *Germany*, the Commission said:

The right to respect for private life is of such a scope as to secure to the individual *a sphere within which he can freely pursue the development and fulfillment of his personality* . . . he must . . . have the possibility of establishing relationships of various kinds, including sexual [and emotional],[71] with other persons . . . whenever the State sets

---

[66] See Girard (1986 Eur), 19.

[67] See ibid. at 9–12. Cf. *Dudgeon* (1981), Ser. A, No. 45, at para. 60 (sexual life described as 'an essentially private manifestation of the human personality'); (1980), Ser. B, No. 40, at para. 109 (Article 10 freedoms, 'with their public aspect, may call for greater regulation . . . than does the carrying on of activities within the essentially private sphere covered by Article 8').

[68] See e.g. *Masterson* v. *Holden*, [1986] 1 WLR 1017 (QB) (two men, seen kissing and cuddling at a bus stop at 1:55 a.m., convicted of 'insulting behaviour'); *The Guardian* (26 April 1988) 7 (two men fined £40 each for kissing in the street).

[69] The Court may be reluctant to deal with discrimination in public employment. See Warbrick (1989 Eur), 717 and (1990 Eur), 1081.

[70] Cf. *The Independent* (7 Aug. 1992) 2 (man and woman fined £50 each for act of vaginal intercourse in crowded second-class compartment of train) with Tatchell (1992 Eur), 87 (37-year-old man jailed for 18 months for '"fondling and kissing" a 17-year-old youth in a deserted church courtyard in the middle of the night').

[71] See *X* v. *Iceland* (No. 6285/74) (1976), 5 D.R. 86 at 87.

up rules for the behaviour of the individual within this sphere, it interferes with . . . private life and such interference must be justified.[72]

Similarly, in *F.* v. *Switzerland*, the Commission observed that 'the *choice* of affirming and assuming one's sexual identity . . . comes under the protection of Article 8 para. 1'.[73] And in *Niemietz* v. *Germany*, the Court said:

it would be too restrictive to limit the notion [of 'private life'] to an 'inner circle' in which the individual may live his own personal life as he chooses and to exclude therefrom entirely the outside world not encompassed within that circle. Respect for private life must also comprise to a certain degree the right to establish and develop relationships with other human beings. There appears . . . to be no reason of principle why this under-standing . . . should be taken to exclude *activities of a professional or business nature* since it is, after all, in the course of their *working lives* that the majority of people have a significant, if not the greatest, opportunity of developing relationships with the outside world.[74]

These statements suggest that rules for the individual's behaviour in 'public' locations, especially employment, can affect the 'private' sphere (i.e. that in which the individual 'pursue[s] the development . . . of [their] personality'). Thus, the Commission's decisions in *F.* v. *Switzerland* that prostitution 'do[es] not belong to the sphere of private life', and in *Dudgeon* that 'offences, which by their very nature appear to concern public activity, [cannot] be said to have affected [the applicant's] private life', would need to be reconsidered.[75]

Second, the Commission would have to take a broader view of 'interference' with private life, and of 'discrimination'. This would mean recognizing that many non-criminal sanctions against same-sex couples or gay, lesbian, and bi-sexual individuals (such as the loss of immigration, housing, and parental rights or employment opportunities) either actively 'interfere' with their private lives (because of the coercive effect on their choice of sexual orientation) or constitute 'discrimination' under Article 14 (in conjunction with Article 8) when compared with the treatment of opposite-sex couples and heterosexual individuals. Third, the Commission would have to subject member state justifications for 'interference' or 'discrimination' under Articles 8(2) or 14 to a more critical review, requiring either the 'particularly serious reasons' of *Dudgeon* for interference with 'sexual life' other than total criminalization or the 'very weighty reasons' of *Abdulaziz* for sex discrimination. And fourth, it would have to eliminate the discrimination (based on sexual orientation or sex) which is inherent in its narrow interpretation of 'family life'[76] and 'marriage' as 'for heterosexual persons only', and which is not required by the text of the Convention.

---

[72] (No. 6959/75) (1977), 10 D.R. 100 at 115 (emphasis added).
[73] (No. 11680/85) (1988), 55 D.R. 178 at 180 (emphasis added).
[74] (1992), Ser. A, No. 251–B, para. 29.
[75] See Ch. 4, notes 49–50 and accompanying text.
[76] See van Dijk (1993 Eur), 190, 198 ('a homosexual relationship between two persons who actually live together would seem to fit very well into the broad, autonomous concept [of 'family life'] developed by the Commission and the Court').

B. Is 'European Consensus' Necessary?

Another view, based on the reality of the Commission's case law (i.e. its four-teen decisions on issues of sexual orientation discrimination other than criminalization since the Court's judgment in *Dudgeon* in 1981),[77] is that *Dudgeon* did not establish a general principle that sexual orientation discrimination violates the Convention, in the absence of 'particularly serious reasons' justifying it.[78] The Court decided the narrow issue before it, whether a total prohibition of sexual activity between men could be justified under Article 8(2), but did not expressly identify any general concept such as 'sexual orientation discrimination', or suggest that other instances of such discrimination could not be justified. Its reference to 'particularly serious reasons'[79] established no requirement of 'strict scrutiny' for the future, which would have placed a heavy onus on member states to justify interferences. Either it applies only to the facts of *Dudgeon* and not to other interferences with 'sexual life' (e.g. a high age of consent) or it is more easily satisfied in such cases.

Indeed, the Court may have indicated its intent that *Dudgeon* have a limited scope by stressing that 'some degree of regulation of male homosexual conduct, as indeed of other forms of sexual conduct, by means of the criminal law can be justified', 'to protect particular sections of society as well as the moral ethos of society as a whole', and by citing the minimally tolerant 1957 report of the Wolfenden Committee.[80] It also observed that '"[d]ecriminalisation" does not imply approval', even though 'some . . . might draw misguided conclusions in this respect from reform'.[81] If this was the Court's intent, it would render ground-less the dissenting judges' fears that 'the applicant . . . [was] seeking . . . a "charter" declaring homosexuality to be an alternative equivalent to heterosexuality, with all the consequences that that would entail (for example, as regards sex education)', and that the Court's judgment would be 'hailed . . . by those who seek to blur the essential difference between homosexual and heterosexual

---

[77] See cases cited in Ch. 4, notes 27–29, 31–34.

[78] See Glendon (1991 Eur), 156: 'The Court avoided suggesting either that the practices in question amounted to fundamental human rights, or that all legal distinctions between homosexuals and heterosexuals were now invalid. . . . [*Dudgeon*] does not seem to prefigure uniform 'Euronorms' regarding homosexuals in employment, housing, adoption, family benefits, and so on.'

[79] (1981), Ser. A, No. 45, at para. 52.

[80] Ibid. at para. 49. See also Home Office (UK) (1957 Eur).

[81] *Dudgeon*, ibid. at para. 61. The references to the Wolfenden Committee's report in *Dudgeon*, and in an age of consent case, *X* v. *UK* (1978), 19 D.R. 66 at 77–8, suggest that the Court and Commission's interpretation of the Convention may rest on a Wolfenden-like notion that same-sex sexual activity is 'immoral', but not the law's business in certain circumstances. Daniel Kane (1988 Eur), 467, 473, and 479, argues that the 'right of privacy' (i.e. Article 8) merely 'limits the degree of state interference with homosexual persons' privacy', but 'does not . . . provide the legal frame-work on which to eliminate that interference', because it 'serves to perpetuate the notion that homosexuality is inherently immoral'. He proposes the recognition of 'sexual self-determination as a fundamental freedom' under Article 14 ('other status'), in conjunction with Article 3.

activities' as 'a declaration . . . that . . . particular homosexual practices . . . virtually amount to fundamental human rights'.[82]

If no general non-discrimination principle has been established under the Convention, how can the Court's apparently 'progressive' decisions in *Dudgeon*, *Norris*, and *Modinos* be reconciled with the Commission's decisions on issues other than criminalization? The explanation may simply be that the approach taken by the Court and Commission to the interpretation of the Convention is fundamentally different from that of the US and Canadian Supreme Courts to the US Constitution and the Canadian Charter. The Court and Commission do not (in spite of statements apparently to the contrary) attempt to identify freedoms or grounds of discrimination that are considered particularly 'sensitive', and therefore require special justifications whenever they are interfered with or used. Instead, as Laurence Helfer has persuasively argued, the Court and Commission appear to look not to the 'sensitivity' of the freedom or ground involved, but to the degree of 'consensus' amongst the member states of the Council of Europe on the justifiability of interfering with the freedom, or using the ground of discrimination, in the particular manner in issue in the case before them.[83] Thus, they are more likely to narrow a government's 'margin of appreciation' and find no justification for an 'interference' or 'discrimination', if few member states have a law or policy similar to the one being challenged. If the majority or a substantial minority of member states have such a law or policy, they are more likely to defer to the respondent government.

C. 'European Consensus' Regarding Sexual Orientation Discrimination

The need for 'European consensus' as a prerequisite for Convention protection may well explain both the change in the Commission's opinion regarding total prohibitions of sexual activity between men, and its decisions on issues other than criminalization, such as the age of consent (to which it does not seem to have applied either the 'particularly serious reasons' requirement of *Dudgeon* or the 'very weighty reasons' requirement of *Abdulaziz*). In December 1966 (just before the Commission's last published upholding of Germany's total prohibition), six of the fourteen member states that had ratified the Convention (forty-three per cent) had such prohibitions, whereas by March 1980 (when violation was found in *Dudgeon*), only three (Cyprus, Ireland, and parts of the UK) out

---

[82] (1981), Ser. A, No. 45 at p. 35 (Judge Matscher), p. 46 (Judge Walsh).

[83] See Helfer (1990 Eur), 1056–9, 1067–75; Helfer (1993 Eur) (proposing a more rigorous approach to 'European consensus' analysis). See also Warbrick (1989 Eur), 707, 715–16 ('strong majority practice [regarded] as important evidence for resolving problems of interpretation'); Yourow (1987 Eur), 158 ('the law of the Convention sometimes seems neither more nor less than consensus, or lack thereof, in the law and practice of the . . . States Parties'); O'Donnell (1982 Eur), 483–4 ('an examination of the laws and practices of the member states in search for consensus or its lack is one of the surest methods for determining the latitude the Court will grant the government when the margin of appreciation is considered').

of twenty (fifteen per cent) still had them, following reforms in England and Wales, Germany, Austria, and Norway.[84] Thus, in *Dudgeon*, the Commission and Court were siding with a Council of Europe majority of eighty-five per cent.

Apart from the single issue of criminalization, however, there may not yet be sufficient 'European consensus' that other kinds of sexual orientation discrimination cannot be justified. Evidence of 'consensus' can be found in experts' studies, and especially in recommendations and resolutions of European institutions.[85] On 1 October 1981, the Parliamentary Assembly of the Council of Europe adopted Recommendation 924, which urged member states to apply the 'same minimum age of consent' for same-sex and opposite-sex sexual activity, and ensure that gay, lesbian, and bisexual persons receive equal treatment in employment and child custody decisions. In 1984, the European Parliament adopted a 'Resolution on sexual discrimination at the workplace', urging EC member states to equalize the age of consent, and calling on the EC Commission to 'submit proposals to ensure that no cases arise in the Member States of discrimination against homosexuals with regard to access to employment and working conditions'.[86] In 1989, it recommended that the 'Community Charter of Fundamental Social Rights' be amended to provide for 'the right of all workers to equal protection regardless of their . . . sexual preference'.[87] And in 1994, it adopted an even broader 'Resolution on equal rights for homosexuals and lesbians in the EC'. This resolution calls on member states to end 'unequal treatment of persons with a homosexual orientation under legal and administrative provisions', and 'to take measures . . . to combat all forms of social discrimination against homosexuals'.[88] It also calls on the EC Commission to present 'a draft Recommendation on equal rights for lesbians and homosexuals' which should, *inter alia*, seek to end 'the barring of lesbians and homosexual couples from marriage or from an equivalent legal framework', and 'any restrictions on the rights of lesbians and homosexuals to be parents or to adopt or foster children'.[89]

But the 'consensus' in these institutions has not yet been sufficiently reflected in changes in the laws of Council of Europe member states.[90] The most promising candidate is the issue of a discriminatory age of consent to sexual activity.[91] In May 1992, when the Commission rendered its most recent age of consent decision (*Zukrigl*),[92] a 'consensus level' of sixty-two per cent (sixteen out of

---

[84] See Council of Europe (1994 Eur) at 114–15; Tatchell (1992 Eur), 139.

[85] See Helfer (1990 Eur), 1086–94; Helfer (1991 Eur), 183–6.

[86] (13 Mar. 1984), 27 O.J., No. C104, pp. 46–8.

[87] (22 Nov. 1989), 32 O.J., No. C323, p. 46.

[88] (8 Feb. 1994), 37 O.J., No. C61, pp. 40–43, paras. 7, 10.   [89] Ibid. at para. 14.

[90] Cf. *Inze* (1987), Ser. A, No. 126, at para. 41 ('consensus' where European Convention on the Legal Status of Children Born out of Wedlock was in force in only 9 out of 21 member states).

[91] See Helfer (1990 Eur), 1075–1100; Waaldijk (1993 Eur), 84–8.

[92] *Zukrigl* v. *Austria* (No. 17279/90) (13 May 1992), unpublished. Equal ages existed in Belgium, Czechoslovakia, Denmark, France, Greece, Italy, Malta, Netherlands, Norway, Poland, Portugal, San Marino, Spain, Sweden, Switzerland, and Turkey. Unequal ages existed in Austria, Cyprus, Finland, Germany, Hungary, Iceland, Ireland, Liechtenstein, Luxembourg, and the UK.

twenty-six member states with an equal age of consent for male–female, male–male, and female–female sexual activity) does not seem to have been sufficient (although the Commission did not expressly make such a calculation). But recent reforms in Germany, Iceland, and Luxembourg, and the admission of three countries with equal ages of consent (Andorra, Slovenia, and the Czech Republic and Slovakia in lieu of Czechoslovakia) have raised the 'consensus level'. Of the thirty-four member states as of 10 February 1995, at least twenty-two (sixty-five per cent) appear to have set an equal (or substantially equal) age.[93] This level (which could be higher, depending on the ages in Estonia, Latvia, and Lithuania) may be enough to tip the scales in favour of a finding that unequal ages are not justified under Article 8(2) or 14. The Commission will soon have a chance to determine whether the 'consensus level' is sufficiently high in a case brought by Euan Sutherland (aged seventeen at the time he made his application) with the support of the Stonewall Group, which challenges the unequal age of consent in the United Kingdom.[94] A survey of the criminal law of the member states might reveal that other examples of sexual orientation discrimination in criminal law (e.g. the 'no more than two persons' restriction in *Johnson*)[95] deviate from a 'European consensus' as to that kind of discrimination.

Outside the area of criminal law, however, there is as yet no 'European

[93] See Appendix IV. The age of consent in Ireland is only equal with regard to consent to being penetrated by a penis (vaginally or anally). It appears to be 17 for female consent to being penetrated vaginally or anally by a man, for male consent to being penetrated anally by a man, for male consent to penetrating a woman or man anally, and for non-penetrative male–male sexual activity, but 15 for male consent to penetrating a woman vaginally, for male or female consent to non-penetrative male–female sexual activity, and for female consent to all female–female sexual activity. See Kingston (1994 Eur), 186–8. In Greece, the equal age of consent of 15 does not appear to apply to anal intercourse resulting from 'seduction' of a person aged 15 or 16. See Tatchell (1992 Eur), 115.

[94] See *Sutherland* v. *UK* (No. 25186/94) (9–20 Jan. 1995 session) (brought to the notice of the UK government for observations on the merits, but not yet declared admissible or inadmissible). The Commission struck from its list, under Article 30(1)(b), another application made by three gay men over 18 (with Stonewall's support), because the age of consent was lowered to 18 in 1994. See *Wilde, Greenhalgh, and Parry* v. *UK* (No. 22382/93) (19 Jan. 1995), unpublished. See notes 17–23 above and accompanying text.

[95] See Ch. 4, notes 66–73 and accompanying text. The Commission has declared admissible under Article 8 a case against the UK which will raise the question of 'European consensus' on the criminalization of consensual, adult, private, sado-masochistic sexual activity (or on the availability of consent as a defence to criminal liability for causing actual bodily harm). *Laskey, Jaggard & Brown* v. *UK* (Nos. 21627/93, 21826/93, 21974/93) (18 Jan. 1995), unpublished, involves three men who were imprisoned for such activity and whose appeals were rejected by the House of Lords in *R* v. *Brown* (1993), [1994] 1 AC 212. The Commission declared inadmissible (under Article 25, for lack of prosecution) a second case (*V.,W.,X.,Y., and Z.* v. *UK* (No. 22170/93) (18 Jan. 1995), unpublished) brought by Liberty, which involved five persons (an opposite-sex couple with children, a heterosexual man, a gay man, and a lesbian woman) who engage in sado-masochistic sexual activity and fear prosecution. The diversity of the applicants in the second case illustrates the fact that criminalization of sado-masochistic sexual activity is an issue of sexual freedom or sexuality and not, prima facie, an issue of sexual orientation discrimination, if all such activity is treated equally. However, the unprecedented prosecutions and harsh prison sentences in *Brown* may have been influenced by the fact that the activity was between men (see the references to 'homosexual sado-masochism', [1994] 1 A.C. at 245–6, 255).

consensus' on eliminating most other kinds of sexual orientation discrimination. Norway, Denmark, Sweden, the Netherlands, France, and Ireland prohibit such discrimination in employment or the provision of goods and services,[96] and each of these countries (except France) prohibits incitement to hatred based on sexual orientation.[97] Denmark, Norway, and Sweden have created a separate (and not quite equal) institution of 'registered partnership', permitting same-sex couples to acquire most of the rights of married opposite-sex couples, while Sweden grants them the same rights as unmarried opposite-sex couples (as does the Netherlands in some areas).[98] In the three Scandinavian countries and the Netherlands, same-sex partners of citizens may immigrate.[99] However, the majority of member states have yet to follow their example, and no member state (including Denmark, Norway, and Sweden) has yet decided expressly to permit same-sex couples to adopt children jointly.[100] It therefore seems unlikely that the Convention will have a significant effect on most of these kinds of discrimination until legislative reforms in these areas take place in a greater number of member states,[101] or the Court and Commission adopt a stricter, less deferential approach to interpreting the Convention than looking for 'European consensus'. Otherwise, they will continue to order changes in a member state's law only where it can be seen as one of a small group of 'recalcitrant laggards' within the Council of Europe.[102]

[96] See Appendix II. See also Waaldijk (1993 Eur), 79–81; Waaldijk (1991 Eur), 45–59; Tatchell (1992 Eur), 132–3. In the area of military employment, at least 10 member states do not ban gay, lesbian, and bisexual persons from any position. See Tatchell (1992 Eur), 81–2; Waaldijk (1993 Eur), 112–113.

[97] See Norway, Penal Code, para. 135a, Law of 8 May 1981, nr. 14 ('homosexual inclination, lifestyle or orientation'); Denmark, Penal Code, para. 266b, Law of 3 June 1987, nr. 357; Sweden, Criminal Code, c. 5, para. 5, Law of 4 June 1987, SFS 1987:610 ('homosexual inclination'); Netherlands, Penal Code, arts. 137c–d–e (Law of 14 Nov. 1991, Staatsblad 1991, nr. 623) ('hetero- or homosexual orientation'); Ireland, Prohibition of Incitement to Hatred Act, 1989, No. 19, s. 1(1) ('hatred'), Video Recordings Act, 1989, No. 22, ss. 3(1)(a)(ii), 7(1)(a)(ii). See also Waaldijk (1993 Eur), 123–4; Waaldijk (1991 Eur), 81–2.

[98] See the Laws on Registered Partnership of Denmark, *Lov om registreret partnerskab*, Law of 7 June 1989, nr. 372; Norway, *Lov om registrert partnerskap*, Law of 30 Apr. 1993, nr. 40; Sweden, *Lag om registrerat partnerskap*, Law of 23 June 1994, SFS 1994:1117. See also Sweden, SFS 1987:232, 813 (unmarried couples); Ch. 4, note 134 (Hungary). See generally Waaldijk (1993 Eur), 91–100; Martin (1994 Eur); Norrie (1994 Eur) at 769–74; Hansen and Jorgenson (1993 Eur); Henson (1993 Eur); Nielsen (1992–93 Eur); Pedersen (1992 Eur); Nielsen (1990 Eur); Bradley (1989 Eur), 327 nn. 29–30; Saldeen (1988–89 Eur), 296–7.

[99] See Waaldijk (1993 Eur), 100–101; Waaldijk (1991 Eur), 35–8; Hendriks and Ruygrok (1993 Eur).

[100] See Waaldijk (1993 Eur), 102–4. In some member states, including the UK, Article 6(1) of the Council of Europe's European Convention on the Adoption of Children (E.T.S. No. 58) presents a problem: 'The law shall not permit a child to be adopted except by either two persons married to each other . . . or by one person.' See Saldeen (1990–91 Eur), 438. Cf. Ch. 6, note 134 (Québec).

[101] Cf. Glendon (1991 Eur), 156–7 ('[a]t present, there is a great deal of variation among the European legal systems with respect to [employment, housing, adoption, family benefits], and the Court's approach in *Dudgeon* suggests that the margin of appreciation to be left to the member states in these areas will be considerable').

[102] Cf. Warbrick (1989 Eur), 716.

Although the presence or absence of 'European consensus' seems to explain the decisions of the Court and Commission, it must be acknowledged that this kind of analysis is not often mentioned expressly in their decisions, and almost never takes the form of an open 'census' of the exact numbers of member states with or without a particular law or policy.[103] In *Dudgeon*, the Court only stated that 'all the member States of the Council of Europe' had legislation on 'male homosexual conduct', but that in the 'great majority of the member States', a total prohibition of sexual activity between men is no longer considered 'necessary or appropriate'.[104] In his dissent, Judge Walsh objected to 'the erroneous inference that a Euro-norm in the law concerning homosexual practices has been or can be evolved'.[105] Nor is 'consensus' analysis consistently used in the age of consent cases. In *X* v. *Germany* (1975), the Commission did refer to the variety of opinions regarding the age of consent within the Council of Europe member states.[106] In *X* v. *UK*, it considered that an age of 21 was high, 'when contrasted with the current position in other member States', but could still be 'necessary in a democratic society', even though 'the majority of European States' have an age of 18 or less.[107] In both these cases and in *Dudgeon*, the Commission and the Court have focused on the 'consensus' as to the need for an age of consent, and on the variety of ages selected, rather than on the growing 'consensus' that the age selected (whether it is 14 or 45) should be equal.[108] This latter 'consensus' appears to have been put to the Commission in the most recent case, *Zukrigl* v. *Austria* (1992). Yet it refused to shift from its 1978 conclusion in *X* v. *UK*, or even discuss the presence or absence of 'consensus', even though

---

[103] See Helfer (1993 Eur), 140 ('the Court and Commission have not specified what percentage of the Contracting States must alter their laws before a right-enhancing norm will achieve consensus status'; instead, they 'speak in vague generalities'); van Dijk and van Hoof (1990 Eur), 602–4 (urging the Court to elaborate common standards by 'reviewing the relevant laws of the Contracting States . . . and setting out that review for all to see'); Yourow (1987 Eur), 158 ('a student of the Court is not informed as to how the Court measures the existence or non-existence of any one particular consensus'). A recent example of consensus analysis is *Casado Coca* v. *Spain* (1994), Ser. A, No. 285–A, paras. 54–7. The Court deferred to national authorities and upheld a ban on advertising by lawyers under Article 10(2), because '[t]he wide range of regulations and the different rates of change in the Council of Europe's member States indicate the complexity of the issue'.

[104] (1981), Ser. A, No. 45 at paras. 49, 60. Cf. O'Donnell (1982 Eur), 492 ('the key appears to have been the European consensus as to male homosexuality').

[105] *Dudgeon*, ibid. at p. 45. The Irish government's reliance on this statement in *Norris* led the Commission to suggest that 'there may indeed be no common, moral, European standard on the criminalization of homosexuality', whereas *Dudgeon* seems at least to have established a common legal standard under the Convention. See *Norris* v. *Ireland* (1987), Ser. A, No. 142 at pp. 30, 33 (report).

[106] (1975), 3 D.R. 46 at 54–5.

[107] (No. 7215/75) (1978), 19 D.R. 66, at pp. 76–7. See also paras. 57, 95–109, 117 (unpublished part), containing consensus arguments by applicant, and especially by the UK (at paras. 104, 106): 'the applicant's argument assumes a consensus of European opinion as to the age beyond which . . . homosexual activity is made criminal', but 'there is no uniform European consensus as to the appropriate age of consent'.

[108] See *X* v. *Germany* (1975), 3 D.R. 46 at 55; *X* v. *UK*, ibid.; *Dudgeon*, (1981), Ser. A, No. 45 at para. 49. See also Helfer (1990 Eur), 1076–86.

'it appear[ed] from the extensive documents submitted by the applicant that attitudes in general may have evolved since 1978'.[109]

Assuming that the presence or absence of 'European consensus' is the most important factor explaining the decisions of the Court and Commission,[110] in spite of its somewhat 'hidden' operation, it is now clear why those decisions have not gone farther in the area of sexual orientation discrimination. Even though logic would permit the extension of *Dudgeon* to other kinds of sexual orientation discrimination, and the text of the Convention presents no insurmountable barriers, the Court and Commission do not appear to be willing to make that extension where it would require them effectively to order a majority, or a substantial minority (greater than fifteen per cent, or perhaps twenty-five per cent?), of member states to change their laws. Rather, they seem to do so only where they have a substantial majority ('the great majority') of member states behind them, thus interpreting 'necessary in a democratic society' as 'necessary in [more than a small minority of Council of Europe] democratic societ[ies]'.[111]

D. Is 'European Consensus' Analysis Desirable?

For a lawyer interested in the protection of human rights, the disappointing aspect of 'European consensus' analysis is that it seems to amount to protection only of those human rights that have been endorsed by 'a substantial majority of majorities'. Where the Court and Commission recognize that a human right is protected by the Convention, and that a particular law violates that right, they do protect a minority in a member state (the group of persons primarily affected by the violation) against the majority in that state. However, they do so only where 'a substantial majority of majorities' in the other member states have effectively recognized that right by not maintaining the kind of law that would violate it. Thus, there is no protection for a 'European minority' against a 'European majority' that rejects recognition of a right,[112] but only for minorities in member states in which the local majority dissents from a 'European consensus' in favour of recognizing a right. The Convention could not help gay and bisexual

[109] See *Zukrigl*, Ch. 4, note 27. In *Bruce* v. *UK* (No. 9237/81) (1983), 34 D.R. 68 at p. 6 (unpublished part), the applicant cited the absence of discrimination against same-sex sexual activity by members of the armed forces in 6 European countries, but the Commission did not comment on it.

[110] Cf. *Johnston* v. *Ireland* (1986), Ser. A, No. 112, at para. 53 ('the Court cannot, by means of an evolutive interpretation, derive ... a right [to divorce] that was not included ... at the outset ... particularly ... where the omission was deliberate'); *Brüggemann* v. *Germany* (1977), 10 D.R. 100, at 117–18 ('no evidence that it was the intention of the Parties to the Convention to bind themselves in favour of any particular solution [to the problem of abortion]'). See also Dillon (1989 Eur).

[111] Cf. O'Donnell (1982 Eur), 493 (suggesting that 'the government can prevail only if it can show that its practice is one prevailing in the great majority of the member states').

[112] Cf. *Cossey* v. *UK* (1990), Ser. A, No. 184 at para. 5.6.3 (Judge Martens, dissenting) ('the Court's policy seems to be to adapt its interpretation to the relevant societal change only if almost all member States have adopted the new ideas ... this caution is in principle not consistent with the Court's mission to protect the individual against the collectivity and to do so by elaborating common standards').

men in (West) Germany in their pre-1969 (and pre-'European consensus') campaign for decriminalization, but has been able to help them in Northern Ireland, Ireland, and Cyprus.

Deciding human rights questions on the basis of 'consensus' rather than 'principle' seems unsatisfactory, and might not be workable where, in a federal system, only one level of government has the power to pass the law in question and the laws of other governments are not available for comparison (e.g. the federal governments in the US and in Canada, or conceivably the European Community, in its areas of exclusive competence). The use of 'consensus' also sheds new light on the assertion that the European Court in *Dudgeon*, *Norris*, and *Modinos* has been more 'progressive' (in the sense of expanding human rights protection) than the US Supreme Court in *Hardwick*. If the US Supreme Court had applied the European Court's reasoning to the situation in the US in 1986, when 24 or 25 of the 50 states and the District of Columbia prohibited same-sex oral or anal intercourse, the US Supreme Court would have had to conclude that there was no 'US consensus' on the issue of criminalization.[113] Yet, if one looks at the issue of abortion and the US Supreme Court's (besieged) decision in *Roe* v. *Wade*, one sees the US Court taking a principled decision to strike down laws prohibiting most abortions in 46 states and the District of Columbia, despite those laws' appearing to constitute an overwhelming 'US consensus' against abortion.[114] The Commission's decision in *Brüggemann* v. *Germany*, in which it found that a woman's being prohibited from choosing an abortion did not 'interfere' with her 'private life', and therefore did not have to be justified under Article 8(2), looks much less 'progressive'.[115] It is not clear whether the Court would agree. It decided its first abortion case (*Open Door and Dublin Well Woman* v. *Ireland*, dealing with access to information about abortion) under Article 10, and declined to consider Articles 2, 8, and 14.[116]

However unsatisfactory 'European consensus' analysis may be, it is probably a defensible result of the Court's role, which is that of an international court interpreting a voluntary, international treaty, and not that of the supra-national constitutional court many would like it to be.[117] Expecting the Court to act as a constitutional court and take decisions as controversial as that in *Roe* v. *Wade*

[113] See Glendon (1991 Eur), 153 ('far from clear that the type of analysis employed in *Dudgeon* would ... have yielded the same result in *Hardwick*'). Cf. Warbrick (1989 Eur), 698–9, 723–4 (comparing 'European consensus' against corporal punishment with absence of 'US consensus' on the issue, and resulting difference in decisions of European Court and US Supreme Court).

[114] See *Roe* v. *Wade*, 410 US 113 at 140 n. 37 (1973) (by 1970, only 4 states had clearly decriminalized abortions in early pregnancy). See also *Texas* v. *Johnson*, 491 US 397 at 428 n. 1 (1989) (invalidating laws against flag burning in 48 states).

[115] (1977), 10 D.R. 100 at 117. The Commission's statement that '[i]n many European countries the problem of abortion is or has been the subject of heated debates on legal reform' suggests that it found insufficient 'consensus'. See the criticism of the Commission's reluctance to require a justification for a prohibition of abortion under Article 8(2) in Connelly (1986 Eur), 586–7, 591–2; Doswald-Beck (1983 Eur), 290–1; Duffy (1982 Eur), 224–5. See also Rendel (1991 Eur).

[116] (1992), Ser. A, No. 246, para. 83.   [117] See Ch. 1, note 6.

(or as a decision holding that Article 12 requires all member states to permit same-sex marriage would be), may be expecting too much. Politically, the Court is not in a position to do so, given the ultimately voluntary nature of the Convention system (i.e. the member states' power to withdraw their consent to the right of individual petition to the Commission under Article 25 and to the compulsory jurisdiction of the Court under Article 46, and their power to denounce the Convention under Article 65).[118] And Colin Warbrick has argued that the structure of the Court is not suited to producing the kind of coherence expected of the decisions of a constitutional court.[119] Thus, the only feasible role for the Court (and the Commission) may be that of identifying and enforcing 'minimum European standards' regarding human rights,[120] and declining to intervene where their existence is not yet sufficiently clear. Gay, lesbian, and bisexual applicants disappointed by the relative absence of such standards in the area of sexual orientation discrimination must look to their national legislatures and courts.[121]

E. Is Amending the Convention an Alternative?

What of countries (e.g. the UK) where national legislatures and courts are reluctant to provide any protection against sexual orientation discrimination? For applicants from such countries, recourse to Strasbourg remains attractive. Yet they may feel that waiting for the development of 'European consensus' on a particular issue could take too long. As a result, in 1990, the International Lesbian and Gay Association drafted a Protocol which would amend the Convention so as to prohibit sexual orientation discrimination, and which is currently being considered by the Parliamentary Assembly of the Council of Europe.[122]

In 1981, the Parliamentary Assembly's Committee on Social and Health Questions prepared a 'Report on discrimination against homosexuals' which

---

[118] If and when Protocol No. 11 comes into force, the current Article 25 and 46 powers will disappear (under a new Article 34), while the current Article 65 power to denounce will remain (renumbered as Article 58). See Council of Europe (1994 Eur), 86–101.

[119] See Warbrick (1990 Eur), 1079–83, 1096.

[120] See Convention preamble, fifth paragraph ('Fundamental Freedoms . . . are best maintained . . . by a common understanding and observance of the Human Rights upon which they depend'). See also Girard (1986 Eur), 6–7 ('[o]ne might expect that the European Court . . . would accord a rather more liberal "margin of appreciation" to States in [reviewing justifications] . . . than the [Canadian] Supreme Court', because it is a supra-national body and the differences among member states are greater than among Canadian provinces).

[121] This is not unlike the post-*Hardwick* situation in the US, where gay, lesbian, and bisexual plaintiffs have turned their attention from the US Supreme Court to state legislatures and courts.

[122] For a thorough discussion of the draft Protocol, the issues it raises and alternatives to it, see Helfer (1991 Eur). See also 'Motion for a Recommendation on the elimination of discrimination based on sexual orientation', Parl. Ass. Doc. 6348 (7 Dec. 1990); and see Danish National Organization for Gays and Lesbians (1990 Eur).

recommended that the Council of Europe's Committee of Ministers 'modify Article 14 ... by adding to it the notion of "sexual preference"'.[123] The Legal Affairs Committee's 'Opinion on the discrimination against homosexuals' objected to the proposed amendment because (1) 'sex' in Article 14 'may well be interpreted in such a way as to cover notions like "sexual orientation" or "sexual preference" ', and (2) the list of grounds in Article 14 is non-exhaustive. '[I]t [would] therefore be better to wait for any case law of the Commission and Court ... to develop. If this case law is unfavourable, one may subsequently propose modification.'[124] On 1 October 1981, an amendment deleting the proposed 'sexual preference' amendment from Recommendation 924 was adopted by the Parliamentary Assembly. Speakers argued that the amendment was unnecessary (for the reasons given by the Legal Affairs Committee), that it was necessary to make the prohibition of such discrimination 'absolutely clear', that '[i]f we sought to make Article 14 exhaustive, it would go on for pages and pages', and that other 'sexual deviations' ('transvestites ... paedophiliacs ... transsexualists ... bigamists') would be included.[125]

It is now clear that the Legal Affairs Committee was wrong and that the development of the case law since 1981 has been 'unfavourable', apart from the criminalization cases. The proposed Protocol seeks to 'overturn' this case law by providing expressly, in Article 2, that '[e]veryone has the right to establish and develop relationships with other human beings, without discrimination on the ground of sexual orientation', and in Article 3, that '[n]o one shall be subjected to discrimination on the ground of sexual orientation in the content or application of the law'. Among the questions the proposed Protocol raises is: why should the Convention expressly provide an independent right to freedom from discrimination based on sexual orientation, but not discrimination based on other grounds, such as race or sex?[126] In spite of Recommendations of the Parliamentary Assembly,[127] the Committee of Ministers has been unwilling to propose an amendment to Article 14 that would delete the requirement that a Convention right or freedom be affected, and make Article 14 more like US equal protection doctrine, Section 15(1) of the Canadian Charter, and Article 26 of the International Covenant.[128] Asbjørn Eide and Torkel Opsahl have suggested that 'fear about the unpredictable scope of such a provision has ... held back the Council

[123] Parl. Ass. Doc. 4755 (8 July 1981), 2. The Committee referred, at p. 19, to the inclusion of 'sexual orientation' in s. 10 of Québec's Charte des droits et libertés de la personne. See Appendix II.
[124] Parl. Ass. Doc. 4777 (22 Sept. 1981), 4–5.
[125] See Parl. Ass., Official Report of Debates, 33rd Session, Vol. 2, Tenth Sitting, 1 Oct. 1981, 257–81 at 260, 262, 270, 274.
[126] See Recommendation 1229 (24 Jan. 1994), para. 8 ('establish the principle of equality of rights between women and men as a fundamental human right in an additional protocol').
[127] See Recommendation 1089 (7 Oct. 1988), para. 21 ('extension of Article 14 ... to prohibit all forms of discrimination'); Recommendation 1134 (1 Oct. 1990) ('introduction of a general non-discrimination clause').
[128] See 'Reply to Recommendation 1089' in Council of Europe, Human Rights Information Sheet No. 27 (May–Nov. 1990), 174–5.

of Europe from adopting [it]'.[129] Indeed, in 1990 the Council's Steering Committee for Human Rights rejected such a provision because 'discriminations could be alleged in many fields . . . such as in social benefits . . . tax law, property law, competition and [media] regulations . . . [which] would provoke such a number of applications that the efficiency of the organs of the Convention would be endangered'.[130]

Another question raised by the proposed Protocol is whether it avoids the problem of insufficient 'European consensus'. It would not apply in any member state that declined to ratify it, and it is possible that the majority of member states would decline to do so. Those most likely to ratify it (Norway, Sweden, Denmark, the Netherlands, France, and Ireland) would be those that had already done the most to prohibit sexual orientation discrimination. In addition, the existence of a separate Protocol on sexual orientation discrimination could affect the Court and Commission's interpretation of the Convention for those member states in which it did not apply.[131]

III. ASSESSMENT OF PROTECTION UNDER THE EUROPEAN CONVENTION

An assessment of the level of protection that the Convention provides against sexual orientation discrimination depends on whether one views 'the glass' as ten per cent full or ninety per cent empty. A fundamental choice ('right to respect for private life') argument under Article 8 has certainly achieved significant success in *Dudgeon*, *Norris*, and *Modinos*, compared both with the Commission's 1955 decision that 'the Convention allows a High Contracting Party to punish homosexuality',[132] and with the US Supreme Court's decision in *Hardwick*. In fact, *Dudgeon* could lead to the elimination of laws prohibiting same-sex sexual activity in the entire continent of Europe (still a distant goal in the US). However, such an approach has yet to succeed in relation to any other issue, and all Article 14 discrimination arguments (which tend to be based on sex, if any ground, and have not used an immutable status argument) have been rejected. Thus, in the absence of a considerable increase in 'European consensus' regarding these issues, or an amendment to the Convention ratified by a substantial number of member states, it appears that the Convention will play a

[129] See Eide and Opsahl (1994 Eur), 128.
[130] 'Reply to Recommendation 1089' op. cit. at 175.
[131] See Helfer (1991 Eur), 191–202. See also Clapham and Weiler (1993 Eur), 62–3; van Dijk (1993 Eur), 203–4. In *Frontiero* v. *Richardson*, 411 US 677 at 691–2 (1973), Justice Powell declined to provide the fifth vote that would have made 'sex' a suspect classification under US equal protection doctrine, partly because the ongoing political campaign to obtain ratification of the Equal Rights Amendment made it inappropriate for the Court to 'pre-empt by judicial action a major political decision'.
[132] *X* v. *Germany* (No. 104/55) (1955), 1 Y.B. 228.

limited role in eliminating other kinds of sexual orientation discrimination in Europe.[133] Gay, lesbian, and bisexual persons will have to look to their national legislatures and courts, or possibly to the European Community.

As interpreted by the Court and Commission (to the end of 1994), the Convention provides essentially the level of protection against sexual orientation discrimination that was recommended by the Wolfenden Committee in 1957 and adopted by the UK Parliament for England and Wales in the Sexual Offences Act 1967 (i.e. the Convention is only violated by criminalization of private, same-sex sexual activity between no more than two persons who are both over 21 and are not in the armed forces).[134] The Commission will only propose that the Court raise this minimal level of protection,[135] if the Commission can be convinced that there exists a sufficient 'European consensus' in favour of a higher level. The only source of hope for frustrated applicants returning from Strasbourg empty-handed, their new arguments and new evidence rejected, has been that if the Commission could eventually change its mind in *Dudgeon* in 1980 (nearly 25 years after the first criminalization case), it can do so again. In *Sutherland* v. *UK*, it has the chance to do so, and to give the Court the opportunity to extend the equality provided in *Dudgeon* to the age of consent.[136]

IV. PROTECTION UNDER THE INTERNATIONAL COVENANT ON CIVIL AND POLITICAL RIGHTS

Until 1994, the European Convention was the only international human rights treaty that had been successfully used to challenge sexual orientation discrimination. In 1994, however, the United Nations Human Rights Committee rendered a decision very similar to *Dudgeon*, which could ultimately have the effect of 'globalizing *Dudgeon*', and has certainly made sexual orientation discrimination an issue of human rights law at the global level. The Committee held, in *Toonen* v. *Australia*, that laws in Tasmania prohibiting same-sex and opposite-sex oral or anal intercourse and all other sexual activity between men constitute

[133] Cf. van Dijk (1993 Eur), 204–5 (despite the lack of a 'dynamic attitude on the part of the Court, and even more so on the part of the Commission, in matters relating to homosexuality', 'it is . . . worthwhile, and . . . even necessary, that complaints are lodged in Strasbourg to elicit a case-law which is more favorable'); van der Veen, Hendriks, & Mattijssen (1993 Eur), 241–2 (limited protection 'not so much a result of textual shortcomings . . . as . . . of the rather conservative interpretation [of the Convention]'; '[o]ngoing pressure is needed to provoke a more liberal interpretation').

[134] The Commission's finding a violation of Article 10 in *Scherer* v. *Switzerland* (1993), Ser. A, No. 287, paras. 59–67 (report) could be seen as a 'liberty' decision in the area of 'obscenity', in which sexual orientation discrimination was not an issue.

[135] Cf. Finnis (1994 Eur), 1049–55 (arguing that this current, minimal level of protection should be the maximum level).

[136] See note 94. Protocol No. 11, if it eventually comes into force, will merge the Commission into the Court. See Council of Europe (1994 Eur) at 86–101. It will then be the Court that will have to depart from the Commission's case law with regard to issues other than criminalization.

an 'arbitrary . . . interference with . . . privacy', contrary to Articles 17(1) and 2(1) of the International Covenant on Civil and Political Rights.[137] It found (like the European Court in *Dudgeon* and unlike the US Supreme Court in *Hardwick*) that 'it is undisputed that adult consensual sexual activity in private is covered by the concept of "privacy"', and that the Tasmanian laws '"interfere" with [Toonen's] privacy, even if [they] have not been enforced for a decade', there being no guarantee that prosecutions will not be brought in the future.[138] As to whether the interference was 'arbitrary', the Committee applied a test of 'reasonableness' under which the interference must be 'proportional to the end sought and . . . necessary in the circumstances'.[139] It rejected both justifications for the interference advanced by the Tasmanian government (the Australian government did not advance any).[140] Criminalization was not 'a reasonable means or proportionate measure to achieve the aim of preventing the spread of AIDS/ HIV'.[141] Nor was criminalization 'essential to the protection of morals in Tasmania', in view of the repeal of similar laws in all other Australian jurisdictions and the non-enforcement of the laws in Tasmania.[142]

Although the Committee did not refer to *Dudgeon*, *Norris*, and *Modinos* (apart from noting Nicholas Toonen's citation of these decisions),[143] its reasoning resembled that of the European Court, particularly in stressing non-enforcement as evidence that the laws were not necessary for the 'protection of morals'. In three important respects, however, the Committee's reasoning differed from, or could be said to go beyond, that of the European Court. First, it rejected a 'prevention of AIDS' justification, which was not raised either in *Dudgeon* (decided before the recognition of AIDS) or in *Norris* or *Modinos* (decided after the recognition of AIDS).[144] Second, it rejected a 'protection of morals' justification by pointing to a 'national consensus' within the six states and two territories of Australia that laws prohibiting same-sex sexual activity are not necessary, rather than to any 'global consensus'.

If the Committee had thought that the European Court's approach to interpreting Article 8 of the Convention in *Dudgeon* (looking for a 'European consensus'

---

[137] (Commun. No. 488/1992) (31 Mar. 1994) (50th Session), UN HR Committee Doc. No. CCPR/ C/50/D/488/1992, 1 I.H.R.R. 97, paras. 8.6, 9–11. See also Morgan (1993 Other); Croome (1992a Other), (1992b Other). On the Covenant, see McGoldrick (1994 Other); Nowak (1993 Other).

[138] *Toonen*, ibid. at para. 8.2. The Committee also concluded, at para. 5.1, that Toonen could be deemed a 'victim' of a violation of Covenant rights, in spite of the absence of prosecutions.

[139] Ibid. at para. 8.3.

[140] An interesting feature of *Toonen* is that the party to the Covenant (the Australian government) agreed with Toonen that there had been a violation, while the Tasmanian government argued that there had not. It is not clear how the Committee will react in a future case where the party to the Covenant actively opposes a communication alleging sexual orientation discrimination.

[141] *Toonen*, ibid. at para. 8.5.

[142] Ibid. at para. 8.6.   [143] Ibid. at para. 7.5.

[144] AIDS was raised by the UK government in *Johnson* v. *UK* (No. 10389/83) (1986), 47 D.R. 72 at p. 7, unpublished part, but the Commission did not address the point. See Clapham and Weiler (1993 Eur), 45–6.

on the question of criminalization) was appropriate under Article 17 of the Covenant, it might have searched for a 'global consensus' on the issue. It might have done so either among the countries that are parties to the International Covenant or among the countries that have ratified the Optional Protocol to the Covenant (permitting individuals to submit communications to the Committee). As of 1 January 1994, 125 countries had ratified the Covenant and 74 had ratified the Optional Protocol.[145] Of the 74 Optional Protocol countries, 19 had laws similar to those in Tasmania (i.e. prohibiting some or all private sexual activity between consenting adult men or between consenting adult women), while 46 did not, with the position being unclear in 8.[146] Of the 125 Covenant countries, 43 had laws similar to those in Tasmania, while 64 did not and the position was not clear in 17.[147] Had the Committee searched for evidence of a 'global consensus', it would have found a 'consensus level' of at least 62% (46 out of 74) against such laws in the Optional Protocol countries, or at least 51% (64 out of 125) in all the Covenant countries, compared with the *Dudgeon* level of 85%.[148]

However, the Committee did not look for a 'global consensus' because it had not used such a concept in its prior decisions, and therefore saw the presence or absence of 'global consensus' as simply irrelevant. Instead, it referred only to a 'national consensus' in Australia (7 of 8 jurisdictions or 88%). The Committee's use of 'national consensus' rather than 'global consensus' cuts both ways. In *Toonen*, it meant that the Committee was able to find a violation whether or not sufficient 'global consensus' was present. However, it could also permit the Committee to distinguish *Toonen* in future cases involving prohibitions of same-sex sexual activity or other kinds of sexual orientation discrimination. If such a 'national consensus' were lacking in the respondent country (because a single national law had been challenged, e.g. in India, or more than a small minority

---

[145] See Marie (1994 Other), 56.

[146] *Similar laws*: Algeria, Angola, Armenia, Barbados, Belarus, Chile, Cyprus, Ecuador, Guyana, Jamaica, Libya, Mauritius, Nepal, Romania, Seychelles, Togo, Trinidad and Tobago, Zaire, Zambia. *No such laws*: Argentina, Austria, Benin, Bulgaria, Cameroon, Canada, Central African Republic, Colombia, Congo, Costa Rica, Czech Republic, Denmark, Dominican Republic, Estonia, Finland, France, Germany, Hungary, Iceland, Ireland, Italy, Korea (South), Lithuania, Luxembourg, Madagascar, Malta, Netherlands, New Zealand, Nicaragua, Norway, Panama, Peru, Philippines, Poland, Portugal, Russia, San Marino, Spain, Senegal, Slovakia, Slovenia, Suriname, Sweden, Ukraine, Uruguay, Venezuela. *Not clear*: Bolivia, Equatorial Guinea, Gambia, Guinea, Mongolia, Niger, St. Vincent and Grenadines, Somalia. The information in notes 146, 147, and 156 is found in Tielman and Hammelburg (1993 Other).

[147] In addition to the countries listed under each category in note 146, there were the following. *Similar laws*: Afghanistan, Albania, Azerbaijan, Bosnia-Herzegovina, Cape Verde, Ethiopia, India, Iran, Jordan, Kenya, Lebanon, Moldova, Morocco, Mozambique, Nigeria, Sri Lanka, Sudan, Syria, Tanzania, Tunisia, U.S.A. (22–3 states), Yemen, Yugoslavia (Serbia), Zimbabwe. *No such laws*: Belgium, Brazil, Croatia, Egypt, El Salvador, Gabon, Guatemala, Haiti, Iraq, Israel, Ivory Coast, Japan, Latvia, Lesotho, Mexico, Paraguay, Switzerland, United Kingdom. *Not clear*: Burundi, Cambodia, Dominica, Grenada, Malawi, Mali, Korea (North), Rwanda, Vietnam.

[148] See Part II.C above. Cf. Morgan (1993 Other), 289 ('[i]t will be impossible for the . . . Committee to find any international consensus in favour of decriminalisation').

of states in a federal system had such a law, e.g. in the US),[149] the Committee could cite the lack of a 'national consensus' in holding that the challenged law could be justified as necessary for the 'protection of morals' or some other aim.[150]

The third respect in which the Committee's reasoning differed from that of the European Court was its brief discussion of the question of discrimination. Like the European Court in *Dudgeon*, the Committee seems to have treated the issue in *Toonen* primarily as one of 'pure liberty' (an interference with freedom to engage in 'adult consensual sexual activity in private' to which no person could be subjected), rather than one of 'discriminatory interference with liberty' or 'pure equality'. It devoted most of its analysis to finding a violation of the 'right to privacy' in Article 17(1) of the Covenant, and found it unnecessary to consider Toonen's 'pure equality' argument: that there had also been a violation of the 'freestanding' right to 'equal protection of the law' in Article 26 of the Covenant.[151] However, it did state, somewhat cryptically, that it had found a violation of Articles 17(1) *'juncto'* Article 2(1), and that Toonen's rights 'under articles 17(1) and 2(1)' had been violated.[152] This implicit reference to the 'non-discrimination' clause of Article 2(1) ('without distinction of any kind, such as race, colour, sex . . . or other status') suggests that it found a 'discriminatory interference with liberty', but it did not clearly specify the ground of distinction used by the Tasmanian laws. It may have done so implicitly by noting that 'the reference to "sex" in Articles [2(1)] and 26 is to be taken as including sexual orientation', and declining to decide whether 'sexual orientation' is an 'other status'.[153] This observation could prove to be of great significance.

---

[149] The examples of India and the US are completely hypothetical because neither has yet signed or ratified the Optional Protocol. But they are the two most populous parties to the Covenant and illustrate the potential impact of *Toonen*.

[150] See Morgan (1993 Other), 289 (Committee could 'adopt a "cultural relativity" attitude to the rights contained in the Covenant', finding a violation by Australia but not by other Optional Protocol countries with laws like Tasmania's); Parliamentary Research Service (1994 Other) at 22 ('[i]f the Committee were to apply the same standard [to a country with strong religious and cultural objections to homosexuality], it could be accused of cultural imperialism, whereas if it allowed different standards, it could be accused of detracting from the universality of human rights').

[151] *Toonen*, note 137 at para. 11. Mr. Bertil Wennergren, in an individual opinion, agreed with the Committee's 'sex' observation (note 153) and found a violation of Article 26. I would agree with the argument of the Australian government and of Toonen (see ibid. paras. 6.13, 7.6) that ss. 122 and 123 of the Tasmanian Criminal Code Act 1924 (as amended by the Criminal Code Amendment (Sexual Offences) Act 1987, No. 71, ss. 3, 6) together discriminate directly on the basis of sex and sexual orientation by prohibiting all male–male sexual activity but not male–female sexual activity (other than oral and anal intercourse) or female–female sexual activity. On its own, s. 122 discriminates indirectly on the basis of sex and sexual orientation because, although it prohibits all penile–oral or penile–anal intercourse, it is either enforced disproportionately against such intercourse between men, or has a disproportionate effect on gay and bisexual men (even if it is enforced equally) who are more likely to engage in such intercourse.

[152] Ibid. at paras. 9–11.

[153] Ibid. at para. 8.7. The Committee has been criticized for failing to give a reason for noting that 'sex' includes 'sexual orientation'. See e.g. Parliamentary Research Service (1994 Other) at 13, 15 ('most unfortunate that the Committee made this bald statement without giving any reason'; 'the Committee's reasons can only be a matter of speculation'). For reasons the Committee could have given, see Chapter 8.

What is the impact of *Toonen* likely to be? Its most immediate effect will be on the laws in Tasmania. The Committee's opinion was that an effective remedy for the violation of the Covenant would be the repeal of those laws.[154] The Australian government acted quickly to achieve that result by passing federal legislation that overrides the Tasmanian laws.[155] But *Toonen* could also be used (as *Dudgeon* has been in Council of Europe countries) to challenge prohibitions of same-sex sexual activity in other Optional Protocol countries. As of 31 December 1994, at least twenty-one Optional Protocol countries (excluding Australia and Council of Europe countries such as Cyprus and Romania) appear to have such prohibitions.[156] However, these countries are all developing countries, or former Soviet or Islamic countries, in which there may be few gay, lesbian or bisexual persons who are sufficiently open about their sexual orientation, or have sufficient resources, to exhaust domestic remedies and take their case to the Committee. If the Committee does receive a communication from one of these twenty-one countries, it could merely apply *Toonen* (as the European Court applied *Dudgeon* in *Norris* and *Modinos*). But it could also choose to distinguish *Toonen* by emphasizing the 'national consensus' in Australia, which would almost certainly be absent in these twenty-one countries (especially Islamic countries such as Algeria and Libya).

In other Covenant countries that have not ratified the Optional Protocol, but prohibit some forms of same-sex sexual activity, *Toonen* could still be invoked before national courts or legislatures. The most striking example of such a country is the United States, which has ratified the Covenant, but not the Optional Protocol, and seems to have precluded the use of the Covenant before US courts.[157] Even if *Toonen* can only be cited as persuasive authority, US courts and legislatures will have to acknowledge the fact that the laws prohibiting oral or anal intercourse which the US Supreme Court upheld in *Hardwick* have been found to violate the International Covenant, an international human rights treaty to which the US is a party.

At a minimum, *Toonen* seems to provide the same level of protection against sexual orientation discrimination under the International Covenant as *Dudgeon* does under the European Convention. Will the Committee be willing to extend

[154] *Toonen*, ibid. at para. 10.

[155] The Human Rights (Sexual Conduct) Act 1994, No. 179, s. 4(1) (in force 19 Dec. 1994), provides (in s. 4(1)) that '[s]exual conduct involving only consenting adults [18 years old or more] acting in private is not to be subject . . . to any arbitrary interference with privacy within the meaning of Article 17 [of the Covenant]'. The Tasmanian government has refused to repeal its laws and may challenge the constitutionality of the federal legislation. See 'Tasmania vows to keep anti-gay laws' *The Independent* (24 Aug. 1994) 6.

[156] The twenty-one countries are the seventeen countries listed under *Similar laws* in note 146 (excluding Australia, which has complied with *Toonen*, and Cyprus and Romania, in which recourse to the European Court and Commission of Human Rights is available), plus Georgia, Kyrgyzstan, Namibia, and Sudan, which were among the 80 countries that had ratified the Optional Protocol by 31 Dec. 1994. See United Nations (1995 Other).

[157] For a thorough analysis of the implications of *Toonen*, especially in the US, see Helfer & Miller (1995 Other). See also Stewart, D. (1993 Other).

Toonen to other kinds of sexual orientation discrimination, e.g. unequal ages of consent or discrimination against gay, lesbian, and bisexual military personnel or against same-sex couples? Its observation that 'sex' in Articles 2(1) and 26 includes 'sexual orientation' seems to mean that the Covenant prima facie prohibits discrimination based on sexual orientation, both in relation to rights specified in the Covenant (Article 2(1)) and in relation to other rights, interests or opportunities not protected by the Covenant (Article 26).[158] This is potentially a very broad principle which could provide comprehensive protection against sexual orientation discrimination, going well beyond that offered by the European Court to date. Whether such protection is forthcoming will depend on the Committee's willingness to accept asserted justifications for sexual orientation discrimination (e.g. 'protection of the family' or 'protection of youth'). If the effect of its treating sexual orientation discrimination as a kind of sex discrimination is that it will require an especially strong justification for the former, then it might indeed grant protection beyond that provided by the European Court. However, if it is as willing to accept justifications as the European Commission (e.g. because it requires the 'national consensus' that was present in *Toonen*), the protection of *Toonen* could be limited to countries where there is a 'national consensus' against criminalization (or other forms of sexual orientation discrimination).

The only evidence of the Committee's possible response is its single pre-*Toonen* decision dealing with an issue of sexual orientation discrimination. In *Hertzberg* v. *Finland*, it upheld the Finnish Broadcasting Company's decision to censor certain radio and television programmes dealing with the lives of gay, lesbian, and bisexual persons in Finland, finding that the restriction on freedom of expression was justified under Article 19(3) as necessary for the protection of 'public morals'.[159] Because 'public morals differ widely' and the Finnish authorities had to be given a certain 'margin of discretion', the Committee could not 'question [their] decision . . . that radio and TV are not the appropriate forums to discuss issues related to homosexuality, as far as the programme could be judged as encouraging homosexual behaviour . . . [T]he audience cannot be controlled . . . [and] harmful effects on minors cannot be excluded.'[160] It is not clear whether the Committee would follow *Hertzberg* today.[161] Having decided

---

[158] The extra protection potentially afforded by Article 26 will only make a difference (vis-à-vis Article 14 of the Convention) if some forms of sexual orientation discrimination do not implicate any Covenant or Convention right. This will not be the case if all such discrimination constitutes interference with the 'right to privacy' in Article 17 of the Covenant, or the 'right to respect for private life' in Article 8 of the Convention.

[159] (Communication No. 61/1979) (2 Apr. 1982), UN Yearbook of the Hum. Rts. Committee, 1981–82, Vol. 2, p. 406, at paras. 10.2–10.4, 11.

[160] *Hertzberg*, ibid. at para. 10.4.

[161] The individual opinion of Mr. Torkel Opsahl in *Hertzberg* may, in effect, reconcile *Toonen* and *Hertzberg*. He began by observing that the Committee's conclusion did not prejudge 'the right to be different and live accordingly, protected by Article 17' (and effectively predicted the outcome

in *Toonen* that 'public morals' do not justify a criminal prohibition of private same-sex sexual activity, and that, under Article 2(1), Covenant rights (including freedom of expression) must be respected without distinctions based on sexual orientation, it might be less ready to permit fears of 'encouraging' such activity or 'harmful effects on minors' to justify censorship. Or it could give a 'protection of morals' justification greater weight in the 'public sphere' than in the 'private sphere', and effectively limit the protection of *Toonen* 'to the bedroom'.

In closing this discussion of the Covenant, I would note that *Toonen* (right of privacy) and *Hertzberg* (freedom of expression) are both examples of the use of fundamental choice arguments, while the Committee seems to have accepted a sex discrimination argument in *Toonen*. In neither case do the communications' authors appear to have made an immutable status argument, although the individual opinion of Mr. Bertil Wennergren in *Toonen* seems implicitly to refer to the concept of 'immutability'.[162] The Committee will certainly have the opportunity to consider these arguments in future cases, and to decide whether to extend *Toonen* to other countries and to other kinds of sexual orientation discrimination. Gay, lesbian, and bisexual persons around the world, their hopes greatly raised by *Toonen*, will be watching.

in *Toonen*). He also noted that, under Article 19, 'everyone . . . [has] the right to impart information—positive or negative—about homosexuality', and suggested that the Finnish law prohibiting 'public[ ] encourage[ment] [of] indecent behaviour between persons of the same sex' (ibid. at para. 2.1) might not be 'necessary' for the protection of 'public morals'. However, he seemed to accept the Committee's conclusion because the Finnish law had not been applied to the authors of the communication, and the broadcaster's self-imposed restrictions did not have to be justified under Article 19. *Hertzberg* could thus be seen as a difficult case pitting the broadcaster's freedom of expression against that of the journalists who had prepared the censored programmes (although it is doubtful whether the broadcaster would have censored the programmes in the absence of the Finnish law). See Ch. 9, note 36.

[162] He agreed with the Committee's observation that 'sex' includes 'sexual orientation', because 'the common denominator for the grounds "race, colour and sex" are biological or genetic factors'. See note 137 above, 1 I.H.R.R. at 106.

6

The Canadian Charter of Rights and Freedoms: Sexual Orientation under Section 15(1)

I. INTRODUCTION

In Chapters 2 to 5, we have seen that the US Supreme Court has yet to provide any protection against sexual orientation discrimination *per se*, and that the European Court and Commission of Human Rights have invalidated only a single form of such discrimination (criminal prohibitions of all private, adult same-sex sexual activity). What are the prospects for protection against such discrimination in Canada? The Canadian Supreme Court has yet to decide a case of sexual orientation discrimination under the Canadian Charter of Rights and Freedoms, which was only proclaimed in 1982, and Section 15(1) of which (the equality rights provision) only came into force in 1985. It is important to note that, when the Canadian Supreme Court does decide its first such case, the issue will not be the threshold question of prohibiting the criminalization of private same-sex sexual activity, at which the US Supreme Court balked in *Hardwick*, and to which the European Court and Commission agreed in *Dudgeon* but beyond which the Commission has refused to go.

This is because Canada is a unitary state for the purposes of criminal law (which falls under federal jurisdiction), and only ever had a single, national law on same-sex sexual activity, rather than the dozens of such laws that existed in the US (where criminal law is mainly under state jurisdiction) and in the Council of Europe countries. In 1969, following the lead of England and Wales in the Sexual Offences Act 1967 and using very similar language, Canada amended the Criminal Code provisions dealing with so-called 'buggery' (which applied to both same-sex and opposite-sex anal intercourse) and 'gross indecency' (which applied to sexual acts between any two persons, and therefore potentially to all sexual activity between men or between women, and to opposite-sex oral intercourse).[1] As a result, the Canadian Supreme Court's first decision on sexual orientation discrimination under the Charter will necessarily deal with an issue other than the validity of a total prohibition of same-sex sexual activity, and will require the Court to consider extending protection beyond that provided to date

---

[1] Criminal Law Amendment Act, 1968–69, SC 1968–69, c. 38, s. 7 (exempting from these offences acts committed in private between two consenting persons 21 and over). The 'gross indecency' offence has been applied to two women 'making love' (see *R. v. C.* (1981), 30 Nfld and PEIR 451 (Nfld Dist Ct), rev'd (1982), 39 Nfld and PEIR 8 (Nfld CA)), and to opposite-sex oral intercourse (see *R. v. Davis*, [1970] 3 CCC 260 (Alta CA)).

by the US Supreme Court or the European Court. This first decision is likely to come in 1995 in *Egan* v. *Canada*,[2] to be discussed below, which concerns discrimination against a same-sex couple in respect of a pension benefit.

Before 1980, the Court's record in sexual orientation discrimination cases was no better than that of the US Supreme Court or the European Commission. In *Klippert* v. *R.* in 1967, the Court (3–2) interpreted the Criminal Code as permitting men like Everett Klippert, who had been convicted of engaging in consensual sexual activity with other men, to be considered 'dangerous sexual offenders' and subjected to 'preventive detention' (imprisonment of indefinite duration, potentially for life).[3] In dissent, Cartwright J. noted that, '[h]owever loathsome conduct of the sort mentioned may appear to all normal persons', it was 'improbable that Parliament should have intended such a result', which could lead to 'serious overcrowding' of prisons.[4] And in *Gay Alliance Toward Equality* v. *Vancouver Sun* in 1979, the Court (6–3) reversed a board of inquiry finding that a newspaper's refusal of a classified advertisement for 'GAY TIDE, gay lib paper' was discrimination 'without reasonable cause' in a service 'customarily available to the public', contrary to British Columbia's (then open-ended) human rights legislation.[5] In concluding that classified newspaper advertisements were not a service 'customarily available to the public', the majority was exceptionally influenced by the guarantee of freedom of the press in the Canadian Bill of Rights,[6] and effectively gave a common law version of that guarantee a surprising precedence over a provincial statute (to which the Bill of Rights did not apply).[7]

Whatever the significance of the Court's reluctance in these cases to interpret statutes as prohibiting, or not aggravating, sexual orientation discrimination, they were decided before the Charter gave it the power to strike down laws depriving individuals of their rights under Sections 7 and 15(1):

7. Everyone has the right to life, liberty and security of the person and the right not to be deprived thereof except in accordance with the principles of fundamental justice.

15(1). Every individual is equal before and under the law and has the right to the equal protection and equal benefit of the law without discrimination and, in particular, without

---

[2] [1993] 3 FC 401 (CA), aff'd (25 May 1995), [1995] 2 SCR. See Ch. 9, Part III.

[3] [1967] SCR 822. See also Kinsman (1987 Can), 161–72.   [4] *Klippert*, ibid. at 831.

[5] [1979] 2 SCR 435. The newspaper 'started accepting such advertising shortly after the court affirmed their right to refuse': *The Advocate* (23 June 1987) 63.

[6] SC 1960, c. 44. See Black (1979 Can), 665, 672–5.

[7] See *Gay Alliance*, ibid. at 454–6. The competing interest of freedom of the press in *Gay Alliance* was emphasized in *University of British Columbia* v. *Berg*, [1993] 2 SCR 353 at 376–9. In *Insurance Corp. of British Columbia* v. *Heerspink*, [1982] 2 SCR 145 at 153, the same British Columbia human rights act as in *Gay Alliance* was described by Lamer J. (at 158) as a 'fundamental law' that would govern in the event of a direct conflict with a British Columbia insurance act. While Black (1979 Can), 650–2, 672–5, saw *Gay Alliance* as a narrow decision turning on freedom of the press, other commentators viewed it as evidencing possible hostility on the part of the Supreme Court to human rights claims by gay, lesbian, and bisexual persons. See e.g. Kopyto (1980 Can), 652; Richstone and Russell (1981 Can), 93.

discrimination based on race, national or ethnic origin, colour, religion, sex, age or mental or physical disability.

These broad guarantees of 'liberty' and 'equality', which Section 32(1) makes applicable to 'the Parliament and government of Canada' and 'the legislature and government of each province', offer potential relief from all forms of legal and other public sector sexual orientation discrimination that can be considered the action of a 'government'.

Should a gay, lesbian or bisexual person challenging an instance of sexual orientation discrimination frame the issue as one of 'pure liberty' under Section 7, as one of 'discriminatory interference with liberty' (under Section 7 or under Section 15(1)), or as one of 'pure equality' under Section 15(1)? In the Canadian context, Section 15(1) would seem to be the more attractive option for at least three reasons. *First*, as has been seen above, a Canadian plaintiff will generally not be challenging a law or policy that purports to apply to all persons, but rather a law or policy that makes an express distinction between gay, lesbian or bisexual persons and heterosexual persons, or between same-sex emotional–sexual conduct and opposite-sex emotional–sexual conduct. Thus, the reason why US plaintiffs have often chosen a 'right of privacy' argument (namely, the application of most US oral or anal intercourse laws to all such intercourse, whether opposite-sex or same-sex) will usually not be applicable. *Second*, the text of Section 15(1) is a hybrid: it combines the advantage which Article 14 of the European Convention has over the US Equal Protection Clause (Section 15(1), like Article 14, has an open-ended list of enumerated grounds of discrimination) with the advantage which the US Equal Protection Clause has over Article 14 (Section 15(1), like the Equal Protection Clause, is a 'freestanding' guarantee of equality which applies to discrimination affecting any right, not just rights protected elsewhere in the Charter). Thus, the reason why European plaintiffs are forced to rely on the rights under Articles 8 and 12 of the European Convention to 'respect for . . . private and family life' and 'to marry and to found a family' (alone or in conjunction with Article 14), rather than on Article 14 alone, is not applicable in the Canadian situation. A 'pure equality' argument can be made under Section 15(1) of the Charter, unlike under Article 14 of the Convention. *Third*, Section 7 (unlike Articles 8 and 12 of the Convention) does not expressly mention 'private and family life' or 'marriage',[8] and a majority of the Canadian

---

[8] In the context of sexual orientation discrimination, the omission of the words 'family' and 'marriage' from the Charter may be beneficial. If a human rights instrument includes these words and they are interpreted as excluding same-sex couples (as a matter of tradition or 'original intent'), this may preclude use of the 'equality' provision of the same instrument to challenge discrimination against same-sex couples. See Ch. 4, Part III.B (marriage decisions of European Court of Human Rights, Netherlands Supreme Court, German Federal Constitutional Court). If a human rights instrument excludes these words, its 'equality' provision could be used to challenge discriminatory definitions and interpretations of 'family' and 'marriage' in subordinate laws or rules: see *Baehr* v. *Lewin*, 852 P 2d 44 (Haw 1993).

Supreme Court has yet to interpret it as including any implied 'right of privacy' similar to that identified by the US Supreme Court.

For these reasons, I will focus in Chapters 6 and 7 on 'pure equality' arguments under Section 15(1) of the Charter (but will suggest that there is an inherent overlap between Sections 7 and 15(1), which could permit a 'discriminatory interference with liberty' argument under Section 15(1)). How can Section 15(1) be applied to a case of sexual orientation discrimination? Under Section 15(1), one can make principled arguments that a new kind of discrimination should be treated as prima facie prohibited (subject to any Section 1 justification). At least two methods can be used. The first method, which was employed by the Supreme Court in *Andrews* v. *Law Society of British Columbia*,[9] its first Section 15(1) decision, involves arguing that the new kind of discrimination is like the kinds of discrimination that Section 15(1) expressly prohibits, i.e. it involves a distinct, independent ground of discrimination that is 'analogous' to the grounds enumerated in Section 15(1). The analogy must be based on certain theoretical criteria that are satisfied both by the enumerated grounds and the proposed analogous ground, which criteria the Court must identify in order to define 'discrimination' in Section 15(1) (instances of discrimination based on enumerated grounds being examples of 'discrimination').[10] In this respect, the Charter differs from human rights legislation (i.e. anti-discrimination legislation), which usually presents a closed list of prohibited grounds of discrimination to which courts are not free to add.[11]

The second method involves arguing that the new kind of discrimination is implicitly included within the scope of a kind of discrimination that Section 15(1) already prohibits (i.e. an enumerated ground or an already recognized analogous ground). This 'included grounds' approach is simpler than the 'analogous grounds' approach in that it should suffice to show the application of the existing ground to cases of the new kind of discrimination. Consistency should require that these cases be treated like any others based on the existing ground (i.e. as prima facie violations of Section 15(1), subject to Section 1), and it should not be necessary to show that the new ground independently satisfies the general theoretical criteria for identifying analogous grounds. The 'included grounds' approach is also available in the context of human rights legislation. New kinds of discrimination can be recognized as coming within existing prohibited grounds without the need for an amendment to expressly add a new ground.[12]

In the remainder of Chapter 6, I will discuss the question of what criteria should be used to identify 'analogous grounds' of discrimination under Section 15(1), and briefly state my reasons for preferring two potential criteria (analogous

---

[9] [1989] 1 SCR 143.   [10] See Gold, M. (1989), 1069.
[11] See *Andrews*, [1989] 1 SCR 143 at 175. But see Ch. 8, notes 111–23 and accompanying text.
[12] See e.g. *Brooks* v. *Canada Safeway Ltd.*, [1989] 1 SCR 1219 ('pregnancy' included in 'sex'); *Janzen* v. *Platy Enterprises Ltd.*, [1989] 1 SCR 1252 ('sexual harassment' included in 'sex').

grounds as either 'immutable statuses' or 'fundamental choices') to alternative
criteria. I will then consider whether sexual orientation is an analogous ground,
by examining the responses given by Canadian legal writers and courts to date,
and the answers suggested by alternative criteria. In Chapter 7, I will apply my
preferred criteria of 'immutable statuses' and 'fundamental choices' to sexual
orientation. In Chapter 8, I will examine the possibility that, whatever the criteria for identifying 'analogous grounds' are or should be, sexual orientation
does not have to be recognized as such a ground because it is in fact an 'included ground', in the sense that virtually every case of sexual orientation discrimination can be seen as a case of discrimination based on 'sex', a ground
expressly enumerated in Section 15(1). I will also assess the level of protection
the Charter provides against sexual orientation discrimination.

II. CRITERIA FOR IDENTIFYING ANALOGOUS GROUNDS

In *Andrews*, the Supreme Court held that a statute limiting admission to the legal
profession to Canadian citizens violated Section 15(1) and could not be justified
under Section 1. In so doing, the Court resolved the problem of interpretation
raised by the relationship between Section 15(1) and Section 1. This problem
arose because of the apparent conflict between a broad reading of Section 15(1)
(and particularly the word 'discrimination') as applying to all legal distinctions,
and the strict test adopted by the Court in *R. v. Oakes*[13] for deciding when, under
Section 1, a 'reasonable limit' on a Charter right or freedom is 'demonstrably
justified in a free and democratic society'. The *Oakes* requirements, namely that
the distinction serve an objective relating to 'pressing and substantial' concerns,
be 'rationally connected' to the objective, 'impair the [Charter] right as little as
possible', and not have effects so severely trenching on rights that the objective
is 'outweighed by the abridgement of rights',[14] appeared so strict that few distinctions would survive Section 1 review.[15] While this result would be desirable
in the case of distinctions based on race, sex or most other grounds traditionally
found in human rights legislation, many distinctions made by 'social and economic' legislation that are generally considered beneficial might not be upheld
if this standard of justification were applied.[16]

In *Andrews*, the Court canvassed four possible descriptions of the kind of
legal distinction that falls within Section 15(1) ('any distinction', 'unreasonable

[13] [1986] 1 SCR 103.

[14] See *R. v. Edwards Books & Art Ltd.*, [1986] 2 SCR 713 at 768.

[15] In fact, many post-*Oakes* decisions have upheld prima facie violations of Charter rights under
Section 1. See e.g. *Edwards Books*, ibid. (Sunday trading legislation); *Reference re ss. 193 and
195.1(1)(c) of the Criminal Code (Man.)*, [1990] 1 SCR 1123 (hereinafter the *Prostitution Reference*) ('solicitation' by prostitutes); *McKinney v. University of Guelph*, [1990] 3 SCR 229 (mandatory retirement); *R. v. Keegstra*, [1990] 3 SCR 697 (incitement of hatred legislation).

[16] See *Andrews*, [1989] 1 SCR 143 at 154, 184.

or unfair distinctions', 'distinctions among the similarly situated', and 'distinctions based on enumerated or analogous grounds'), and selected the fourth one as consistent with its interpretation of the respective roles of Section 15(1) and Section 1 and the meaning of 'discrimination' in Section 15(1).[17] It found that the 'any distinction' approach trivialized Section 15(1), the 'unreasonable distinctions' approach left a very minor role to Section 1,[18] and the test of 'similarity of situation' was 'mechanical' and not 'helpful'.[19] The Court's selection of an 'enumerated or analogous grounds' interpretation of Section 15(1) has had the apparent effect of excluding all legal distinctions based on non-enumerated and non-analogous grounds from judicial review under Section 15(1).[20] Thus, the Court seems, for now, to have rejected the kind of 'rational basis' review to which any legal distinction may be subjected under US equal protection doctrine.

After *Andrews*, a prima facie violation of Section 15(1) requires, at least, that the challenged distinction be one that is enumerated in Section 15(1) or analogous to the enumerated grounds.[21] However, the Court provided little guidance in *Andrews* as to what makes a ground 'analogous', apart from isolated references to factors that might be significant. Rather than attempt to state any criteria or tests, it preferred to conclude that 'non-citizenship' (or at least 'being a non-citizen permanent resident') is an analogous ground (at least in the employment context) and to defer to future cases the definition of 'the limits, if any, on grounds for discrimination'.[22] Subsequent Supreme Court decisions have provided little clarification regarding the criteria, and have identified no other analogous grounds.

The question of what criteria should be used to identify prohibited grounds of discrimination under Section 15(1) of the Charter (or under any constitution or treaty that contains an open-ended guarantee of 'equality' or prohibition of 'discrimination') is one that is extremely interesting, but which exceeds the scope of this book.[23] As a result, I can only present the various criteria that have been proposed in *Andrews* (and subsequent cases) and by legal commentators, and briefly state my reasons for thinking that only the 'immutable statuses' and 'fundamental choices' criteria should be used in deciding whether a ground is 'analogous'.

The diverse array of potential criteria (many of which are familiar from US

[17] Ibid. at 177–82.   [18] Ibid. at 181–2.
[19] Ibid. at 165–8. See Wintemute (1994 Can), 442–3 on why this test had to be rejected. This test is used by the US Supreme Court as part of 'rational basis' review, see e.g. *Cleburne* v. *Cleburne Living Center, Inc.*, 473 US 432 at 439 (1985) ('[t]he Equal Protection Clause . . . is essentially a direction that all persons similarly situated should be treated alike'), and by the European Court of Human Rights under Article 14, see e.g. Ch. 5, note 10; *Darby* v. *Sweden* (1990), Ser. A, No. 187, at para. 31 ('Article 14 protects individuals placed in similar situations from discrimination in their enjoyment of their [Convention] rights').
[20] See e.g. *R.* v. *Turpin*, [1989] 1 SCR 1296; *Reference re Workers' Compensation Act, 1983 (Nfld)*, [1989] 1 SCR 922.
[21] [1989] 1 SCR 143 at 182.   [22] Ibid. at 153, 175.   [23] See Ch. 1, note 40.

equal protection case law) can be divided into two broad categories: those that focus on the nature of the ground on which the unequal treatment (at issue in the specific case) is based, and those that focus on how that ground is or has been used (in society generally) as a basis for unequal treatment. The following list sorts the criteria into these two broad categories, and refers the reader to passages in *Andrews*, other Supreme Court decisions, and commentaries where each criterion has been mentioned or discussed:

A. Nature of the Ground on Which the Unequal Treatment Is Based

1. *Personal Characteristics.* The ground is a personal characteristic[24] (or the group(s) defined by the ground have a non-economic basis[25]).
2. *Immutable Statuses.* The ground represents a status that is immutable, uncontrollable or acquired at birth.[26]
3. *Fundamental Choices.* The ground represents the exercise of a right deemed 'fundamental' in the Charter or elsewhere in the law, or the making of a choice that is important or 'inhérent' or 'essentiel' to the individual.[27]
4. *Irrelevance.* The ground is generally irrelevant to legitimate public purposes.[28]
5. *Importance to Individual or Group Identity.* The ground is a characteristic that is important to individual or group identity.[29]
6. *Individual Interest Analysis.* Use of the ground in the circumstances constitutes an affront to individual dignity or otherwise harms important individual interests.[30]
7. *Inclusion in Human Rights Legislation.* The ground is included as a prohibited ground of discrimination in federal, provincial, or territorial human rights legislation.[31]

---

[24] See e.g. *Andrews*, [1989] 1 SCR 143 at 151, 165, 174, 195; *Turpin*, [1989] 1 SCR 1296 at 1331, 1333; *R.* v. *S(S)*, [1990] 2 SCR 254 at 287–9, 291–2. See also Gibson (1991a Can), 775–82; Hogg (1990 Can), 834–5; Ryder (1990 Can), 79; Proulx (1988 Can), 594; MacLauchlan (1986 Can), 228; Ross (1986 Can), 459; Duplé (1984 Can), 818–21; Black (1979 Can), 652 n. 16.

[25] See Leopold and King (1985 Can), 182–4.

[26] See *Andrews*, [1989] 1 SCR 143 at 195. See also Gibson (1991a Can), 786–8 ('stability'); Hawkins (1990 Can), 298, 303; Gold, M. (1989 Can), 1069; Proulx (1988 Can), 594; Smith (1988 Can), 83; Harris (1987 Can), 424; Ross (1986 Can), 459; Bayefsky (1985 Can), 51; Jefferson (1985 Can), 82; Leopold and King (1985 Can), 182–3; Duplé (1984 Can), 820.

[27] See Gold, M. (1989 Can), 1069; Proulx (1988a Can), 594–5; Brudner (1986 Can), 484; Bayefsky (1985 Can), 51; Jefferson (1985 Can), 81–2; Duplé (1984 Can), 820, 824; Smith (1984 Can), 372–3; Bender (1983 Can).

[28] See *Andrews*, [1989] 1 SCR 143 at 165, 193, 196–7. See also Gibson (1991a Can), 791; Gold, M. (1989 Can), 1069; Grey (1988 Can), 214 n. 93; Ross (1986 Can), 460; Bayefsky (1985 Can), 51; Jefferson (1985 Can), 81.

[29] See Moon (1988 Can), 698; Smith (1988 Can), 83; MacLauchlan (1986 Can), 228; Leopold and King (1985 Can), 183.

[30] See Harris (1987 Can), 408, 424, 426–7; Ross (1986 Can), 458–9.

[31] See *Andrews*, [1989] 1 SCR 143 at 175–6, 193 (relationship between Section 15(1) and human rights legislation). See also Baker (1987 Can), 552; Gall (1986 Can), 473; Leopold and King (1985 Can), 182.

B. Use of the Ground as a Basis for Unequal Treatment

1. *History of Use.* There has historically been widespread use of the ground as a basis for unequal treatment in the public and private sectors.[32]
2. *Motivation for Use.* Justifications for use of the ground as a basis for unequal treatment have often involved, or could be suspected to have involved, reliance on prejudice (i.e. bias)[33] or stereotypes.[34]
3. *Characteristics of Groups Affected by Use.* The groups affected by use of the ground as a basis for unequal treatment: (a) are identifiable, have 'distinctive marks', or are 'discrete and insular' minorities;[35] (b) lack political power and cannot influence the legislature so as to prevent or reverse unequal treatment;[36] (c) are economically or socially disadvantaged.[37]

At this early stage of Section 15(1) jurisprudence, has the Supreme Court made a clear selection amongst these candidates? The answer would seem to be no, because the Court has cited a variety of different criteria and provided no explanation for its lack of consistency from case to case. Dale Gibson has concluded 'that the case law on this question is in a grossly confused state, and that the most useful future development would be to abandon what has been decided so far, and begin afresh'.[38] If no particular criteria have been selected, does the Court at least appear generally to favour either the individual-focused

---

[32] See e.g. *Andrews*, [1989] 1 SCR 143 at 175, 180, 195–6; *Turpin*, [1989] 1 SCR 1296 at 1333; *McKinney*, [1990] 3 SCR 229 at 393 ('legal disadvantage'); *R.* v. *Swain*, [1991] 1 SCR 933 at 992, 994 ('historical disadvantage', 'legal disadvantage'). See also Ryder (1990 Can), 79–80; Brodsky and Day (1989 Can), 194; Gold, M. (1989 Can), 1069; Smith (1988 Can), 83; Brudner (1986 Can), 497; Ross (1986 Can), 460; Bayefsky (1985 Can), 51; Jefferson (1985 Can), 81; Leopold and King (1985 Can), 182; Duplé (1984 Can), 819.

[33] See e.g. *Andrews*, [1989] 1 SCR 143 at 180–1; *Turpin*, [1989] 1 SCR 1296 at 1333; *McKinney*, [1990] 3 SCR 229 at 387, 391–3; *Swain*, [1991] 1 SCR 933 at 992. See also Hogg (1990 Can), 834–5, 837; Moon (1988 Can), 686–7; Proulx (1988 Can), 589–90, 592, 594; Harris (1987 Can), 424; Brudner (1986 Can), 497.

[34] See e.g. *Andrews*, [1989] 1 SCR 143 at 174–5, 180, 183; *Turpin*, [1989] 1 SCR 1296 at 1333; *McKinney*, [1990] 3 SCR 229 at 387, 391–3, and 413; *Swain*, [1991] 1 SCR 933 at 992. See also Hogg (1990 Can), 834–5, 837; Proulx (1988 Can), 590, 592; Harris (1987 Can), 424; Brudner (1986 Can), 497; Ross (1986), 446.

[35] See e.g. *Andrews*, [1989] 1 SCR 143 at 152–3, 183; *Turpin*, [1989] 1 SCR 1296 at 1333. See also Gibson (1991a Can), 782–6; Gibson (1991b Can), 3–8; Proulx (1988 Can), 592, 594; Leopold and King (1985 Can), 183–4; Woehrling (1985 Can), 278 nn. 22, 24, 281 n. 29; Duplé (1984 Can), 819–20; Black (1979 Can), 653 n. 20.

[36] See e.g. *Andrews*, [1989] 1 SCR 143 at 152, 195; *Turpin*, [1989] 1 SCR 1296 at 1333 ('political . . . prejudice', 'political . . . disadvantage'). See also Hogg (1990 Can), 835, 837; Gold, M. (1989 Can), 1069; Proulx (1988 Can), 590, 592; Smith (1988 Can), 83; Harris (1987 Can), 424; Brudner (1986 Can), 497; Bayefsky (1985 Can), 51; Leopold and King (1985 Can), 184–5; Woehrling (1985 Can), 286 n. 38; Duplé (1984 Can), 819.

[37] See e.g. *Andrews*, [1989] 1 SCR 143 at 152, 154, 180; *Turpin*, [1989] 1 SCR 1296 at 1332–3. See also Gibson (1991a Can), 782–6; Gibson (1991b Can), 3–8; Black and Grant (1990 Can), 375–6, 378; Hogg (1990 Can), 834–7; Ryder (1990 Can), 79–80; Brodsky and Day (1989 Can), 193–4; Sheppard (1989 Can), 222–5; Moon (1988 Can), 677, 697; Proulx (1988 Can), 589–93; Smith (1988 Can), 83–4; Brudner (1986 Can), 484, 500; Woehrling (1985 Can), 278, 286 n. 38.

[38] Gibson (1991a Can), 773.

'nature of ground' criteria or the group-focused 'use of ground' criteria? In *Andrews*, McIntyre J. referred both to 'irrelevant personal differences' and 'personal characteristics', and to 'historically practised bases of discrimination', 'stereotyping', 'distinctions . . . which involve prejudice [detriment] or disadvantage', and non-citizen permanent residents' being 'a good example of a "discrete and insular minority"'.[39] His preference was therefore not clear. Likewise, La Forest J. described citizenship as 'a personal characteristic which shares many similarities with those enumerated in s. 15', as 'immutable' and 'in general, irrelevant', and non-citizens as 'a group of persons who are relatively powerless politically' and who have historically had their employment opportunities limited by legislation.[40] Wilson J. was much less equivocal. Although she agreed with McIntyre J. that the challenged rule discriminated against non-citizens 'on the ground of their personal characteristics', she stressed that 'non-citizens are a group lacking in political power' and vulnerable 'to becoming a disadvantaged group'.[41] She also observed that 's. 15 is designed to protect those groups who suffer social, political and legal disadvantage in our society', that 'the framers of the Charter . . . addressed themselves to the difficulties experienced by the disadvantaged' on the enumerated grounds, and that legislative distinctions 'should not bring about or re-inforce the disadvantage of certain groups or individuals'.[42] Indeed, rather than hold that 'being or not being a citizen' is an 'analogous ground', she concluded that non-citizens are an 'analogous group'.[43]

While *Andrews* did not produce a clear consensus on whether 'nature of ground' or 'use of ground' criteria are to be employed, the subsequent case of *R.* v. *Turpin* may have done so. Writing for a unanimous Supreme Court, Justice Wilson held that persons charged with murder outside Alberta (who could not elect trial by judge alone, as could persons charged with murder in Alberta) 'do not constitute a disadvantaged group in Canadian society within the contemplation of s. 15', and therefore did not suffer 'discrimination' under Section 15(1).[44] She did use a 'nature of ground' criterion as her starting point, by defining 'discrimination' (and implicitly analogous grounds) as distinctions 'based on grounds related to personal characteristics of the individual or group', and noted that she did not want to suggest that 'a person's province of residence or place of trial could not in some circumstances be a personal characteristic of the individual or group capable of constituting a ground of discrimination'.[45]

However, she determined whether the case involved a 'personal characteristic'

---

[39] See *Andrews*, [1989] 1 SCR 143 at 165, 174–5, 180–81, 183. For criticism of the importation of this vague concept into Canadian law, see Gibson (1991b Can), 3–8; Gibson (1991a Can), 785; Black and Grant (1990 Can), 381.

[40] [1989] 1 SCR 143 at 195–7.   [41] Ibid. at 151–2.   [42] Ibid. at 152–4.

[43] Ibid. at 152–3.   [44] See *Turpin*, [1989] 1 SCR 1296 at 1330, 1333.

[45] Ibid. at 1331, 1333. See also *R.* v. *S. (S.)*, [1990] 2 SCR 254 at 291–2 ('province of residence' not in the circumstances a 'distinction which is based upon a "personal characteristic" for the purposes of s. 15(1)').

by referring mainly to 'use of ground' criteria: (1) the Court must look not only at the legislative distinction but also to 'the larger social, political and legal context' to decide whether differential or identical treatment will result in 'equality';[46] (2) a finding of 'discrimination' will, 'in most but perhaps not all cases, necessarily entail a search for disadvantage that exists apart from and independent of the particular legal distinction being challenged';[47] (3) the purpose of Section 15(1) is 'remedying or preventing discrimination against groups suffering social, political and legal disadvantage in our society';[48] (4) 'it would be stretching the imagination' to characterize persons in the appellants' position as members of a 'discrete and insular minority';[49] and (5) 'a search for indicia of discrimination such as stereotyping, historical disadvantage or vulnerability to political and social prejudice [bias] would be fruitless in [their] case'.[50]

The tension between individual-focused 'nature of ground' and group-focused 'use of ground' criteria also arises in interpreting enumerated grounds. In *R.* v. *Hess*, section 146(1) of the Criminal Code prohibited a male person from having 'sexual intercourse' with a female person (not his wife) under the age of fourteen. Justice Wilson reaffirmed the group-focused interpretation of Section 15(1) in *Turpin*, noting that 'we must not assume that simply because a provision addresses a group that is defined by reference to a characteristic that is enumerated in s. 15(1) [sex] . . . we are automatically faced with an infringement of s. 15(1)'.[51] She cautioned against 'rigid formalism', i.e. 'an overly simple comparison of men charged under s. 146(1) . . . with women who engage in intercourse with males to whom they are not married who are under fourteen'.[52] However, she did not apply her reasoning in *Turpin* by arguing that men were not a 'discrete and insular minority' or a 'disadvantaged group', and therefore could not suffer 'discrimination based on . . . sex' under Section 15(1). Instead, she asserted that 's. 15(1) does not prevent the creation of [a criminal] offence which, as a matter of biological fact, can only be committed by one of the sexes because of the unique nature of the acts that are proscribed'.[53] Because only a man can penetrate (a vagina with a penis), the sex-based distinction did not

---

[46] *Turpin*, ibid. at 1331.   [47] Ibid. at 1332.

[48] Ibid. at 1333. See also *Andrews*, [1989] 1 SCR 143 at 154; *McKinney*, [1990] 3 SCR 229 at 393 (the 'common characteristic [of enumerated grounds] is political, social and legal disadvantage and vulnerability'). Wilson J. gave no reasons in *Turpin* for limiting the purpose of Section 15(1) to the protection of such groups.

[49] *Turpin*, ibid. at 1332–3. Several cases have held that particular groups were not 'discrete and insular minorities' or 'disadvantaged groups'. See *R.* v. *Finta*, [1994] 1 SCR 701 at 875–6 ('persons who commit a war crime outside of Canada'); *Haig* v. *Canada*, [1993] 2 SCR 995 at 1044 (persons resident in Québec for less than six months); *R.* v. *Généreux*, [1992] 1 SCR 259 at 310–11 (military personnel); *Wolff (Rudolph) & Co.* v. *Canada*, [1990] 1 SCR 695 at 702 (plaintiffs were a 'disparate group with the sole common interest of seeking to bring a claim against the Crown before a court'); *Reference re Workers' Compensation Act*, [1989] 1 SCR 922 at 924 ('situation of workers and dependents [deprived of tort actions against employers] is in no way analogous to those listed in s. 15(1)').

[50] *Turpin*, ibid. at 1333.   [51] [1990] 2 SCR 906 at 928.

[52] Ibid. at 929.   [53] Ibid.

prima facie violate Section 15(1), any more than a prohibition of self-induced abortion that applies only to women.[54]

Justice McLachlin, in dissent, rejected 'the suggestion that *Turpin* may characterize discrimination more restrictively than *Andrews*'.[55] She read *Andrews* as requiring a showing 'that a distinction is drawn on the enumerated or analogous grounds, and that the distinction results in a burden being placed on the complaining individual or group'.[56] In her view, *Turpin* should not be interpreted as adding to these requirements, and thus as excluding men from the protection of Section 15(1) 'because they do not constitute a "discrete and insular minority" disadvantaged independently of the legislation under consideration'.[57] Applying the *Andrews* requirements, section 146(1) constituted discrimination under Section 15(1), because it made distinctions based on the enumerated ground 'sex' by burdening males (over 14) but not females (over 14), and by protecting females (under 14) but not males (under 14).[58]

Several recent cases suggest that the preference for group-focused 'use of ground' criteria expressed in *Turpin* continues. In *R.* v. *Swain*, which dealt with mental disability (an enumerated ground), Chief Justice Lamer said that 'the court must consider whether the personal characteristic in question falls within the grounds enumerated in [Section 15(1)] or within an analogous ground, so as to ensure that the claim fits within the overall purpose of s. 15—namely, to remedy or prevent discrimination against groups subject to stereotyping, historical disadvantage and political and social prejudice in Canadian society'.[59] In *Rodriguez* v. *British Columbia (Attorney-General)*, he described 'physical disability' as 'among the personal characteristics listed in s. 15(1)', and found 'no need to consider . . . the connection between [this] ground . . . and the general purpose of s. 15 [described in *Swain*]', because '[n]o one would seriously question the fact that persons with disabilities are the subject of unfavourable treatment in Canadian society'.[60] And in *Haig* v. *Canada*, Justice L'Heureux-Dubé cited the *Turpin* criteria of 'stereotyping, historical disadvantage or vulnerability to political and social prejudice' as relevant in 'determining whether a group is analogous', adding that the plaintiff 'must establish that he or she is a member of a discrete and insular minority group'.[61] She found that 'persons moving to Québec less than six months before a referendum date' are not 'analogous to persons suffering discrimination on the basis of race, religion or gender', do not satisfy the *Turpin* criteria, and are not a 'discrete and insular' group.[62]

---

[54] Ibid. at 929–30. Justice Wilson's conclusion is arguably correct, but only if one interprets '[having] sexual intercourse' narrowly as 'penetrating a vagina with a penis', rather than as 'engaging in penile-vaginal intercourse', which a woman could commit.

[55] Ibid. at 941.   [56] Ibid.   [57] Ibid. at 943–4.

[58] Ibid. Justice McLachlin apparently did not adopt Justice Wilson's narrow interpretation of 'sexual intercourse' as an act that only a man could commit (see note 54), but did uphold the prima facie violation of Section 15(1) under Section 1: ibid. at 956–7.

[59] [1991] 1 SCR 933 at 992.   [60] [1993] 3 SCR 519 at 555.
[61] [1993] 2 SCR 995 at 1043.   [62] Ibid. at 1044.

If the *Turpin* view of Section 15(1) prevails, analogous grounds will be those that define 'disadvantaged groups', and a Section 15(1) plaintiff will have to show that they are a member of such a group (possibly even where the ground of discrimination is enumerated). This interpretation of Section 15(1) is certainly popular among Canadian legal academics.[63] I would argue that this interpretation is mistaken and that individual-focused 'nature of ground' criteria should be used rather than group-focused 'use of ground' criteria.[64] Space limitations permit only a brief summary of my reasons.[65]

First, the 'use of ground' criteria (unlike several of the 'nature of ground' criteria) do not provide any normative standard that would suggest what is inherently unjust about unequal treatment based on the ground in question.[66] Burglars, paedophiles, heroin users, and prostitutes[67] could all be regarded as disadvantaged groups. Is public sector discrimination against all of them a prima facie violation of Section 15(1)? Or does it depend on the nature of their conduct?

Second, the 'use of ground' criteria focus on characteristics of particular groups, and therefore tend to lead to asymmetrical protection against discrimination, i.e. discrimination against members of a 'disadvantaged group' (e.g. a racial minority or women) defined by a particular manifestation of a ground is prima facie prohibited, whereas discrimination against members of an 'advantaged group' (e.g. the racial majority or men) defined by a different manifestation of the same ground is not. This focus on groups is inconsistent with the text of Section 15(1), which confers the right to be free from discrimination on '[e]very individual'.[68] 'Nature of ground' criteria focus on the nature of general characteristics possessed, or general choices made, by all (or most) individuals. Because these criteria will be satisfied regardless of the specific manifestation of the characteristic or the specific choice made (e.g. race and sex are as 'immutable' for members of the racial majority and men as for members of a racial minority and women; religion is as 'fundamental' a choice for Christians as for Jews or Muslims), they suggest that protection against discrimination should be symmetrical, applying to all individuals affected by unequal treatment based on a particular ground rather than only to members of particular groups.

Among the 'nature of ground' criteria, I prefer the combination of 'immutable statuses' (physical or historical statuses that are initially unchosen and impossible to change, excluding change that would constitute a violation of bodily

---

[63] See note 37. See also Gold, R. (1989 Can), 225–6; Petter (1989 Can), 362; Black and Smith (1989 Can), 607–8; Bankier (1985 Can). For a seminal exposition of a 'disadvantaged groups' argument (under the US Constitution), see Fiss (1976 US), 108, 154–5.

[64] Cf. Hogg (1992 Can), 1167–8, 1175–6 ('[a]nalogous grounds involve immutable personal characteristics'; membership of a disadvantaged group not necessary under Section 15(1)).

[65] See Ch. 1, note 40.   [66] See Tribe (1980 US), 1075–7.

[67] In the *Prostitution Reference* (see note 15), which rejected a challenge to the prohibition of 'solicitation' argued under Sections 2 and 7, it could have been argued that prostitutes are a 'disadvantaged group' under Section 15(1). See MacLauchlan (1986 Can), 225–31.

[68] See e.g. Gibson (1991b Can), 6–8; Hawkins (1990 Can), 300–2.

integrity if coerced) and 'fundamental choices' (rights or freedoms guaranteed elsewhere in the Charter or the Constitution). Together, these criteria cover grounds involving no choice and grounds involving choices that must be respected.[69] Of the nine enumerated grounds in Section 15(1), eight are arguably immutable (race, national origin, ethnic origin, colour, sex, age, mental disability and physical disability), while religion is a 'fundamental choice' expressly protected in Section 2(a) of the Charter.[70] I would discard 'personal characteristics' as potentially limitless, 'irrelevance' as more appropriate to Section 1 analysis (there being no clear threshold level of 'infrequency of relevance' amongst such diverse enumerated grounds as race, sex, age, and disability), 'importance to individual or group identity' as potentially both over-inclusive and under-inclusive,[71] 'individual interest analysis' as placing no limit on the kinds of distinctions that can be challenged under Section 15(1), and 'inclusion in human rights legislation' as being merely persuasive but not conclusive (in view of the differences between constitutions and statutes).

III. IS A DISTINCTION BASED ON AN ANALOGOUS GROUND 'DISCRIMINATION'?

Once it has been determined that a particular ground is 'analogous', does it automatically follow that any distinction based on that ground prima facie violates Section 15(1) (subject to Section 1)? I would argue that the answer should be yes, and that the doctrine of 'enumerated and analogous grounds' sufficiently limits the scope of Section 15(1).[72] However, Justice McIntyre cast doubt on this in *Andrews* by adding to the requirements (1) that there be a distinction[73] (denying one of the Section 15(1) rights to equality before or under the law, or to the equal protection or equal benefit of the law), and (2) that the distinction involve an enumerated or analogous ground, a further requirement (3) that the plaintiff show that 'the legislative impact of the law is discriminatory'.[74] This third requirement has been interpreted differently by commentators, with some

---

[69] Cf. *Kask* v. *Shimizu* (1986), 69 Alta Rep 343 (QB) at 349 (each enumerated ground is either an 'immutable physical or other characteristic' or a 'characteristic ... protected by some other *Charter*-guaranteed right or freedom'); Gold, M. (1989 Can), 1069 ('whether the basis of classification concerns those aspects of one's person that are either beyond one's control or within that sphere independently protected by the Constitution'); Proulx (1988 Can), 594 (an enumerated or analogous ground is a personal characteristic that is either a 'caractéristique inhérente ou incontrôlable' or a 'choix fondamental'). The categories of 'immutable status' and 'fundamental choice' are similar in many respects to the categories of 'suspect classification' and 'fundamental right', used in US equal protection doctrine to determine when 'strict scrutiny' is appropriate.

[70] Cf. Hogg (1992 Can), 1168 (the nine grounds 'do not reflect a voluntary choice ... but an involuntary inheritance. They describe what a person is, rather than what a person does.')

[71] See Ch. 1, note 25.   [72] See Wintemute (1994 Can), 455–8.

[73] A distinction is present where there is unequal treatment (i.e. direct discrimination) or equal treatment with a differential impact (i.e. indirect or adverse effect discrimination). See e.g. *Symes* v. *Canada*, [1993] 4 SCR 695, 755–6, 761–2; *Rodriguez*, note 60 at 547–52.

[74] See *Andrews*, [1989] 1 SCR 143 at 182.

seeing it as adding nothing,[75] and others treating it as a requirement that the plaintiff show that they suffer 'prejudice [detriment] or disadvantage' as a result of a distinction based on an enumerated or analogous ground.[76] Justice McIntyre's discussion in *Andrews* of the effect of the rule that lawyers must be citizens seems to indicate the meaning of his third requirement: merely 'not receiving equal treatment' or a 'differential impact' is not enough; the law must impose a 'burden' on the plaintiff, so that 'obviously trivial and vexatious' claims will be screened out.[77] In post-*Andrews* decisions, however, Justice Wilson transformed the third requirement into a requirement that the plaintiff show that they are a member of a 'disadvantaged group',[78] or that the distinction involves 'prejudice [bias] or stereotype'.[79] A full analysis of this requirement, and other aspects of Section 15(1) jurisprudence, is beyond the scope of this Chapter.[80] But it will be seen below that the requirement of 'discriminatory impact' represents a significant, additional hurdle for a plaintiff arguing that a distinction based on sexual orientation constitutes prima facie discrimination under Section 15(1).

IV. IS SEXUAL ORIENTATION AN ANALOGOUS GROUND?

A. *Response of the Canadian Legal Community to Date*

There is a clear consensus in the Canadian legal community that sexual orientation is an analogous ground of discrimination under Section 15(1). This consensus is most evident among legal writers, who are virtually unanimous in concluding that sexual orientation should be recognized as an analogous ground.[81]

---

[75] See Bayefsky (1990 Can), 513 (not 'a significant hurdle'); Gold, M. (1989 Can), 1072; Elliott (1989 Can), 242.

[76] See Flanagan (1989 Can), 580; Sheppard (1989 Can), 222–3. Justice McIntyre's reference to distinctions involving 'prejudice or disadvantage' was in the context of identifying enumerated or analogous grounds, not in assessing the 'discriminatory impact' of such a ground on the plaintiff. See *Andrews*, [1989] 1 SCR 143 at 179–81.

[77] See *Andrews*, ibid. at 151, 182–83. See also text accompanying note 56; *McKinney*, [1990] 3 SCR 229 at 278, La Forest J. (a distinction based on an enumerated ground that 'impose[s] burdens on' affected individuals is enough for a prima facie violation of Section 15(1)); *Haig*, [1993] 2 SCR 995 at 1043 (a complainant must show that 'the law has a negative impact'); *Rodriguez*, [1993] 3 SCR 519 at 552 (the inequality must 'impose . . . a disadvantage or burden').

[78] See *Turpin*, [1989] 1 SCR 1296 at 1330–3. In *Haig*, ibid., L'Heureux-Dubé J. required that the complainant's group be not only one defined by an enumerated or analogous ground, but also a 'discrete and insular minority group'.

[79] See *McKinney*, [1990] 3 SCR 229 at 387, 391–3, 413 ('[t]he listing of sex, age and race . . . is not meant to suggest that any distinction drawn on these grounds is per se discriminatory').

[80] See Ch. 1, note 40.

[81] See Ryder (1990 Can), 77, 81, 89; Brodsky and Day (1989 Can), 206; Lepofsky and Schwartz (1988 Can), 121; Proulx (1988 Can), 594; Smith (1988 Can), 83; MacLauchlan (1986 Can), 228; Spitz (1986 Can), 401; Bruner (1985 Can), 465–66; Eberts (1985 Can), 213; Hogg (1985 Can), 799; Hughes (1985 Can), 80–82; Jefferson (1985 Can), 84; Leopold and King (1985 Can), 179–86; McLellan (1985 Can), 415 n. 76; Duplé (1984 Can), 825; Williams (1983 Can), C/83–5 n. 33.

The consensus disappears, however, when it comes to specifying the reasons for this conclusion. Those writers who have given reasons cite, alone or in various combinations, almost all of the criteria discussed above (or criteria that are substantially similar). For example, sexual orientation has been described as a personal characteristic,[82] a non-economic classification,[83] immutable or 'incontrôlable',[84] 'inhérent' or 'essentiel',[85] important to individual identity,[86] similar to religion,[87] an essential aspect of reproductive and sexual choice,[88] possibly protected under Section 2(b) or 2(d) of the Charter or by a 'right of privacy',[89] irrelevant,[90] and included in provincial human rights legislation.[91] Similarly, gay, lesbian, and bisexual persons have been referred to as having a history of discrimination,[92] prejudice (bias),[93] and stereotyping,[94] and as being an identifiable[95] and politically powerless[96] group. In fact, the only criterion not mentioned is economic and social disadvantage.

Although the Supreme Court has yet to decide whether or not sexual orientation is an analogous ground, a number of lower courts and administrative tribunals have considered the question since *Andrews*.[97] Most have clearly held that sexual orientation is an analogous ground, and none has clearly held that it is not such a ground. But, because the government defendants in most of these cases have elected to concede the point, few judges have found it necessary to state any reasons for their conclusions.

The Federal Court Trial Division was the first to consider the issue in *Veysey* v. *Canada (Commissioner of the Correctional Service)*,[98] where a gay prisoner challenged a refusal to allow him to participate in his prison's 'Private Family Visiting Program' with his male partner. In holding that sexual orientation is an analogous ground under Section 15(1) and that the plaintiff's exclusion from the

[82] See Duplé (1984 Can), 823–4.   [83] See Leopold and King (1985 Can), 184.
[84] See Gibson (1991a Can), 787; Proulx (1988 Can), 594; Jefferson (1985 Can), 83–4; Leopold and King (1985 Can), 182–3.
[85] See Duplé (1984 Can), 820, 824–5; Proulx (1988 Can), 594.
[86] See Leopold and King (1985 Can), 183.   [87] See Duplé (1984 Can), 825.
[88] See Hughes (1985 Can), 82.   [89] See Jefferson (1985 Can), 83, 85.
[90] See Jefferson (1985 Can), 84; Hughes (1985 Can), 82; Bergeron (1980 Can), C/18.
[91] See Leopold and King (1985 Can), 182.
[92] See Sheppard (1989 Can), 226 n. 72; Jefferson (1985 Can), 71, 82–3; Leopold and King (1985 Can), 182; Bruner (1985 Can), 468–90; Duplé (1984 Can), 824.
[93] See Bruner (1985 Can), 459, 482–3; Jefferson (1985 Can), 71, 82, 87–8.
[94] See Bruner (1985 Can), 481–4; Jefferson (1985 Can), 71, 84, 88.
[95] See Leopold and King (1985 Can), 183–4.
[96] See Ryder (1990 Can), 71–2; Girard (1986 Can), 267, 276–7; Leopold and King (1985 Can), 184–5; Bruner (1985 Can), 462–4; Duplé (1984 Can), 824.
[97] Two pre-*Andrews* cases rejected sexual orientation discrimination claims under Section 15(1). See *Andrews* v. *Ontario (Minister of Health)* (1988) 49 DLR (4th) 584 (Ont HC) (*Karen Andrews*) (using the 'similarity of situation' test, later rejected in *Andrews*, to uphold the denial of health care benefits to Karen Andrews' partner Mary Trenholm and Trenholm's children); *Anderson* v. *Luoma* (1986) 50 Rep Fam L (2d) 127 at 141–2 (BCSC) (Section 1 justified any violation of Section 15(1) by a statutory definition of 'step-parent', for purpose of obligation to support children, as including a man vis-à-vis the children of his unmarried female partner but not a woman vis-à-vis the children of her female partner).
[98] (1989), [1990] 1 FC 321 (TD).

programme was not justified under Section 1, the court noted that 'sexual orientation would fit within one of [the] levels of immutability' displayed by the
enumerated grounds, that 'those who have deviated from accepted sexual norms'
'have been victimized and stigmatized throughout history because of prejudice
[bias]', that four of the thirteen federal, provincial and territorial human rights
acts had included sexual orientation,[99] and that the Parliamentary Committee on
Equality Rights had recommended in 1985 that sexual orientation be added to
the Canadian Human Rights Act.[100] The court in *Brown* v. *British Columbia
(Minister of Health)* agreed that 'discrimination based on sexual orientation
contravenes [Section 15(1)]', citing the history of discrimination 'from biblical
times to our own' against 'homosexuals', and the injustice of the failure 'to take
account of individual merit'.[101]

In *R.* v. *Schnare*[102], Crowell J. found 'considerable merit' in the Crown's
submission that 'the Charter . . . does not prohibit discrimination based on "sexual
preference"', which could encompass 'the confirmed rapist or paedophile', but
noted the inclusion of 'sexual orientation' in human rights legislation and acknowledged that there could be situations where 'sexual orientation' is an analogous ground under Section 15(1). However, he refused to find that 'the
accused . . . and others who may be similarly situated' (i.e. persons over 18
charged with violating section 159(1) of the Criminal Code by engaging in anal
intercourse with a person under 18) are 'a discrete and insular minority', or that
there were 'any indicia of discrimination such as stereotyping, historical disadvantage or vulnerability to political and social prejudice'. His conclusion probably stemmed from his prior finding that section 159(1) applies equally to
same-sex and opposite-sex anal intercourse, in spite of the accused's argument
that section 159(1) 'discriminates against homosexuals on the basis of sexual
orientation' because 'its effect is to criminalize a predominantly homosexual
act'.

Veysey was affirmed by the Federal Court of Appeal, without discussing the
Charter issue, on the ground that the term 'common law partner' in the prison's
policy included same-sex partners.[103] The court noted that counsel for the federal
government had conceded that sexual orientation is an analogous ground.[104]
Such a concession has been made in four subsequent cases: *Knodel* v. *British
Columbia (Medical Services Commission)*,[105] *Egan* v. *Canada*,[106] *Haig* v. *Canada*,[107]

---

[99] It is interesting to compare this rather low level of 'consensus' with that apparently required
under the European Convention. See Ch. 5, Part II.B.–D.

[100] (1989), [1990] 1 FC 321 (TD) at 327–9.

[101] (1990) 66 DLR (4th) 444 at 457–9 (BCSC).

[102] (15 Feb. 1990) Kentville K89–2326, K89–2327 at 9–12, 19–22 (NS Prov Ct).

[103] (1990) 109 NR 300 (FCA).

[104] Ibid. at 304. The concession was consistent with a 1986 statement that '[t]he Department of
Justice is of the view that the courts will find that sexual orientation is encompassed by the guarantees in section 15 of the Charter': Department of Justice (Canada) (1986 Can), 13.

[105] [1991] 6 WWR 728 at 743.

[106] (1991), [1992] 1 FC 687 at 700 (TD), aff'd, [1993] 3 FC 401 (CA).

[107] (1992) 94 DLR (4th) 1 at 6–7 (Ont CA).

and *Leshner* v. *Ontario*.[108] In each, the defendant government conceded that sexual orientation is an analogous ground and the court apparently agreed, finding it unnecessary to state any reasons for its acceptance of this proposition. Perhaps the most surprising silence was that of the Ontario Court of Appeal in *Haig*, where it became the first appellate court in Canada to hold that sexual orientation is an analogous ground. Krever J.A. said only that '[c]ourts in Canada have acted on the premise that sexual orientation is an analogous ground', citing the conclusion in *Veysey* (Federal Court Trial Division) and the concessions in *Veysey* (Federal Court of Appeal) and *Knodel*. He then referred to the federal government's concession in *Haig* and said: 'I agree and add that, as a matter of law, the concession is right. No further analysis of this point need be undertaken.'[109]

Krever J.A. did go on to consider whether failure to include 'sexual orientation' in the Canadian Human Rights Act had a 'discriminatory impact' on the plaintiff, applying the arguably redundant third requirement mentioned by McIntyre J. in *Andrews* and discussed above in Part III. He described '[h]omosexual persons' as falling 'within a ground analogous to . . . sex' and having 'historically been the object of discrimination on analogous grounds'. But, under *Turpin*, '[t]he larger context, social, political and legal, must also be considered . . . to find disadvantage that exists apart from and independent of the legal distinction created by the omission of sexual orientation'. This 'social context' includes 'the pain and humiliation undergone by homosexuals by reason of prejudice towards them' and 'the enlightened [post-war] evolution of human rights, social and legislative policy in Canada'. 'The failure to provide an avenue for redress for prejudicial treatment of homosexual members of society, and the possible inference from the omission that such treatment is acceptable, create the effect of discrimination offending s. 15(1).'[110]

Likewise in *Knodel*, as part of a 'discriminatory impact' analysis similar to that in *Haig*, Rowles J. considered criteria one would have thought relevant to the question of whether sexual orientation is an analogous ground. She noted that 'the distinction [denial of medical care benefits to Timothy Knodel's partner Ray Garneau] is not related to the petitioner's merit or capacity', and that, because 'homosexual people as a group are stigmatized in our society', '[t]he petitioner falls within a group that constitutes a "discrete and insular minority".'[111]

In three recent decisions, several judges have departed from the trend of assuming that sexual orientation is an analogous ground and have analyzed the question. In *Egan*, the majority of the Federal Court of Appeal did not do so, merely echoing the conclusion in *Haig*. Robertson J.A. saw the government's concession as correct because it is 'settled law that sexual orientation can be invoked as an analogous ground', even though 'the Supreme Court has yet to

---

[108] (1992) 16 CHRR D/184 at D/200 (Ont HRC).
[109] (1992) 94 DLR (4th) 1 at 6–7 (Ont CA).
[110] Ibid. at 7–10.   [111] [1991] 6 WWR 728 at 757–8.

adjudicate on whether homosexuals constitute a disadvantaged group entitled to Charter protection'.[112] The majority then demonstrated how some Canadian courts have been able to make the concession that sexual orientation is an analogous ground, but still hold that discrimination against a same-sex couple is not a prima facie violation of Section 15(1). They did so by finding, *inter alia*, that the distinction is based not on sexual orientation but on 'spousal status', and that there is insufficient 'discriminatory impact' on same-sex couples because they are excluded along with other 'non-spousal couples' and are not an 'economically disadvantaged group'.[113]

In dissenting and finding a violation of Section 15(1), Linden J.A. gave reasons for concluding that sexual orientation is an analogous ground. He referred to legislation prohibiting sexual orientation discrimination in Canada and the US, and to 'a person's sexual orientation [having] been a basis for discrimination and persecution throughout history'. He also described gay men and lesbian women as 'two historically disadvantaged groups', which are 'legally, economically, socially and politically disadvantaged', 'suffer widespread stereotyping and prejudice', 'endure the constant threat of verbal [and] physical abuse' and harassment, have experienced criminalization of their sexual activity and exclusion from the armed forces, and 'have often felt that they must conceal their lifestyles'.[114]

In *Layland* v. *Ontario (Minister of Consumer and Commercial Relations)*, the first same-sex marriage case under the Charter, the majority of the Ontario Divisional Court made the contradictory suggestions that same-sex couples are not 'independently disadvantaged', and that 'professed homosexuals . . . make up a discrete and insular minority', before citing the conclusion in *Haig* that sexual orientation is an analogous ground.[115] They then avoided finding a prima facie violation of Section 15(1) by citing, *inter alia*, the common law definition of 'marriage' and a same-sex couple's lack of procreative capacity.[116] Greer J., in dissenting and finding a violation, also cited the conclusion in *Haig*, after observing that 'homosexuals have been politically powerless' (like non-citizens) and 'subject to negative treatment and bigotry'.[117]

Finally, in *Vriend* v. *Alberta*, the government of Alberta did not concede that sexual orientation is an analogous ground, but Russell J. effectively found that it is.[118] She asked whether 'homosexuals are a 'discrete and insular minority' which has historically suffered discrimination, prejudice or stereotyping by virtue of a personal characteristic'. She found that 'discrimination against homosexuals is an historical, universal, notorious, and indisputable social reality', that

---

[112] [1993] 3 FC 401 at 461 (CA). See also Mahoney J.A. at 410 ('the weight of authority supports that concession as a matter of law').

[113] For an analysis of the majority's reasoning, see Wintemute (1994 Can), 442–8.

[114] *Egan*, ibid. at 481–6.   [115] (1993) 14 OR (3d) 658 at 664–5 (Ont Div Ct).

[116] For an analysis of the majority's reasoning, see Wintemute (1994 Can), 451–4.

[117] *Layland*, ibid. at 674–5.   [118] (1994) 20 CHRR D/358 at D/364 (Alta QB).

it 'is already the subject of provincial legislation elsewhere in Canada', and that she could take judicial notice of it.[119]

B. Which Criteria Should Be Applied?

Given the relative absence of detailed analysis in the lower courts, and the lack of clarity in the Supreme Court's decisions as to which criteria are relevant, how exactly does one decide whether or not sexual orientation is an analogous ground? Is the answer really so obviously yes, as several lower courts seem to think, that '[n]o further analysis . . . need be undertaken'? At this point, I must make a distinction between the criteria that may be *satisfied* in the case of sexual orientation as a ground of discrimination, or in the case of gay, lesbian, and bisexual persons as a group (defined by a specific manifestation of that ground), and the criteria that I consider *appropriate* for finding that a ground is analogous. A very good case can be made that sexual orientation satisfies virtually all the criteria that were rejected above as inappropriate. It is certainly a non-economic personal characteristic that could be said to be 'generally irrelevant'[120] and 'important to individual or group identity'.[121] And by the end of 1994, sexual orientation had been expressly included in eight of the thirteen human rights acts in Canada.[122] It is easy to document the history of violence[123] and discrimination[124] against gay, lesbian, and bisexual persons in Canada, including discrimination in such areas as: the criminal law relating to sexual activity[125] or 'obscenity';[126]

---

[119] Ibid. at D/363.

[120] See Ryder (1990 Can), 77 ('clearly there is no correlation between an individual's sexual orientation and his or her merit or capacities').

[121] See e.g. Halley (1989 US).   [122] See Appendix II.

[123] Fear of discrimination precludes most gay, lesbian, and bisexual persons from being as open about their personal lives and relationships as heterosexual persons are, and in particular, from expressing affection in public. Fear of violence is probably an even greater deterrent. See Petersen (1991 Can); Ryder (1990 Can), 41–2.

[124] See e.g. Commission des droits de la personne du Québec (1994 Can); Alberta Human Rights Commission (1992 Can).

[125] See Demers (1984 Can). The process of decriminalization begun in 1969 (see note 1), was continued by An Act to amend the Criminal Code and the Canada Evidence Act, SC 1987, c. 24, ss. 1–4 (RSC 1985 (3d Supp), c. 19, ss. 1–4), which abolished the offence of 'gross indecency' (thereby lowering the age of consent for all sexual activity, other than anal intercourse, to 14) and replaced 'buggery' with 'anal intercourse' (for which the age of consent was lowered from 21 to 18, compared with 14 for vaginal and oral intercourse). See s. 159 of the Criminal Code, RSC 1985 (3d Supp), c. 19, s. 3. The 'common bawdy-house' provision (ss. 197 and 210 of the Criminal Code, RSC 1985, c. C–46), which prohibits keeping or being 'found in' a place that is used for prostitution or 'the practice of acts of indecency', has often been used to harass gay bars and bathhouses. See Russell (1982 Can); Ryder (1990 Can), 64 n. 104.

[126] See e.g. Jeffrey Toobin, 'X-Rated' *The New Yorker* (3 Oct. 1994) 70 (discussing impact of *R. v. Butler*, [1992] 1 SCR 452, on gay and lesbian bookstores); *Glad Day Bookshop Inc. v. Canada (Customs & Excise)* (14 July 1992), No. 619/90 (Ont Ct Justice) (finding various books and magazines describing or depicting oral or anal intercourse between men 'degrading' and therefore 'obscene', and upholding their seizure against a Section 2(b) challenge); 'Lesbian porn mag seized by

employment, both civilian[127] and military;[128] housing, education, and other services;[129] parades and official proclamations;[130] rights of couples,[131] including the

[127] Canadian police' *Gay Times* (June 1992) 21; *Glad Day Bookshop Inc.* v. *Canada (Customs & Excise)* (20 March 1987), No. 300/86 (Ont Dist Ct) (invalidating attempt to prevent importation of *The Joy of Gay Sex*); *R.* v. *Popert* (1981), 58 CCC (2d) 505 (Ont CA) (officers of national gay and lesbian newspaper, *The Body Politic*, charged with using the mails to transmit 'obscene, indecent, immoral or scurrilous' matter).

[127] See e.g. *Waterman* v. *National Life Assurance Co. of Canada* (1993) 18 CHRR D/176 (Ont HRC) (lesbian insurance underwriter dismissed); *Re Board of Governors of the University of Saskatchewan and Saskatchewan Human Rights Commission* (1976) 66 DLR (3d) 561 (Sask QB) (gay lecturer denied permission to supervise practice teaching in public schools); *Damien* v. *Ontario Racing Commission* (1975) 11 OR (2d) 489 (HC) (gay horse racing steward dismissed).

[128] Until Feb. 1987, the armed forces had a policy of refusing to enlist or discharging any person known to be gay, lesbian or bisexual. See, e.g. *Gallant* v. *R.* (1978) 91 DLR (3d) 695 (FCTD). See also Bruner (1985 Can), 478–91; Jefferson (1985 Can), 86–8; Leopold and King (1985 Can), 179–80. From Feb. 1987 until Oct. 1992, the ban on enlistments and promotions remained, but the armed forces ceased discharging those who had already enlisted, freezing their careers instead. An end to the discriminatory policy was announced on 27 Oct. 1992. See Ch. 8, Part III. Both the Royal Canadian Mounted Police and the Canadian Security and Intelligence Service had already abandoned similar policies following the settlement of Charter litigation by gay 'Mountie' James Stiles. See *Stiles* v. *Canada (Attorney-General)* (1986) 3 FTR 234; 'Homosexual Mountie gets badge back in out-of-court deal' *The Ottawa Citizen* (19 July 1988) A1.

[129] See e.g. *Gay Alliance*, [1979] 2 SCR 435 (refusal of classified advertisement in newspaper); *Association pour les droits des gai(e)s du Québec* v. *Commission des écoles catholiques de Montréal*, (1979) [1980] Cour Supér. 93, 112 DLR (3d) 230 (refusal to rent school for weekend conference); *Winnipeg Free Press* (14 July 1992) A3 (pub owner's sign says: 'Dogs must be on a leash. Gays not welcome.'); *Perceptions* (6 Nov. 1991) 17 (two lesbian women expelled from café for kissing in public); *GO Info* (June 1990) 19 (lesbian couple not allowed to skate together during 'couples only' skate; two gay men told not to apply for rental accommodation); Girard (1986 Can), 271–2 (two gay men forbidden to dance together in predominantly heterosexual bar; gay education student failed by professor who did not believe gay men should teach).

[130] See *Geller* v. *Reimer* (1994) 21 CHRR D/156 (Sask HRC) (police chief's denial of permit for Regina gay and lesbian pride parade violated rights to freedom of expression and assembly under Saskatchewan Human Rights Code); *Perceptions* (6 March 1991) 10 (Winnipeg's mayor proclaims 'German Shepherd Dog Week' but refuses to proclaim 'Lesbian and Gay Pride Week'). An Ontario Human Rights Commission board of inquiry held (on 6 March 1995) that the mayor of Hamilton's refusal to proclaim 'Lesbian and Gay Pride Week' was discriminatory and ordered him to pay C$5,000 in compensation and to issue a proclamation in 1995 if asked to do so. See *Xtra* (17 March 1995) 1.

[131] See *Canada (A.-G.)* v. *Mossop*, [1993] 1 SCR 554; *Egan*, [1992] 1 FC 687 (TD), aff'd, [1993] 3 FC 401 (CA); *Layland*, (1993) 14 OR (3d) 658 (Ont Div Ct); *Clinton* v. *Ontario Blue Cross* (1993) 18 CHRR D/377 (Ont HRC), rev'd, (1994), 21 CHRR D/342 (Ont Div Ct); *Vogel* v. *Manitoba (A.-G.)* (1992) 90 DLR (4th) 84 (Man QB) (*Vogel II*); *Nielsen* v. *Canada (Human Rights Commission)*, [1992] 2 FC 561 (TD); *Leshner*, (1992) 16 CHRR D/184 (Ont Hum Rts Comm); *Knodel*, [1991] 6 WWR 728; *Veysey*, [1990] 1 FC 321 (TD); *Karen Andrews* (1988) 49 DLR (4th) 584 (Ont HC); *Anderson* (1986), 50 Rep Fam L (2d) 127 (BCSC); *Vogel* v. *Manitoba* (1983) 4 CHRR D/1654 (Man HRC) (*Vogel I*); *Re North and Matheson* (1974) 52 DLR (3d) 280 (Man Co Ct). See also *Re Canada (Treasury Board—Environment Canada) and Lorenzen* (1993) 38 LAC (4th) 29; *Re Canada Post Corporation and P.S.A.C. (Guevremont)* (1993) 34 LAC (4th) 104; *Re Parkwood Hospital and McCormick House and London and District Service Workers' Union* (1992) 24 LAC (4th) 149; *Re Canada (Treasury Board—Indian and Northern Affairs) and Watson* (1990) 11 LAC (4th) 120; *Re Carleton University and CUPE Local 2424* (1988) 35 LAC (3d) 96. See generally Rusk (1993 Can), 174–82; Ryder (1990 Can), 48–59; Bruner (1985 Can), 468–76; Leopold and King (1985 Can), 166–70; Veitch (1976 Can).

right of a partner to immigrate[132]; and rights of existing or prospective parents to obtain custody[133] of, or to adopt,[134] children, or to use alternative means of reproduction.[135] The existence of many prejudices and stereotypes about them is also easily demonstrated.[136] Although their 'identifiability' as a group depends on the degree of 'visibility' this entails,[137] their lack of political power should be evident in view of the very small number of people who are openly gay, lesbian or bisexual, and therefore willing to lobby politicians, and the risk of political backlash faced by any politician opposing sexual orientation discrimination. In the federal Parliament, for example, only two of the 295 members of the House of Commons are openly gay men.[138]

[132] One of the most serious consequences of the non-recognition of same-sex couple relationships occurs in the area of immigration. Unlike the Canadian wife of the British plaintiff in *Andrews*, who met her husband while studying in Oxford and returned to Canada with him (see 27 DLR (4th) 600 at 602 (BCCA)), a gay, lesbian or bisexual Canadian citizen is not permitted to sponsor a non-Canadian same-sex partner for immigration to Canada. Only non-Canadian opposite-sex legal spouses may be sponsored. See Wintemute (1994 Can), 431 n. 4. This could prevent a same-sex couple from living in the same country and cause their relationship to end. See the briefs of the Lesbian and Gay Immigration Task-Force to the federal Minister of Immigration: *Growing Old Together* (May 1992), *Taking the Next Step* (12 Nov. 1993). See also Ryder (1990 Can), 61–2; Bruner (1985 Can), 477–8. Same-sex partners are currently being admitted on 'humanitarian and compassionate' grounds rather than as 'spouses'. See *Xtra* (28 Oct. 1994) 11 (at least 62 same-sex partners admitted since 1993).

[133] See e.g. *Saunders* v. *Saunders* (1989) 20 Rep Fam L (3d) 368 (BC Co Ct) (gay father); *Droit de la famille—31* (1983) 34 Rep Fam L (2d) 127 (Qué Super. Ct) (lesbian mother). Cf. *Johnson* v. *Rochette* (1982) 3 CHRR D/1133 (Qué Super. Ct) (attempt to deny access by lesbian mother to her children was sexual orientation discrimination contrary to human rights act).

[134] Some provincial legislation expressly permits only one adult person or a married opposite-sex couple to adopt, but not two unmarried persons. See e.g. British Columbia's Adoption Act, R.S.B.C. 1979, c. 4, s. 3(1) ('[a]n adult person, or an adult husband and his wife together, may apply to adopt a child'). Under s. 66(1) of Manitoba's Child and Family Services Act, SM 1985–86, c. 8, an opposite-sex couple (married or 'cohabiting as spouses') or a single adult may adopt. Article 546 of the Code Civil du Québec, S.Q. 1991, c. 64 provides that '[a]ny person of full age may, alone or jointly with another person, adopt a child'.

[135] See Coffey (1986 Can); *Anderson* (1986) 50 Rep Fam L (2d) 127 (BCSC) (female–female couple had two children by donor insemination).

[136] See Ryder (1990 Can), 67–9; Ruse (1988 Other), 236–65; Bruner (1985 Can), 459, 481–4; Jefferson (1985 Can), 71, 82, 84, 87–8; Miller (1984 US), 821–4. See also *Maclean's* (14 March 1988) 13 (Svend Robinson's coming out as a gay MP caused Saskatchewan premier Grant Devine to compare 'homosexuals with bank robbers' and vandals to throw rocks through the window of his constituency office). From 1952 to 1977, the federal Immigration Act prohibited non-Canadian 'homosexuals' from entering Canada because of the 'security risk' they posed. See Girard (1987 Can); Green (1987 Can).

[137] See Leopold and King (1985 Can), 183–4 (argument against including sexual orientation in Alberta's human rights act because it is not 'publicly practiced' like religion); Duplé (1984 Can), 824–5. In some neighbourhoods, the gay, lesbian, and bisexual community becomes 'visible' through its cafés, bars, restaurants, bookstores and community centres. And openly gay, lesbian or bisexual persons, a minority of a minority, may make themselves 'visible' through their conduct, statements (e.g. on job applications), dress, etc. A 'visibility' requirement creates a Catch 22 for members of 'invisible' minorities. They are forced to hide, and remain 'invisible', to avoid discrimination, but will not receive legal protection unless they make themselves 'visible' and expose themselves to the risk of discrimination.

[138] See 'Svend Robinson: An MP who happens to be gay' *Saturday Night* (May 1989) 33. See also note 96. Any political influence gay, lesbian, and bisexual persons may have is probably limited to a few neighbourhoods in the centres of large cities.

As for economic and social disadvantage, the stigma that still attaches to being a gay, lesbian or bisexual person would seem to constitute a social disadvantage, which causes the majority of such persons to remain 'in the closet', especially in the workplace, and to refrain from public displays of affection with a same-sex partner. As for economic disadvantage, although the sub-minority of openly gay, lesbian, and bisexual persons may face discrimination, limited job opportunities, and therefore economic disadvantage, it is not clear whether gay, lesbian, and bisexual persons as a whole (including the 'closeted' majority of such persons) are 'economically advantaged' or 'disadvantaged' compared with the heterosexual majority. A 1991 US survey purported to find that average household incomes were US$51,325 for gay men and US$45,927 for lesbian women, compared with a national average of US$36,520, and that sixty per cent of 'homosexuals' have college degrees, compared with a national average of twenty per cent.[139] A group in Saskatchewan cited surveys of this kind in arguing against legislation prohibiting sexual orientation discrimination.[140] While the accuracy of these figures is doubtful,[141] what is far more doubtful is the appropriateness of 'economic disadvantage' as a criterion. The same situation of 'economic advantage' might be true of Jews or recent immigrants from Hong Kong, yet would surely not preclude their being protected by Section 15(1).[142]

The only criterion that sexual orientation clearly does not satisfy is one that was not discussed above and is almost certainly inappropriate, i.e. whether or not the drafters of the Charter intended it to be implicitly included in Section 15(1) as an unenumerated ground. Although it is clear that the inclusion of sexual orientation was urged by both gay and lesbian groups and women's groups,[143] the fact that it did not become an enumerated ground does not mean that it is forever excluded. As one writer has argued, such a theory would punish unsuccessful lobbying and relies on an imputed intention of the drafters that is difficult to discern.[144] And in the absence of an express intention to exclude, one should assume that the drafters left the decision to the courts under the

---

[139] See 'More Companies Lure Gay Consumers' Dollars' *International Herald Tribune* (4 Mar. 1992) 11 (survey by Overlooked Opinions).

[140] See *Perceptions* (28 Oct. 1992) 9. See also Duncan (1994 US), 407–9.

[141] Other studies by Lee Badgett of the University of Maryland and by Yankelovich Partners Inc. have found that the average annual incomes of gay men and lesbian women, respectively, are the same as, or slighter lower than, those of heterosexual men and heterosexual women: see *Perceptions* (26 Oct. 1994) 29. See Badgett (1995 US).

[142] See Hogg (1992 Can), 1175.

[143] See Bayefsky and Eberts (1985 Can), 634, 639–41; Jefferson (1985 Can), 75–6. The inclusion of marital status and political belief was also recommended. On 29 Jan. 1981, a parliamentary committee rejected (by 22–2) an amendment adding sexual orientation, proposed by Svend Robinson MP. See Canada (1981 Can), at 48:20–21, 48:31–34. Jean Chrétien, then Minister of Justice, said at 48:33: 'We have explained that there are other grounds of discrimination that will be defined by the courts. We wanted to have an enumeration of grounds and we do not think it should be a list that can go on forever.'

[144] See Jefferson (1985 Can), 73–4.

open-ended language of Section 15(1).[145] This approach would seem to be consistent with the Supreme Court's decision in the *Reference re s. 94(2) of the Motor Vehicle Act, R.S.B.C. 1979*,[146] in which it gave 'minimal weight' to evidence of legislative intent ('a fact which is nearly impossible of proof'), so that Charter rights do not 'become frozen in time to the moment of adoption with little or no possibility of . . . adjustment to changing societal needs'. In *Andrews*, any intent of the drafters with respect to citizenship was not considered.

It is thus relatively easy to show that sexual orientation satisifies certain popular criteria (e.g. gay, lesbian, and bisexual persons can easily be characterized as a 'disadvantaged group').[147] However, because I view these criteria as inappropriate, I prefer to devote Chapter 7 to an examination of whether sexual orientation is either an 'immutable status' or a 'fundamental choice', the two criteria selected above as appropriate for identifying analogous Section 15(1) grounds. I have several reasons for what may appear to be an abrupt departure from the format adopted in Chapters 2 to 5: examining and criticizing existing criteria used by the US Supreme Court and the European Court of Human Rights, and by gay, lesbian, and bisexual plaintiffs, rather than proposing new criteria.

First, the Section 15(1) jurisprudence of the Canadian Supreme Court is sufficiently young (dating from 1989), and the criteria for identifying analogous grounds are sufficiently fluid and uncertain, that it should still be possible to propose new criteria.

Second, an analysis limited to the use of existing criteria by gay, lesbian, and bisexual plaintiffs under the Charter would not be particularly satisfying. Because courts frequently accept a government's concession that sexual orientation is an analogous ground, they have usually not examined the arguments in favour of this conclusion, whether based on the Supreme Court's existing criteria or any other criteria. (In view of the Supreme Court's apparent preference for 'membership of a disadvantaged group' as the main requirement for Section 15(1) protection, any more explicit arguments advanced in future cases may merely seek to demonstrate that gay, lesbian, and bisexual persons are such a group.) And, as seen above, it is often the requirement of 'discriminatory impact', and not that of an analogous ground, which has proved a stumbling block for plaintiffs.

Third, plaintiffs may have to consider making 'immutable status' or 'fundamental choice' arguments in future cases. In cases to date, courts have not had to consider the connection between being gay, lesbian or bisexual and (to some) morally controversial same-sex sexual activity. (The absence of any blanket

---

[145] See ibid. Cf. Hawkins (1990 Can), 315 (Charter should be given 'the same meaning which it was generally understood to have by the informed public at the time of its ratification').

[146] [1985] 2 SCR 486 at 507–9 (the *Motor Vehicle Reference*).

[147] See *Egan*, [1993] 3 FC 401 at 429, 433, 441 (CA) (Linden J.A., dissenting); Ryder (1990 Can), 76–7.

criminal prohibition of sexual activity between men or between women in Canada since 1969 may explain why this issue is not raised, unlike in the US and in Council of Europe countries, where such prohibitions persist.) Yet, it must be implicit in a finding that sexual orientation is an analogous ground under Section 15(1) and that the Charter prohibits some kinds of sexual orientation discrimination (against gay, lesbian or bisexual individuals in employment, or against same-sex couples), that the Charter would prohibit the crudest form of sexual orientation discrimination (criminalization of same-sex sexual activity) if Parliament were to re-enact such a prohibition. But what principle would explain the Charter's protection in such a case? Would it be enough that gay, lesbian, and bisexual persons are a 'disadvantaged group'? Or would an 'immutable status' or 'fundamental choice' argument be necessary? It is the connection between sexual orientation and sexual activity that makes the question of whether sexual orientation is an analogous ground more difficult than it appears, and has led to the differing responses to criminalization of the US Supreme Court in *Hardwick*, the European Court in *Dudgeon*, and the UN Human Rights Committee in *Toonen*.

This change in format means that I will mainly be considering the merits of 'immutable status' and 'fundamental choice' arguments, rather than their actual use by plaintiffs or acceptance by courts, and will do so in somewhat greater detail than was possible in previous chapters. I must acknowledge the speculative nature of this discussion, in that it assumes that the Supreme Court might at some stage adopt 'immutable statuses' or 'fundamental choices' as criteria for identifying analogous grounds. But the novelty and fluidity of Section 15(1) doctrine, mentioned above, and the absence of any constraining Supreme Court precedent on sexual orientation discrimination under the Charter, make such a discussion possible.

I will also reverse the order in which 'immutable status' and 'fundamental choice' arguments are discussed. Fundamental choice arguments were the appropriate starting point under the US Constitution, because of the importance of challenges to generally applicable oral or anal intercourse laws and the extensive 'right of privacy' case law, and under the European Convention, because of the textual advantage of Article 8 over Article 14. Under the Canadian Charter, an immutable status argument is the more attractive starting point. This is because, as seen above, Section 15(1) is to be preferred to Section 7, and because eight of the nine enumerated grounds in Section 15(1) are arguably immutable statuses.

Finally, I would point out that, although the evaluations of immutable status and fundamental choice arguments in Chapter 7, and of a sex discrimination argument in Chapter 8, are conducted in the context of the Canadian Charter, they are intended to be of general interest and potentially of general application (i.e. to the US Constitution and the European Convention as well).

7

The Canadian Charter of Rights and Freedoms: Is Sexual Orientation an Immutable Status or a Fundamental Choice?

I. IS SEXUAL ORIENTATION AN IMMUTABLE STATUS?

To answer this question, one must attempt to determine to what degree sexual orientation could be said to be 'immutable', and decide whether this degree of immutability is sufficient. Having done so, one must then ask a second question: does it matter? Would recognition of sexual orientation as an 'immutable status' provide an effective solution to the problem of public sector discrimination against gay, lesbian, and bisexual persons and same-sex emotional–sexual conduct?

In considering whether sexual orientation is immutable, one should look at the direction of a person's emotional–sexual attraction, because the direction of their conduct is almost certainly chosen. Is the direction of a person's attraction something they cannot change, or is it something they can choose? It is certainly true that many gay men and lesbian women sincerely believe that the direction of their attraction is something they did not choose and cannot change, which makes same-sex emotional–sexual conduct the only viable choice for them. Their own subjective belief in the immutability of their own sexual orientation (as direction of attraction) will often make an immutable status argument seem to them the most appealing response to sexual orientation discrimination. (Indeed, during the first year of my doctoral studies, I was convinced that an immutable status argument was 'the answer', that the connection between attraction and conduct was irrelevant, and that gay men and lesbian women who see their sexual orientation as a choice, as well as all bisexual persons, could be 'swept under the carpet'.)

A court could merely accept the sincerity of this belief of many gay men and lesbian women, or could find it credible in view of the overwhelming social pressure on them to change.[1] However, there is not yet any way for them to prove the existence and immutability of the direction of their attraction through scientific measurement or observation (e.g. an x-ray, blood test, brain scan or chromosome count), in the way that a person's sex, height, weight or HIV antibody status might be established. A number of recent, highly publicized

[1] See Mohr (1988 US), 39–40.

scientific studies have suggested that:[2] (1) certain structures found in the brains of gay men may differ in size from those found in heterosexual men;[3] (2) there may be a genetic component to sexual orientation because 52% of the identical twin brothers of selected gay or bisexual men and 48% of the identical twin sisters of selected lesbian or bisexual women were also gay, lesbian, or bisexual;[4] (3) ' "one form of male homosexuality [may be] . . . transmitted through the maternal side and [may be] genetically linked to chromosomal region Xq28" ' because 64% of selected pairs of gay brothers, 'shared an identifiable genetic sequence on the X chromosome';[5] (4) the cognitive abilities (spatial and verbal) of gay men may be different from those of heterosexual men and those of heterosexual women;[6] and (5) gay men and lesbian women may be more likely to be left-handed.[7] While these studies are certainly interesting, scientists are still a very long way from conclusively proving that sexual orientation (as direction of attraction) has a 'cause' or combination of 'causes' that precludes individual choice and renders it an 'immutable status'.

Nor do all gay men or all lesbian women share this belief. Research does suggest that it is extremely difficult to change the direction of attraction of gay men.[8] But there are gay men who claim that, even though the direction of their attraction may initially have been unchosen, they have succeeded in changing it from same-sex to heterosexual or bisexual. In addition, there are lesbian women who say that they freely and rationally chose the direction of their attraction. For some women, choosing couple relationships with other women may be a rational response to male domination of many opposite-sex couple relationships and thus a 'political choice'.[9] Perceiving female–female couple relationships as a choice would certainly be easier for bisexual women, and it has been suggested that women may be more likely than men to have a bisexual sexual orientation (as direction of attraction).[10] The possibility of choice for lesbian and bisexual women has led Didi Herman to question the use of an immutable status argument under Section 15(1).[11]

---

[2] For a thorough analysis of these studies, see Halley (1994 US), 529–46. See also Levay (1993 Other), 105–30 (and bibliography at 144–7); Green (1992 Other), 63–87; Ruse (1988 Other).

[3] See Levay (1991 Other), 1036 ('the results do not allow one to decide if the size of [the cell group] in an individual is the cause or consequence of that individual's sexual orientation'); Allen and Gorski (1992 Other).

[4] See Bailey and Pillard (1991 Other); Bailey, Pillard, et al. (1993 Other).

[5] See Halley (1994 US), 532, citing Hamer, et al. (1993 Other). See also Hamer and Copeland (1994 Other).

[6] See McCormick and Witelson (1991 Other).

[7] See McCormick, Witelson, and Kingstone (1990 Other).

[8] See Green (1992 Other), 77–83; Green (1988 Other), 555–67.

[9] See e.g. Leopold and King (1985 Can), 162–4; Hughes (1985 Can), 47–9; Crane (1982 Eur), 4.

[10] See Ruse (1988 Other), 172–3.

[11] See Herman (1990 Can), 810–15 (discussing inconsistencies between immutability and both feminist theory and the reality of lesbianism). For a sceptical view of immutability, see also Stychin (1995 Can).

Thus, it would appear that sexual orientation (as direction of attraction) may be immutable (i.e. impossible to change) for many (perhaps even for most) persons but not for all, and that this immutability cannot be proven conclusively even in those cases where it is said to exist. Is this degree of immutability sufficient under Section 15(1)? Several commentators have concluded that it is,[12] while at least one has argued that the possibility of change, even if limited to 'highly motivated' individuals, precludes immutability.[13] Courts have had little to say on this question, either because they have accepted a concession that sexual orientation is an analogous ground, or because they have found it sufficient that gay, lesbian, and bisexual persons are a 'disadvantaged group'.[14] In *Veysey*, Dubé J. observed that race, national or ethnic origin, colour, and age are immutable, that religion may be changed 'with some difficulty', and that sex or a mental or physical disability may be changed with 'even greater difficulty'.[15] He concluded that 'sexual orientation would fit within one of these levels of immutability'.[16]

Immutability has received greater consideration in the context of claims to refugee status by non-Canadian gay, lesbian, and bisexual persons, which require the interpretation of the phrase 'fear of persecution for reasons of ... membership in a particular social group' in the Immigration Act.[17] In *Jorge Alberto Inaudi*, the Immigration and Refugee Board ruled that a gay man who had been raped by police in Argentina was a member of such a group. Citing *Veysey*, Ethel Teitelbaum found that '[i]f ... homosexuality is an immutable characteristic, that alone ... suffices to place homosexuals in a particular social group'.[18] This view has since received the support of an *obiter* statement by Justice La Forest in the Supreme Court. In *Canada (Attorney-General)* v. *Ward*, he defined a 'particular social group' as including the category of 'groups defined by an innate or unchangeable characteristic', which 'would embrace individuals

---

[12] See Leopold and King (1985 Can), 182–3 (difficult to change); Jefferson (1985 Can), 83 (unlikely that anyone would choose 'homosexuality'); Proulx (1988 Can), 594.

[13] See Duplé (1984 Can), 824–5.

[14] In *Egan*, [1993] 3 FC 401 at 427–30 (CA), Linden J.A., in dissent, held that sexual orientation is an analogous ground without mentioning immutability.

[15] See *Veysey* [1990] 1 FC 321 at 329 (TD).

[16] Ibid. Cf. *Re Board of Governors of University of Saskatchewan*, (1976) 66 DLR (3d) 561 at 566 (Sask QB) ('if a homosexual has certain characteristics related to his condition I am unable to say that they are "immutable"'); *Knodel* [1991] 6 WWR 728 at 736 (citing psychiatrist's testimony that 'same sex affectionate and erotic feelings' have a 'biological' explanation and 'are not a deliberate choice', but not discussing immutability in Section 15(1) analysis).

[17] RSC 1985, c. I-2, s. 2(1) (definition of 'Convention refugee').

[18] (9 Apr. 1992), No. T91–04459, at 5–6. She also found that 'even if homosexuality were a voluntary condition, it is one so fundamental to a person's identity that a claimant ought not to be compelled to change it'. On Canadian and US refugee law and sexual orientation, see Grider (1994 US), Vagelos (1994 Can), Goldberg (1993 US). See also *Vraciu* v. *Secretary of State for the Home Department* (21 Nov. 1994), Appeal No. HX/70517/94 (11559) at p. 15 (UK Imm App Trib) ('[w]e find ... that in Romania homosexuals are a particular social group within the meaning of the Refugee Convention').

fearing persecution on such bases as gender, linguistic background and sexual orientation'.[19]

While I believe that 'immutability' is a useful criterion for identifying Section 15(1) grounds of discrimination (and grounds on which persecution may be based), I would argue that difficulty of change is not sufficient and that immutability must mean impossibility of change (combined with absence of initial choice) so as to place a manageable limit on the number of 'immutable statuses'. Consequently, while sex and certain disabilities are immutable (because chromosomal sex can only be disguised, not changed, and a disability that can be completely removed usually will be), religion is not.[20] Likewise, the facts that some persons believe they can choose to change their sexual orientation (as direction of attraction), and that those who do not believe they can change theirs cannot conclusively prove either its existence or the impossibility of changing it, mean that sexual orientation cannot be viewed as an 'immutable status' for the purposes of Section 15(1).[21]

Assuming that it were impossible for anyone to change their sexual orientation (as direction of attraction), and that this could be proved, would recognition as an 'immutable status' raise a prima facie prohibition against most sexual orientation discrimination? It is quite possible that such recognition would provide inadequate protection from much discrimination against gay, lesbian, and bisexual persons. This is because most such discrimination is based on sexual orientation (as direction of conduct), e.g. criminal laws dealing with private sexual activity or public displays of affection,[22] or civil laws that deny rights to same-sex couples. Even where discrimination purports to be based on sexual orientation (as direction of attraction), such as discrimination in public employment (including the armed forces) or child custody decisions, the basis for the discrimination can easily be recast as the presumed direction of the person's past or future conduct, assuming that it will be consistent with the stated or presumed direction of the person's attraction. Thus, an employer could argue that a person is being dismissed not because the employer believes (as a result of their statements, conduct or appearance) that they *are* gay or lesbian (i.e. the direction of

---

[19] [1993] 2 SCR 689 at 739.

[20] See Ryder (1990 Can), 80; Mohr (1988 US), 189–91; Duplé (1984 Can), 820.

[21] Of course, this conclusion assumes that 'immutability' is defined strictly as 'impossibility'. If 'difficulty of change' were sufficient, the conclusion would be different.

[22] S. 173(1) of the Criminal Code, RSC 1985 (3d Supp), c. 19, s. 7, prohibits 'indecent acts' in public places and could be used to prosecute two men or two women for kissing, hugging or holding hands in public. In Toronto in 1976, two gay men were arrested for committing an 'indecent act' in a public place after kissing at the corner of Yonge and Bloor. They were found guilty and fined $50. See Coalition for Lesbian and Gay Rights in Ontario, *Discrimination Against Lesbians and Gay Men: A Brief to the Members of the Ontario Legislature* (1986), 24. See also *Priape Enrg.* v. *Canada (Deputy-Minister of National Revenue)*, [1980] Cour Supér. 86 at 88–9 ('a young man and woman lying on the grass in a sunny city park ... kissing and embracing ... will draw hardly a passing glance [;] [t]he same conduct ... by two men together would almost certainly lead to a disturbance and to the police being called').

178   *Canadian Charter of Rights and Freedoms*

their attraction is same-sex), but because they are presumed to engage in private
same-sex sexual activity, or because they have engaged in some public aspect
of same-sex emotional–sexual conduct (e.g. they have been observed publicly
expressing affection for a person of the same sex or bringing a person of the
same sex to a social event,[23] or they have spoken publicly about their same-sex
partner).[24] An excellent example of this distinction is the US case of *Shahar* v.
Bowers, where an offer of employment was withdrawn from a woman who
planned to marry another woman. The court accepted the defendant's argument
that 'he [did] not discriminate against homosexuals as a general class' and that
his action was 'not based on mere sexual orientation, but on sexual orientation
plus conduct viewed . . . as inconsistent with state law'.[25]

If such an argument were successful, the protection provided by recognizing
sexual orientation (as direction of attraction) as an 'immutable status' would
apply in extremely narrow circumstances. It would effectively cover only gay,
lesbian, and bisexual persons who do not act on their attraction, and thus have
always been celibate or engaged only in opposite-sex sexual activity (and intend
to continue to do so). Even if they could avoid discrimination by asserting (often
falsely) that they have not engaged in, and do not intend to engage in, any
private same-sex sexual activity (which assertion would be difficult to disprove),
they could not engage in any public same-sex emotional–sexual conduct, and
might not even be able to make any public statements related to such conduct
(unless the statements were protected by Section 2(b) of the Charter). This low
level of protection, which is the result of protecting an immutable status but not
related conduct (as in *Watkins* v. *US Army*), is grossly inadequate (although, as
was seen in Chapter 3, it is probably the best that can currently be provided
under the US Constitution, in view of *Hardwick*).[26]

Clearly, then treating sexual orientation as an immutable status could only
provide effective protection if the status (a person's direction of attraction) also
includes the direction of conduct to which the status makes them attracted. But
the direction of a person's conduct, regardless of their direction of attraction, is
most definitely voluntary and chosen.[27] It certainly is true that for heterosexual
persons and for gay men and lesbian women, as opposed to bisexual persons, the
choice may seem 'constrained' and therefore 'unfair', i.e. the alternatives are

[23] See *Krolikowski* v. *AGFA Compugraphic*, [1991] *Lesbian/Gay Law Notes* 10 (sexual orientation discrimination complaint filed in Massachusetts where employee was laid off after he actively
participated in an AIDS fund-raising event, brought a male date to a company dinner, and began to
wear a stud earring).
[24] Some heterosexual persons assert that gay men and lesbian women who engage in such public
conduct or make such public statements are 'flaunting' their sexual orientation. They do not realize
that they are constantly (if unconsciously) 'flaunting' their heterosexual sexual orientation by engaging in similar public conduct or making similar public statements.
[25] 836 F Supp 859 at 867–8 (ND Ga 1993).   [26] See Ch. 3, Part I.C. and D.
[27] See Halley (1994 US), 520 (immutability 'fails to address the anti-gay argument that homosexuality, whether it is mutable or not, is expressed through elected behavior, ranging from same-
sex erotic acts to practices of self-identification'). See also Ch. 3, notes 57–58 and accompanying
text.

celibacy, or conduct of which they may feel physically incapable or to which any attraction they may feel is minimal or non-existent.[28] However, the choice of celibacy versus opposite-sex conduct versus same-sex conduct versus both kinds of conduct is nonetheless a choice.[29] And for bisexual persons, the choice is not constrained.[30] As the Fifth Circuit observed in *Baker* v. *Wade*, '[t]hough the conduct be the desire of the bisexually or homosexually inclined, there is no necessity that they engage in it. The [same-sex oral or anal intercourse law] affects only those who *choose* to act in the manner proscribed'.[31]

Can protection of an immutable status include chosen conduct? I would suggest that it cannot, because the protection of the status is premised on the absence of choice in possessing the status, which is generally not true of conduct.[32] However, conduct that is closely related to an immutable status (e.g. non-religious cultural practices, such as choice of clothing, food, music, name, language or housing,[33] in the case of race, national or ethnic origin and colour; using contraception, continuing a pregnancy or having an abortion, in the case of sex; and using an aid, in the case of a mental or physical disability)[34] may be protected in a number of ways.[35] First, a direct distinction on the basis of many of these kinds of conduct (e.g. no person wearing their hair in African-style braids, or using a wheelchair or a guide dog, may enter a public building) would appear so irrational that it would be hard to believe that the exclusion of persons with an immutable status likely to be engaging in the conduct (i.e. persons of African origin or disabled persons) was not intentional. Second, regardless of any intention to exclude, direct distinctions of the kind made in the previous examples would certainly have a grossly unequal effect on persons of African origin or disabled persons, thereby creating an indirect distinction on the basis of race or physical disability. Third, the conduct in question may itself constitute a fundamental choice. I would argue that this is true of using an aid to alleviate a disability,[36] using contraception, continuing a pregnancy or having an abortion.

[28] Cf. *Hardwick*, 478 US 1986 at 202 n. 2 (1986) (Blackmun J., dissenting) ('[a]n individual's ability to make . . . "decisions concerning sexual relations" . . . is rendered empty indeed if he or she is given no real choice but a life without physical intimacy').

[29] See Ruse (1988 Other), 170–75, for a discussion of the ultimately voluntary nature of emotional–sexual conduct. See also Halley (1989 US), 915, 932–63 (discussing the mutability of sexual identity and openness about it, as opposed to sexual attraction); *State* v. *Walsh*, 713 SW 2d 508 at 510 (Mo 1986) ('[i]t cannot be said in the usual circumstance that refraining from certain conduct is beyond control').

[30] See Halley (1994 US), 526–8 (observing, at 528, that immutability 'does not explain why bisexuals—by hypothesis capable of satisfactory [opposite-sex] sexual encounters . . . — should not be encouraged or forced to do so').

[31] 774 F 2d 1285 at 1287 (5th Cir 1985) (emphasis added).

[32] Some immutable statuses (e.g. epilepsy) may give rise to completely involuntary 'conduct' (e.g. epileptic seizures).

[33] E.g. gypsy caravans in Britain.   [34] Cf. text accompanying Ch. 3, note 55.

[35] See Black (1979 Can), 652 (discussing possibility of circumventing human rights legislation by prohibiting guide dogs or white canes or imposing dress requirements).

[36] See e.g. Manitoba Human Rights Code, SM 1987–88, c. 45, s. 9(2)(1)(d) (prohibiting discrimination based on 'physical or mental disability or related characteristics or circumstances, including reliance on a dog guide . . . a wheelchair, or any other remedial . . . device').

If an immutable status is the reason for desiring to engage in a particular kind of conduct, it may be seen as compelling the conduct and therefore strengthening the argument that the conduct is a fundamental choice (e.g. a mental or physical disability compels the use of an aid to alleviate the disability). If a fundamental choice (e.g. of religion) is the reason for desiring to engage in a particular kind of conduct that is compelled by the choice (e.g. a particular religious practice, such as sabbath observance), the conduct may be seen as included within the fundamental choice, even though it might not be considered a fundamental choice on its own if a different reason were given for desiring to engage in it (e.g. an employee seeks an exemption from Saturday work to play golf).

Applying this analysis to sexual orientation, it is clear that treating sexual orientation (as direction of attraction) as an immutable status cannot directly protect sexual orientation (as direction of conduct). It might strengthen an argument that sexual orientation (as direction of conduct) is a fundamental choice by establishing a protected reason that compels the conduct.[37] However, the element of compulsion (with respect to same-sex emotional–sexual conduct) would only be present in the case of gay men and lesbian women, and not in the case of bisexual or heterosexual persons.[38] Permitting the protection of same-sex emotional–sexual conduct to vary depending on one's reason for wishing to engage in it (however that might be determined) would seem highly undesirable.[39] If sexual orientation (as direction of conduct) were not a fundamental choice and sexual orientation (as direction of attraction) were an immutable status, restrictions on a particular direction of conduct (e.g. same-sex) would have an unequal effect on persons whose direction of attraction made them especially interested in such conduct (e.g. gay, lesbian, and bisexual persons).[40] However, there is a risk that distinctions indirectly creating unequal effects might be more easily upheld under Section 1, than distinctions directly based on an enumerated or analogous ground.[41]

[37] See Duplé (1984 Can), 825 ('l'homosexualité est un choix dicté par la sexualité').

[38] Cf. Goldstein (1988 US), 1077 n. 29 (category of 'persons with an exclusive, lifelong [same-sex] sexual preference' not the same as that of persons engaging in same-sex sexual activity).

[39] But see Murphy (1993 US), 694, 697–8 (proposing 'a policy of tolerance and containment' under which same-sex oral or anal intercourse would be prohibited except among 'true homosexuals'). Cf. *R.* v. *Edwards Books & Art Ltd.*, [1986] 2 SCR 713 at 779–81 (state-conducted inquiries into religious beliefs undesirable).

[40] Striking down a restriction on this basis (disproportionate impact on a group versus exclusive impact on every individual in the group) would be for the benefit of all (including bisexual and heterosexual persons). See e.g. *R.* v. *Hayden* (1983), 3 DLR (4th) 361 (Man CA) (striking down, under the Canadian Bill of Rights, the offence of being found intoxicated on an Indian reserve because of disproportionate impact on aboriginal persons). See also *Anglin* v. *City of Minneapolis*, [1992] *Lesbian/Gay Law Notes* 86 (denial of health coverage to lesbian employee's female partner was 'affectional orientation' discrimination because of 'disparate impact on lesbians').

[41] See Black (1986 Can), 121, 151–2; Hughes (1985 Can), 83; *Edwards Books*, [1986] 2 SCR 713 at 758–9. Compare the decisions in *R.* v. *Big M Drug Mart Ltd.*, [1985] 1 SCR 295 (Sunday trading law with discriminatory purpose struck down) and *Edwards Books* (similar law with indirectly discriminatory effect upheld). See also *Symes* v. *Canada*, [1993] 4 SCR 695 (upholding non-deductibility of child care expenses as business expenses because disproportionate effect on women not established).

In the US, some judges have used an 'immutable attraction versus chosen conduct' distinction to try to provide constitutional protection against sexual orientation discrimination in public employment in the face of oral or anal intercourse laws and *Hardwick*. In Canada, there is no oral or anal intercourse law and no *Hardwick* problem, and most litigated cases of sexual orientation discrimination have involved denials of benefits to same-sex partners. However, some courts seem to have used an implicit 'immutable attraction versus chosen conduct' distinction[42] to limit protection against sexual orientation discrimination to gay, lesbian, and bisexual *individuals* (with regard to dismissals or refusals to hire or promote, or denial of a benefit to an individual), and avoid extending it to same-sex *couples* (with regard to benefits provided to an individual's partner, in connection with the individual's employment or otherwise, or with regard to the right to marry).

An example of this kind of 'immutable attraction versus chosen conduct' distinction is *Egan* v. *Canada*, in which pensioner James Egan is seeking a 'spouse's allowance' for John Nesbit, his partner since 1948. Under the federal Old Age Security Act, such an allowance is payable to the 'spouse' of a pensioner aged 65 and over, if the 'spouse' is aged 60 to 64 (and certain other requirements are met). Egan and Nesbit argue that the Act's definition of 'spouse' as including a cohabiting 'person of the opposite sex' (if the 'spouse' and the pensioner 'have publicly represented themselves as husband and wife') discriminates against them on the ground of their sexual orientation, contrary to Section 15(1). The trial judge, Martin J., conceded that 'a woman cohabiting with Egan . . . would have been eligible for the spouse's allowance' and that sexual orientation is an analogous ground.[43] But, he argued, 'the parties to a [same-sex] relationship cannot expect to share the benefits accorded to those in spousal relationships, not because of their sexual orientation, but because their relationship is not a spousal one'. The plaintiffs were treated the same as other 'non-spousal couples' such as 'brother and brother, . . . two friends, or parent and child'. He thus concluded that 'the plaintiffs . . . do not benefit because of their non-spousal status rather than because of their sexual orientation'.[44] In reaching this conclusion, which was adopted by the majority of the Federal Court of Appeal,[45] Martin J. lumped the plaintiffs' relationship with relationships that are clearly not 'couple relationships' (i.e. have no sexual aspect), and failed to recognize that the only difference between their relationship and that of an unmarried opposite-sex couple is their individual sexual orientations (as direction of conduct), or the sexual orientation of their relationship.

---

[42] Peter Hogg's interpretation of Section 15(1) as confined to 'immutable personal characteristics' would support this distinction: see Hogg (1992 Can), 1168 ('Section 15 prohibits laws that distinguish between people on the basis of their inherent attributes as opposed to their behaviour').

[43] (1991), [1992] 1 FC 687 at 695 (TD).

[44] Ibid. at 695. See McEvoy (1994 Can), 74 (Egan-Nesbit relationship 'not a brother-brother relationship').

[45] [1993] 3 FC 401 at 413, 486.

Martin J.'s reasoning in *Egan* was applied in *Vogel* v. *Manitoba* (*A-G*) (*Vogel II*), in which Chris Vogel, a government employee, sought various dental, health, and pension benefits for Richard North, his partner of twenty years.[46] He argued that the denial of these benefits (which were provided to 'common law spouses') violated the Manitoba Human Rights Code's statutory prohibition of sexual orientation discrimination in employment. Citing *Egan*, Hirschfield J. found no such discrimination, holding that, absent a 'clear and unambiguous' statement of legislative intent, '[a] common law relationship does not include a homosexual relationship and therefore does not give to one homosexual partner the status of spouse'.[47] It was not clear whether his conclusion rested on an 'immutable attraction versus chosen conduct' distinction, or a rigid definition of 'common law spouse', in view of his statement that: '[t]he sexual orientation of the complainants is a matter of their individual preference or life-style. The fact that they choose to live together in what they call a married or spousal relationship does not in my opinion give to them the status of spouses'. But he also cited the board of adjudication's reasoning, which did clearly make such a distinction:

there has not been discrimination based on sexual orientation. Benefits are provided based upon whether employees are married as defined in the various programs . . . The sexual orientation of the employee is irrelevant. A person may very well be married to a person of the opposite sex and yet be homosexual . . . Similarly, a person may be heterosexual and yet receive no benefit . . . because he or she is [not] married . . . as contemplated in the plans.[48]

The board might have extended its analogy and asserted that a heterosexual employee with a same-sex partner would receive the same treatment,[49] the distinction being based not on their 'immutable attraction' (being heterosexual) but on their 'chosen conduct' (choosing a same-sex partner who, by definition, cannot be a 'spouse').

Similar reasoning can be seen in *Layland*, where the majority said: 'The law

---

[46] (1992) 90 DLR (4th) 84 (Man QB). Vogel and North were denied the right to marry in *Re North and Matheson* (1974) 52 DLR (3d) 280 (Man Co Ct). Vogel's argument that denial of dental benefits to North was discrimination based on sex or marital status was rejected in *Vogel* v. *Manitoba* (1983) 4 CHRR D/1654 (Man HRC) (*Vogel I*), before sexual orientation was added to Manitoba's legislation.

[47] *Vogel II*, ibid at 102.   [48] Ibid. at 101–2.

[49] Three US courts have employed such reasoning in finding that discrimination against same-sex couples is not based on sexual orientation. In *Baehr*, the court defined sexual orientation narrowly as direction of attraction, and neither saw it as including the choice of direction of conduct nor saw particular instances of conduct (e.g. a marriage) as having sexual orientations: 852 P 2d 44 at 58 n. 17 (Haw 1993) ('it is irrelevant . . . whether homosexuals constitute a "suspect class" because it is immaterial whether the plaintiffs . . . are homosexuals'), 51 n. 11 ('[p]arties to a same-sex marriage could theoretically be either homosexuals or heterosexuals'). See also *Engel* v. *Worthington* 23 Cal. Rptr 2d 329 at 331 (Ct App 1993) ('it matters not whether Engel is homosexual or heterosexual'); *Dean* v. *District of Columbia*, 653 A 2d 307 at 363 n. 1 (not all opposite-sex marriages are between heterosexual persons, not all same-sex marriages are between gay, lesbian, and bisexual persons). The *Baehr* and *Engel* courts found sex discrimination instead. The *Dean* court did not.

does not prohibit marriage by homosexuals provided it takes place between persons of the opposite sex. Some homosexuals do marry. The fact that many homosexuals do not choose' to marry, because they do not want unions with persons of the opposite sex, is the result of their own preferences, not a require-ment of the law.'[50] Thus, any protection enjoyed by gay, lesbian, and bisexual individuals because of the immutability of the direction of their attraction does not extend to same-sex couples who freely choose the direction of their conduct (e.g. by entering into a same-sex marriage).

II. IS SEXUAL ORIENTATION A FUNDAMENTAL CHOICE?

In considering whether sexual orientation is a 'fundamental choice', one should look at sexual orientation solely as the direction of a person's actual emotional–sexual conduct, without regard to the direction of their attraction, either *per se* or as a reason for their choice of direction of conduct.[51] A person's choice of the direction of their emotional–sexual conduct can be defined in a number of ways: (1) it is their choice of the sex of the person with whom they engage in such conduct (this definition might be more appropriate for heterosexual persons, gay men, and lesbian women); (2) it is their choice of the person with whom they engage in such conduct, without regard to the sex of that person (this definition might be more appropriate for bisexual persons); and (3) it is their choice of opposite-sex conduct, same-sex conduct, both types of conduct or celibacy (this definition stresses the choice of conduct over the choice of sex or of person, perhaps thereby implying misleadingly that there is something inherently differ-ent about the two types of conduct apart from the sexes of the participants).

Is a person's choice of the direction of their emotional–sexual conduct[52] 'fun-damental'? The first issue that arises is whether this question is to be answered under Section 15(1) or under another provision of the Charter. 'Religion' is the only enumerated ground of discrimination in Section 15(1) that appears to be a 'fundamental choice'. Because it is also an enumerated 'fundamental freedom' in Section 2(a), one could argue that a choice can only be 'fundamental' and an analogous ground under Section 15(1) if it is also a freedom expressly or impliedly protected by another provision of the Charter (i.e. an 'enumerated or analogous

---

[50] (1993) 14 OR (3d) 658 at 666–7 (Ont Div Ct).

[51] Alfred Kinsey described the search for the 'cause' of a person's choice of same-sex sexual activity as 'part of the broader problem of choices in general: the choice of the road that one takes, of the clothes that one wears, of the food that one eats, of the place in which one sleeps, and of the endless other things that one is constantly choosing. A choice of a partner in a sexual relation becomes more significant, only because society demands that there be a particular choice in this matter, and does not so often dictate one's choice of food or clothing.' See Kinsey (1948 Other), 661.

[52] It is important to describe the choice in this broad manner so as to include public aspects of emotional–sexual conduct that might not be covered by a 'right of privacy' linked to the location where decisions are carried out.

freedom'). (This requirement would not apply to 'immutable statuses', because the absence of choice makes it unnecessary to look outside Section 15(1) for protection of 'freedom of [e.g. race or sex]'.) An example of such a choice might be 'political opinion', which is not enumerated in Section 15(1) but is arguably an analogous ground[53] because it comes within the express protection of 'thought, belief, opinion, and expression' in Section 2(b).

Where does one look in the case of sexual orientation (as direction of conduct), which is not expressly mentioned either in Section 15(1) or Section 2 or elsewhere in the Charter?[54] In this respect, it is like other potential analogous grounds, such as marital status and pregnancy, which are arguably 'fundamental choices',[55] not 'immutable statuses', and are not expressly mentioned in Section 15(1) or elsewhere in the Charter. I would argue that the appropriate provision is Section 7, which guarantees that '[e]veryone has the right to . . . liberty . . . and the right not to be deprived thereof except in accordance with the principles of fundamental justice'. This guarantee of 'liberty' could serve as a residual, open-ended protection of analogous 'fundamental' freedoms or choices not enumerated elsewhere in the Charter, just as the prohibition of 'discrimination' in Section 15(1) provides a residual, open-ended prohibition of discrimination based on analogous grounds not enumerated elsewhere in Section 15(1). Justice Wilson has suggested that such enumerated freedoms as religion, association, expression, and inter-provincial mobility (Sections 2 and 6) 'are all examples of the basic theory underlying the Charter, namely that the state will respect choices made by individuals'.[56]

However, it is not yet clear whether the Supreme Court will develop Section 7 as a residual guarantee of 'liberty'. Although it has declined to limit Section 7 to dealing with the 'procedure' for enforcing legislation, as opposed to dealing with the legislation's 'substance',[57] a majority of the Court has yet to use 'liberty' in Section 7 to identify any 'analogous freedoms', every interference with which (regardless of the procedure used) would have to be justified under Section 1. In *R. v. Morgentaler*, five out of seven judges struck down a law permitting abortions only where approved by a hospital's abortion committee, but four of the five did so only on the ground that the law interfered with a woman's

[53] See Proulx (1988 Can), 595; Gall (1986 Can), 473; Hughes (1985 Can), 80–81.

[54] In *Sylvestre* v. *R.*, [1984] 2 FC 516 at 519 (TD) (denying motion to dismiss action of lesbian woman released from Armed Forces), rev'd, [1986] 3 FC 51 (CA), Denault J. observed that '[s]exual orientation is not the subject of a fundamental freedom or legal right recognized in the Charter, but the provisions [requiring the release of gay, lesbian, and bisexual persons], which are different from those that apply to other Canadian citizens, may be reviewed on the merits'.

[55] Regarding pregnancy, see Turnbull (1989 Can), 183; Proulx (1988 Can), 595. Cf. *Leroux* v. *Co-operators General Insurance Co.* (1991), 83 DLR (4th) 694 at 705–6 (Ont CA) (marital status discrimination did not violate Section 15(1) because 'unmarried persons who live together' are not a 'disadvantaged group' or 'discrete and insular minority' and 'the characteristic of being an unmarried partner is not . . . immutable').

[56] See *R. v. Morgentaler*, [1988] 1 SCR 30 at 166.

[57] See *Motor Vehicle Reference*, [1985] 2 SCR 486 at 498–9, 512–13.

Section 7 right to 'security of the person', by delaying her access to medical treatment.[58] Only Justice Wilson was willing to consider the Section 7 right to 'liberty'. After examining US 'right of privacy' case law, she concluded that Section 7 'guarantees to every individual a degree of personal autonomy over important decisions intimately affecting their private lives', and that a woman's decision to terminate her pregnancy is clearly such a decision.[59] In the *Prostitution Reference*, the majority did consider 'liberty', but dismissed the claim that Section 7 protects the right to earn one's livelihood by prostitution as one of 'economic liberty'.[60]

More recently, in *Rodriguez* v. *British Columbia (Attorney-General)*, the Court again avoided 'liberty'. Justice Sopinka, for the majority, found that a prohibition of assisted suicide (as applied to disabled persons) engages 'security of the person', which encompasses 'personal autonomy, at least with respect to the right to make choices concerning one's own body, control over one's physical and psychological integrity, and basic human dignity . . . , at least to the extent of freedom from criminal prohibitions which interfere with these'.[61] However, he found no violation of any principle of fundamental justice (and therefore of Section 7).[62] Justice McLachlan, in dissent, invoked a similar concept of 'security of the person' as protecting 'decisions concerning [one's] own body',[63] but held that 'Section 7 protects [the] choice [to end one's life with dignity] against arbitrary state action which would remove it'.[64] One could argue that these descriptions of 'security of the person' are broad enough to cover the choice of direction of emotional–sexual conduct, which concerns individuals' bodies (in relation to sexual activity) and interference with which may affect 'psychological integrity' and 'basic human dignity'. But such a broad concept of 'security of the person' would seem to absorb much of the potential content of 'liberty'.

A reference to 'liberty' in Section 7 in order to identify 'fundamental choices' for the purposes of Section 15(1) would recognize the inherent overlap between 'pure liberty', 'discriminatory interference with liberty', and 'pure equality' issues, where a ground of discrimination involves a choice.[65] 'Discrimination' that is based on the making of a choice is an interference with the 'liberty' to make that choice, and any interference with the 'liberty' to make a choice may 'discriminate' directly (by applying to less than all persons or only to particular options related to the choice) or indirectly (by having a disproportionate impact on persons desiring to make the choice). Reference to Section 7 in order to identify 'fundamental choices' would also permit the Supreme Court to achieve consistent results, which would not depend on whether the plaintiff stressed the abstract interference with the choice they had made (a Section 7 'pure liberty'

---

[58] See *R.* v. *Morgentaler*, [1988] 1 SCR 30 at 51, 89.
[59] Ibid. at 171.   [60] [1990] 1 SCR 1123 at 1162–71, 1179.
[61] [1993] 3 SCR 519 at 588.   [62] Ibid. at 608.
[63] Ibid. at 618.   [64] Ibid. at 624.
[65] See Tribe and Dorf (1990 US), 1094–5 ('the inseparability of liberty and equality').

issue), the relative interference resulting from the more favourable treatment accorded some persons in relation to the same choice (a Section 7 or Section 15(1) 'discriminatory interference with liberty' issue), or the use of the plaintiff's choice as a ground of discrimination (a Section 15(1) 'pure equality' issue). For example, the 'fundamentality' of a woman's choice to have an abortion should be the same whatever the nature of the potential interference with her choice and however she decides to frame her case. It should be the same whether she elects to frame it as one of 'pure liberty' under Section 7 (in response to a criminal sanction); or as one of 'discriminatory interference with liberty', when her position is compared to that of women choosing to continue their pregnancies, under Sections 7 or 15(1) (in response to a denial of public funding); or as one of 'pure equality' under Section 15(1) (in response to discrimination in public employment against women choosing abortions).[66]

It is possible, however, that the Supreme Court will decline to find this link between Section 15(1) and Section 7, and will identify 'fundamental choices' only under Section 15(1) (if at all). This could result from a desire to avoid the controversy which 'substantive due process' has generated in the US, or a desire to avoid incorporating a US-style 'fundamental rights branch' into Section 15(1),[67] or from the Court's expressed preference for dealing with discrimination issues under Section 15(1).[68] Assuming that the Supreme Court is willing to identify 'fundamental choices' as analogous grounds, and regardless of which provision of the Charter it relies on in doing so, is sexual orientation (as direction of conduct) such a choice?

The answer to this question depends, of course, on what is meant by 'fundamental', but providing a definition of 'fundamentality' is an extremely difficult task. Whereas 'immutability' may have some objective content arising from the impossibility of changing a physical or historical fact, 'fundamentality' is inevitably far more subjective. A choice that seems 'trivial' to one person (e.g. riding a motorcycle) may well be 'fundamental' to another. Several attempts in the US to define a general 'right of privacy' principle were discussed above[69], but, as Norman Vieira has observed, 'the task of devising standards for determining which unenumerated freedoms are entitled to heightened protection remains intractable'.[70] Jed Rubenfeld, in proposing an 'anti-totalitarian principle', seeks

---

[66] Section 7 arguments were made by plaintiffs challenging sexual orientation discrimination in *Sylvestre* [1984] 2 FC 516 (TD) (military employment), and *Andrews* v. *Ontario (Minister of Health)* (1988) 49 DLR (4th) 584 (Ont HC) (health care benefits for same-sex partner), but were summarily rejected.

[67] See Black and Smith (1989 Can), 606 n. 72; Ross (1986 Can), 459. The doctrine of 'enumerated and analogous grounds' under Section 15(1) resembles (by including age and disability) a broader version of the 'suspect and quasi-suspect classifications' branch of US equal protection doctrine, but so far does not seem to permit an equivalent of a 'fundamental rights' branch or 'rational basis' review.

[68] See e.g. *Edwards Books*, [1986] 2 SCR 713 at 785, 790–91, 804.

[69] See Ch. 2, Part II.A.3.   [70] Vieira (1988 US), 1188.

to avoid the difficulty of measuring the 'importance' of a specific option to an individual by looking instead to the effect on their life of being forced to select another option. Thus, he argues that '[t]he privacy argument against laws forbidding homosexual sex cannot be rested on the claim that they deprive certain persons of something deeply important to them, crucial to their happiness, or even central to their identity', but must point to the fact that such laws 'forceably channel certain individuals . . . into a network of social institutions and relations that will occupy their lives to a substantial degree'.[71] His alternative is appealing, but seems to involve merely a different means of measuring the 'importance' to the individual of freedom to choose, i.e. the negative effects of being forced to select another option rather than the positive effects of being permitted to select the preferred option. He does not tell us what degree of 'occupation of one's life' renders a choice such that governments should not prima facie be allowed to interfere with it; and he does not explain why, in the case of same-sex sexual activity, he treats opposite-sex marriage with children as the imposed option, rather than celibacy or opposite-sex sexual activity alone.[72]

The Canadian Supreme Court's only attempt to date to define what choices are protected by 'liberty' in Section 7 of the Charter was Justice Wilson's in *Morgentaler*. Her finding of a right to 'a degree of personal autonomy over important decisions intimately affecting [every individual's] private [life]'[73] stresses 'autonomy' and 'decisions', thus potentially avoiding the spatial limitations inherent in the US concept of 'privacy', and permitting the inclusion of public aspects of emotional–sexual conduct. However, the definition of what decisions are sufficiently 'important', or what effects are sufficiently 'intimate', or what constitutes 'private life', will not prove to be any easier under the Charter than under the US Constitution.

I do not propose to attempt to offer any 'test' of what is 'fundamental', primarily because it is beyond the scope of this book. But I also doubt whether any such 'test' is possible. Ultimately, whether or not one thinks that judges should use a vague guarantee of 'liberty' to identify 'fundamental' choices, rights, freedoms or liberties depends on whether one would rather see judges interpret the guarantee as granting them this power (trusting that they will exercise it wisely on a case-by-case basis, conscious of a need not to strike down statutes indiscriminately, especially those interfering only with 'economic' liberty), or whether one would prefer that judges refrained from doing so and confined themselves to interpreting enumerated freedoms (making it impossible to challenge laws interfering with important choices that fall outside the enumerated freedoms). I can only suggest that a person's choice of the sex of the partner with whom they engage in emotional–sexual conduct would certainly seem to be an 'important decision[ ] intimately affecting their private [life]', as

---

[71] Rubenfeld (1989 US), 799.   [72] Ibid. at 800.   [73] [1988] 1 SCR 30 at 171.

important to them (and as controversial to others) as their choice of religion or political opinion.[74] It is therefore an excellent candidate for recognition as a 'fundamental choice'.

Whatever test of 'fundamentality' one uses, two further issues will arise in applying it to sexual orientation, and in deciding when interference with a 'fundamental choice' may be justified under Section 1. The first issue is the level of generality used to define the proposed 'fundamental choice'. One's conclusion as to whether a choice is fundamental may depend on whether it is defined either as a general freedom to choose in a particular sphere or as the freedom to choose one of the specific options available in that sphere (e.g. freedom of expression, freedom to choose whether or not to continue a pregnancy, freedom to choose what you eat versus freedom to express racist views, read pornography, have an abortion or eat a cat or dog). This is because some might argue that specific options that are unpopular, controversial or associated with a minority could not possibly be 'fundamental', rather than accept that they come within a more general 'fundamental choice' but seek to justify interferences with them under Section 1.

Thus, if a 'fundamentality' test were applied to the particular option of same-sex emotional–sexual conduct, some heterosexual persons might argue that such a choice cannot be 'important' because it is of no interest to them. In *Hardwick*, Justice Blackmun rejected the majority's characterization of the case as about 'a fundamental right to engage in homosexual sodomy', seeing it as involving 'the right [of individuals] to decide for themselves whether to engage in particular forms of private, consensual sexual activity'.[75] He recognized that 'a necessary corollary of giving individuals freedom to choose . . . is acceptance of the fact that different individuals will make different choices', some of which will 'upset the majority'.[76] Even stating the choice more generally, as a person's choice of their sexual orientation (in the sense of the direction of their emotional–sexual conduct), some heterosexual persons might claim that the more general choice is the same as the particular option, because they often do not see themselves as having a sexual orientation (whether as direction of attraction or conduct).[77]

Having moved from the particular option of same-sex emotional–sexual conduct to the more general choice of direction of emotional–sexual conduct, it might be necessary to proceed to even higher levels of generality to situate sexual orientation within an area of choice that most would concede is 'fundamental'.

---

[74] See also *R. v. LeBeau* (1988) 41 CCC (3d) 163 at 176 (Ont CA) ('it may be that if any constitutional right is implicated [by a statutory interference with sexual activity] it would . . . be a form of "liberty" protected by s. 7 of the Charter').

[75] 478 US 186 at 199 (1986).   [76] Ibid. at 205–6, 211.

[77] Because they do not realize that they have a sexual orientation and frequently exercise their right to be open about it without fear of discrimination, some heterosexual persons (especially in the US) assert that gay, lesbian, and bisexual persons seeking the same right are demanding 'special rights'.

The next level of generality would be choice in the area of emotional–sexual conduct generally, which includes not just its direction (determined by the sexes of the participants), but also its 'content' (i.e. the precise nature of sexual activities, characteristics of a chosen partner other than their sex, whether and how to express affection in public, and whether to form a couple relationship, be monogamous, live together, marry, etc.). Choice in this area might be described as 'freedom of sexuality' (a person's freedom to exercise their capacity to engage in emotional–sexual conduct, i.e. their 'sexuality', and to choose every aspect of that conduct) as opposed to 'freedom of sexual orientation' (a person's freedom to choose a single aspect of their emotional–sexual conduct, i.e. its direction as between the sexes). The problem with resting the case for the 'fundamentality' of sexual orientation on its coming within such a broad area of choice is that, although many might agree that the choice of emotional–sexual conduct is 'fundamental' and that sexual orientation prima facie comes within its protection, many other controversial aspects of emotional–sexual conduct would also prima facie merit such protection (subject to any Section 1 justifications that could be established). However easy or difficult it might be to do so, the need to justify any existing or future restrictions on sexual activity with minors or in public places, or on incest, prostitution, polygamy, sado-masochism or bestiality, might deter recognition of the choice as fundamental.[78] But if the Supreme Court can give Section 1 an interpretation that is flexible enough to deal with the many justifiable instances of age or disability discrimination, it should be able to distinguish between those aspects of emotional–sexual conduct where individuals must be permitted the freedom to choose from those where restrictions are necessary.

Although the choice of emotional–sexual conduct with other persons should be sufficiently general to accommodate sexual orientation, one could also look to an even more general sphere of choice, i.e. the sphere encompassing the three closely related 'sub-spheres' of emotional–sexual conduct, procreative decisions, and parent–child relationships. The sub-sphere of procreative decisions includes all decisions about whether or not to attempt to create a child, either through opposite-sex sexual activity (i.e. penile–vaginal intercourse) or alternative means (such as *in vitro* fertilization, donor insemination or surrogate motherhood). The sub-sphere of parent–child relationships includes the creation of such relationships by non-procreative or legal means (e.g. adoption or fostering) and all decisions regarding the custody, education, or welfare of the child.

The degree to which these three sub-spheres overlap will vary greatly. For fertile heterosexual persons, the decision whether or not to attempt to procreate is inextricably linked to the decision whether or not to engage in any kind of

---

[78] In *Hardwick*, 478 US 186 at 195 (1986), the US Supreme Court refused to consider the choice 'in the privacy of the home' of 'voluntary sexual conduct between consenting adults' as fundamental, so as to avoid having to deal with 'adultery, incest and other sexual crimes . . . committed in the home'.

opposite-sex sexual activity that could cause pregnancy. For infertile opposite-sex couples and all same-sex couples, the decision whether or not to attempt to procreate through alternative means, or to adopt or foster a child, may be an important one addressed in the context of their couple relationship. Yet an individual woman might choose to attempt to procreate (e.g. by donor insemination) without engaging in any sexual activity or forming a couple relationship. And in many instances of opposite-sex sexual activity (where effective contraception is used or one person is infertile), as well as all instances of same-sex sexual activity, procreation will not be possible. Similarly, the parties to a decision to procreate will usually become the parents who care for the child, but not necessarily. The biological parents may be unwilling or unable to raise the child and may place it in the care of adoptive or foster parents.

The purpose of discussing these three overlapping sub-spheres is to illustrate the connection between emotional–sexual conduct and other areas of choice that have been or may be deemed 'fundamental'.[79] In particular, the potentially fundamental choices whether or not to use contraceptives and whether or not to continue a pregnancy or have an abortion (e.g. in the event of contraceptive failure) permit fertile heterosexual persons to sever the link between certain opposite-sex sexual activity (i.e. penile–vaginal intercourse) and procreation. This raises the questions of whether penile–vaginal intercourse without procreative potential because of contraception might itself be protected; of whether sexual activity without procreative potential for other reasons is also protected (e.g. penile–vaginal intercourse involving an infertile person, opposite-sex sexual activity other than penile–vaginal intercourse, or same-sex sexual activity) is also protected; and the question of whether decisions to procreate by means other than opposite-sex sexual activity might be protected.[80] But because the potential area covered by these three sub-spheres is so broad (like that of emotional–sexual conduct alone), it is difficult for a court to say that everything coming within any of the three sub-spheres is prima facie 'fundamental' (subject to Section 1). Instead, a court might find it easier to select particular elements from these broad areas of choice and declare them fundamental on a case-by-case basis.

Thus, 'choice of sexual orientation (as direction of emotional–sexual conduct)' could be recognized as a fundamental choice, rather than 'choice of emotional–sexual conduct' or 'choice of emotional–sexual/procreative/parental conduct'. This is because sexual orientation involves only the choice of the

[79] See *Morgentaler*, [1988] 1 SCR 30 at 171–2, Wilson J. (a woman's right to choose an abortion); *R.* v. *Jones*, [1986] 2 SCR 284 at 319–20, Wilson J. (dissenting) (parent's right to educate their child in accordance with their conscientious beliefs); *Schachter* v. *Canada*, [1988] 3 FC 515 (TD), aff'd, [1990] 2 FC 129 (CA), rev'd, [1992] 2 SCR 679 (violation of Section 15(1) where child-care benefits made available to adoptive parents but not biological parents); *E. (Mrs.)* v. *Eve*, [1986] 2 SCR 388 at 431, 435–7 (involuntary sterilization). Cf. Ch. 2, notes 13–17.

[80] See Hughes (1985 Can), 82 (recognizing link between sexual orientation and reproductive/sexual choice). Cf. *Hardwick*, 478 US 186 at 190–91 (1986) (refusal to see any connection).

direction of emotional–sexual conduct (i.e. the sex of one's partner) and not any aspect of its 'content'. 'Content' might include, for instance: the age of one's partner, the degree of blood or legal relation to one's partner, the existence of any relationship of trust or authority, the number of persons involved (over two), the location of the activity, the 'decency' of a public or semi-public activity, the presence of any financial consideration, the consensual use of force, the duration of a couple relationship. Restrictions based on any of these aspects of the 'content' of emotional–sexual conduct could be imposed without interfering with sexual orientation, so long as they were imposed without regard to the direction of the conduct.[81] By selecting sexual orientation as the relevant choice, one can separate the narrower, easier 'equality' issue, raised by the unequal treatment of same-sex emotional–sexual conduct (vis-à-vis opposite-sex conduct), from the broader, more difficult 'liberty' issues raised by restrictions on other aspects of emotional–sexual conduct.

If sexual orientation were recognized as a 'fundamental choice', the second issue that would arise, in applying Section 1 (or perhaps in deciding whether there existed a sufficient 'burden' to constitute 'discrimination' under Section 15(1)), would be what degrees of interference could be justified. Some choices might be considered fundamental only when the government seeks to dictate them (by prohibiting the only alternative, e.g. abortion versus continuing a pregnancy). Others might be considered fundamental when the government seeks to restrict them (by prohibiting one or more but not all alternatives, e.g. same-sex sexual activity versus celibacy versus opposite-sex sexual activity). Still others might be considered fundamental when the government merely attempts to influence them (by attaching a sanction less than outright prohibition to a particular option, e.g. loss of a benefit such as employment or funding; or using state-sponsored education or publicity to promote one option over another). It is submitted that sexual orientation, like religion, is in the last category of 'most sensitive' choices, and therefore that neither restrictions (in the form of criminal prohibitions) nor attempts to influence (in the form of civil sanctions—for example, discrimination against same-sex couples in respect of benefits, or state-sponsored education or publicity intended to promote one sexual orientation over another) should be permitted (in the absence of a strong justification).[82] Yet several Canadian courts have held (as has the European Commission) that attempts to influence (through sanctions other than a blanket criminal prohibition

---

[81] Legislation prohibiting sexual orientation discrimination often expressly excludes distinctions based on illegal conduct. See e.g. Manitoba Human Rights Code, SM 1987–88, c. 45, s. 9(4) ('[sexual orientation] shall [not] be interpreted as extending to any conduct prohibited by the Criminal Code of Canada'); Massachusetts Gen Laws Ann c. 151B, s. 4.1 (prohibiting employment discrimination based on 'sexual orientation, which shall not include persons whose sexual orientation involves minor children as the sex object').

[82] See Ryder (1990 Can), 81 ('legislation that has the effect of compelling the abandonment of, or creating an inducement to abandon, the expression of one's sexual orientation' prima facie violates Section 15(1)).

of all same-sex sexual activity) do not 'interfere' with freedom of sexual orientation.[83]

Drawing an analogy between sexual orientation and religion raises a difficult question (beyond the scope of this Chapter): could any kind of assistance to the gay, lesbian, and bisexual community (e.g. funding of cultural, sports or social services organizations), or any discussion of the existence of gay, lesbian, and bisexual persons and same-sex emotional–sexual conduct in public schools, be construed as 'promoting' same-sex or bisexual sexual orientation (as direction of attraction or conduct), thereby interfering with the freedom of each individual to choose their sexual orientation (as direction of attraction or conduct)? Most such assistance will be extended to gay, lesbian or bisexual organizations on an equal footing with other (predominantly heterosexual) organizations providing similar activities or services, and thus will not involve any 'preference' or 'promotion' of one sexual orientation over another. Only where a real 'preference' could be shown would it be necessary, under Section 15(2) or Section 1, to consider any special needs the gay, lesbian, and bisexual community may have as a minority group facing discrimination.[84] (Of course, if one adopts the 'disadvantaged groups' interpretation of Section 15(1), 'discrimination' against heterosexual persons is an impossibility.) In schools, actual 'promotion' of same-sex sexual activity (in the sense of active encouragement of experimentation with it, as opposed to any neutral or positive statement about it) will be extremely rare, and as inappropriate as similar promotion of opposite-sex sexual activity.[85] However, this has not prevented legislatures or voters in several jurisdictions from attempting to prohibit perceived 'promotion'.[86]

---

[83] See *Sylvestre* [1986] 3 FC 51 at 53 (CA) (dismissal of lesbian member of Armed Forces 'in no way impaired [her] liberty to be a homosexual'); *Schnare* (15 Feb. 1990) Kentville K89–2326, K89–2327 at 20 (NS Prov Ct) (prohibition of anal intercourse with person under 18 did not 'interfere with the accused's liberty to be a homosexual'); *Karen Andrews* (1988) 49 DLR (4th) 584 at 590 (Ont HC) (no basis for argument, under Section 7, that denial of health insurance to woman's female partner and partner's children threatened her liberty to 'engage in an adult, intimate and consensual relationship with a person of the same sex').

[84] For example, proclamations of Lesbian and Gay Pride Days by mayors might be justified in that the heterosexual majority has no need for such proclamations (i.e. every day is Heterosexual Pride Day). See Ch. 6, note 130.

[85] See Ryder (1990 Can), 80–81 (as with religion, 'the state is free to provide education regarding sexuality, but it must do so in an even-handed manner, avoiding indoctrination').

[86] See Ch. 2, notes 269–71; Great Britain, the Local Government Act 1988, s. 28 ('a local authority shall not intentionally promote homosexuality or . . . the teaching in any . . . school of the acceptability of homosexuality as a pretended family relationship'); in Isle of Man, the Sexual Offences Act 1992, s. 38 (same as Great Britain but applies to any 'public body'); in Western Australia, the Law Reform (Decriminalization of Sodomy) Act 1989, SWA 1989, No. 32, ss. 23–24 (encouraging or promoting 'homosexual behaviour' is contrary to public policy and shall not be part of the teaching in primary or secondary schools); in Connecticut, Conn Gen Stat s. 46a–81r(2) (anti-discrimination law shall not be construed 'to authorize the promotion of homosexuality or bisexuality in educational institutions or require the teaching . . . of homosexuality or bisexuality as an acceptable lifestyle'); in Minnesota, Minn Stat Ann s. 363.021(2) (same as Connecticut). See also Austria Penal Code, ss. 220–221 (making it unlawful to 'publicly advocate, promote or encourage

If express or implied protection of a 'fundamental choice' had to be found outside Section 15(1), and sexual orientation could not be recognized as a 'fundamental choice' under Section 7,[87] it is unlikely that this would be possible under any other provision of the Charter, in particular Section 2. Freedom of association will probably not be interpreted as protecting any particular kind of emotional, sexual or other conduct in which an association of two or more persons chooses to engage.[88] Freedom of expression would have to be stretched considerably to cover many of the aspects of emotional–sexual conduct that are most significant in the context of sexual orientation (e.g. private sexual activity).[89] And freedom of conscience and religion, although it may serve as a 'shield', by providing protection against Section 1 arguments based on religious morality, probably cannot serve as a 'sword', i.e. it probably does not protect conduct merely because it is consistent with a person's own moral beliefs and

homosexual acts' or to 'establish or belong to an organization which supports "homosexual lewdness" and which causes public offence') and Finland Penal Code, s. 20:9.2 (prohibiting 'the public encouragement of fornication between members of the same sex'), both cited in Tatchell (1992 Eur) at 102, 109–110. The Nicaragua Supreme Court has upheld as constitutional Penal Code article 204, which imposes up to three years imprisonment on anyone who 'induces, promotes or practises in a scandalous form sexual relations between persons of the same sex': see *Capital Gay* (4 Nov. 1994) 11. Examples of 'anti-promotion' provisions that are neutral as among sexual orientations include Manitoba, Human Rights Code, SM 1987–88, c. 45, ss. 9(5), 14(11) (Code does not condone or condemn any 'beliefs, values or lifestyles' based upon a protected characteristic, or prohibit discipline where a job is improperly used 'as a forum for promoting beliefs or values' based upon a protected characteristic), and 42 USCA s. 300ee(c) (no funds for AIDS prevention programmes may be used to 'promote or encourage, directly, homosexual or heterosexual sexual activity').

[87] In the *Prostitution Reference*, [1990] 1 SCR 1123, the Supreme Court upheld, against a Section 7 challenge, the Criminal Code's prohibition of keeping a 'common bawdy-house' (including a place used for prostitution). Lamer J. (at 1162–71, 1179), focusing on the commercial aspect of the case, treated prostitution as an 'economic liberty' but did not consider the fact that the liberty involves sexual activity. A non-commercial case of private sexual activity would serve as a much better vehicle for recognizing choices in the area of sexual activity as 'fundamental'.

[88] See *Reference re Public Service Employee Relations Act (Alta.)*, [1987] 1 SCR 313 at 406 (McIntyre J.) ('marriage and the family ... do not fall easily or completely under the rubric of freedom of association.... [M]arriage ... might well be protected by freedom of association in combination with other rights and freedoms. Freedom of association alone, however, is not concerned with conduct; its purpose is to guarantee that activities ... may be pursued in common. .... [Section] 2(d) cannot be interpreted as guaranteeing specific acts ..., whether or not they are fundamental in our society'). A Section 2(d) argument was rejected in *Karen Andrews*, (1988) 49 DLR (4th) 584 at 590 (Ont HC), but was accepted by a Security Intelligence Review Committee in *Douglas* v. *Chief of the Defence Staff* (14 Aug. 1990), No. 1170, at 46 (policy of dismissing gay, lesbian, and bisexual military personnel 'inconsistent with the provisions of [Sections 2(d) and 15(1)]'). In *R.* v. *Skinner*, [1990] 1 SCR 1235 at 1249–51, Wilson J. held that Section 2(d) protects only the right of prostitutes to meet and negotiate with their clients and not their right to engage in sexual activity with them.

[89] See *LeBeau* (1988) 41 CCC (3d) 163 at 176–7 (Ont CA) (not necessary to decide whether some forms of sexual conduct may be a form of 'expression' under Section 2(b), but any right implicated would more reasonably be a form of 'liberty' under Section 7); *Prostitution Reference*, [1990] 1 SCR 1123 at 1206, Wilson J. (keeping a 'common bawdy-house' is not expression). Cf. Ryder (1990 Can), 80–81 ('there is a strong connection between recognizing sexual orientation as a protected ground of discrimination under s. 15 and the fundamental freedoms of [expression and association] in s. 2').

inconsistent with other (religious) persons' moral beliefs.[90] Without express or implied protection under Sections 2 or 7, sexual orientation (as direction of conduct) could probably only be made a fundamental choice by amending the Charter to add provisions similar to the rights 'to respect for ... private and family life' and 'to marry and found a family' in Articles 8 and 12 of the European Convention. If such an amendment were necessary, because protection of emotional–sexual conduct, procreative decisions, and parent-child relationships has no express textual basis (as in the European Convention), and cannot be found by implication (as in the US Constitution), it would suggest that the Canadian Charter is 'defective' in this respect.

We saw in Part I. that, if sexual orientation (as direction of attraction) were recognized as an analogous ground because it is an 'immutable status', sexual orientation (as direction of conduct) would not be covered, permitting courts to find (as in *Egan* (F.C.T.D.), *Vogel II*, and *Layland*) that discrimination against same-sex couples in respect of benefits, or the right to marry, does not constitute sexual orientation discrimination. If sexual orientation (as direction of conduct) were recognized as an analogous ground because it is a 'fundamental choice', it would preclude the making of a distinction between an 'immutable attraction' and 'chosen conduct'. The reasoning in several cases reflects a rejection of such a distinction.

In *Veysey*, the federal government argued that Timothy Veysey 'cannot have the man with whom he formerly lived [Leslie Beu] approved for a private family visit, not because of [Veysey's] sexual orientation, but because [Beu] is not his [legal or common law opposite-sex] spouse'. Veysey responded that 'the program is discriminatory because it excludes homosexual relationships'.[91] Dubé J. implicitly rejected the federal government's argument by finding 'differential treatment based on sexual orientation'.[92] Similarly, in *Knodel*, the British Columbia government argued that the denial of medical insurance coverage to Timothy Knodel's partner Ray Garneau was based, 'not ... on sexual orientation, but rather on a distinction between [legal or common law opposite-sex] "spouses" and the wider class of "non-spouses" who do not hold themselves out as man and wife, ... such as brother/sister, or parent/adult child'.[93] Rowles J. also implicitly rejected this argument, holding that Knodel's Section 15(1) right 'is infringed by the denial of coverage to homosexual couples, the denial being discrimination on the basis of sexual orientation', and declaring that 'same sex couples are included in the definition of "spouse"' in the applicable regulations.[94]

In *Egan* (F.C.A.), Linden J.A. in dissent described the majority's acceptance of a distinction between 'spousal status' and sexual orientation as 'circular',

---

[90] See *Edwards Books*, [1986] 2 SCR 713 at 762 ('legislation with a secular inspiration does not abridge the freedom from conformity to religious dogma merely because ... [it] coincide[s] with the tenets of a religion', unless perhaps the 'conduct [which the legislation precludes] is governed by an intention to express ... non-conformity with religious doctrine').

[91] (1989) [1990] 1 FC 321 at 325–6 (TD).   [92] Ibid. at 330.

[93] [1991] 6 WWR 728 at 731.   [94] Ibid. at 763.

because the issue before the court was whether 'the definition of "spouse" . . . creates a distinction . . . which is discriminatory on the basis of sexual orientation'.[95] He then made his own 'immutable attraction versus chosen conduct' distinction by finding that a distinction between same-sex and opposite-sex couples is 'strictly speaking, . . . not a distinction based directly on sexual orientation, since being in a same-sex relationship is not necessarily the defining characteristic of being gay or lesbian'. He was still able to find a prima facie violation of Section 15(1), however, because the distinction was based 'on a characteristic or matter related to sexual orientation, since it is lesbians and gay men who may enter into same-sex relationships'.[96] In *Layland*, Greer J. in dissent did not expressly address the majority's 'immutable attraction versus chosen conduct' distinction, but referred to the denial of the plaintiffs' 'right to choose whom they wish to marry'. She described 'the right to choose' as 'a fundamental right' and Section 15(1) as 'designed to protect the individual's right to choose'.[97]

More explicit statements regarding the 'immutable attraction versus chosen conduct' distinction were made in *Leshner*, in which a board of inquiry under the Ontario Human Rights Code considered the denial of pension benefits to Michael Stark, the partner of Michael Leshner, an Ontario government employee. In interpreting the Code's statutory requirement of 'equal treatment with respect to employment without discrimination because of . . . sexual orientation',[98] two members of the board concluded that 'discriminatory conduct prejudicial to an established relationship between gays or lesbians ought to be challengeable as discrimination based on "sexual orientation" within the meaning of the Code. Such a relationship is a major aspect of an individual's "sexual orientation".'[99] The third member agreed that 'the ground of sexual orientation protects gay men and lesbian women from discrimination directed against their same-sex relationships. Where the reason for discrimination is "gayness", whether of an individual *or a relationship*, it is "sexual orientation" which has been used to make a distinction unrelated to personal characteristics or merit.'[100] Indeed, the Ontario government had conceded that 'the only reason for excluding Mr. Leshner from the employment benefits was *the sexual orientation of his relationship* with Mr. Stark',[101] and that 'equal treatment with respect to employment' meant that '[g]ay and lesbian relationships must be treated as equal in status to heterosexual unions'.[102]

Even though there was prima facie sexual orientation discrimination, the

---

[95] [1993] 3 FC 401 at 417 (CA).   [96] Ibid. at 432.
[97] (1993) 14 OR (3d) 658 at 672 (Ont Div Ct).   [98] RSO 1990, c. H.19, s. 5(1).
[99] (1992) 16 CHRR D/184 at D/197 (Ont Hum Rts Comm).
[100] Ibid. at D/212 (emphasis added).   [101] Ibid. at D/213 (emphasis added).
[102] Ibid. at D/197. See also *Re Canada (Treasury Board—Environment Canada) and Lorenzen*, (1993) 38 LAC (4th) 29 at 46–7: 'a characteristic of the grievor's sexual orientation is a natural inclination to favouring a spousal relationship with a person of the same sex, just as a heterosexual's natural inclination is to favour a spousal relationship with a person of the opposite sex. The fact that the grievor has chosen as a spouse a person of the same sex cannot be separated from his sexual orientation.'

majority concluded that it was condoned by several contradictory provisions of the Code, which themselves discriminated on the basis of sexual orientation: section 10(1), defining a 'spouse' as 'a person of the opposite sex' and 'marital status' as including 'the status of living with a person of the opposite sex in a conjugal relationship', and section 25(2), exempting marital status discrimination in pension plans.[103] The Ontario government conceded that 'these provisions are subject to scrutiny under section 15 of the Charter on the basis that "sexual orientation" is an analogous ground . . . , and . . . that [they] infringe upon the equality rights protected by section 15'.[104] But because the discrimination was necessary to maintain favourable treatment of the government's pension plan under the federal Income Tax Act (which contains an opposite-sex definition of 'spouse'),[105] the government sought to justify it under Section 1. The board rejected the government's asserted justifications[106] and ordered: that 'the definition of "marital status" [in s. 10(1)] . . . be read down by omitting the words "of the opposite sex"'; that s. 25(2) be of 'no force or effect' to the extent of the inconsistency with Section 15(1), so that 'there is no discrimination as between employees living in conjugal relationships outside marriage, irrespective of whether or not those relationships are heterosexual or homosexual'; and that the government provide 'equivalent survivor benefits . . . to persons living in homosexual conjugal relationships' (but outside of the pension plan, so as not to jeopardize its federal tax status).[107]

The realization that a prohibition of sexual orientation discrimination in employment may be interpreted as applying to discrimination against same-sex couples in respect of employment benefits seems to have led several legislatures that have recently enacted such prohibitions to insert language intended to preclude such an interpretation. In Canada, this has taken the form of definitions of 'marital status' (very similar to Ontario's) that include unmarried couples only if they are of opposite sexes.[108] These definitions have been adopted or proposed at the same time as prohibitions of sexual orientation discrimination and with full knowledge of litigation over benefits for same-sex partners of employees (whereas the Ontario definition existed before the prohibition of sexual orientation discrimination was introduced and may have been overlooked). In the US, legislators have been more explicit. Vermont's prohibition of sexual orientation

[103] *Leshner*, ibid. at D/198–9. A similar view of the effect of these provisions has been taken, without considering the Charter, in *Clinton* (Ont Div Ct), *Parkwood*, and *Carleton* (each cited in Ch. 6, note 131).

[104] *Leshner*, ibid. at D/200.   [105] Ibid. at D/189.   [106] Ibid. at D/201–D/206.

[107] Ibid. at D/223–D/224. The Board found that, in the circumstances, 'separate but equal treatment' was justifiable and not comparable to that in *Brown* v. *Board of Education*, 347 US 483 (1954): see *Leshner*, ibid. at D/195–D/196.

[108] See Nova Scotia, Human Rights Act, RSNS 1989, c. 214, s. 3(i) (as amended by SNS 1991, c. 12); Bill C–108, 3rd Sess., 34th Parl., 1992, s. 10 (unsuccessful proposal to amend Canadian Human Rights Act). Cf. Québec, Charter of Human Rights and Freedoms, RSQ c. C–12, s. 137 (prohibitions of sexual orientation and sex discrimination do not apply to pension and other social benefit plans).

discrimination 'shall not be construed to change the definition of family or dependent in an employee benefit plan',[109] Massachusetts' shall not 'be construed so as to . . . provide health insurance or related employee benefits to a "homosexual spouse", so-called',[110] while California's 'shall [not] invalidate any marital status classification that is otherwise valid'.[111] In the US, the issue of benefits for same-sex partners is complicated by the fact that employment benefits are often extended only to the married opposite-sex partners of employees, whereas in Canada they are usually extended to all opposite-sex partners (married or unmarried). Thus, in the US discrimination against a same-sex couple may be treated as based, not on sexual orientation, but on marital status, because unmarried opposite-sex couples are also excluded from the benefit.[112]

[109] Vt Stat Ann tit. 21, s. 495(f).
[110] Mass Gen Laws Ann c. 151B, s. 4 (note referring to Mass Stat 1989, c. 516, s. 19).
[111] Cal Labor Code, s. 1102.1(c).
[112] See *Ross* v. *Denver Department of Health and Hospitals*, 883 P 2d 516 (Colo Ct App 1994); *Phillips* v. *Wisconsin Personnel Commission*, 482 NW 2d 121 at 127 (Wis Ct App 1992); *Hinman* v. *Department of Personnel Administration*, 213 Cal Rptr 410 (Ct App 1985).

8

The Canadian Charter of Rights and Freedoms:
Is Sexual Orientation Discrimination
Sex Discrimination?

I. INTRODUCTION

In Chapter 7, I concluded that sexual orientation is an excellent candidate for recognition as an analogous ground under Section 15(1), but as a 'fundamental choice' (and therefore in the sense of a chosen direction of conduct) and not as an 'immutable status' (and therefore not in the sense of an unchosen direction of attraction). This would, however, require the Canadian Supreme Court to develop the kind of substantive protection of 'liberty' initiated by Wilson J. in *Morgentaler*, and to apply it either specifically to sexual orientation (as direction of conduct) or, more generally, to all emotional–sexual conduct, or perhaps to all emotional–sexual conduct, procreative decisions, and parent–child relationships. Is there another approach that does not depend on the expansion of a doctrine that has yet to be accepted by a majority of Supreme Court justices? In this Chapter, I will argue that sexual orientation (as direction of attraction or conduct) is already implicitly included in an enumerated Section 15(1) ground, i.e. 'sex', because almost every case of sexual orientation discrimination can be analysed as one of sex discrimination.

Could sexual orientation be included in any other grounds? Plaintiffs using human rights legislation to challenge sexual orientation discrimination (where sexual orientation was not a listed ground) have also invoked such grounds as 'marital status' or 'family status'.[1] I will not consider their potential use under Section 15(1) because they are not enumerated grounds (which means that they

---

[1] 'Physical disability' (an enumerated Section 15(1) ground) could conceivably be invoked: see *Biggs* v. *Hudson* (1988), 9 CHRR D/5391 at para. 40360 (BC Council of HR) (interpreting 'physical disability' in the BC Human Rights Act as protecting members of 'groups widely regarded as especially vulnerable to HIV infection'). Cf. *Blackwell* v. *US Department of the Treasury*, 830 F 2d 1183 (DC Cir 1987) (sexual orientation or preference does not come within statute prohibiting 'handicap' discrimination); the Americans With Disabilities Act, 42 USCA s. 12211(a) ('homosexuality and bisexuality . . . are not disabilities'). The only 'disability' related to same-sex or bisexual sexual orientation is the inability of same-sex couples to have children with genetic input from both partners, but this 'reproductive disability' results from the choice of a same-sex partner, not from any physical impairment. (The same is true of a fertile heterosexual person who chooses to remain with an infertile opposite-sex partner.) And the current association of gay and bisexual men (but not lesbian and bisexual women) with the HIV epidemic is not a sound (or comprehensive) basis for legal protection against sexual orientation discrimination.

must first be shown to be analogous), and they are difficult to apply to many kinds of sexual orientation discrimination that do not involve a same-sex couple relationship. Moreover, much discrimination against same-sex couples in Canada (unlike in the US and the UK) is arguably not based on the marital status of the couple because the benefit is provided to unmarried opposite-sex couples.[2] It can certainly be argued that the concept of discrimination based on 'family status' can be applied to discrimination against same-sex couples.[3] But the exclusion of same-sex couples from a definition of 'family' that includes unmarried opposite-sex couples without children can more easily be analysed as discrimination based on 'sexual orientation' or 'sex' than as discrimination based on the vague ground of 'family status'. Indeed, treating such an exclusion as 'family status' discrimination may amount to treating a same-sex couple's relationship as equivalent to that of two brothers or two sisters (rather than to that of an opposite-sex couple), where relatives other than partners or children qualify for the benefit in question.[4]

II. IS SEXUAL ORIENTATION DISCRIMINATION SEX DISCRIMINATION?

In treating sexual orientation as the direction of a person's emotional–sexual attraction, or as the direction of a person's emotional–sexual conduct, one focuses on the *direction* of desired or actual emotional–sexual conduct, i.e. the *sex of the partner* with whom the person desires to engage, or actually engages, in the conduct. However, the direction of a particular instance of conduct (i.e. opposite-sex or same-sex) is merely the combination of the sexes of the two persons (A, the choosing person, and B the chosen partner) engaging in the conduct. (These choices are, of course, reciprocal.) Suppose that A has been treated unequally because of their choice of B. Instead of taking the sex of A as given (i.e. a person of a particular sex is choosing a partner), and looking at the sex of B to determine whether it is A's choice of B that has caused A to be treated unequally, one can take the sex of B as given (i.e. a person of a particular sex is being chosen), and look at the sex of A to determine whether it is A's sex,

---

[2] See *Vogel* v. *Manitoba* (1983) 4 CHRR D/1654 (Man HRC) (*Vogel I*), at D/1657–8.

[3] In *Mossop* v. *Canada (Secretary of State)* (1989) 10 CHRR D/6064, a Canadian Human Rights Commission tribunal held (at D/6094) that 'homosexual couples may constitute a family' and (at D/6097) that denying a male employee bereavement leave to attend the funeral of his male partner's father was discrimination based on his 'family status'. The decision was reversed by the Federal Court of Appeal in 1990, see [1991] 1 FC 18, and the Supreme Court dismissed an appeal. See *Canada (A-G)* v. *Mossop*, [1993] 1 SCR 554 at 582 (a 'homosexual couple' not a 'family' for the purposes of the Canadian Human Rights Act). See also *Vogel* v. *Manitoba (A-G)* (1992) 90 DLR (4th) 84 at 99 (Man QB) (*Vogel II*) ('homosexual couples without children and without the potential . . . for procreation . . . are not families').

[4] This was the case in *Mossop*, [1993] 1 SCR 554 at 590. For a discussion of *Mossop*, see Wintemute (1994 Can), 432–41.

rather than A's choice of B, that has caused A to be treated unequally. In other words, if a man chooses a man, it is just as much his sex (male) that is the source of the objection (because only a woman may choose a man) as it is his choice of a man (because a man may only choose a woman). When one focuses on the *sex of the choosing person*, rather than the sex of the chosen partner, one realizes that it is the choosing person's sex which makes both their choice of direction of emotional–sexual conduct (sex of partner) and their direction of emotional–sexual attraction objectionable, and which therefore constitutes the ground of distinction. Why then is it not obvious that discrimination on the basis of sexual orientation is nothing more than discrimination on the basis of sex?[5]

A. The Traditional Response

At least six reported decisions in Canada appear to have dealt with the argument that sexual orientation discrimination is sex discrimination:[6] *University of Saskatchewan* and *Vogel I* under provincial human rights legislation, *Knodel* and *Egan* under the Charter, and *Nielsen* and *Guevremont* under the Canadian Human Rights Act (CHRA).[7] In *University of Saskatchewan*, a gay lecturer, Douglas Wilson, challenged the suspension of his right to supervise practice teaching in public schools. Johnson J. prohibited the Human Rights Commission from investigating the complaint, holding that the 'sex' of a person meant 'whether or not that person was a man or a woman', not their 'sexual orientation, . . . sexual proclivity, or sexual activity'.[8] In *Vogel I*, a Board of Adjudication relied on *University of Saskatchewan* in upholding the denial of dental plan benefits to Richard North, the male partner of Chris Vogel, a male government employee

[5] The owner of the copyright to Cole Porter's musical 'Anything Goes' refused to permit a production that changed the sex of a character, casting a male actor in the lead female role and 'turning the tuneful 1920s romp into a gay romance': *The Economist* (4 May 1991) 122.

[6] *Gay Alliance Toward Equality* v. *Vancouver Sun* [1979] 2 SCR 435 at 461, is often cited as an authority rejecting this interpretation. See Bruner (1985 Can), 461–3; Eberts (1985 Can), 213 n. 77; Tarnopolsky (1982 Can), 257–8. However, the statement of Dickson J. that sexual orientation was not included in the list of prohibited grounds in the former British Columbia Human Rights Code must be treated as an observation that sexual orientation was not *expressly* included in the list. An attempt to infer a rejection of the argument that sexual orientation was *implicitly* included in the ground 'sex' is not warranted because the argument does not appear to have been made (at least, the Supreme Court's decision does not mention it). See Black (1979 Can), 650 n. 7.

[7] RSC 1985, c. H-6. See Ch. 6, notes 105, 106, 127, 131. Cf. *Haig* (1992) 94 DLR (4th) 1 at 13 (Ont CA) ('homosexual persons . . . fall within a ground analogous to the . . . ground of sex'); *Egan*, [1993] 3 FC 401 at 410 (CA) ('sexual orientation . . . conceded to be a ground analogous to discrimination based on "sex"'); *Vriend* (1994) 20 CHRR D/358 at D/365 (QB) ('discrimination on the basis of sexual orientation is directly associated with discrimination on the basis of sex').

[8] (1976) 66 DLR (3d) 561 at 564 (Sask QB). See also *Re Damien and Ontario Human Rights Commission* (1976) 12 OR (2d) 262 (Div Ct), where a gay employee of the Ontario Racing Commission was dismissed and the Ontario Human Rights Commission refused to investigate his complaint, holding that 'sex' did not include 'sexual orientation'. The decision containing the reasoning for this holding does not appear to have been reported. Cf. *Perceptions* (12 June 1991) 18 (Nova Scotia Human Rights Commission announced in 1990 that it would investigate sexual orientation discrimination complaints using a statutory prohibition of sex discrimination).

(the male 'common-law spouse' of a female employee would have qualified for the benefits).[9] More recently, in *Knodel*[10], *Egan* (F.C.T.D.),[11] *Nielsen*,[12] and *Guevremont*,[13] each of which concerned a denial of benefits to a same-sex partner, sex discrimination arguments under Section 15(1) or the CHRA were rejected.

The reasoning in *University of Saskatchewan* and *Vogel I*, which will be examined below, has not been seriously questioned by commentators. Most have accepted these decisions as conclusive authority that 'sex' in human rights legislation, and by extension in Section 15(1) of the Charter, does not include sexual orientation.[14] In the Charter context, Anne Bayefsky has suggested that the open-endedness of Section 15(1) makes it unnecessary to determine whether 'sex' includes 'sexual orientation' (or 'pregnancy').[15] But Nicole Duplé has observed that sex, rather than sexual orientation (understood narrowly as direction of attraction), will often be the ground of distinction used in legislation (e.g. providing the right to marry or claim tax benefits) that treats same-sex couples unequally.[16] (No man may marry another man; it is not the case that heterosexual men may marry each other, but gay and bisexual men may not.) And Wendy Williams has recognized that 'discrimination against homosexuals and sex-distinct grooming codes . . . are the ultimate sex discrimination (in the sense of sex distinction) and therefore invisible to us as such'.[17]

B. Why the Answer Is Not So Obvious

The logic underlying the view that sexual orientation discrimination is not sex discrimination is spelled out clearly in *Vogel I*:

Both males and females are treated the same under the Dental Services Plan . . . The entire issue in this case arises *not because Mr. Vogel is a male but because he chooses to live with another male* for whom he seeks dental benefits . . . Denial of benefits to [his male partner] arises because of Mr. Vogel's sexual preference [i.e. his choice of a same-sex partner] and not his gender.[18]

[9] (1983) 4 CHRR D/1654 at D/1656–7 (Man HRC). Chris Vogel filed his complaint again in 1988 after sexual orientation was included in the new Manitoba Human Rights Code. His complaint was dismissed again in *Vogel II* (1992) 90 DLR (4th) 84 (Man QB). In refusing to permit him to relitigate the sex discrimination issue, Hirschfield J. said (at 97) that '[s]ex in the Code still refers to gender and not sexual preference'.

[10] [1991] 6 WWR 728 at 742–3. [11] [1992] 1 FC 687 at 701–2 (TD).

[12] [1992] 2 FC 561 at 570, 573–4 (TD). [13] (1993) 34 LAC (4th) 104 at 115.

[14] See Hickling (1988 Can), 137; Bruner (1985 Can), 459–63; Eberts (1985 Can), 213 (argument against inclusion described as 'technical'); Hughes (1985 Can), 81–2; Leopold and King (1985 Can), 176–7; Tarnopolsky (1982 Can), 257–8.

[15] Bayefsky (1985 Can), 48–9. Cf. *Bordeleau* v. *Canada* (1989), 32 FTR 21 at 26 (it 'must be resolved [under Section 15(1)] . . . whether discrimination based on sex also covers discrimination involving sexual orientation').

[16] Duplé (1984 Can), 825.

[17] Williams (1983 Can), C/83–9, C/83–10. See also Brodsky and Day (1989 Can), 54 (supporting a sex discrimination argument); Turnbull (1989 Can), 182–3 ('sex' equals 'gender' view described as narrow).

[18] (1983) 4 CHRR D/1654 at D/1657 (Man HRC) (emphasis added).

This kind of analysis implicitly assumes that the discrimination is based, not on the plaintiff's sex, but on the plaintiff's choice between two different kinds of conduct (same-sex and opposite-sex).[19] However, the sex discrimination at work here is rendered invisible (i) by incorporating the sex-based distinction into the definitions of the two kinds of conduct, and (ii) by creating the illusion of equal treatment of men and women, in that the same treatment seems to be applied to both men and women choosing each kind of conduct. Thus, the reasoning in *Vogel I* permits the assertion that a denial of benefits to persons choosing same-sex conduct applies to all equally, regardless of sex, because men choosing such conduct with men are treated the same as women choosing such conduct with women. Similarly, a grant of benefits to persons choosing opposite-sex conduct applies to all equally, regardless of sex, because every man or woman is permitted to choose such conduct.

This illusion of equal treatment was accepted by Rowles J. in *Knodel*:

[T]he effect of the legislation is not aimed at a characteristic related to gender. The definition of 'spouse' . . . affects both men and women who are engaged in a homosexual relationship. Further, there is no indication that the discriminatory effects fall entirely on men . . . Sexual orientation is not gender specific nor is it a characteristic that affects one gender primarily.[20]

In *Egan* (F.C.T.D.), Martin J. merely quoted this reasoning and stated his agreement with it.[21] In order to unmask the sex discrimination that occurs in cases such as *Vogel I*, *Knodel*, and *Egan*, one must (i) expose the sex-based distinction that is being used, and (ii) show that the 'mirror-image symmetry' of its application to both sexes does not constitute equal treatment.

1. The Hidden Sex-based Distinction

Presenting the choice in *Vogel I* as between (a) living (in a couple relationship) with a person of the same sex as the choosing person (same-sex conduct, prohibited to all without regard to sex) or (b) living with a person of the sex opposite to that of the choosing person (opposite-sex conduct, permitted to all without regard to sex), incorporates the choosing person's sex into the definitions of the two kinds of conduct in respect of which there is discrimination. This misrepresents the choice between these two kinds of conduct (and hides the sex discrimination) by assuming that the choosing person's sex is (together with the chosen partner's sex) an inherent part of the definitions of these two kinds of conduct. Excluding the choosing person's sex from the definitions and looking only at the possible sexes of the chosen partner reveals the true nature of the

[19] See Hickling (1988 Can), 137 (the protected class is defined 'by reference to the kind of sexual activity involved').
[20] [1991] 6 WWR 728 at 743. See also *Guevremont* (1993) 34 LAC (4th) 104 at 115.
[21] [1992] 1 FC 687 at 701–2 (TD).

choice: it is between living with a man and living with a woman.[22] Viewed in this way, it is immediately clear on what basis the choice is restricted: a woman, but not a man, may choose to live with a man; a man, but not a woman, may choose to live with a woman.[23] Thus, the reason Mr. Vogel cannot 'choose[ ] to live with another male' (and obtain benefits for his partner) *is* 'because Mr. Vogel is a male'.[24]

The same kind of analysis can be applied to almost all cases of discrimination directed against individuals or particular aspects of emotional–sexual conduct. Thus, the discrimination in *University of Saskatchewan* was not, without regard to sex, between gay, lesbian, and bisexual lecturers (male or female) and hetero-sexual lecturers (male or female). Rather, it was between men choosing emotional–sexual conduct with men, and women choosing such conduct with men (or between women choosing such conduct with women, and men choosing such conduct with women). Discrimination between private same-sex sexual activity, public same-sex kissing or same-sex marriage and the equivalent opposite-sex conduct, allegedly without regard to sex, actually constitutes discrimination on the basis of sex as to who may choose to engage in sexual activity with a man in private, to kiss a man in public or to marry a man, and who may choose the equivalent conduct with a woman.

One can attempt to escape this conclusion by using an argument similar to that of Wilson J. in *Hess*:[25] a man's choice of emotional–sexual conduct with a man and a woman's choice of emotional–sexual conduct with a man are 'bio-logically different' acts or choices, of which only men and only women respec-tively are capable. However, such an argument relies entirely on the difference in the choosing person's sex and cannot point to any significant 'biological difference' between the conduct chosen by a man and that chosen by a woman. For example, there is no more 'biological' difference between a man performing oral intercourse on a man and a woman doing so on a man,[26] or between a woman living with a woman and a man living with a woman, than between a

---

[22] This means that a sex discrimination argument, unlike immutable status and fundamental choice arguments, does not use the concept of 'directions' of emotional–sexual conduct (opposite-sex or same-sex). Rather than consider 'directions' (combinations of the choosing person's sex and the chosen person's sex), one takes the chosen person's sex as given and asks who may choose emotional–sexual conduct with a person of that sex.

[23] See Pannick (1985 Eur), 203. ('The differentiation is on the ground of sex: women may have relationships with Mr. X and retain their jobs; if men have such relationships they will be sacked.') See *O'Rourke and Wallace* v. *B.G. Turnkey Services (Scotland) Ltd.* (7 June 1993), Nos. S/457/93, S/458/93 (preliminary ruling by Scottish Industrial Tribunal under the Great Britain Sex Discrim-ination Act 1975) (impossible to lay down a categoric rule that 'the dismissal of a woman, because she is carrying on a lesbian relationship, is never sex discrimination'). See also *The Independent* (9 June 1993) 7; *Pink Paper* (22 Oct. 1993) 3 (cash settlement prior to hearing on merits).

[24] See note 18 and accompanying text.   [25] [1990] 2 SCR 906.

[26] See Harvard Survey (1989 US), 1527, n. 57 (no 'biological differences' because '[t]he physical acts themselves—anal and oral sex—are the same whether between a man and a woman or two persons of the same sex; the difference is the cultural significance attached to the gender of the participants').

male lawyer advising a male client and a female lawyer advising a male client. The only 'biological differences' between same-sex emotional–sexual conduct and opposite-sex emotional–sexual conduct are that the former never has potential for unassisted procreation (which the latter may have in some but not all cases), and that the former can never involve penile–vaginal intercourse (which the latter may involve).

However, these differences are virtually never the basis of legislative and other distinctions. A public employer might refuse to hire 'men who choose emotional–sexual conduct with men' (but hire women who do so), or refuse to hire 'women who choose emotional–sexual conduct with women' (but hire men who do so). But a public employer would not refuse to hire 'persons who engage in sexual activity that does not have procreative potential or does not involve penile–vaginal intercourse' or 'persons who are unable to procreate with their partners without assistance'. Such policies would arguably not discriminate on the basis of sex, in that the choice (e.g. of sexual activity with a person of a given sex that has procreative potential) is one of which only persons of the opposite sex are biologically capable. But such policies would exclude many heterosexual persons and would therefore not be adopted.[27]

Neither race discrimination nor other forms of sex discrimination could be hidden by incorporating the choosing person's race or sex into the definition of the kinds of conduct (or opportunity) at issue. A boy of African origin, excluded from a school for children of European origin, could not be told that his choice of a school reserved for a particular race was the reason for his exclusion rather than his own race (attending a 'same-race' school being open to all, without regard to race, and attending a 'mixed-race' school being prohibited to all, without regard to race).[28] Nor could a refusal to permit a woman of East Asian origin to marry a man of European origin be explained as resulting from her choice of a spouse of a particular race rather than her own race ('same-race' marriage being open to all, without regard to race, and 'mixed-race' marriage being prohibited to all, without regard to race).[29] Similarly, a girl barred from a boys' ice hockey league would not have her claim of sex discrimination denied on the ground that her exclusion was based on her choice of the league of the other sex rather than on her own sex ('same-sex' ice hockey being open to all, without regard to sex, and 'mixed-sex' ice hockey being prohibited to all, without regard to sex).[30]

---

[27] Most opposite-sex sexual activity involves the use of contraception and is not intended to have any procreative potential.

[28] See *Brown* v. *Board of Education*, 347 US 483 (1954).

[29] See *Loving* v. *Virginia*, 388 US 1 (1967) (mixed-race marriage); *McLaughlin* v. *Florida*, 379 US 184 (1964) (mixed-race cohabitation).

[30] *Re Blainey and Ontario Hockey Association* (1986) 26 DLR (4th) 728 (CA).

2. The Illusion of Equal Treatment

Once the sex-based distinctions that underlie virtually all sexual orientation discrimination have been exposed, the next step is to challenge the argument that these distinctions do not constitute sex discrimination, and do not need to be justified, because they are made 'symmetrically', in the sense that the choices of both men and women are restricted. Thus, even though we have established that Chris Vogel is treated differently 'because [he] is a male', we must refute the claim that '[b]oth males and females are treated the same under the Dental Services Plan'.[31] Clearly, this claim is false if it means that the Plan permits each individual man and woman the same choices. As was demonstrated above, these choices are plainly not the same (i.e. they are unequal): a man can live with a woman, a woman cannot; a woman can live with a man, a man cannot. This is 'mirror-image symmetry', in that the treatment on one side is the reverse of that on the other, and therefore different. It is not 'symmetry' in the sense in which I use it, i.e., treatment is the same on both sides. The claim that the treatment is 'the same' can only be defended if it is interpreted as a claim that the treatment is 'different but equivalent', in the sense that all individuals of both sexes are denied one option and no one is permitted to choose a person of their own sex.

The short answer to this claim is that it attempts to justify one case of discrimination by invoking the existence of another related case (i.e. the discrimination against men in *Vogel I* is justified by a related, but different, discrimination against women).[32] This is something that can only be done under Section 1 of the Charter. A second, allegedly 'offsetting' sex-based distinction simply cannot negate the sex-based distinction that was initially challenged, nor cause it to

---

[31] See text accompanying note 18. See also *Nielsen*, [1992] 2 FC 561 at 570 (TD) ('the dental care plan is . . . available to both women and men equally'); *Guevremont* (1993) 34 LAC (4th) 104 at 115 (opposite-sex definition of 'common law spouse' in collective agreement 'applies equally to the corporation's male and female employees'); *DeSantis* v. *Pacific Telephone & Telegraph Co.*, 608 F 2d 327 at 331 (9th Cir 1979) ('whether dealing with men or women the employer is using the same criterion: it will not hire or promote a person who prefers sexual partners of the same sex'); *State* v. *Walsh*, 713 SW 2d 508 at 510 (Mo 1986) (law prohibiting same-sex sexual activity applies equally to men and women); *Dean* v. *District of Columbia*, 653 A 2d 307 at 363 n. 2 ('marriage statute applies equally to men and women'); *Phillips* v. *Wisconsin Personnel Commission* 482 NW 2d 121 at 127–8 (Wis Ct App 1992) (woman denied health insurance for her female partner treated the same as 'similarly situated males', i.e. those with male partners); *Dillon* v. *Frank*, 58 Empl. Prac. Dec. (CCH) para. 41332 at p. 70108 (6th Cir 1992) (gay man did not argue that his co-workers would not have harassed a lesbian woman); *X & Y* v. *UK* (No. 9369/81) (1983), 32 D.R. 220, 5 E.H.R.R. 601 at 602 (immigration law treated male–male and female–female couples in same way). Cf. *Valdes* v. *Lumbermen's Mutual Casualty Co.*, 507 F Supp 10 (SD Fla 1980) (sex discrimination argued where gay men preferred over lesbian women).

[32] See Pannick (1985 Eur), 204. ('It is no defence to a charge of sex discrimination in one's treatment of men that one has discriminated against women in another respect . . . employers [cannot] . . . impose detriment X on men, and . . . justify it by the fact that they impose detriment Y on women, and [do so] by reference to what they believe to be relevant differences between the sexes'.) See also *Symes* v. *Canada*, [1993] 4 SCR 695 at 825 (L'Heureux-Dubé J., dissenting) ('[d]iscrimination cannot be justified by pointing to other discrimination').

cease to be a prima facie violation of Section 15(1). Some pairs of sex-based distinctions would surely survive Section 1 review (e.g. separate toilets for men and women). Other pairs (e.g. a law that only men could be doctors and only women could be nurses) would not.[33]

If there were a principle that 'mirror-image symmetry' precludes a finding of a prima facie violation of Section 15(1), it could be stated as follows: a first distinction based on an enumerated or analogous ground that excludes group A, but not group B, from opportunity C, is not discriminatory if a second distinction, based on the same ground as the first distinction, excludes group B, but not group A, from opportunity D, in a way that could be said to correspond to, offset or compensate for, the first distinction. Such a principle focuses on the net effect of a set of distinctions on groups, rather than on the effect of the specific distinctions on the choices of individuals, and would insulate from Section 1 review all forms of segregation or 'separate but equal' (or 'different but equivalent') treatment, whether they are based on sex, race, or another enumerated or analogous ground.

The 'discriminatory impact' requirement in *Andrews*,[34] as interpreted in subsequent cases, makes it more difficult to dismiss such an argument than if a distinction based on an enumerated or analogous ground were automatically a prima facie violation of Section 15(1). Assuming that substantially equivalent opportunities are in fact provided separately to each group (e.g. in separate locations), one may have to show that the justification for the separation is based on some prejudice or stereotype, or that the separation actually inflicts some kind of harm on one of the groups, if only by stigmatizing its members as inferior.[35] In the case of sexual orientation, one could argue that the different options for each sex (which combine to make integration of the sexes, and opposite-sex emotional–sexual conduct, compulsory) harm women by stigmatizing them as inferior (i.e. they are incomplete without a man, and any man who seeks a relationship with another man degrades himself by 'acting like a woman'), or constitute the imposition of traditional sex roles and the prejudices or stereotypes inherent in those roles.[36]

If one succeeds in establishing that the different treatment is harmful, it does not necessarily follow under the 'discriminatory impact' requirement that the

---

[33] See *Loving*, 388 US 1 at 7–12 (1967) (holding that a prohibition of mixed-race marriages is race discrimination in spite of the 'mirror-image symmetry' of its application to all races); *Barnes* v. *Costle*, 561 F 2d 983 at 990 n. 55 (DC Cir 1977) (sexual harassment of woman by man was sex discrimination even though 'a similar condition could be imposed on a male subordinate by a ... female').

[34] See Ch. 6, Part III.

[35] See Rogers (1986 Can), 155–6 (advantage of anti-discrimination principle over group-disadvantaging principle in cases of 'separate but equal' treatment).

[36] See Fajer (1992 US), 617–50; Capers (1991 US), 1163–7; Harvard Survey (1989 US), 1526–8, 1570, 1578–81; Harvard Note (1989 US), 627–30; Koppelman (1988 US), 158–60; Law (1988 US), 196; Rosales Arriola (1988 US), 164; Hughes (1985 Can), 49–73; Leopold and King (1985 Can), 163–5; Karst (1980 US), 683–4; Babcock et al. (1975 US), 179–80.

prohibition of discrimination is symmetrical (i.e. the same on both sides). A number of writers have argued that Section 15(1) should be interpreted as protecting only members of 'disadvantaged groups'.[37] This would mean that the prima facie prohibition of sex discrimination in Section 15(1) protects only women (a 'disadvantaged group') and not men (an 'advantaged group'), and therefore that the only kind of sexual orientation discrimination that would constitute sex discrimination would be discrimination against lesbian and bisexual women and against emotional–sexual conduct (including couple relationships) between women. One can avoid this conclusion by arguing that discrimination against gay and bisexual men and emotional–sexual conduct (including couple relationships) between men harms women in the ways referred to above.[38] However, no such argument should be necessary, because I would argue that both the text of Section 15(1) (which applies to 'every individual', not 'every member of a disadvantaged group', and to 'discrimination . . . based on sex', not 'discrimination against women'), and the text of Section 28 ('the rights referred to in [this Charter] are guaranteed equally to male and female persons'),[39] make it impossible to read men out of 'sex' in Section 15(1).

3. Form versus Substance?

If the sex-based distinctions inherent in virtually all sexual orientation discrimination are sufficient to trigger prima facie violations of Section 15(1), then any justifications that might be asserted for restricting same-sex and not opposite-sex emotional–sexual conduct (e.g. same-sex sexual activity is 'immoral', 'unnatural' or 'offensive', or lacks procreative potential or potential for penile–vaginal intercourse; same-sex couple relationships are 'inherently unstable', are not 'financially interdependent' or require assistance with procreation) could only be raised under Section 1. Thus, the 'formal' similarity of same-sex and opposite-sex emotional–sexual conduct (but for the sex of one of the persons involved) would permit a gay, lesbian or bisexual plaintiff to move from Section 15(1) to Section 1. At this stage, in rebutting any asserted justifications, the plaintiff could establish that the similarity is not just a matter of 'form' but of 'substance'; that the feelings arising from same-sex conduct are as intense as those

---

[37] See Ch. 6, note 63. Cf. *R.* v. *Hess* [1990] 2 SCR 906 at 943–4 (not essential for Section 15(1) protection that men be 'a "discrete and insular minority" disadvantaged independently of the legislation under consideration').

[38] See note 36. One could also argue that gay and bisexual men, as opposed to heterosexual men, are members of a 'disadvantaged group' and are therefore entitled to benefit from the prima facie prohibition of sex discrimination in Section 15(1).

[39] See *Hess*, [1990] 2 SCR 906 at 932–3, 943–4 (Section 28 protects men as well as women); Black and Grant (1990 Can), 380 ('[t]he complete exclusion of men from s. 15 would be difficult to reconcile with the language of s. 28'). But see Brodsky and Day (1989 Can), 37, 62, 82 (interpreting Section 28 as protecting men is 'cruel' and 'perverse'). Cf. *J.E.B.* v. *Alabama ex rel. T.B.* 128 L Ed 2d 89 at 104–5 (US Sup Ct 1994) (that discrimination is against men does not 'exempt it from scrutiny or reduce the standard of review' under equal protection doctrine).

arising from opposite-sex conduct; and that being in love, making love, strolling hand in hand in a park, and setting up a home with a partner have the same importance and value regardless of the sexes of the persons involved. This 'substantive' similarity should help counter any asserted Section 1 justifications.[40]

Assuming that crude, sex-based distinctions could not be used to discriminate between same-sex and opposite-sex couples, other neutral criteria (e.g. a monogamous sexual relationship, living together, owning property jointly, merging finances) might exclude a disproportionate number of same-sex couples from a particular benefit, in spite of their long-term emotional commitment. This would raise issues under Section 15(1) of indirect discrimination based on sex (or sexual orientation), accommodation of difference, and the inadequacy of 'formal' equality where same-sex couples are in fact different from opposite-sex couples. As Douglas Sanders has pointed out, in discussing the use of '"we are the same" data' by same-sex couples, '[t]he idea of good homosexuals and bad homosexuals, judged by the degree to which their lives parallel ideal heterosexual models, is rejected by many lesbians and gays'.[41] Thus, the Board of Inquiry in *Leshner* hastened to add:

People organize their intimate relationships differently depending on a variety of factors . . . This is . . . true for heterosexuals as it is for homosexuals . . . [I]t [is not] necessary for same-sex relationships to mirror the idealized model perceived with respect to a heterosexual conjugal relationship. An administrative need for identification should be met by neutral, objective criteria rather than the prospect of detailed personal inquiries, which we do not believe are the business of employers.[42]

C. Other Not So Obvious Kinds of Sex Discrimination: Sexual Harassment and Pregnancy Discrimination

Because sexual orientation involves a choice (of emotional–sexual conduct), because the choice is restricted (on the basis of sex) on what appears to be a 'symmetrical' basis, and because the restrictions do not affect most women or men (who are heterosexual), it is a less obvious example of sex discrimination. Similarly, because sexual harassment and pregnancy discrimination may not affect all women, some courts have been reluctant (for this and other reasons) to treat these phenomena as sex discrimination. The Supreme Court has, however, settled this issue (at least with respect to human rights legislation) by

[40] Courts and tribunals have tended not to question the substantial similarity between a long-term same-sex couple relationship and a long-term opposite-sex couple relationship. See e.g. *Egan*, [1992] 1 FC 687 at 695–7 (TD); *Knodel*, [1991] 6 WWR 728 at 745; *Leshner* (1992) 16 CHRR D/184 at D/188-D/189 (Ont Hum Rts Comm); *Vogel II* (1992) 90 DLR (4th) 84 at 95 (Man QB).
[41] 'Drawing Lines on Lesbian and Gay Rights' (7 Jan. 1993) at 19, 28–9, draft of Sanders (1994 Can).
[42] (1992) 16 CHRR D/184 at D/189 (Ont Hum Rts Comm).

interpreting 'sex' in the former Manitoba Human Rights Act as including sexual harassment, in *Janzen* v. *Platy Enterprises Ltd.*,[43] and pregnancy discrimination, in *Brooks* v. *Canada Safeway Ltd.*[44] This Part will examine the conceptual difficulties that arise when sexual harassment and pregnancy discrimination are treated as sex discrimination and suggest that, because sexual orientation does not present these difficulties, it should be an easier case for the Supreme Court (under Section 15(1)).[45]

Treating sexual harassment as sex discrimination is problematic for a number of reasons. Where sexual harassment involves requests for, or actual, unwanted physical contact of a sexual nature, the harasser's motive for selecting the victim may be a combination of the victim's sex and her or his physical attractiveness (as opposed to a general hostility toward the presence of women or men in the workplace). The Supreme Court dealt with this problem in *Janzen* by concluding that it is sufficient for sex to be *a* factor in the decision to treat an employee differently (and therefore that not all women or men need be affected), and that 'sexual attractiveness cannot be separated from gender'.[46]

While the first conclusion is certainly correct, I would suggest that the second is not and fails to recognise a 'loophole' in the protection against sexual harassment that a prohibition of sex discrimination can provide. Sexual or physical 'attractiveness', like height or hair colour, is a separate phenomenon from that of male or female sex, and a bisexual person could choose to discriminate only on the basis of physical 'attractiveness' and not on the basis of sex by sexually harassing both physically attractive women and physically attractive men.[47] This hypothetical defence to a charge of sex discrimination has been noted by US

[43] [1989] 1 SCR 1252. Dickson C.J. (at 1279) defined sex discrimination as unequal treatment 'on the basis of a characteristic related to gender'. In *Knodel*, [1991] 6 WWR 728 at 742–3, Rowles J. purported to apply this statement and found that sexual orientation is not such a characteristic.

[44] [1989] 1 SCR 1219. Cf. *Dekker* v. *Stichting Vormingscentrum voor Jong Volwassenen (VJV-Centrum) Plus* (Case C-177/88), [1990] ECR I-3941 at I-3973 (Eur Ct Justice) (pregnancy discrimination is 'direct discrimination on grounds of sex'); *Webb* v. *EMO Air Cargo (UK) Ltd.*, [1992] 4 All ER 929 at 934 (HL) ('in general to dismiss a woman because she is pregnant . . . is unlawful direct [sex] discrimination'); *General Electric Co.* v. *Gilbert*, 429 US 125 (1976) (pregnancy discrimination not sex discrimination under Title VII of the Civil Rights Act of 1964); *Geduldig* v. *Aiello*, 417 US 484 (1974) (pregnancy discrimination not sex discrimination under Equal Protection Clause of Fourteenth Amendment).

[45] In Wisconsin, employment discrimination based on sexual orientation is prohibited by a prohibition of employment discrimination based on sex. See Wis Stat Ann ss. 111.321, 111.36(1). S. 111.36(1) states: 'Employment discrimination because of sex includes, but is not limited to . . . (b) [e]ngaging in sexual harassment . . . (c) [d]iscriminating against any woman on the basis of pregnancy, child-birth, maternity leave or related medical conditions . . . (d) 1. . . . [discriminating] against an individual . . . because of the individual's sexual orientation.'

[46] [1989] 1 SCR 1252 at 1290.

[47] For examples of male–male and female–female sexual harassment, see *Romman* v. *Sea-West Holdings Ltd.* (1984), 5 CHRR D/2312 (male–male); Ch. 3, notes 143–7 (US cases); *Gates* v. *Security Express Guards* (5 July 1993), No. 45142/92 (Industrial Tribunal), *The Independent* (22 June 1993) 5 (male–male) (damages awarded under Great Britain Sex Discrimination Act 1975).

courts.[48] Indeed, the harasser could be heterosexual, gay or lesbian and harass both men and women if their criterion for selecting victims were 'being a person the harasser would like to humiliate through words or conduct of a sexual nature'. Rather than rely solely on a prohibition of sex discrimination, it would be better to acknowledge the gap in protection and propose an express, general prohibition of all forms of harassment in the workplace, defined in terms of conduct rather than the basis for choosing victims.[49]

This minor defect in the sex discrimination approach (and consequent need for a general prohibition) results from the fact that discrimination principles (which identify prima facie prohibited grounds of distinction in areas where distinctions are usually permitted, e.g. employment decisions) are being used in an area of conduct that is objectionable *per se* (regardless of the ground of distinction or the existence of any distinction) and does not become acceptable when the distinction is eliminated. Sex discrimination against women which takes the form of their exclusion from a benefit available to men can be remedied by extending the benefit to women. Sex discrimination against women which takes the form of sexual harassment is not remedied by removing the distinction and extending the burden to men (i.e. when a bisexual man becomes an 'equal opportunity harasser').[50] Murder, assault, and harassment (whether verbal or involving unwanted physical contact) should be prohibited regardless of the basis on which a victim is selected.

The purpose of this discussion is only to point out an 'imperfection' in the fit of sexual harassment into the category of sex discrimination, and not to suggest that the sex discrimination approach and the decision in *Janzen* are wrong. Sexual harassment is properly characterized as an issue of sex discrimination, because the majority of cases will involve a heterosexual man selecting a woman for different treatment (harassment) on the basis of her sex. The existence of hypothetical cases that may escape the net of sex discrimination is an argument for a more general prohibition, but not for the abandonment of an approach that permits existing legislation to be used to deal with most cases of sexual harassment.

Pregnancy discrimination resembles sexual orientation discrimination in that,

[48] See e.g. *Bundy* v. *Jackson*, 641 F 2d 934, 942 n. 7 (DC Cir 1981); *Barnes*, 561 F 2d 983 at 990 n. 55 (DC Cir 1977). Cf. *Chiapuzio* v. *BLT Operating Corporation*, 826 F Supp 1334 (D Wyo 1993) (rejecting argument that no sex discrimination occurred where a male supervisor harassed both male and female employees).

[49] See e.g. Manitoba Human Rights Code, SM 1987–88, c. 45, s. 19 (defining 'harassment' as including 'unwelcome sexual solicitations or advances').

[50] This problem can also arise with harassment of gay, lesbian, and bisexual workers. In *Dillon*, 58 Empl. Prac. Dec. (CCH) para. 41, 332 (6th Cir 1992), the Sixth Circuit held that physical harassment of a gay man by his male co-workers was not sex discrimination because there was no evidence that they would not also have harassed a woman known to engage in oral or anal intercourse. Even if the court had asked the relevant question of how they would have treated a woman presumed to engage in unspecified sexual activity with men (since Dillon presumably had not discussed the details of his sexual activity with them), it may still have found no sex discrimination if these (presumably heterosexual) male workers harassed both heterosexual women and gay or bisexual men equally. See generally Marcosson (1992 US).

under the Charter, there are at least four potential approaches to finding protection: (a) pregnancy (sexual orientation) is included within the enumerated ground 'sex'; (b) pregnancy discrimination has a disproportionate, and indeed exclusive, impact on women[51] and therefore has the same effect as sex discrimination (discrimination against same-sex emotional–sexual conduct has a disproportionate impact on gay, lesbian, and bisexual persons); (c) pregnancy (sexual orientation) is an immutable status and therefore an analogous ground; and (d) pregnancy (sexual orientation) is a fundamental choice and therefore an analogous ground. In the context of human rights legislation, however, the third and fourth approaches would require an amendment to the statute (there being a closed list of grounds of discrimination rather than an open-ended list as in Section 15(1)), and are therefore not available in the judicial arena.[52] In *Brooks*, the Supreme Court accepted the first approach (the second apparently was not argued). The Court concluded that, because only women have the capacity to become pregnant, they are pregnant because of their sex, and that the fact that not all women are pregnant at any one time makes no difference.[53] In *Janzen*, the Court added that 'pregnancy cannot be separated from gender'.[54]

The decision in *Brooks* achieves an extremely desirable result by stretching the meaning of female sex as an immutable status. Pregnancy is not something over which a woman has no control. It requires her to make choices, usually to engage in opposite-sex sexual activity and not to use contraception, and always (whether insemination occurs as a result of consensual or non-consensual opposite-sex sexual activity or alternative methods, and whether contraception was used or not) not to terminate the pregnancy by having an abortion.[55] The analysis in *Brooks* disregards these choices. This is certainly appropriate with respect to the choice of abortion, because although it makes a wanted pregnancy theoretically mutable, a coerced abortion would be a gross violation of bodily integrity. However, the choices with regard to opposite-sex sexual activity and contraception or donor insemination would remain in most cases, supplying the element of initial choice that would prevent pregnancy from being considered an immutable status, either independently or as part of female sex.[56] But whether or not pregnancy is an immutable status, I would argue that the related choices to become pregnant and not to have an abortion, or to have an abortion and not to remain pregnant, should be considered fundamental.[57]

[51] See Sheppard (1989 Can), 232. A disproportionate (but not exclusive) impact on women is also true of sexual harassment.
[52] But see notes 111–23 and accompanying text.
[53] [1989] 1 SCR 1219 at 1242–9.   [54] [1989] 1 SCR 1252 at 1289.
[55] This discussion assumes that abortion is legally available and that all cases of pregnancy discrimination therefore involve wanted pregnancies.
[56] Pregnancy would be an initially unchosen and currently immutable status where a woman had been raped and did not want an abortion. On the 'voluntariness' of pregnancy, see Smith (1991 Can), 387–9.
[57] See Ch. 7, note 55. See also *Brooks*, [1989] 1 SCR 1219 at 1237 ('It is to state the obvious to say that pregnancy is of fundamental importance in our society').

It would be preferable to treat pregnancy as an independent fundamental choice, rather than as part of the immutable status of being a woman, for two reasons. First, if pregnancy discrimination is sex discrimination, then it is difficult to see why interference of any kind (including criminal regulation) with a woman's decision to have an abortion is not also sex discrimination.[58] The majority of the Supreme Court dealt with abortion under Section 7 in *Morgentaler*. To hold that interference with abortion is sex discrimination under Section 15(1), the Supreme Court would have to conclude, as it did in *Brooks*, that, because only women have abortions, women have abortions because of their sex, and that 'abortion cannot be separated from gender'. However much one might support a woman's right to choose an abortion, one can hardly fail to acknowledge that it *is* a choice and does not follow inevitably from a woman's sex.

Second, if discrimination based on any chosen physical condition that happens only to one sex (or any chosen conduct of which only one sex is physically capable) is sex discrimination,[59] which seems to follow from the *Brooks* reasoning, then a 'no beards' rule must constitute sex discrimination. The Supreme Court in *Brooks* dismissed the analogy between beards and pregnancy as trivializing 'the procreative and socially vital function of women and [elevating] the growing of facial hair to a constitutional right'.[60] This statement points to the reason why the analogy is invalid. Although only women can become pregnant and only men can grow beards, neither is an immutable status. Both usually involve choices (opposite-sex sexual activity or donor insemination; not shaving), but becoming pregnant should be considered a fundamental choice, whereas growing a beard is unlikely to be viewed as such (unless it is required by one's religious beliefs).[61]

Although the *Brooks* decision may stretch the meaning of sex, this interpretation can be justified by recalling that the Supreme Court was dealing with a human rights statute, not the Charter, and could not therefore find that pregnancy was a fundamental choice and an analogous ground.[62] The Court avoided an unjust result by interpreting 'sex' as including pregnancy, and may well have given effect to the Manitoba legislature's intent. In adopting sex discrimination legislation, primarily to protect women, it probably intended protection to extend to pregnancy as a fundamental choice of the utmost importance to women. However, the Court's approach in *Brooks* would not be necessary in a Charter

---

[58] See Sheppard (1989 Can), 216 n. 32, 218 n. 37. Cf. *Hess*, [1990] 2 SCR 906 at 930 (it is absurd 'to suggest that a provision that prohibits self-induced abortion is discriminatory because it does not include men').

[59] In *Hess*, ibid. at 929, Wilson J. took the opposite position, holding that the prohibition of sex discrimination in Section 15(1) 'does not prevent the creation of an offence which, as a matter of biological fact, can only be committed by one of the sexes'. I would agree with her statement, but would not agree that 'penile–vaginal intercourse with a person under 14' is such an offence.

[60] [1989] 1 SCR 1219 at 1249–50.

[61] See Proulx (1988 Can), 594. Treating pregnancy as a fundamental choice also shows why the analogy between pregnancy and cosmetic surgery, referred to in *Brooks*, ibid. at 1237, is fallacious (at least if the surgery is not essential to psychological health).

[62] But see notes 111–23 and accompanying text.

case, because the flexibility of Section 15(1) would allow the Court to find that pregnancy is a fundamental choice and analogous ground under Section 15(1), rather than included in the enumerated ground 'sex'.[63]

Putting aside any justifications that might be asserted under Section 1, it should be easier for the Supreme Court to find that sexual orientation discrimination is sex discrimination under Section 15(1) than to find that either sexual harassment or pregnancy discrimination is sex discrimination. First, unlike sexual harassment, the basis on which a person's choice of sexual orientation is restricted will almost always be only their sex and not a combination of their sex and some other factor. Second, unlike pregnancy, which usually involves an initial choice of sexual activity, one does not initially choose one's sex; the theoretical ability to escape a restriction on one's choice of sexual orientation by having a sex-change operation would (like an abortion) be a gross violation of bodily integrity if coerced.[64] Indeed, the fact that one chooses one's sexual orientation (as direction of conduct) obscures the fact that the restriction of that choice is based on an effectively immutable and inescapable status. The existence of the choice is a 'red herring', just as the fact that a non-citizen might seek a job in their country of citizenship or a woman might seek a job across the street is a 'red herring'. The choice of opportunity (country or company where job is sought) may be mutable, but the basis on which the individual's choice is restricted (citizenship or sex) is not.

Finally, it should be noted that, although sanctions against same-sex emotional–sexual attraction or conduct apply to all men and all women, one could argue that they affect only those men and women who have such an attraction or engage in such conduct. But the fact that only some men or some women are affected is irrelevant. As the Supreme Court held in *Janzen* and *Brooks*, they will be treated differently because they are men or because they are women.[65] A refusal to hire Muslim women (but not Muslim men) or to hire women with small children (but not men with small children)[66] is nonetheless sex

---

[63] See Bayefsky (1985 Can), 49 (not necessary to find 'pregnancy' included in 'sex'). If the Supreme Court declined to identify fundamental choices and treat them as analogous grounds, there would be an incentive to invoke the *Brooks* reasoning under Section 15(1).

[64] A sex-change operation would permit one to escape a sex-based restriction on one's choice of sexual orientation only if the distinction were based on genital (as opposed to chromosomal) sex. It is worth noting that many transsexual persons challenge the definition of 'sex' as 'chromosomal', but are prepared to comply with sex-based distinctions. Most gay, lesbian, and bisexual persons accept the definition of sex and have no desire to change their sex, but challenge instead the making of sex-based distinctions, including the sex-based distinction in the traditional definition of marriage. Thus, a male-to-female transsexual person seeks recognition as a woman so as to enjoy a woman's existing right to marry a man. See *Cossey* (1990), Ser. A, No. 184. A gay or bisexual man seeks recognition of a man's right to marry a man, and a lesbian or bisexual woman seeks recognition of a woman's right to marry a woman.

[65] See *Janzen*, [1989] 1 SCR 1252 at 1288–90; *Brooks*, [1989] 1 SCR 1219 at 1247–9. See also *Symes*, [1993] 4 SCR 695 at 769–70 ('an adverse effect felt by a subgroup of women can still constitute sex-based discrimination'; 'a finding of sex discrimination need not necessarily have widespread effects').

[66] See Hickling (1988 Can), 139–40.

discrimination, even though only a subset of women is affected. The same is true where an employer refuses to hire or provide benefits to women with female partners (but not men with female partners), or men with male partners (but not women with male partners).

D. *The Drafters' 'Original Intent' as to What Sex Discrimination Is*

Even if a plaintiff succeeds in convincing a court that sexual orientation discrimination is 'literally'[67] sex discrimination because it involves sex distinctions that are different for each sex, they must confront a final hurdle: Was the constitutional or statutory prohibition of sex discrimination intended to apply to cases of sexual orientation discrimination? A number of courts and human rights tribunals in Canada and the US have refused to interpret prohibitions of sex discrimination in human rights legislation as extending to sexual orientation discrimination, because they assumed that the legislature could not have intended such a result,[68] especially if it had rejected a proposed amendment that would have added 'sexual orientation' expressly.[69]

It is questionable whether a narrow interpretation of 'sex', as circumscribed by the legislature's 'original intent', is appropriate in the case of human rights legislation, especially in Canada where the Supreme Court has held that such legislation 'is of a special nature, not quite constitutional but certainly more than ordinary', and is to be given 'an interpretation which will advance its broad purposes'.[70] The 'original intent' of the Manitoba legislature did not seem to be a significant factor in determining whether 'sexual harassment' and 'pregnancy' were implicitly included in 'sex' in *Janzen* and *Brooks*.[71] If a court concludes

[67] See *Macauley* v. *Massachusetts Commission Against Discrimination*, 397 NE 2d 670 at 671 (Mass 1979): '[a]s a matter of literal meaning, discrimination against homosexuals could be treated as a species of discrimination because of sex. We treat distinctions based on pregnancy as distinctions based on sex, calling them "sex-linked" . . . In a somewhat different sense, homosexuality is also sex-linked.'

[68] See *Macauley*, ibid.; *University of Saskatchewan* (1976) 66 DLR (3d) 561 at 564–5 (Sask QB); *Vogel I*, (1983) 4 CHRR D/1654 at D/1658 (Man HRC); *DeSantis*, 608 F 2d 327 at 329–30 (9th Cir 1979) ('Congress has not shown any intent other than to restrict the term "sex" to its traditional meaning'); *Gay Law Students*, 595 P 2d 592 at 612 (Cal 1979) ('[a]lthough, as a semantic argument, the contention may have some appeal . . . when viewed in terms of expressed intent, the Legislature . . . did not contemplate discrimination against homosexuals'); *Singer* v. *Hara*, 522 P 2d 1187 at 1194 (Wash Ct App 1974) (the majority that voted for Washington's Equal Rights Amendment did not intend it to permit same-sex marriages).

[69] See *DeSantis*, ibid. at 329. Cf. *Mossop*, [1993] 1 SCR 554 ('family status').

[70] *Ontario Human Rights Commission* v. *Simpsons-Sears Ltd.*, [1985] 2 SCR 536 at 547 (*O'Malley*).

[71] See *Brooks*, [1989] 1 SCR 1219 at 1228, 1250 ('[o]ne cannot conclude from the fact that some provinces [including Manitoba] have added pregnancy . . . that discrimination on the basis of sex does not encompass pregnancy-based discrimination'); *Janzen*, [1989] 1 SCR 1252 at 1261, 1286 (amendments in Manitoba and other jurisdictions expressly prohibiting sexual harassment 'were no doubt intended to make . . . explicit what had previously been implicit'). Similarly, it is highly doubtful that Parliament 'intended' or 'foresaw' that the CHRA's prohibition of sex discrimination would be applied to the exclusion of women from combat duties in the armed forces. Nevertheless, this absence of 'original intent' did not preclude the perfectly logical conclusion that such exclusion violates the CHRA. See *Gauthier* v. *Canada (Attorney-General)* (1989), 10 CHRR D/6014 (Can HRC).

that sexual orientation discrimination is sex discrimination, it need not ask whether the legislature 'intended' an unambiguous prohibition of sex discrimination to apply to cases where the sex discrimination interferes with a person's choice of the direction of their emotional–sexual conduct. It should ask only whether there is any statutory language expressly excluding the application of such a prohibition to such cases. If not, and if no other statutory exception (such as a bona fide occupational qualification) can be established, the conclusion that the legislation has been violated should be inescapable.

An 'original intent' argument is even weaker in the context of Section 15(1) of the Charter, which is to be given a 'broad and generous' interpretation,[72] and with respect to which evidence of legislative intent is given 'minimal weight'.[73] As has been demonstrated above, sexual orientation discrimination clearly falls within the prima facie scope of the prohibition of sex discrimination in Section 15(1). That prohibition should be given its full prima facie effect. Any special justification for excluding a particular case of sexual orientation discrimination from the prima facie protection offered by 'sex' in Section 15(1) must be raised under Section 1.

Whatever weight is given to the 'original intent' of the drafters of the Charter (or of human rights legislation), it can be argued that treating sexual orientation discrimination as sex discrimination is entirely consistent with that intent. This is true if the 'original intent' or purpose behind a prohibition of sex discrimination is defined, not with respect to specific applications of the prohibition, but in terms of a general goal of eliminating the enforcement of traditional sex roles by legislatures and public (or private) employers.[74] The obligation of men to choose emotional–sexual conduct only with women, and the obligation of women to do so only with men, are perhaps the most fundamental (and therefore invisible[75] and unchallenged) aspects of traditional sex roles. The legal and social persecution of gay and bisexual men (who violate the traditional male role by engaging in conduct that is only permitted to women, thereby betraying and forfeiting their superior male status),[76] and lesbian and bisexual women (who violate their traditional female role by seeking to live independently of men) is an integral aspect of enforcing traditional sex roles (men in the workplace and

---

[72] Justice McIntyre said in *Andrews*, [1989] 1 SCR 143 at 175: 'Both the enumerated grounds ... and other possible grounds of discrimination recognized under s. 15(1) must be interpreted in a broad and generous manner, reflecting the fact that they are constitutional provisions not easily repealed or amended but intended to provide a "continuing framework for the legitimate exercise of governmental power" and, at the same time, for "the unremitting protection" of equality rights.' See also Ch. 6, notes 143–6 and accompanying text.

[73] See Ch. 6, note 146.

[74] For a discussion of how 'original intent' can be defined more broadly, see Dworkin (1987 US), 3–10. See also Pannick (1985 Eur), 204 (the Great Britain Sex Discrimination Act 1975 'was introduced precisely to prevent reliance on real or perceived biological or cultural differences between the sexes, except where Parliament expressly provided an exception to the anti-discrimination principle').

[75] See text accompanying note 17 above.

[76] See, e.g. Boswell (1980 Other), 74–5 (discussing loss of status of adult male citizens of Rome if they permitted themselves to be penetrated by another man's penis, which only politically powerless women, adolescent males, and slaves were supposed to do).

women in the home, joined exclusively by traditional opposite-sex marriages).[77]
As conservative writer William Gairdner argues:

[H]omosexuality . . . thrives when male/female role distinctions are discouraged. Cultures that want to guard against the threat of homosexuality must therefore drive a cultural wedge down hard between maleness and femaleness, for it is no simple coincidence that homosexuality is flourishing in a time of feminism. They go together like the two sides of a coin. The attempt of the state to neutralize male and female differences is manifest in its effort to 'normalize' homosexuality, marketing it to us in its agencies and schools as a 'value-free' matter of sexual 'orientation'.[78]

Of such writers, Kenneth Karst has observed: 'It is not just coincidence that [those] most disturbed about the liberalization of society's response to same-sex orientation are also the most concerned to see that women return to "the family" . . . to domesticity'.[79]

E. Single-sex Situations

A sex discrimination argument is almost perfectly suited to cases of sexual orientation discrimination that involve a mixed-sex situation, i.e. where both men and women are present. The fact that both men and women are present (e.g. in a workplace) permits the treatment of gay and bisexual men to be compared with that of heterosexual women (because members of both groups may choose emotional–sexual conduct with men), and the treatment of lesbian and bisexual women to be compared with that of heterosexual men (because members of both groups may choose emotional–sexual conduct with women).[80]

However, the application of a sex discrimination argument appears, at first glance, to break down in single-sex situations, i.e. those where only men or only women are present, because the prima facie sex discrimination that excludes the other sex is considered justified. These situations arise where a bona fide

---

[77] See note 36 and accompanying text. Cf. Gairdner (1990 Can), 73, 82–3, 209–10, 273–84 (suggesting that traditional sex roles, that assign women to the home and insist on traditional opposite-sex marriage as the only option, are essential to the success of a capitalist economy); Honoré (1978 Eur), 103–5 ('[h]omosexual men are less likely to marry and support wives', which 'tends to undermine the economic position of women').

[78] Gairdner (1990 Can), 281.   [79] See Karst (1991 US), 509.

[80] Such a comparison is easier where the sex discrimination is direct rather than indirect. In cases of indirect sex discrimination against gay and bisexual men or against lesbian and bisexual women, it will be difficult to show a disproportionate impact on men as a group or women as a group (unless one wishes to argue that same-sex and bisexual sexual orientations are more common among men or among women). However, a disproportionate impact on a subgroup of men (men choosing emotional–sexual conduct with men versus women choosing such conduct with men) or a subgroup of women (women choosing emotional–sexual conduct with women versus men doing so with women) could be established and should be sufficient. In *Symes*, [1993] 4 SCR 695 at 763–5, 769–71, a claim that the non-deductibility of child care expenses (as business expenses for income tax purposes) was indirect sex discrimination (i.e. had a disproportionate impact on self-employed women with children versus self-employed men with children) failed for lack of evidence of the disproportionate impact, not because such precisely defined subgroups of men and of women could not be compared.

occupational requirement or 'public decency' are deemed to permit either the exclusion of one sex altogether or the segregation of the sexes (e.g. public toilets and changing rooms, single-sex residences, the armed forces or jobs involving viewing or having physical contact with a person in a state of undress). They also arise where 'biological differences' confine the ability to make a particular choice to persons of one sex. In such situations, one could argue that exclusion of a gay, lesbian, or bisexual person does not constitute sex discrimination, in that the 'but for sex' test is not satisfied. A gay or bisexual man denied a job as a men's locker room attendant at a public swimming pool could not claim that a heterosexual woman would have been employed (assuming that women could legally be excluded from the job). Similarly, a lesbian or bisexual woman denied donor insemination could not assert that a heterosexual man would have been provided the service.

In spite of this apparent difficulty, a sex discrimination argument can be applied to single-sex situations. To do so, one must recall that a major purpose of prohibiting sex discrimination is to prevent the penalizing of persons who fail to comply with a stereotype about the proper role or behaviour of a person of their sex (e.g. women seeking employment in traditionally 'male' jobs, and vice versa). In mixed-sex situations, it is often unnecessary to consider the traditional sex roles in identifying a particular case of discrimination as sex discrimination, because explicit sex-based distinctions must be made to force men into one role and women into another (e.g. only men may be janitors; only women may be secretaries). The enforcement of traditional sex roles may often be raised as a justification for the sex-based distinctions, but will almost always be rejected.

In single-sex situations, however, it is essential to consider these roles because no explicit sex-based distinctions are or can be made, in that there is no other sex present that could be treated more or less favourably. The distinctions are not based explicitly on 'biological sex', but on compliance with social 'sex roles' (or 'gender') (although those roles are ultimately determined by 'biological sex'). The kind of sex discrimination that occurs in these situations involves penalizing a person because they fail to comply with the social role traditionally associated with their sex. One of the most fundamental elements of this role is the assumption that men will engage in emotional–sexual conduct only with women, and that women will do so only with men. Thus, refusing to hire the gay or bisexual man or serve the lesbian or bisexual woman in the situations mentioned above (because they do not comply with the male and female sex roles respectively) constitutes prima facie discrimination because of their sex under Section 15(1) and must be justified under Section 1.[81]

The above discussion of single-sex situations has sought to demonstrate that cases of sexual orientation discrimination in such situations fall within the principle

---

[81] Cf. Capers (1991 US), 1158 (arguing that 'discrimination based on sexual orientation is essentially discrimination based on sex stereotyping').

of a prima facie prohibition of sex discrimination, whether in the Charter or human rights legislation. But an additional issue may arise when one considers the 'public decency' exceptions to such a principle, in single-sex situations, that may be upheld as justified under Section 1 or may be expressly included in human rights legislation.[82] On its face, any such exception deals only with the exclusion of one sex or the segregation of the sexes, and thus does not apply to distinctions within one sex (e.g. the exclusion of gay and bisexual men from a men-only situation or the exclusion of lesbian and bisexual women from a women-only situation). However, it could be argued that, just as the principle of a prima facie prohibition of sex discrimination can be interpreted as applying to cases of sexual orientation discrimination, 'public decency' exceptions to that principle can also be interpreted as applying to such cases. To do so, one would have to assert that the rationale for these exceptions is the protection of individuals (in circumstances where privacy is minimal or non-existent) from being viewed or touched by any person (regardless of sex) who might be sexually attracted to them.[83]

I would argue that the rationale for these exceptions must be confined to the protection of individuals (in such circumstances) from being viewed or touched by a person who is not of their own sex (i.e. who is visibly different). Even the justification for this narrower version is not unchallengeable. There is no reason to assume that a person, solely because of their sex, is unable to act profession-ally or otherwise respect the privacy of a person of the opposite sex who is undressed and may or must be viewed (or, where it is necessary to touch the other person, that they will abuse the situation). Most doctors and nurses are able to do so, as are most patrons of mixed-sex nude beaches. Persons who cannot do so (or who abuse such a situation) could be dismissed or disciplined.[84]

---

[82] See e.g. Ontario Human Rights Code, RSO 1990, c. H.19, s. 20(1) ('use of . . . services or facilities is restricted to persons of the same sex on the ground of public decency') and s. 21(2) (single-sex accommodation); Manitoba Human Rights Code, SM 1987–88, c. 45, ss. 13–17 ('*bona fide* and reasonable' causes or requirements).

[83] In *Steffan I* 780 F Supp 1 at 13 (DDC 1991), the court discussed 'the military interest in maintaining a semblance of privacy for its members', asserting that '[t]he quite rational assumption in the [US] Navy is that with no one present who has a homosexual orientation, men and women alike can undress, sleep, bathe, and use the bathroom without fear or embarrassment that they are being viewed as sexual objects'. This 'staring in the showers' argument was rejected by the DC Circuit panel in *Steffan II*, 8 F 3d 57 at 69 (DC Cir 1993), and by the minority in *Steffan III*, 41 F 3d 677 at 719–20, as either presuming misconduct on the part of gay, lesbian, and bisexual persons or catering to the irrational fears and prejudices of heterosexual persons. See also *Dahl* v. *Secretary of the US Navy*, 830 F Supp 1319 at 1329, 1332 (ED Cal 1993); *Able* v. *US*, 1995 US Dist LEXIS 3928 at *27–*29.

[84] See *Watkins* v. *US Army*, 875 F 2d 699 at 728 n. 31 (9th Cir 1989): '[e]ven if the Army had raised the argument that excluding homosexuals from barracks reduces sexual tension and had shown that reducing sexual tension serves a compelling interest, nothing in the record even suggests that a *per se* ban would be the least restrictive method of advancing this interest.' See also Karst (1991 US), 556: '[i]n the barracks, in the shower room, gay and lesbian servicemembers are already present. If the exclusion rule were dropped . . . there would be no reason to expect a flood of unwelcome sexual advances.'

However, the segregation of the sexes in minimal privacy situations is so well entrenched that prohibiting single-sex toilets, changing rooms, dormitories, etc. would constitute a radical and, for some, alarming[85] departure from tradition. Assuming that these kinds of segregation of the (visibly different) sexes can be justified, there is no reason to extend them to segregation *within* sexes so as to permit discrimination based on sexual orientation (a generally invisible difference). 'Intra-sex' segregation would stigmatize persons excluded (e.g. from 'heterosexual' public toilets), and would be extremely difficult to enforce. Instead, the presumption of professional and respectful conduct mentioned above should prevail, with only those persons (heterosexual, bisexual, gay or lesbian) unable or unwilling to comply being excluded from a single-sex situation.

F. Sex Discrimination Against Same-sex Couples

We have seen in Chapter 7 that a fundamental choice argument can deal with cases of discrimination against same-sex couples in respect of benefits, but that an immutable status argument cannot (at least as direct discrimination). A sex discrimination argument is also well suited to such cases. One need only ask whether, if the plaintiff were a person of the opposite sex, their partner would qualify for the benefit in question. In *Vogel I*, *Karen Andrews*, *Mossop*, *Veysey*, *Knodel*, *Egan*, *Vogel II*, and *Leshner*[86] the answer was yes because, in each case, the benefit was made available to unmarried opposite-sex couples. Courts have failed to recognize this because they have focused solely on the sex of the (chosen) partner, and not on the sex of the plaintiff (the choosing partner). In *Mossop*, the tribunal noted that Brian Mossop's partner, Ken Popert, would have qualified as a 'common-law spouse' 'but for [his] gender' or 'except for [his] sex'.[87] Similarly, in *Egan* (F.C.T.D.), Martin J. said that 'had [John] Nesbit [the partner] been a woman cohabiting with [James] Egan [the plaintiff] . . . [Nesbit] would have been eligible for the spouse's allowance'.[88] What courts need to do is to shift their focus from the sex of the (chosen) partner, which gives the relationship its sexual orientation, to the sex of the plaintiff (the choosing partner). If Martin J. had merely reversed the names of Nesbit and Egan (i.e. 'had Egan [the plaintiff] been a woman cohabiting with Nesbit [the partner] . . . [Nesbit] would have been eligible for the spouse's allowance'), he would have stated a prima facie case of sex discrimination under Section 15(1).[89]

---

[85] It must be acknowledged that the continuing problem of sexual violence by (presumably mostly heterosexual) men against women may provide a justification for some forms of segregation.

[86] See Ch. 6, notes 97, 98, 105, 106, 108, 131.

[87] (1989) 10 Can Hum Rts Rep D/6064 at D/6097–99 (Can. HRC).

[88] [1992] 1 FC 687 at 695 (TD).

[89] Although the partner is often a co-plaintiff (as Nesbit is in *Egan*), and also suffers sex discrimination, it simplifies the analysis to treat the party who has the relationship with the defendant government (e.g. the pensioner, employee or prisoner) as the plaintiff, and the other party (who has no such relationship) as the partner.

A sex discrimination argument can also be applied to same-sex marriage.[90] In *Layland*, if Todd Layland were a woman, he would have been permitted to marry Pierre Beaulne (and vice versa). Until *Baehr* v. *Lewin*, the Canadian and US courts that had considered the issue had all concluded that marriage is 'by definition' opposite-sex (as voters were once 'by definition' male).[91] They did so even when the plaintiff relied on *Loving* v. *Virginia*, in which the US Supreme Court struck down laws prohibiting mixed-race marriage as racially discriminatory, in spite of the 'mirror-image symmetry' of the treatment of races.[92] In *Singer* v. *Hara*, a Washington Court of Appeals considered whether the 'definition of marriage . . . in and of itself . . . constitutes a violation of [the Washington Equal Rights Amendment]', prohibiting discrimination 'on account of sex'. It held that the Amendment did not apply to distinctions 'founded upon the unique physical characteristics of the sexes', and that 'the refusal of the state to authorize same-sex marriage results from . . . impossibility of reproduction rather than . . . discrimination "on account of sex".' The fact that opposite-sex couples are permitted to marry even when one or both partners is infertile or when they do not want to have children was dismissed as an 'exceptional situation',[93] as it was by the majority in *Layland*.[94] But this fact cannot be ignored and clearly demonstrates that the distinction *is* based on sex, and not on 'impossibility of reproduction' (meaning inability to have children with genetic input from both partners).

In *Baehr* v. *Lewin*, the Hawaii Supreme Court became possibly the first court in the world[95] to accept the argument that sexual orientation discrimination is

---

[90] See e.g. Eskridge (1993 US), 1504–10; Trosino (1993 US); Strasser (1991a US); Yale Note (1973 US). There is a debate within the gay, lesbian, and bisexual community as to whether same-sex couples should be seeking the right to marry or an end to the ways in which married couple relationships are preferred over other relationships. See, e.g. Polikoff (1993 US); Ettelbrick (1992 US); Stoddard (1992 US); Duclos (1991 Can); Herman (1990 Can), 794–804. I would argue that, in the short term, the heterosexual majority is unlikely to abolish civil marriage or remove all of the benefits it may bring. As long as it exists, and even if the only additional benefit is a symbolic one, same-sex couples will not have the same range of options as opposite-sex couples, and will not be 'equal' to them, unless they are permitted to marry. It is true that, although burdens tied to the benefits of marriage could be avoided by not marrying, certain 'involuntary' burdens would accompany equal treatment of unmarried same-sex and opposite-sex couples (e.g. calculation of welfare benefits based on combined incomes). See Duclos (1991 Can), 52–5. Perhaps 'involuntary' burdens must be accepted as part of the 'package' that equality with opposite-sex couples represents, and their elimination sought by other means for all unmarried couples or all couples.

[91] See *Layland* v. *Ontario (Minister of Consumer and Commercial Relations)* (1993) 14 OR (3d) 658 (Ont Div Ct); *Re North and Matheson* (1974), 52 DLR (3d) 280 (Man Co Ct); *Singer* v. *Hara*, 522 P 2d 1187 at 1191–2 (Wash Ct App 1974); *Baker* v. *Nelson*, 191 NW 2d 185 at 186 (Minn 1971); *Jones* v. *Hallahan*, 501 SW 2d 588 (Ky Ct App 1973); *Dean* v. *District of Columbia*, 653 A 2d 307 at 361 (DC 1995) ('same-sex "marriages" are legally and factually—i.e., definitionally—impossible'). See also Ch. 4, Part III.B.

[92] *Singer* v. *Hara*, ibid.; *Baker* v. *Nelson*, ibid. at 187 ('there is a clear distinction between a marital distinction based merely upon race and one based upon the fundamental difference in sex').

[93] *Singer* v. *Hara*, ibid. at 1193–5.

[94] See (1993) 14 OR (3d) 658 at 666 (Ont Div Ct).

[95] Cf. *Toonen* v. *Australia* (for reference see Chapter 5, note 137, and see Ch. 5, note 153) (UN Human Rights Committee); *Engel* v. *Worthington* 23 Cal Rptr 2d 329 (Ct App 1993) (publisher's refusal to include a picture of a male–male couple in a high school reunion memory book was sex

sex discrimination, in holding that exclusion of same-sex couples from marriage is at least prima facie sex discrimination (contrary to Article I, Section 5 of the Hawaii Constitution)[96] and must be justified.[97] It rejected the 'liberty' or 'privacy' argument of the plaintiffs, three same-sex couples, that they had 'a fundamental constitutional right to same-sex marriage arising out of the right to privacy or otherwise.'[98] However, the Court accepted their 'equality' or 'equal protection' argument, not on the basis that 'homosexuals' are a 'suspect class',[99] but on the basis that 'sex' is a 'suspect category' under the Hawaii Constitution[100] and that the marriage law 'denies same-sex couples access to the marital status and its concomitant rights and benefits . . . on the basis of the applicants' sex.'[101] It rejected the dissent's argument that 'all males and females are treated alike. A male cannot obtain a license to marry another male, and a female cannot obtain a license to marry another female.'[102] In so doing, it accepted the analogy to *Loving* v. *Virginia*[103] and the US Supreme Court's rejection of 'mirror-image symmetry' of the treatment of races as precluding a finding of race discrimination. The Hawaii Supreme Court described as 'tautological and circular' and as 'tortured and conclusory sophistry' the arguments that 'same sex marriage is an innate impossibility' and that the plaintiffs 'were denied a marriage license because of the nature of marriage itself.' Instead it observed that, 'as *Loving* amply demonstrates, constitutional law may mandate, like it or not, that customs change with an evolving social order.'[104]

Same-sex couples should not book their flights to Hawaii quite yet, as the Hawaii Supreme Court did not strike down the 'opposite-sex couples only' marriage law. Rather, it held that the law 'is presumed to be unconstitutional . . . [unless the State of Hawaii] can show that (a) the statute's sex-based classification is justified by compelling state interests and (b) the statute is narrowly drawn to avoid unnecessary abridgments of the [plaintiffs'] constitutional rights.'[105]

discrimination contrary to s. 51 of the California Civil Code). A sex discrimination argument does not appear to have been made in two same-sex marriage cases in the Netherlands and Germany: see Ch. 4, notes 132 and 134.

[96] 852 P 2d 44 at 50 n. 5 (Haw 1993): 'No person shall . . . be denied the equal protection of the laws . . . or be discriminated against . . . because of . . . sex . . .'

[97] The argument was initially accepted by two judges, with one concurring on other grounds, and two dissenting. A motion for reconsideration, together with a change in the composition of the court, seems to have altered the result to three judges accepting the argument, one concurring on other grounds, and one dissenting. Ibid. at 48, 68, 70, 74–5.

[98] Ibid. at 57. See also *Dean*, 653 A 2d 307 at 331–3, 363 n. 5. Cf. Hohengarten (1994 US), 1524–5 (in spite of *Hardwick*, prohibitions of same-sex marriage violate 'the right of privacy, which encompasses the right to marry, [and] concerns choices about familial relationships', because 'the right to marry [does not] depend[ ] on a prior right to engage in sexual activity').

[99] See Ch. 7, note 49.   [100] *Baehr*, 852 P 2d 44 at 67 (Haw 1993).

[101] Ibid. at 60.   [102] Ibid. at 67–8, 71.

[103] See Koppelman (1988 US); *Engel*, 23 Cal Rptr 2d 329 at 331 (Ct App 1993).

[104] *Baehr*, ibid. at 63. In *Dean*, 653 A 2d 307, the District of Columbia Court of Appeals declined to follow *Baehr* and upheld the exclusion of same-sex couples from marriage. It rejected (at 363 n. 2) the *Loving* analogy and the sex discrimination argument as 'stretch[ing] the concept of gender discrimination'.

[105] *Baehr*, ibid. at 67.

It remains to be seen whether the State can discharge this heavy burden, but an argument such as 'lack of procreative capacity' should not be enough. If the Hawaii Supreme Court ultimately holds that the State has failed to do so, and the Hawaii Constitution is not amended to overturn the decision,[106] 'the State of Hawaii will no longer be permitted to refuse marriage licenses to couples merely on the basis that they are of the same sex.'[107] Business could boom both for travel agents and experts on inter-jurisdictional recognition of marriages.[108]

III. ASSESSMENT OF PROTECTION UNDER THE CANADIAN CHARTER

Since 1989, Charter litigation by gay and lesbian plaintiffs has resulted in at least six declarations by Canadian courts or human rights tribunals that particular instances of sexual orientation discrimination violated the plaintiff's rights under Section 15(1): *Veysey* (3 November 1989), *Knodel* (30 August 1991), *Haig* (6 August 1992), *Leshner* (31 August 1992), *Douglas* v. *R.* (27 October 1992), and *Vriend* (12 April 1994). In at least two cases, however, courts have declined to find violations of Section 15(1): *Layland* (15 March 1993) and *Egan* (Federal Court of Appeal) (29 April 1993). Although the results have been mixed, the Charter has had a significant impact in three areas: (i) exclusion of gay, lesbian, and bisexual persons from military employment; (ii) inclusion of sexual orientation as a prohibited ground of discrimination in federal, provincial, and territorial human rights legislation; and (iii) discrimination against same-sex couples.

In the area of military employment, Charter litigation seems to have hastened the end of the ban on gay, lesbian, and bisexual personnel. *Douglas* v. *R.* involved the settlement of an action for damages brought by Michelle Douglas, a lesbian woman who had been released from the armed forces. MacKay J. of the Federal Court Trial Division signed a judgment granting declarations that her Section 15(1) rights had been violated and that 'the Defendant's polic[ies] . . . regarding the service of homosexuals in the Canadian Armed Forces are contrary to the Charter'.[109] The same day, the Chief of Defence Staff issued a statement that 'Canadians, regardless of their sexual orientation, will now be able to serve their country . . . without restriction'.[110] The decision of the Canadian armed forces to concede defeat and rescind their policy, without even a trial court decision against them, is startling in view of the US military's tenacious defence of their policies.

---

[106] Attempts to have the Hawaii legislature propose a referendum, under Article XVII, Section 3 of the Hawaii Constitution, on a constitutional amendment prohibiting same-sex marriage have so far been unsuccessful. See *The Washington Blade* (25 Mar. 1994) 1; (31 Mar. 1995) 21.

[107] *Baehr*, ibid. at 57.

[108] See e.g. Keane (1995 US), Cox (1994 US), Henson (1993–94 US), Hovermill (1994 US).

[109] See *Douglas* v. *R.* (1992) 98 DLR (4th) 129 (FCTD). In 1990, a Security Intelligence Review Committee had recommended her reinstatement. See Ch. 7, note 88.

[110] *The Globe and Mail* (28 Oct. 1992) A1.

In the area of human rights legislation, Charter litigation may prove to have even more sweeping consequences. In *Haig* (an action by Joshua Birch, a gay armed forces officer who had been released), the Ontario Court of Appeal held that the failure to include 'sexual orientation' in the list of prohibited grounds of discrimination in the CHRA was a violation of Section 15(1) (the federal government not having attempted to justify it under Section 1).[111] It then determined that the appropriate remedy was to 'read in' the missing words, and ordered that 'the Canadian Human Rights Act . . . be interpreted, applied and administered as though it contained "sexual orientation" as a prohibited ground of discrimination'.[112] The federal government declined to appeal the decision and, after some hesitation, decided to carry out a 1986 promise[113] by introducing legislation that would have expressly amended the Act.[114] This amendment was not passed before the 1993 federal election, but the new government has promised to introduce an amendment.

Relying on *Haig*, the Canadian Human Rights Commission and the human rights commissions of Alberta, Prince Edward Island, and Newfoundland have decided to accept complaints of sexual orientation discrimination, even though the human rights legislation they enforce does not expressly include sexual orientation. Because eight jurisdictions have legislation that does expressly include sexual orientation, this means that the human rights commissions of twelve out of the thirteen Canadian jurisdictions (all but the Northwest Territories) now accept complaints of sexual orientation discrimination (compared with one prior to December 1986, and four prior to 1990).[115] In deciding to accept such complaints, the Alberta, Prince Edward Island, and Newfoundland commissions presumably acted on the assumption that, if *Haig* is correct, their provincial human rights acts must also be read as including 'sexual orientation'. This reasoning was accepted with regard to the Alberta legislation in *Vriend*, which involves the dismissal of Delwin Vriend, a gay chemistry teacher, by a private (but thirty-five per cent publicly funded) Christian college.[116] Russell J. cited *Haig* in declaring that various sections of the Individual's Rights Protection Act must be 'interpreted, applied and administered as though they contained the words "sexual orientation"'.[117] The Alberta government has appealed her decision

---

[111] (1992) 94 DLR (4th) 1 at 10 (Ont CA).

[112] Ibid. at 14–15. Charter remedies of this kind ('reading in') were approved by the Supreme Court in *Schachter* v. *Canada*, [1992] 2 SCR 679. If *Haig* is correct, courts do in fact have power, under Section 15(1), to add to the list of grounds in human rights legislation by inserting enumerated and analogous grounds.

[113] See Department of Justice (Canada) (1986 Can), 13 ('The Government will take whatever measures are necessary to ensure that sexual orientation is a prohibited ground of discrimination in relation to all areas of federal jurisdiction').

[114] See Ch. 7, note 108.

[115] Letter from Charles Mojsej, Canadian Human Rights Commission, Ottawa, 23 December 1992.

[116] See *Perceptions* (6 Mar. 1991) 9, (29 July 1992) 10.

[117] *Vriend* v. *Alberta* (1994) 20 CHRR D/358 at D/369 (QB).

to the Alberta Court of Appeal. The losing side could take the case to the Supreme Court and ask it to approve, overrule or limit *Haig*.

The reasoning in *Haig* is certainly open to challenge in that it seems to require each human rights act to contain both the enumerated Section 15(1) grounds (which most do contain) and every ground that has been identified as analogous. This result is defensible insofar as it affects public sector defendants (or at least those that are part of 'government'), because Section 15(1) could be interpreted as precluding a government from only providing the 'plaintiff-friendly' procedures which a human rights act offers in respect of some of the kinds of discrimination Section 15(1) prohibits. But it seems to constitute an indirect use of the Charter to prohibit private sector sexual orientation discrimination, to which Section 15(1) does not apply directly.[118] As Marceau J. said in *Mossop*:

I do not see the Charter as capable of being used as a kind of *ipso facto* amendment machine requiring its doctrine to be incorporated in the human rights legislation . . . [H]uman rights codes impact on areas of the private sector of economic life which are not readily seen to fall within the scope of the Charter. It may well be that the legislatures who entrenched the Charter were willing to impose a more demanding standard of conduct on themselves and on the executive than . . . on the population at large.[119]

It seems clear that discriminatory language in a human rights act may be a prima facie violation of Section 15(1).[120] Some commentators have argued that the same should be true of a discriminatory omission,[121] but the Supreme Court has yet to decide the point.[122] Perhaps *Haig* can be explained on the basis that, whether or not Section 15(1) requires the enactment of human rights legislation, a legislature that elects to make such an enactment (and to extend the legislation to the private sector) must treat all enumerated and analogous grounds of discrimination equally. The omission of sexual orientation certainly has a disproportionate impact on gay, lesbian, and bisexual persons, in that heterosexual persons would rarely need such protection.[123]

---

[118] See *Retail, Wholesale & Department Store Union* v. *Dolphin Delivery Ltd.*, [1986] 2 SCR 573.

[119] [1991] 1 FC 18 at 38 (FCA). Cf. Stone J. at ibid. 43 ('the absence of "sexual orientation" . . . as infringing a right enshrined in the Charter is not raised in this appeal, and I refrain from expressing an opinion on the matter').

[120] See *McKinney* v. *University of Guelph*, [1990] 3 SCR 229 (statutory exception expressly permitting age discrimination against persons 65 and over); *Blainey* (1986) 26 DLR (4th) 728 (CA) (statutory exception expressly permitting sex discrimination in athletics).

[121] See Bruner (1985 Can), 467–8; Jefferson (1985 Can), 76–7.

[122] In *McKinney*, [1990] 3 SCR 229, L'Heureux-Dubé J. said (at 436) that an omission is not enough ('if the provinces chose to enact human rights legislation which only prohibited discrimination on the basis of sex, and not age, this legislation could not be held to violate the Charter'); Wilson J. left the point open (at 412–13) ('[i]t is not self-evident to me that government could not be found to be in breach of the Charter for failing to act'); and the majority were silent. See Pothier (1993 Can), 279–83.

[123] See Pothier (1993 Can), 284–6. Cf. *Hunter* v. *Erickson*, 393 US 385 at 391 (1969) ('although the law [treating race or religion discrimination differently] on its face treats Negro and white, Jew and gentile in an identical manner, the reality is that the law's impact falls on the minority. The majority needs no protection against discrimination').

Finally, it is in the area of discrimination against same-sex couples that the Charter may have its greatest impact. Even if *Haig* is correct, its effect would be limited to discrimination against gay, lesbian, and bisexual individuals (the kind at issue in *Haig* and *Vriend*), if discrimination against same-sex couples were held not to violate Section 15(1) or statutory prohibitions of sexual orientation discrimination. *Veysey, Knodel,* and *Leshner* have held that discrimination against same-sex couples is sexual orientation discrimination contrary to Section 15(1),[124] while two post-*Andrews* decisions, *Layland* and *Egan* (F.C.A.), have rejected this conclusion.[125] This split in the lower courts will probably be resolved by the Supreme Court in 1995. On 1 November 1994, it heard oral argument in *Egan* v. *Canada*, which will be its first decision in a case of sexual orientation discrimination under the Charter.[126]

In *Egan*,[127] the Supreme Court of Canada is presented with the opportunity of deciding that sexual orientation is an analogous ground under Section 15(1) of the Charter, and that discrimination against same-sex couples is discrimination on the basis of sexual orientation (or sex), and must be justified under Section 1. If it were to adopt such a principle (and find no Section 1 justifications), it would establish that same-sex couples are generally entitled to the same benefits as unmarried opposite-sex couples, where such benefits are provided for by statute or are otherwise provided by 'government'. But its reasoning, in interpreting an analogous ground (sexual orientation) or an enumerated ground (sex) in Section 15(1) as applying to discrimination against same-sex couples in the provision of benefits, would probably apply to human rights acts that expressly prohibit discrimination based on sexual orientation (or sex). It would thereby lend support to the reasoning in *Leshner*, that a prohibition of sexual orientation discrimination in a human rights act protects same-sex couples, and that Section 15(1) of the Charter precludes attempts to limit protection to gay, lesbian, and bisexual individuals, by using opposite-sex definitions of 'spouse' or 'marital status' to exclude same-sex couples.[128] If the reasoning in *Leshner* is ultimately accepted by appellate courts,[129] it could mean that the recent attempt to insert

[124] See also *Re Canada (Treasury Board—Environment Canada) and Lorenzen* (1993) 38 LAC (4th) 29 (under a collective agreement and the CHRA).

[125] *Karen Andrews* and *Anderson* (for references see Chapter 6, note 97) rejected it before *Andrews*. *Vogel II* and *Clinton* (Ont. Div. Ct.) have done so under provincial human rights legislation, as have *Guevremont, Parkwood, Watson,* and *Carleton* under collective agreements that prohibit sexual orientation discrimination: for references, see Ch. 6, note 131.

[126] For comments on the Federal Court of Appeal's reasoning in *Egan*, [1993] 3 FC 401 (CA), see Wintemute (1994 Can), 442–51, 455–8; McEvoy (1994 Can). For the outcome in the Supreme Court, see Ch. 9, Part III.

[127] See Ch. 7, notes 43–5 and accompanying text for the facts.

[128] (1992) 16 CHRR D/184 at D/200–D/206 (Ont Hum Rts Comm).

[129] The Ontario government did not appeal in *Leshner*. In *Clinton* v. *Ontario Blue Cross* (1993) 18 CHRR D/377 (Ont HRC), an Ontario Human Rights Commission board of inquiry held, without relying on Section 15(1), that the denial of benefits to Elizabeth Clinton's partner, Laurie Anne Mercer, constituted sexual orientation discrimination, in spite of the 'person of the opposite sex'

such a limit into the Nova Scotia Human Rights Act could be struck down,[130] and that all Canadian employers (public and private sector) bound by legislation expressly prohibiting sexual orientation (or sex) discrimination would have to extend employment benefits provided to unmarried opposite-sex partners to the same-sex partners of their employees.[131]

After *Egan*, the Supreme Court may soon have two[132] additional opportunities to consider issues of sexual orientation discrimination under the Charter. If there is an appeal from the Ontario Court of Appeal's decision in *Layland*, the Supreme Court will have to decide whether any principle it adopts in *Egan* applies to the most fundamental and historically entrenched kind of discrimination against same-sex couples: their exclusion from the right to marry and any benefits that may justifiably be restricted to married couples. By then it may be able to cite the final decision of the Supreme Court of Hawaii in *Baehr* v. *Lewin*, which could be the first to interpret a constitution as prohibiting the exclusion of same-sex couples from marriage. Further, if there is an appeal from the Alberta Court of Appeal's decision in *Vriend*, the Supreme Court will have to consider the reasoning in *Haig*. It is worth noting that in *Egan* (discrimination between same-sex couples and unmarried opposite-sex couples), *Layland* (exclusion of same-sex couples from marriage), and *Vriend* (omission of sexual orientation from anti-discrimination legislation), the Supreme Court is or may be examining issues of sexual orientation discrimination that have yet to be addressed by any of the US Supreme Court, the European Court of Human Rights or the UN Human Rights Committee.

What is the Supreme Court likely to decide in *Egan*? Since 1982, it has adopted a very liberal approach to interpreting both human rights legislation and

definitions of 'marital status' and 'spouse' in the Ontario Human Rights Code, RSO 1990, c. H.19, s. 10(1). The Ontario Divisional Court relied on these definitions (and did not permit a Charter argument) in reversing the Board of Inquiry's decision. See *Clinton, Parkwood* and *Carleton* (references in Chapter 6, note 131). On 9 June 1994, the Ontario legislature voted (68–59) against a bill (Bill 167, the Equality Rights Statute Law Amendment Act, 1994) that would have amended 57 statutes that discriminate against same-sex couples (including the 'person of the opposite sex' definitions in the Human Rights Code, which would have been replaced by 'person of either sex'), and that would have permitted same-sex couples to adopt children jointly but not to marry (a matter seen as falling within federal jurisdiction): see *The Globe and Mail* (10 June 1994) A1. See also Child and Family Services Act, RSO 1990, c. C.11, s. 146(4) ('[a]n application [for an adoption order] . . . may only be made (a) by one individual, or (b) jointly, by two individuals who are spouses of one another'); s. 136(1) ('"spouse" ' has the same meaning as in . . . the Human Rights Code; see text accompanying Ch. 7, note 103). Cf. Ch. 6, note 134 (Québec).

[130] See Ch. 7, note 108.

[131] This could include private sector employers in every jurisdiction of Canada, if the Supreme Court approves the reasoning in *Haig* or accepts a sex discrimination argument. In *Clinton* (1993) 18 CHRR D/377 at D/384 (Ont HRC), the board of inquiry ordered that 'no employee benefit plan be offered in . . . Ontario which limits common-law conjugal benefits to persons of the opposite sex', but the Divisional Court reversed its decision (see note 129 above). In the case of pension plans, an additional obstacle is the opposite-sex definition of 'spouse' in the federal Income Tax Act: see *Leshner* (1992) 16 CHRR D/184 at D/196 (Ont Hum Rts Comm).

[132] See also *R.* v. *Carmen M.* discussed in Chapter 9, note 20.

the Charter.[133] This change of approach has brought it a long way from its position in 1967, when it was able to decide in *Klippert* that all men who engage in sexual activity with other men are 'dangerous sexual offenders'.[134] Thus, it seems likely that it will agree that sexual orientation is an analogous ground under Section 15(1) and that discrimination against same-sex couples in respect of benefits is sexual orientation discrimination. But it is not clear what reasons (if any) it will give for finding that sexual orientation is an analogous ground or whether it will find sex discrimination. If the Court does find in favour of James Egan and John Nesbit, it will have to distinguish two recent decisions.

In *Canada (Attorney-General)* v. *Mossop*, the Court held (4–3) that discrimination against a same-sex couple is not discrimination based on 'family status' under the Canadian Human Rights Act.[135] In so doing, it seemed to depart from the approach of giving human rights legislation a 'large, purposive and liberal interpretation' by relying on 'parliamentary intent'.[136] But its decision that the discrimination was based on sexual orientation, not family status, can be defended.[137] It left open the question of how it would decide a similar case under the Charter (no Charter argument having been made),[138] implying that the outcome might be different.[139]

Egan also bears a superficial resemblance to *Symes* v. *Canada*, in which the Supreme Court held that the non-deductibility of child care expenses as business expenses under the federal Income Tax Act is not indirect sex discrimination against women contrary to Section 15(1). In *Symes* and *Egan*, the plaintiff's group and another group were both excluded from the benefit (self-employed parents and salaried parents in *Symes*,[140] same-sex couples and non-couples in *Egan*),[141] and the plaintiff benefited under another programme (a fixed child-care expenses deduction in *Symes*,[142] and a provincial social assistance plan in *Egan*).[143] But the major difference between *Symes* and *Egan* is that *Symes* was a case of *indirect* sex discrimination where insufficient evidence of adverse impact on women was found, and which would have required the Court to second-guess the federal government's attempt to provide tax relief for child-care expenses.[144]

---

[133] See e.g. *Andrews* v. *Law Society of British Columbia* [1989] 1 SCR 143; *Brooks* v. *Canada Safeway Ltd.*, [1989] 1 SCR 1219; *Janzen* v. *Platy Enterprises Ltd.*, [1989] 1 SCR 1252; *Ontario Human Rights Commission* v. *Simpson-Sears Ltd.*, [1985] 2 SCR 536.
[134] See Ch. 6, Part I.   [135] [1993] 1 SCR 554.
[136] See Wintemute (1994 Can), 433–5.
[137] Ibid. at 436–40. For other comments on *Mossop*, see e.g. Freeman (1994 Can); Herman (1994 Can), 133–9;
[138] The plaintiff did not argue either that discrimination against same-sex couples (as in *Egan*) or the omission of sexual orientation from the CHRA (as in *Haig*), violated Section 15(1).
[139] See *Mossop*, [1993] 1 SCR 554 at 581–2, 587; Wintemute (1994 Can), 440–41. In *Lorenzen*, (1993) 38 LAC (4th) 29, a labour arbitrator found that discrimination (identical, in part, to that in *Mossop*) against a same-sex couple violated prohibitions of sexual orientation discrimination in a collective agreement and (applying *Haig*) in the CHRA.
[140] [1993] 4 SCR 695 at 776, 773–4.   [141] [1993] 3 FC 401 at 479–81 (CA).
[142] *Symes*, ibid. at 706.   [143] (1991), [1992] 1 FC 687 at 697 (TD).
[144] *Symes*, ibid. at 773–4.

Had there been a tax deduction that discriminated directly (or expressly) on the basis of sex (e.g. a deduction limited to fathers), it would almost certainly have been struck down under Section 15(1). *Egan*, however, involves *direct* discrimination on the basis of sexual orientation (or sex) because the statute is expressly limited to opposite-sex couples (who actually receive the benefit—in *Symes*, no group received the benefit sought by the plaintiff).[145] It should therefore be irrelevant whether other groups are excluded,[146] and whether the plaintiffs actually received greater benefits under another programme.[147] The existence of other opportunities or benefits is a 'red herring' in cases of direct discrimination. If a person were denied a job because of their race or sex, it would not be a defence to show that they had obtained a better-paying job across the street. Exclusion from the particular opportunity or benefit is the issue. While mitigation may affect damages, it is irrelevant to the existence of direct discrimination.

If the Supreme Court finds for the plaintiffs in *Egan*, and in *Layland* and *Vriend* (should those two cases reach the Court), the Charter could provide comprehensive protection against sexual orientation discrimination by the legislature and other 'government' actors, and possibly even by private sector actors (if the reasoning in *Haig* is upheld). In particular, the Charter could require that same-sex couples receive the same benefits as opposite-sex couples, married or unmarried, and be permitted the same choice of whether or not to marry.[148] Such protection would of course go far beyond anything provided to date under the US Constitution, the European Convention or the International Covenant. It remains to be seen whether the Supreme Court will be willing to provide it. After the defeats in *Gay Alliance* and *Mossop*,[149] gay, lesbian, and bisexual persons in Canada can only hope that, in *Egan*, it will be a case of 'third time lucky'.

---

[145] *Egan* involves provision of a benefit in a way that discriminates directly on the basis of sexual orientation or sex. *Symes* involved a failure to provide a benefit that discriminated indirectly on the basis of sex because of its disproportionate impact on women.

[146] Wintemute (1994 Can), 444, 447, 449.

[147] The federal government appeared to rely heavily on this fact in the oral argument, leading Chief Justice Lamer to reply: '[t]his leads to the conclusion that heterosexuals have a good case [presumably of discrimination against opposite-sex couples].' See 'Judge ridicules Ottawa's claim in benefits case' *The Globe and Mail* (2 Nov. 1994).

[148] The Ontario Law Reform Commission (1993 Can), 53–5, 70–1, has recommended that legislation be enacted that would permit any two unmarried adults to register a 'Registered Domestic Partnership'. See also Commission des droits de la personne du Québec (1994 Can), 119 (recommending a Québec Ministry of Justice study of the possibility of a voluntary registry for unmarried couples, same-sex and opposite-sex). Like the Ontario proposal, and unlike the Scandinavian 'same-sex couple only' registered partnership laws (see Chapter 5, note 98), procedures for registering 'domestic partnerships' that have been established in a number of US cities are open *both* to same-sex couples and to unmarried opposite-sex couples, giving the former one recognition option (registration), and the latter two (registration or marriage). See Bowman and Cornish (1992 US) at 1188–91. See also Sanders (1994 Can), 134–5 (discussing various ways of recognizing same-sex couples); Rubenstein (1993 US), 439–41 (text of San Francisco ordinance).

[149] The two cases of sexual orientation discrimination decided by the Supreme Court since the decriminalization of same-sex sexual activity in 1969. See Ch. 6, note 1.

9

Comparison and Conclusion

I. COMPARISON OF THE THREE ARGUMENTS UNDER THE THREE HUMAN RIGHTS INSTRUMENTS

A. Why Is a Comparative Perspective Useful?

Although it may be useful to compare different arguments that can be made in relation to sexual orientation discrimination, is there any point in doing so across several human rights instruments? Anyone setting out to compare the solutions of several legal systems to a single problem must certainly observe the 'Proceed With Caution' sign at the side of the road. As Otto Kahn-Freund warned in 1973:

we cannot take for granted that rules ... are transplantable ... [and] any attempt to use a pattern of law outside the environment of its origin ... entail[s] the risk of rejection ... [U]sing the comparative method ... requires a knowledge not only of the foreign law, but also of its social, and above all its political, context. The use of comparative law ... becomes an abuse only if it is informed by a legalistic spirit which ignores this context of the law.[1]

Likewise, Bernhard Grossfeld has stressed the need for caution, arguing that law is culture, that every legal system is unique, and that a comparatist can only have a superficial grasp of a foreign legal culture.[2]

Bearing these warnings in mind, I would submit that the contexts in which the three human rights instruments operate, and the issues of sexual orientation discrimination that may arise under them, are sufficiently similar to permit a comparison. Kahn-Freund acknowledged that the 'environmental obstacles to legal transplantation' will not be as great where the countries involved are economically, socially, culturally, and politically similar, and where the area of law in question is substantive rather than procedural.[3] The US, the Council of Europe countries, and Canada share a common 'Western' or 'Greater European' culture, democratic governments committed to the protection of human rights, and similar levels of economic and social development. Thus, the comparison does not attempt to straddle the differences between these countries and developing, Communist, East Asian, or Islamic-law countries.

In addition, the comparison deals with the substantive (rather than procedural)

---

[1] Kahn-Freund (1974 Other), 27.   [2] Grossfeld (1990 Other), 39, 41.
[3] Kahn-Freund (1974 Other), 8–11, 17–20.

aspects of human rights or anti-discrimination law. Kahn-Freund conceded that '[c]omparative law has far greater utility in substantive law than in the law of procedure'.[4] Human rights law is substantive and, by definition, aspires to universality. As a result, the characterization by one country of a particular kind of discrimination as a violation of a 'human right' may have a highly persuasive influence on another country that prides itself on its record of respecting human rights. Although sexual orientation discrimination touches on particular areas of substantive law in which Kahn-Freund observed that obstacles to comparison may be high (e.g. criminal law and family law),[5] it also relates to areas of law (e.g. individual, rather than collective, labour law and racial discrimination law) in which he acknowledged the potential for transplantation.[6] In addition, he did note the considerable amount of comparison that has taken place even in the supposedly inhospitable area of family law, especially with regard to divorce.[7]

The phenomenon of sexual orientation discrimination itself displays a degree of universality within these countries, as illustrated by the similarity in the kinds of cases that have been litigated before US and Canadian courts and the European Court and Commission of Human Rights. This is not surprising in that the level of organization of the gay, lesbian, and bisexual communities in these countries is similar, as are the issues these communities are raising (e.g. military employment, marriage or benefits for partners, parental rights). As Kahn-Freund said with regard to accident liability, 'the nature of accidents . . . is much the same everywhere. No wonder then that precisely the same problems . . . are discussed wherever you go.'[8] The same is true of sexual orientation discrimination.

As for grasping foreign legal cultures, I have had the advantage of doing first degrees in law in Canada, practising law in the US, and pursuing graduate studies in the UK (a Council of Europe member state). I hope that this has reduced somewhat the superficiality of my grasp of the cultures of the three human rights instruments. I would be less confident that this was the case had I attempted a comparison with the constitutions of, for example, the Netherlands or Denmark (which were, in any event, ruled out by linguistic barriers).

Perhaps a final (and most important) justification for this comparison is that litigants have begun to cite, before the US Supreme Court, the European Court of Human Rights, and the Canadian Supreme Court, the other courts' decisions in the area of sexual orientation discrimination. In the world of instant communications in which we now live, and with these courts publishing their decisions in English or both English and French, both litigants and judges are much less likely to be ignorant of developments under another instrument, and can increasingly be expected to cite decisions under another instrument that support their arguments. Before the European Court, this has already occurred in *Dudgeon*, in which Judge Walsh referred to negative pre-*Hardwick* authority in the US;[9] and

---

[4] Ibid. at 20.   [5] Ibid. at 10, 15–17.   [6] Ibid. at 5, 21, 23.   [7] Ibid. at 13–15.
[8] Ibid. at 9.   [9] *Dudgeon* v. *UK* (1981), Ser. A, No. 45 at pp. 46–7.

in *Norris*, the Irish government relied on *Hardwick*, *Doe*, and other US privacy cases,[10] while Norris cited *Gay Rights Coalition of Georgetown University Law Center* v. *Georgetown University*.[11] Before the US Supreme Court, *Dudgeon* was mentioned very briefly by an *amicus curiae* in *Hardwick*,[12] causing some commentators to wonder whether the outcome might have been different if the parties had made the European Court's decision more prominent. Anthony Lester has pointed out that:

No one drew the Supreme Court's attention to the importance of *Dudgeon* as a recent decision by the strongest international court of human rights, dealing with a closely analogous problem and having potential persuasive value. . . . If *Dudgeon* had been relied upon, Justice White might not have characterized [Hardwick's] claim . . . as being 'at best, facetious' . . . [and] one of the negative majority might have been persuaded.[13]

Before the Canadian Supreme Court, although the issue of criminalization cannot currently be presented, any party citing *Hardwick* in another kind of sexual orientation discrimination case would almost certainly be faced with the counter-citation of *Dudgeon*, *Norris*, *Modinos* (and *Toonen*). Apart from the litigants' interest in marshalling every available authority, national and international courts seeking to protect the individual against the state should be interested in hearing about the level of protection that has been provided elsewhere. As Mary Ann Glendon has observed, with regard to the US:

Our rights jurisprudence . . . could only benefit if American judges and lawyers in difficult and novel cases followed the practice (now routine in many other nations) of examining important decisions of leading courts elsewhere. . . . [T]he writers of all the [*Hardwick*] opinions could have benefited if they had taken a look at the way the European judges struggled with the issues in *Dudgeon*.[14]

I will therefore proceed with the comparison and attempt to determine the relative merits of the three arguments, referring where appropriate to their success under the three instruments. However, it will be important to remember that lack of success of a particular argument under a particular instrument will not necessarily indicate any inherent problem with the argument, but may result from peculiarities of the instrument's text or the court charged with interpreting it, or from the general political conditions in which the court operates.

[10] See Memorial of the Government of Ireland, Cour (87) 117 at pp. 40–46.
[11] 536 A 2d 1 (DC 1987). See Verbatim Record (25 Apr. 1988, morning hearings), Cour/Misc. (88) 100, at p. 21.
[12] See *Amicus Curiae* Brief on Behalf of the Respondents by Lambda Legal Defense, et al. (Case No. 85–140) (31 Jan. 1986), 15 n. 10, 24 (incorrectly citing the Commission's report as the Court's judgment).
[13] Lester (1988 Eur), 560. See also Helfer (1990 Eur), 1044.
[14] Glendon (1991 Eur), 152–3. See also Lester (1988 Eur), 560 (*Hardwick* 'illustrates . . . the continuing isolation of American constitutional law from international human rights law'); Michael (1988 Eur) ('one lesson from *Hardwick* is . . . that comparative law could be of assistance [to the US Supreme Court]').

B. Comparison of the Three Arguments

In Chapters 2 to 8, I have examined three ways to argue that the US Constitution, the European Convention, and the Canadian Charter implicitly contain prima facie prohibitions of sexual orientation discrimination. As was seen in Chapter 1, these three arguments correspond to three different ways of looking at the phenomenon of sexual orientation: (i) as an immutable attraction which constitutes the reason for a person's choice of the direction of their emotional–sexual conduct (an immutable status argument); (ii) as a person's choice of the direction of their emotional–sexual conduct (a fundamental choice argument); and (iii) as a choice (of direction of emotional–sexual conduct) which is restricted according to the choosing person's sex (a sex discrimination argument). This Part will compare the extent to which each of these three arguments satisfies four criteria (factual support, availability of legal doctrine, comprehensiveness of protection, and capacity to counter potential justifications for discrimination), and attempt to determine which argument is potentially the most effective in providing protection against sexual orientation discrimination.

1. Factual Support

Only an immutable status argument is open to challenge as lacking factual support. This is because it relies on the assumption that sexual orientation (as direction of attraction) is initially unchosen and currently immutable. This assumption does not appear to be valid for all gay men and lesbian women, and cannot be scientifically proved with respect to those gay men and lesbian women who believe it is true in their cases.[15] Fundamental choice and sex discrimination arguments do not suffer from a lack of factual support, because they do not rest on any controversial assumptions about the nature of sexual orientation (as direction of attraction). Instead, they assume that sexual orientation (as direction of conduct) is freely chosen and seek to protect the choice of direction of conduct rather than the reason for making it.

2. Availability of Legal Doctrine

The application of this criterion to a particular argument depends on which human rights instrument is considered. Under the US Constitution, a sex discrimination argument is to be preferred, because *Hardwick* has so far been interpreted as precluding both fundamental choice ('right of privacy') and immutable status ('suspect classification') arguments. A sex discrimination argument could rely on existing equal protection doctrine, and thus might avoid both the controversy generated by the US Supreme Court's creation and expansion of

---

[15] See Ch. 7, Part I. On the reluctance of some courts to intervene in this scientific controversy, see Halley (1994 US), 513–16.

the 'right of privacy', and the murkiness surrounding the criteria for identifying new 'suspect' or 'quasi-suspect' classifications. Such an argument now has the support of the Hawaii Supreme Court in *Baehr* v. *Lewin*.[16] Although a defendant (e.g. a public employer) might try to use *Hardwick* to block a sex discrimination argument, by asserting that they do not discriminate on the basis of sex because they dismiss all employees who engage in oral or anal intercourse, it is unlikely that they could prove that heterosexual employees were dismissed for this reason.

Under the European Convention, the limited scope of Article 14 pre-empts this debate altogether, by mandating some form of fundamental choice argument. But a sex discrimination argument relying on *Abdulaziz* is probably the better way to supplement it, because a general concept of 'suspect classifications' or 'analogous grounds', based on 'immutability' or some other criterion, has yet to be developed under Article 14.

As for the Canadian Charter, the argument that requires the least development of new legal doctrine is also clearly a sex discrimination argument, because sex is an enumerated ground under Section 15(1) and need only be interpreted as including sexual orientation. However, in Canada, unlike the US, a sex discrimination argument is not necessarily the preferred candidate because Canadian courts have been able (in the absence of any negative Supreme Court authority) and willing to find that sexual orientation is an analogous ground under Section 15(1).[17] An immutable status argument could rely on the 'enumerated and analogous grounds' interpretation of Section 15(1) adopted by the Supreme Court in *Andrews* and the recognition in that decision of the 'citizenship status of non-citizen permanent residents' as a temporarily immutable analogous ground. It would still have to be shown that sexual orientation (as direction of attraction) is an immutable status, and therefore an analogous ground. A fundamental choice argument requires the exploration of relatively new constitutional territory. A majority of the Supreme Court would have to agree that fundamental choices are analogous grounds, and can be identified under Section 15(1) or Section 7, and would have to conclude that sexual orientation (as direction of conduct) is such a choice.

3. Comprehensiveness of Protection

In considering the comprehensiveness of protection against sexual orientation discrimination which each argument could potentially provide, at least four questions can be raised: (i) is discrimination based on chosen conduct covered? (ii) is discrimination based on an unchosen attraction covered? (iii) is discrimination against persons who are bisexual or asexual/celibate covered? (iv) is discrimination resulting from the ways in which gay, lesbian, and bisexual persons

[16] See discussion in Ch. 3, Part II; Ch. 8, Part II.F.
[17] See Wintemute (1994 Can), 459 n. 175.

may be different from heterosexual persons covered as direct discrimination, or only as indirect discrimination?

With regard to the first two questions, there is a clear difference between the three arguments. An immutable status argument cannot directly protect a person's actual choice of the direction of their emotional–sexual conduct. It can only stress that the asserted immutability of the direction of the person's emotional–sexual attraction tends to compel their choice of direction of emotional–sexual conduct, and therefore strengthens the case for protecting that choice. In so doing, however, it may imply that protection of that choice should be limited to persons whose direction of attraction tends to compel their making it (i.e. the choice of same-sex emotional–sexual conduct should be limited to gay men and lesbian women, and denied to bisexual and heterosexual persons).[18] However, fundamental choice and sex discrimination arguments can protect the choice of direction of emotional–sexual conduct regardless of the reason for making it (and whether or not it is consistent with a person's direction of emotional–sexual attraction). But can these latter two arguments also protect a person against discrimination based on the direction of their emotional–sexual attraction (chosen or unchosen)? Protection of sexual orientation as a fundamental choice of the actual direction of emotional–sexual conduct should include the reason for making that choice, and therefore a person's interest in or desire for a particular direction of conduct (i.e. the direction of their emotional–sexual attraction, chosen or unchosen). A sex discrimination argument should provide similar protection, because a man's attraction to men (or a woman's to women) will be considered objectionable solely because of his (or her) sex.

With regard to the third question, the protection provided by immutable status and fundamental choice arguments should extend to persons who are bisexual (are attracted to, or engage in conduct with, both sexes), asexual (are attracted to neither sex) or celibate (engage in conduct with neither sex). This will be the case if possible directions of attraction or conduct are defined as to or with persons of the opposite sex, the same sex, both sexes or neither sex. However, like the argument that sexual harassment is sex discrimination, the argument that sexual orientation discrimination is sex discrimination theoretically suffers from a loophole. This is because restrictions on persons whose direction of attraction is bisexual or asexual, or on the choices of bisexual conduct or celibacy, could be imposed on all men and women without discriminating on the basis of sex. This 'bisexual/asexual/celibate' loophole is not likely to have much practical significance. Discrimination against persons who are asexual or celibate (as opposed to unmarried) must be extremely rare; and discrimination against bisexual persons will almost always be based on the same-sex component of their attraction or conduct.

The fourth question arises because it will often be preferable to show that a

---

[18] See Murphy (1993 US), 697–8.

particular instance of sexual orientation discrimination constitutes direct discrimination rather than indirect discrimination, where the latter might be seen as
easier to justify (e.g. under Section 1 of the Canadian Charter) or might violate
a particular human rights instrument only if it is intentional (e.g. the US Constitution).[19] Under an immutable status argument, any discrimination based on
chosen conduct or statements may have to be treated as indirect rather than
direct discrimination, because the conduct or statement could be engaged in or
made by any person, regardless of sexual orientation (as direction of attraction).
Fundamental choice and sex discrimination arguments can apply to discrimination against gay, lesbian, and bisexual persons which is based on chosen conduct
and statements and treat it as direct discrimination, provided that comparable
conduct or a comparable statement by a heterosexual person is or would be
treated more favourably. But both the latter two arguments may be unable to
bring a particular instance of sexual orientation discrimination within the net of
direct discrimination, where an apparently neutral rule is applied equally to all
persons (heterosexual, bisexual, gay or lesbian) or to all emotional–sexual conduct (opposite-sex or same-sex), or where direct discrimination is difficult to
prove because there appears to be no comparable conduct or statements by
heterosexual persons.

Neutral rules could be applied in the area of private sexual activity. By defining sexual orientation narrowly as a person's choice of the *direction* of their
emotional–sexual conduct (including private sexual activity), as opposed to their
choice of the *content* of such conduct, a fundamental choice argument avoids the
difficult task of defining any justifiable limits on such conduct. However, because it does not assert that every interference with private sexual activity prima
facie violates a human rights instrument (rather, only those interferences that
discriminate on the basis of the direction of such conduct), a fundamental choice
argument will not provide protection where the interference is applied equally
to opposite-sex and same-sex conduct. A sex discrimination argument faces the
same difficulty, because any restriction applying equally to the choices of opposite-
sex and same-sex conduct arguably does not discriminate on the basis of sex.
Although in many cases, the heterosexual majority could be expected not to
want to restrict their own conduct, there could be cases where they might be
willing to tolerate restrictions that may be unacceptable to the gay, lesbian, and
bisexual minority.

For example, most US oral or anal intercourse laws purport to apply to all
such intercourse, whether its direction is opposite-sex or same-sex. And in Canada,
section 159 of the Criminal Code continues to prohibit both opposite-sex and
same-sex anal intercourse involving a person aged between 14 and 18 (even
though such a person could consent to vaginal or oral intercourse).[20] To attack

[19] See e.g. *Washington* v. *Davis*, 426 US 229 (1976).
[20] See Ch. 6, note 125. In *R.* v. *Carmen M.* (27 July 1992), No. P3137/91 (Ont Ct Just) (appeal
heard by Ont CA in Nov. 1994), Corbett J. held (at 19–20) that '[t]he failure of s. 159 . . . to afford

a sex-neutral prohibition of oral or anal intercourse, one would have to argue that it is applied unequally (i.e. enforced only against same-sex conduct), that it is intended to discriminate against the choice of same-sex conduct (e.g. by permitting penile–vaginal intercourse, the direction of which can only be opposite-sex),[21] or that it disproportionately affects gay, lesbian, and bisexual persons, whether or not this effect was intended (i.e. it is indirectly discriminatory).[22] If none of these arguments were available, one would have to argue that the law interfered with a more general choice of the content of emotional–sexual conduct, rather than with the specific choice of the direction of emotional–sexual conduct (sexual orientation). Under the European Convention, this could be done under Article 8. A challenge to a US-style total prohibition of opposite-sex and same-sex oral and anal intercourse should succeed, under *Dudgeon, Norris*, and *Modinos*. But a challenge to a Canadian-style discriminatory age of consent for opposite-sex and same-sex anal intercourse would be more difficult, in view of the Commission's age of consent case law to date.[23]

Neutral rules could also be applied in relation to 'other public manifestations of sexual orientation',[24] including aspects of a person's appearance, manner or dress, and their statements or expressive acts. These 'other public manifestations' will usually serve merely as evidence of the direction of a person's attraction or conduct, either of which will ultimately be the ground on which an act of discrimination is based. However, it is possible that a public employer might argue that, regardless of the direction of an employee's attraction or conduct, a particular 'other public manifestation' is objectionable *per se*, and justifies the dismissal of the employee.[25] One could attempt to establish an intent to discriminate on the basis of sexual orientation, or a disproportionate (and unjustifiable) impact on gay, lesbian or bisexual persons, or one could invoke freedom of

---

the accused the defence of consent to acts of anal intercourse . . . with a young person between . . . 14 and 18 deprives him of [a Section 7] right' and is not justified under Section 1. She allowed the accused, a man of 23 who had engaged in consensual anal intercourse with a girl of 14, the defence of consent and acquitted him, finding it unnecessary to consider his Section 15(1) argument that the law discriminates 'on account of . . . sexual preference' because of its 'disparate effect on homosexuals'. In *Halm* v. *Canada (Minister of Employment and Immigration)* (24 Feb. 1995), No. IMM-7073–93 (F.C.T.D.), Reed J. held, at 21–2, 31, that s. 159 'has a disparate impact insofar as homosexual males are concerned and therefore discriminates against them', contrary to Section 15(1), and that the discrimination cannot be justified under Section 1. Cf. *R.* v. *Schnare* (15 Feb. 1990) Kentville K89–2326, K89–2327 (NS Prov Ct) (rejecting Section 15(1) argument because s. 159 applies to both opposite-sex and same-sex anal intercourse); Ryder (1990 Can), 64.

[21] See Koppelman (1988 US), 151–3 and 153 n. 54.

[22] See *Halm* (cited note 20) (accepting this argument); *Schnare*, (cited ibid.) and text accompanying Ch. 6, note 102 (rejecting it). Cf. *Watkins* v. *US Army*, 847 F 2d 1329 at 1357 (9th Cir 1988) (Reinhardt J., dissenting) (if 'homosexuals' were a 'suspect class', a statute criminalizing both opposite-sex and same-sex oral and anal intercourse would have to include opposite-sex vaginal intercourse to be an equal prohibition and 'survive equal protection analysis').

[23] See Ch. 4, note 27; Ch. 5, note 94.   [24] See Ch. 1, text accompanying notes 36–39.

[25] See *Williamson* v. *A.G. Edwards & Sons, Inc.*, 876 F 2d 69 at 70 (8th Cir 1989) (dismissed gay employee accused of 'openly discuss[ing] his sex li[fe] while at work').

expression (where a statement or expressive act was involved). But it would be preferable, whenever possible, to treat such a case as involving direct discrimination based on sexual orientation or sex.

In the case of appearance, manner, and dress, a sex discrimination argument may be useful because a rule that appears neutral as among sexual orientations (e.g. no 'masculine' women or 'feminine' men, regardless of sexual orientation) may in fact discriminate directly on the basis of sex. This is because both involuntary and voluntary 'masculine' traits in a woman's appearance, manner or dress (or 'feminine' traits in a man's) will often be considered objectionable solely because of her (or his) sex.[26]

Where a statement or expressive act relates to another person (e.g. a reference to a partner or to the attractiveness of another person, or a picture on a desk), a comparison of the treatment of an 'opposite-sex statement' with that of a 'same-sex statement' permits a finding of direct discrimination based on sexual orientation or sex. In the case of statements and expressive acts that do not relate to a particular person, a 'lack of comparator' problem could arise,[27] whether a fundamental choice or sex discrimination argument is used, where heterosexual persons do not customarily make equivalent statements or do equivalent acts (e.g. 'I am gay, lesbian, bisexual' or 'I went to the Gay, Lesbian, and Bisexual Pride Day Parade on Sunday'). This is because, as members of the majority, heterosexual persons rarely need to identify themselves or their community events as heterosexual. Even if equivalent statements or acts by heterosexual persons are rare or only hypothetical, it should be sufficient to establish direct sexual orientation or sex discrimination that those equivalent statements would attract no penalty.[28] If all variants of a particular statement or act were banned (e.g. no

---

[26] See e.g. *Re Wardair Canada Inc. and Canadian Air Line Flight Attendants Association* (1987), 28 LAC (3d) 142 at 150 (rule against men wearing earrings is prima facie sex discrimination). Cf. *Williamson*, ibid. at 70 (dismissed male employee 'reprimanded for wearing makeup at work'); *Smith* v. *Liberty Mutual Insurance Co.*, 569 F 2d 325 (5th Cir 1978) (denying job to man considered 'effeminate' not sex discrimination); *DeSantis* v. *Pacific Telephone & Telegraph Co.*, 608 F 2d 327 at 331–2 (9th Cir 1979) ('discrimination because of effeminacy [man wearing an earring] . . . does not fall within the purview of Title VII'). The authority of *Smith* and *DeSantis* regarding 'effeminacy' is doubtful after *Price Waterhouse* v. *Hopkins*, 490 US 228 at 235 (1989) (sex was motivating factor in decision not to make woman a partner, where partners described her as 'macho', needing 'a course at charm school' and 'somewhat masculine', and advised her to walk, talk, and dress 'more femininely', wear make-up and jewelry and have her hair styled). See Capers (1991 US), 1180.

[27] Distinctions were held to be based on the 'content' of a statement rather than the sexual orientation of the person making it in *Gay Alliance Toward Equality* v. *Vancouver Sun* [1979] 2 SCR 435 at 456, and *Gay News Ltd.* v. *UK* (No. 8710/79) (1982), 28 D.R. 77 at p. 6 (unpublished part). In neither case was the treatment of a statement with 'gay content' compared with that of a statement with equivalent 'heterosexual content'.

[28] See *Rowland* v. *Mad River Local School District* 470 US 1009 at 1016 n. 11 (1985) (Brennan J., dissenting) (teacher's statement that she was bisexual was 'a natural consequence of her sexual orientation, in the same way that co-workers generally know whom their [heterosexual] fellow employees are dating or to whom they are married'); *Rowland* 730 F 2d 444 at 453 (6th Cir 1984) (Edwards J., dissenting) (race discrimination if 'teacher whose appearance was consistent with majority race status . . . revealed she had a black parent').

statements regarding pride in one's sexual orientation are permitted), gay, lesbian, and bisexual persons would have to argue disproportionate impact (intentional or unintentional)[29] or freedom of expression.

4. Capacity to Counter Potential Justifications for Prima Facie Discrimination

It must be remembered that proving a prima facie violation of one of the three human rights instruments is not sufficient to establish that a particular instance of sexual orientation discrimination is prohibited by that instrument. The plaintiff must be prepared to counter compelling government interests that might be asserted under the US Constitution, or justifications that might be raised under Articles 8(2), 12 or 14 of the European Convention or under Section 1 of the Canadian Charter. Discussion of the justifications for discrimination against gay, lesbian, and bisexual persons and same-sex emotional–sexual conduct that are most likely to be asserted (such as 'morality', the HIV epidemic, protection of the 'traditional family', and protection of adolescents and children) is beyond the scope of this book,[30] which is concerned only with the case for finding prima facie violations of the three instruments. However, it is worth considering these asserted justifications briefly to determine whether they might influence one's choice of argument.

In view of the way the three arguments have been structured, the cases that trigger prima facie violations and require justification will involve discrimination on the basis of sexual orientation, i.e. treating gay, lesbian, and bisexual persons and same-sex emotional–sexual conduct less favourably than heterosexual persons and opposite-sex emotional–sexual conduct. Thus, thorny debates about the justifiability of interferences with many controversial areas of emotional–sexual conduct, such as paedophilia, incest, prostitution, pornography, sado-masochism or polygamy, will not arise where the interference applies both to opposite-sex and same-sex conduct. The justifications that will be raised in a case of sexual orientation discrimination will relate, not to whether a minimum age of consent should be required or whether payment of money or consensual use of force should be prohibited, but to whether same-sex conduct should be prohibited or discouraged where comparable opposite-sex conduct is not.

The strength of some asserted justifications,[31] such as 'morality',[32] the

---

[29] In *Georgetown*, 536 A 2d 1 at 26–30 (DC 1987), the court held that a denial of benefits to gay and lesbian student groups was not based on the 'purposes and activities' of the groups but on the sexual orientation of the groups' members, either intentionally or with the same effect as intentional discrimination.

[30] Justifications have been discussed in Chs. 2 to 8 only where it seemed essential to do so.

[31] One justification that should not be accepted is prejudice of third parties (e.g., co-workers, customers, neighbours) against gay, lesbian or bisexual persons. See *Gay Alliance*, [1979] 2 SCR 435 at 445 (Laskin J., dissenting); *Palmore* v. *Sidoti*, 466 US 429 (1984) (court could not give effect to prejudice against mixed-race couples, by reversing a post-divorce child custody award in favour of a mother of European origin because she had begun living with a man of African origin). See also *Rolon* v. *Kulwitzky*, 200 Cal Rptr 217 at 219 (Ct App 1984) (restaurant could not exclude same-sex

HIV epidemic,[33] freedom of religion,[34] freedom of association,[35] or freedom of expression[36] will not vary with the argument used. However, the plausibility of a related pair of potential justifications, 'protection of the traditional

couples from romantic dining booths, open to public view, to protect patrons from 'acts of "intimacy" between homosexuals').

[32] I would suggest that giving any weight to purely religious or 'moral' justifications would violate freedom of conscience and religion (US Constitution, First Amendment; European Convention, Article 9(1); Canadian Charter, Section 2(a)). The Convention, however, seems to contradict itself by expressly including 'protection of morals' as a justification in Articles 8(2), 9(2), 10(2), and 11(2). See Ch. 4, Part III.A.1(c) (treatment of this justification in *Dudgeon* and *Norris*). I would also suggest that accepting religious or 'moral' objections to conduct, not based on any effects the conduct may have, would constitute giving effect to 'prejudice' (bias), and would not be a legitimate public purpose: see Ch. 2, Part II.A.2 (e); Ch. 3, Part I.D. Cf. *Watkins* v. *US Army*, 875 F 2d 699 at 729–30 (9th Cir 1989) (Norris J., concurring) (even if US military regulations are based on 'morality', and not 'prejudice masking as morality', 'equal protection doctrine does not permit majoritarian notions of morality to serve as compelling justifications for laws that discriminate against suspect classes', citing rejection of 'immorality' of mixed-race marriage in *Loving*); *Steffan* v. *Cheney*, 780 F Supp 1 at 13 (DDC 1991) (*Steffan I*) (regulations based on 'a standard of morality', not prejudice).

[33] Discrimination against gay or bisexual men, or against emotional–sexual conduct between men, that relies on risk of HIV transmission as a justification will be based on exactly the kind of stereotype that prohibitions of discrimination are intended to exclude. The UN Human Rights Committee rejected this justification in *Toonen* (reference Ch. 5, note 137) at para. 8.5. Cf. *Steffan I*, ibid. at 13–16 (court cites AIDS, *sua sponte*, as 'rational basis' for US military's policy); *State* v. *Walsh*, 713 SW 2d 508 at 512 (Mo 1986) (AIDS cited as 'rational basis' for Missouri's prohibition of same-sex oral or anal intercourse). Discrimination against lesbian or bisexual women or emotional–sexual conduct between women that relies on risk of HIV transmission as a justification is completely irrational.

[34] When legislation prohibiting discrimination in employment or services is drafted or interpreted, the conflict between freedom of religion and freedom from discrimination is often resolved in favour of the religious institution. See e.g. *Dignity Twin Cities* v. *Newman Center*, 472 NW 2d 355 (Minn Ct App 1991) (Roman Catholic church's refusal to rent secular meeting space to gay and lesbian Roman Catholic group upheld); *Lewis ex rel Murphy* v. *Buchanan*, 21 Fair Empl Prac Cases (BNA) 696 (Minn Dist Ct 1979) (Roman Catholic school's refusal to hire gay music teacher upheld); *Walker* v. *First Presbyterian Church*, 22 Fair Empl Prac Cases (BNA) 762 (Cal Super Ct 1980) (church's dismissal of gay organist upheld). Cf. *Association pour les droits des gai(e)s du Québec* v. *Commission des écoles catholiques de Montréal* (1979) [1980] Cour Supér. 93, 112 DLR (3d) 230 (religious institution exception must be interpreted restrictively and did not permit refusal to rent school for weekend conference, where schools were offered to public in general and had been rented to atheist political parties); *Georgetown*, 536 A 2d 1 at 30–39 (DC 1987) (neither statutory exception for religious organizations nor First Amendment exempted Roman Catholic university). But see DC Code s. 1–2520(3) (subsequent amendment permitting 'any educational institution that is affiliated with a religious organization' to deny benefits to 'persons that are organized for, or engaged in, promoting, encouraging or condoning any homosexual act, lifestyle, orientation or belief'). See also Duncan (1994 US); Minn Stat Ann s. 363.02 subdiv. 8 (broad exemption for religious institutions in relation to sexual orientation discrimination in education and employment does not apply to their 'secular business activities').

[35] Freedom from discrimination also conflicts with the right of a private non-profit association to exclude persons it does not wish to have as members. See e.g. *Curran* v. *Mount Diablo Council of the Boy Scouts of America*, 29 Cal Rptr 2d 580 (Ct App 1994), rev'g in part (after trial) 195 Cal Rptr 325 (Ct App 1983) (a Boy Scouts organization could not be required to hire an openly gay man as scoutmaster, under s. 51 of the California Civil Code, because this would violate its First Amendment right to freedom of expressive and intimate association and because it was not a 'business establishment' to which s. 51 applies).

[36] Freedom from discrimination may also be seen as conflicting with freedom of expression (see Ch. 2, notes 224–226 (St. Patrick's Day parade litigation in US)), and especially with freedom of

family'[37] and 'protection of adolescents and children',[38] may be affected by one's choice of argument. For fundamental choice and sex discrimination arguments protect a person's actual choice of the direction of their emotional–sexual conduct, regardless of any attraction they may have to that direction of conduct (and regardless, therefore, of their reason for choosing that direction). This is potentially threatening to the 'traditional family' (married opposite-sex couple with children), because if the choice of same-sex conduct is protected for everyone, regardless of the direction of their attraction, the theoretical possibility is raised that a large percentage (up to one hundred per cent) of the population could make that choice.

Evidence that legislatures perceive such a threat can be seen in laws prohibiting the 'promotion of homosexuality'.[39] One example of fear of 'promotion' is the US Hate Crime Statistics Act.[40] It provides, in section 1(b)(1), that the Attorney-General shall acquire data 'about crimes that manifest evidence of prejudice based on . . . sexual orientation'. But the Act expressly states that it does not create a cause of action for sexual orientation discrimination (section 1(b)(3)), and is not to be construed (nor shall funds be used) 'to promote or encourage homosexuality' (section 2(b)). Section 2(a) states the findings of Congress that: '(1) the [traditional] American family life [i.e. married opposite-sex couple with children] is the foundation of American Society, (2) Federal policy should encourage the well-being, financial security, and health of the

the press. In both *Gay Alliance*, [1979] 2 SCR 435, and *Hatheway* v. *Gannett Satellite Information Network, Inc.*, 459 NW 2d 873 (Wis Ct App 1990), courts refused to interpret anti-discrimination legislation as applying to refusals by newspapers to accept advertisements containing the words 'gay' or 'lesbian'. In *Gay Alliance*, ibid. at 469, Dickson J. (dissenting) sought to resolve the conflict by distinguishing between a newspaper's editorial content and its commercial advertising. Cf. *Lambda Amateur Radio Club* v. *American Radio Relay League*, [1994] *Lesbian/Gay Law Notes* 54 (Conn Comm on Hum Rts) (refusal of gay club's advertisement in newsletter violated Connecticut law prohibiting sexual orientation discrimination, where other 'issue-oriented' groups such as Jehovah's Witnesses were permitted to advertise).

[37] The European Commission has accepted this justification in same-sex couple cases. See Ch. 5, text accompanying notes 24–8. Cf. *Leshner* (1992) 16 CHRR D/184 at D/203–D/204 (Ont Hum Rts Comm) (government declined to assert this justification for denying pension to same-sex partner, and argued greater financial dependency of women in opposite-sex couple relationships).

[38] 'Protection of adolescents and children' may be viewed as seeking to prevent the perceived harm of *any* individual adolescent or child being exposed to any influence that might cause them to choose same-sex emotional–sexual conduct later in life. 'Protection of the traditional family' may be viewed as seeking to prevent the perceived harm of significant numbers of persons choosing same-sex emotional–sexual conduct. Thus, it focuses on the cumulative effect rather than on individual cases.

[39] See Ch. 7, note 86. See also Ryder (1990 Can), 43, 68–73, 94–5 (discussing dichotomy in legal responses to discrimination against gay, lesbian, and bisexual persons between 'compassion for . . . misguided souls' and 'no promotion or condonation of "their lifestyle"'); Black (1979 Can), 658 (Board of Inquiry statement in *Gay Alliance* that '[a]cceptance . . . does not require that society . . . encourage or promote homosexuality or convert those who are not naturally so inclined').

[40] 28 USCA s. 534 (note, referring to Pub L 101–275, 23 Apr. 1990). Gairdner (1990 Can) refers, at 81, to the promotion of 'perverse anti-family sexual "orientations"', and claims, at 282, that 'the homosexual underculture always vies for normality with the core culture, destroying core values and stealing otherwise procreative males from women'.

American family, (3) schools shall not de-emphasize the critical value of American family life.'

John Boswell discussed this 'threat' to society[41] and noted the similarity between 'deviance in sexual matters' and religious heresy or political dissent:

Gay people seem as dangerous in kinship societies as heretics once did in Catholic Europe or as socialists more recently in Western democracies. In all such cases dissent or deviance may appear to be treason at first; only time, familiarity, and education can make for room for harmless nonconformity and enable the majority to distinguish between those forms of atypical behavior which actually are destructive of the social order and those which are not.[42]

He also observed that '[m]ost societies . . . which freely tolerate religious diversity also accept sexual variation, and the fate of Jews and gay people has been almost identical throughout European history, from early Christian hostility to extermination in concentration camps'.[43]

To discard this perceived threat (however unlikely it may be),[44] one must ultimately be prepared to defend the right of every adult and adolescent to choose same-sex emotional–sexual conduct and argue that the government's legitimate interests are (possibly) in encouraging procreation,[45] and (certainly) in ensuring that children receive proper care, neither of which requires the suppression of same-sex emotional–sexual conduct. The government should no more be able to dictate a person's choice of sexual orientation than their choice of religion or political party. Although one may accept that this should be true, as a matter of principle, the political reality is that tolerance of religious, political, and racial minorities seems to decrease as their numbers increase. Thus, openly gay, lesbian, and bisexual persons in a state that defines itself as 'heterosexual' may be no more welcome than Muslim immigrants in a state that defines itself as 'Christian'.[46]

---

[41] See Boswell (1980 Other), 8–10.   [42] Ibid. at 33–4.

[43] Ibid. at 15–16. See also Honoré (1978 Eur), 89, 102–3 ('homosexuality . . . resembles political or religious dissent, being an atheist in Catholic Ireland or a dissident in Soviet Russia'); Posner (1992 US), 346 ('statutes that criminalize homosexual behavior express an irrational fear and loathing of a group that has been subjected to discrimination, much like that directed against the Jews, with whom indeed homosexuals—who, like Jews, are despised more for what they are than for what they do—were frequently bracketed in medieval persecutions'). An English legal textbook of about 1300 stated that 'those who have connection with Jews or Jewesses or are guilty of bestiality or sodomy shall be buried alive in the ground': see Crane (1982 Eur), 11.

[44] It may be greater in the case of lesbian or bisexual women. The problems that women often face in traditional opposite-sex couple relationships (e.g. violence or the entire burden of childcare and domestic work) may give women a greater incentive than men to consider same-sex couple relationships. See e.g. Rich (1983 Other), 191–2, 196–7. See also Ch. 7, notes 9–11 and accompanying text. And it is far easier for a female–female couple (who will usually have eggs and two wombs and need only a sperm donation) to have children than for an (eggless and wombless) male–male couple.

[45] See Ryder (1990 Can), 84 ('[t]he state interest in encouraging people to bring babies into an already over-crowded world is not self-evident').

[46] This raises the question whether any state should define itself in terms of a particular religion, ethnic origin, political opinion (more specific than a general belief in democracy and certain human rights) or sexual orientation.

An immutable status argument attempts to avoid this difficulty by claiming that same-sex emotional–sexual conduct is mainly of interest only to a small, fixed minority of gay men and lesbian women (consisting of ten per cent of the population or less). Whether or not this claim is factually correct will depend on what percentage of the population is bisexual (and also potentially interested in same-sex conduct), and what effect the elimination of discrimination would have on the number of persons identifying themselves as gay, lesbian or bisexual. Assuming that this claim is correct, it defuses one asserted justification ('protection of the traditional family') at the possible expense of giving credence to another ('protection of adolescents and children'). Whereas, under the other two arguments, the choice of same-sex conduct can be viewed as a free choice that must be respected and protected, an immutable status argument rests on the assumption that a person's sexual orientation (as direction of attraction) constrains their choice of the direction of their emotional–sexual conduct (unless their direction of attraction is bisexual, in which case their choice may not be constrained, because both opposite-sex and same-sex conduct are of interest). Thus, an advocate of this argument must concede that being gay or lesbian may make it difficult to choose opposite-sex conduct (just as being heterosexual may make it difficult to choose same-sex conduct).

Advocates of sexual orientation discrimination incorrectly equate difficulty in choosing opposite-sex emotional–sexual conduct with impossibility of having or raising children. They then conclude that, because it limits a person's ability to choose opposite-sex conduct, an attraction to same-sex conduct is an unfortunate difference that no-one would choose and against which others must be protected (i.e. a potentially contagious 'affliction').[47] This characterization of same-sex attraction is used to justify not only attempts to 'cure' 'afflicted' adults, but also to prevent the 'affliction' from 'spreading' involuntarily to adolescents or children by prohibiting their exposure to gay, lesbian or bisexual adults (expressing affection in public places, working in schools or daycare centres, or acting as parents),[48] or their engaging in same-sex sexual activity at the same age they

[47] See Ryder (1990 Can), 71. See also Finnis (1994 Eur), 1052 (referring to 'the judgment that a life involving homosexual conduct is bad even for anyone unfortunate enough to have innate or quasi-innate homosexual tendencies').

[48] Florida and New Hampshire have legislation expressly prohibiting 'homosexuals' from adopting or fostering children. See Fla Stat Ann s. 63.042(3) (adoption); Rubenstein (1993 US), 517–22; NH Rev Stat Ann ss. 170–B:4 (adoption), 161:2(IV) (fostering); *Opinion of the Justices*, 530 A 2d 21 at 25 (NH 1987) ('exclusion of homosexuals . . . from foster parentage and adoption . . . [is] rationally related to the bill's [legitimate] purpose . . . to provide appropriate role models for children'). Connecticut and Massachusetts expressly exclude adoption and fostering from laws prohibiting sexual orientation discrimination, and Minnesota has an exemption for 'programs providing . . . role models for minors'. See Conn Gen Stat s. 45a–726a; Mass Gen Laws Ann ch. 151B, s. 4 (note, referring to Mass Stat 1989, c. 516, s. 18); Minn Stat Ann s. 363.021(1); *Big Brothers, Inc.* v. *Minneapolis Commission on Civil Rights*, 284 NW 2d 823 at 828 (Minn 1979) (permitting Big Brothers to inform mother of applicant's same-sex sexual orientation, as with 'any other atypical trait'). Cf. Rubenstein (1993 US), 532 n. 1 (New York State regulations providing that 'applicants for adoption shall not be rejected solely on the basis of homosexuality'); *Kippen* v. *Big*

could engage in opposite-sex sexual activity (to prevent their becoming 'corrupted' by same-sex sexual activity and therefore 'addicted' to it).

Using the terminology of disease or drug addiction in the context of sexual orientation is certainly inappropriate. But it illustrates the tone of arguments one must be prepared to counter ·if one relies on an immutable status argument. In *Ratchford* v. *Gay Lib*, Justice Rehnquist observed that:

[f]rom the point of view of the University [which had refused to recognize a gay and lesbian student organization to prevent an increase in violations of Missouri's oral or anal intercourse law] . . . the question is more akin to whether those suffering from measles have a constitutional right, in violation of quarantine regulations, to associate together and with others who do not presently have measles, in order to urge repeal of a state law providing that measles sufferers be quarantined.[49]

Bruce Ryder's compassion/condonation dichotomy results from this negative view of same-sex sexual orientation as a 'contagious affliction' (or an 'addiction').[50] 'Compassion' for the 'victims' of the 'affliction' (or 'addiction') is warranted, but there must be no 'condonation'[51] or 'promotion' of their conduct so as to prevent the 'affliction' (or 'addiction') from 'spreading'. Advocates of discrimination against gay, lesbian, and bisexual persons seem to alternate between portraying same-sex sexual orientation as a 'contagious disease' (like measles) or an 'addiction' (like alcoholism) depending on whether they see it as caused by mere social contact with such persons (e.g. teachers) or by actually trying same-sex sexual activity and becoming 'addicted' to it. The 'addiction' argument is more common where the issue is decriminalizing same-sex sexual activity or lowering the age at which a person may consent to it.

One can respond to this 'contagious affliction' argument either by denying that a same-sex attraction is an 'affliction', or by denying that a same-sex attraction is 'contagious' (or both). The first response involves asserting that a same-sex attraction has no significant disadvantages (other than legal and social discrimination), because same-sex conduct has no such disadvantages. Putting discrimination aside, the only inherent disadvantage of same-sex conduct is that, like infertile opposite-sex couples, same-sex couples require the assistance of a

---

Brothers Association of Winnipeg, Inc. (1993), 20 CHRR D/483 (Man HRC) (statutory prohibitions of sexual orientation discrimination in services and employment apply to the matching of prospective Big Brothers with Little Brothers).

[49] 434 US 1080, 1084 (1978) (dissenting from denial of cert.).

[50] See note 39 above. See also *Maclean's* (27 July 1987) 11 (statement of former Governor-General Edward Schreyer that 'homosexuality' is an 'affliction' that, '[i]f allowed to become too visible in society . . . cannot help but have a negative and detrimental effect on the younger generation'); *The Advocate* (20 Jan. 1987) 14 (remark of Ontario legislator that 'homosexuality' is like alcoholism).

[51] Several legislatures have expressly stated, in passing anti-discrimination laws, that they did not intent to 'condone', 'approve', or 'endorse' 'homosexuality or bisexuality or any equivalent lifestyle'. See Conn Gen Stat s. 46a–81r(1); Mass Gen Laws Ann ch. 151B, s. 4 (note, referring to Mass Stat 1989, c. 516, s. 18); Minn Stat Ann s. 363.021(1).

third party to have children and cannot have children with genetic input from both partners. (A female–female couple is in the same position as a male–female couple in which the man is infertile. Both couples can procreate using donor insemination, which is relatively easy to arrange, or they can adopt a child. A male–male couple is in the same position as a male–female couple in which the woman is infertile. Both couples can procreate with the assistance of a surrogate mother, which could be very difficult to arrange, or they can adopt a child.)[52] Each individual considering a same-sex couple relationship must weigh this 'objective' disadvantage (the difficulty, rather than the impossibility, of having children) against the advantages of such a relationship, both 'subjective' (e.g. it may satisfy a person's emotional–sexual attraction to persons of their own sex) and potentially 'objective' (e.g. any advantage persons of the same sex may have in understanding and satisfying each other's emotional and sexual needs, and in building a relationship as equals that does not duplicate the strict social roles common in opposite-sex couple relationships).

However, persons who rely on an immutable status argument tend to use only the second response. Rather than defend the ultimate choice of same-sex emotional–sexual conduct (as those using the other two arguments must do), they focus on same-sex emotional–sexual attraction and deny that it is chosen or can be changed or 'spread' involuntarily. Thus, they often assert that 'no-one chooses to be gay or lesbian'. It is true that many gay men and lesbian women do feel that their same-sex attraction is immutable (i.e. initially unchosen and currently impossible to change); and it is true that the immutability of a status does not necessarily mean that particular manifestations of the status are undesirable and such that no-one would choose them. But emphasizing the absence of choice of gay men and lesbian women tends to give credence to the 'contagious affliction' argument (even though an immutable opposite-sex attraction involves the same absence of choice) and imply that, if there were any significant risk of adolescents or children acquiring a same-sex attraction, steps could justifiably be taken to protect them from it.[53]

Proponents of an immutable status argument are thus forced to show that same-sex emotional-sexual attraction cannot 'spread' and are plunged into the scientific debate regarding the cause of sexual orientation. They must seek to prove that sexual orientation (as direction of attraction) is fixed at an early age

[52] See Ryder (1990 Can), 87–9. A significant percentage of opposite-sex couples may experience fertility problems. See e.g. *The New York Times* (13 Sept. 1990) B11 (8% of married opposite-sex couples with wives aged 15 to 44 are infertile). It could be argued that the infertility of a same-sex couple (where both partners are fertile) is 'wilful', in that it is caused by each partner's choice of a person of the same sex rather than a medical problem. However, the same is true of an opposite-sex couple with one fertile partner, who could terminate the relationship and seek a new, fertile partner, but prefers to remain with their infertile partner. The only difference between an infertile opposite-sex couple and a same-sex couple is that the latter's fertility problem is obvious at the start of their relationship.

[53] See Halley (1994 US), 523 (immutability 'fails to contest the argument[ ] . . . that homosexuality is bad').

(if not at birth), that there is no evidence that the same-sex attraction of adult gay men or lesbian women can be 'transmitted' before (or after) this age to children[54] or adolescents (or that same-sex sexual activity is any more 'addictive' for adolescents than opposite-sex sexual activity), and that the effects of sexual orientation discrimination on adult gay men and lesbian women outweigh any highly speculative risk of 'transmission' to adolescents and children.

Of course, the 'protection of adolescents and children' justification can also be asserted where fundamental choice or sex discrimination arguments are used. Since these do not depend on the existence of immutable directions of emotional–sexual attraction, an advocate of any of them must be prepared to concede that a child or adolescent's ultimate choice of sexual orientation (as direction of conduct), when they begin to choose emotional–sexual conduct (as an adolescent or as an adult), may have been influenced by the examples of their parents, teachers, and other adults they come in to contact with (most of whom will be heterosexual, but some of whom may be openly gay, lesbian or bisexual) and by social attitudes (which overwhelmingly encourage opposite-sex emotional–sexual conduct). But they can then argue that the ultimate choice that an adolescent or adult makes will be their own and must be respected, just as an adolescent or adult is free to choose the religion they practise (if any), and to accept or disregard the examples of their parents and other adults they meet (whose religion may be different from their parents') or any religious education they may have received.[55]

Before leaving this question, it is worth noting one difference between fundamental choice and sex discrimination arguments in the context of justifications. Although a sex discrimination argument makes it comparatively easy to find a prima facie violation of a prohibition of such discrimination, it says nothing about the importance of the choice that has been restricted on the basis of sex. To avoid characterization as a 'trivial' choice that may justifiably be restricted on the basis of sex (e.g. choice of public toilet), the importance of the choice of sexual orientation to the individual (and possibly its 'fundamentality') would have to be stressed in refuting any asserted justifications.[56]

5. Which Argument Is the Best?

On balance, it would appear that a sex discrimination argument is the most effective, in that it would provide the most comprehensive protection against sexual orientation discrimination while requiring the least innovation, in terms

[54] See e.g. Tasker and Golombok (1991 Other).

[55] No one would argue that persons who are Jewish or Muslim should not be permitted to raise children or teach in state schools because their own children or those they teach may decide to be 'like them'.

[56] See Ch. 7, Part II.

of developing legal doctrine.[57] (Under the European Convention, however, it could only supplement a fundamental choice argument, because of the textual limits of Article 14.) An immutable status argument is probably best abandoned[58] because of its factual problems, its inability to encompass directly the actual choice of direction of conduct, and its potentially negative connotations when countering asserted justifications. A fundamental choice argument, although it is the mirror image of a sex discrimination argument in most respects (by focusing on the sex of the chosen person, rather than the sex of the choosing person), is hampered by the controversy surrounding the 'right of privacy' under the US Constitution, and the infancy of 'liberty' review under Section 7 (or identification of fundamental choices under Section 15(1)) of the Canadian Charter. Under the European Convention, however, it is the only feasible argument (of the three), and is less controversial because there is a textual basis for it in the inclusion of express rights to 'respect for . . . private and family life' in Article 8, and to 'marry and to found a family' in Article 12.

This leaves a sex discrimination argument (alone, under the US Constitution or the Canadian Charter, or as a supplement to a fundamental choice argument, under the European Convention) as the preferred candidate. It avoids factual assumptions about the immutability of directions of emotional–sexual attraction; it uses a ground of discrimination that is expressly enumerated in Article 14 of the European Convention and Section 15(1) of the Canadian Charter, and well established in US equal protection doctrine; it covers discrimination based on direction of attraction or on direction of conduct (subject to a hypothetical 'bisexual/asexual/celibate loophole');[59] it permits apparently neutral rules relating to a person's appearance, manner or dress to be challenged as direct sex discrimination; and it permits a more positive response to potential justifications.

In *R.* v. *Turpin*, Justice Wilson observed that:

[t]he argument that s. 15 is not violated because departures from its principles have been widely condoned in the past and that the consequences of finding a violation would be novel and disturbing is not . . . an acceptable approach to the interpretation of Charter provisions.[60]

It must be acknowledged, however, that there may be considerable resistance to finding that sexual orientation discrimination is sex discrimination and must be justified. Although logic makes the conclusion inescapable, emotion and fear of its 'novel and disturbing' consequences may cause it to be rejected.[61] Sex

[57] For the avoidance of doubt, I have not reached this conclusion because a sex discrimination argument involves a 'legal technicality' and is thus useful for 'tactical' reasons. I sincerely believe that sexual orientation discrimination *is* one of the most fundamental forms of sex discrimination. See Ch. 8, text accompanying notes 74–79.

[58] Cf. Halley (1994 US), 506, 516.

[59] See Part I.B.3.   [60] [1989] 1 SCR 1296 at 1328.

[61] Cf. *Re Section 24 of the British North America Act, 1867*, [1928] SCR 276 (women are not 'qualified persons', who can be summoned to the Senate), rev'd, [1930] AC 124 at 127 (PC) ('the word "persons" in s. 24 does include women').

discrimination is seen as a principle that primarily protects an 'established' human rights movement, i.e. the women's movement. Some would be reluctant to see this principle 'tainted' (and perhaps 'discredited') by using it to shelter a human rights movement that is still viewed as controversial, i.e. the gay, lesbian, and bisexual movement.[62] Rather than meet the heavy onus of justifying sexual orientation discrimination (treated as sex discrimination), which onus they per- haps fear would be weakened for all sex discrimination cases were sexual ori- entation included, they would rather exclude it at the definitional stage and force it to find protection in its own right (e.g. as a 'fundamental right', a 'suspect classification' or an 'analogous ground').[63] As a result, it might be necessary to argue that sexual orientation is a fundamental choice. A fundamental choice argument could provide a viable alternative under the US Constitution and the Canadian Charter (and is essential under the European Convention). It does require greater development of legal doctrine in Canada (and would require the overruling of *Hardwick* in the US), but has most of the same advantages as a sex discrimination argument (except possibly in the area of appearance, manner, and dress), and can avoid the hypothetical 'bisexual/asexual/celibate loophole'.

The relevance of both 'sex' and a 'fundamental choice' causes sexual orienta- tion discrimination (including the restriction of marriage to opposite-sex couples) to resemble the kind of racial discrimination seen in *Loving* v. *Virginia*. There, the US Supreme Court struck down a ban on mixed-race marriage holding that it implicated both 'liberty' (by interfering with the fundamental choice of whether or not to marry) and 'equality' (by basing the interference on a racial distinc- tion). Similarly, all sexual orientation discrimination implicates both 'liberty' (because it interferes with a fundamental choice of the direction of emotional– sexual conduct) and 'equality' (because the interference with that choice takes the form of distinctions based on sex). In other words, each individual's funda- mental choice of the direction of their emotional–sexual conduct is restricted on the basis of their sex.[64]

Although a sex discrimination argument is probably the 'best', and a funda- mental choice argument an alternative, it should be clear by now that all three arguments considered give rise to particular problems. In the case of an im- mutable status argument, the problems arise not so much from the principle of

[62] This may explain the reluctance of courts to treat sexual orientation discrimination as sex discrimination in the absence of express legislative authorization. Opponents of the Equal Rights Amendment to the US Constitution argued that it would require states to issue marriage licenses to same-sex couples. The chief sponsor of the Amendment rejected this interpretation: see Yale Note (1973 US), 583–8. Cf. Williams (1983 Can), C/83–10 ('[t]he citizenry would far rather give up the ideal of gender equality than settle for [men wearing dresses to work]').

[63] See Williams, ibid. ('discrimination against homosexuals should be forbidden by law . . . [but] it will be on its own merits and not as a part of sex discrimination doctrine').

[64] Thus, exclusion of gay and bisexual men is sexual orientation discrimination vis-à-vis hetero- sexual men and sex discrimination vis-à-vis heterosexual women, jut as exclusion of Muslim women is religious discrimination vis-à-vis non-Muslim women and sex discrimination vis-à-vis Muslim men.

'immutable statuses', a relatively objective concept, but from its application to 'the facts' of sexual orientation. In the case of a fundamental choice argument, the problems arise more from the indeterminacy of the principle of 'fundamental choices', than from its application to 'the facts' of sexual orientation. In the case of a sex discrimination argument, the problems do not arise from the well-established principle of non-discrimination on the basis of sex, or (upon analysis) from its logical application to 'the facts' of sexual orientation, but rather from the emotional resistance to concluding that sexual orientation discrimination is sex discrimination, which causes recourse to 'original intent' to avoid that conclusion.

C. Comparison of Protection Under the Three Human Rights Instruments

In addition to comparing the three arguments, it is also interesting to compare the results that have been achieved to date under the three human rights instruments. Under the US Constitution, neither the Supreme Court nor any of the federal Courts of Appeals has been willing or able (in a decision that was not reversed or vacated) to apply strict or intermediate scrutiny to any aspect of sexual orientation discrimination, other than discrimination affecting expression or association protected by the First Amendment.[65] As yet, there is no 'fundamental right' to engage in same-sex sexual activity and sexual orientation is not a 'suspect or quasi-suspect classification'. Under the European Convention, criminalization of private same-sex sexual activity between no more than two persons who are both over 21 and are not in the armed forces violates Article 8, but every other kind of sexual orientation discrimination has so far been held to be consistent with the Convention. Yet under the Canadian Charter, it seems likely that the Supreme Court will agree with the lower courts that have held that sexual orientation is an analogous ground under Section 15(1). Thus, it may be possible to challenge every kind of public sector sexual orientation discrimination under the Charter, including discrimination against same-sex couples and the omission of sexual orientation from human rights legislation (if the Supreme Court were to uphold the reasoning in *Haig*).

Why have litigants in Canada had much greater success before the lower courts, and appear likely to have greater success before the Supreme Court, than litigants in the US or under the European Convention? Is it because they have been using the 'best argument' selected above, whereas US and European litigants have not, or because they have argued their cases in a more coherent manner and more carefully identified the principles of human rights law at

[65] State supreme courts have been willing to provide protection under state constitutions that extends beyond freedom of expression or association. See e.g. *Baehr* v. *Lewin* 852 P 2d 44 (Haw 1993); *Commonwealth* v. *Wasson*, 842 SW 2d 487 (Ky 1992).

stake? As a human rights lawyer, I wish I could say that this was the case, and that differences in the principles used had led to the results in Canada. However, the decisions to date holding that particular instances of sexual orientation dis-crimination violated Section 15(1) of the Canadian Charter do not disclose any clear principle (i.e. defining analogous grounds of discrimination) or any clear argument that sexual orientation is such a ground. Indeed, there seems to be a consensus amongst Canadian lawyers that the answer to the question whether Section 15(1) includes sexual orientation is so obviously yes that no reason needs to be given for reaching that conclusion. Nor have judges been forced to provide any reasons, because the defendant government has conceded the point in most of the cases that have raised it.

This legal consensus reflects a growing political consensus in Canada that sexual orientation discrimination is wrong, that human rights legislation should be amended so as to prohibit it (as has been done in eight out of thirteen juris-dictions), and that the Charter should be interpreted as prima facie prohibiting it. Such a political consensus, rather than any textual advantage of the Charter or of its case law, or any superiority of the principles invoked by litigants, probably explains the greater success achieved in Canada (and may make it a moot question whether the Canadian Supreme Court would provide protection, as a matter of principle, in the absence of such a consensus). A similar degree of consensus has simply not yet been achieved in the US, or the Council of Europe countries as a whole (as opposed to individual European countries). Without 'European consensus', the European Court and Commission of Human Rights do not seem to be willing to move forward. And although the US Su-preme Court was willing to act in the absence of consensus in *Brown* v. *Board of Education* and *Roe* v. *Wade*, the controversy over *Roe* and the 'right of privacy' case law has inhibited its extension.

Why should consensus take longer to develop in the US and in the Council of Europe countries? It may be that the US as a whole, or certain regions of the US (see Appendix III), and particular member states of the Council of Europe, are politically more conservative than Canada. But a simpler explanation could be the size of the populations governed by the US Constitution and the European Convention, as well as their cultural diversity or the geographic diversity of the territory over which they are spread. The US has over 260 million people, and the Council of Europe countries have over 500 million. Both populations are spread over large areas, and the Council of Europe population speaks more than 20 languages. Canada has around 30 million people, most of whom speak one of two official languages and live in roughly the same latitude (along the south-ern border). It may thus be far easier to achieve a political consensus regarding sexual orientation discrimination in a smaller, more geographically or linguistic-ally homogeneous entity, such as Canada or the individual European countries where such a consensus seems to prevail (e.g. Norway, Sweden, Denmark, and the Netherlands[66]), than in a much larger entity such as the US or the Council of Europe countries taken together.

II. CONCLUSION

In the quotation that opens Chapter 1, Max asks 'What's wrong with [same-sex love]?' In so doing, Max was asking for a justification for discrimination against gay, lesbian, and bisexual persons. The rest of this book has sought to show why a justification is required by attempting to answer a different, and prior, question under three human rights instruments: 'Does sexual orientation discrimination require a strong justification under constitutional and international human rights law?' To some persons, the intuitive answer to this question is obviously 'yes', while to others, it is most emphatically 'no'. Those on both sides of the debate are likely to be clear about the arguments they would use, in response to Max's question, in attempting to justify a prima facie violation of a particular human rights instrument, or in refuting an asserted justification. But at the prior stage of showing that this issue is not an ordinary one of legislative policy, but one implicating principles of constitutional and international human rights law, those on the 'yes' side may experience some difficulty in translating their 'gut feeling' into concrete arguments.

At first glance, sexual orientation does not fit neatly into a list of other traditional grounds of discrimination (such as race, religion, and sex), making it not entirely clear how discrimination against gay, lesbian, and bisexual persons is like discrimination against persons of African origin, Jews or women. Nor is a reference to a human rights act necessarily helpful, because when a legislature inserts 'sexual orientation' into such an act, alongside 'race', 'religion', and 'sex', it may not be clear on what conceptual basis (if any) it has done so, or what it has sought to protect (direction of attraction or conduct) by doing so. Thus, those who believe that national constitutions and international human rights treaties should be interpreted as containing prima facie prohibitions of sexual orientation discrimination may display a certain vagueness about what principle justifies that conclusion, or refer only to a history of discrimination or prejudice against gay, lesbian, and bisexual persons, or to their being a 'disadvantaged group'.

I have attempted to show how, under three human rights instruments, sexual orientation discrimination does implicate principles of constitutional and international human rights law, how a conceptual basis for including sexual orientation in these instruments can be supplied, and what inclusion would protect.

---

[66] A consensus that the open-ended equality/non-discrimination provision (Section 1) of the Netherlands Constitution (1983) includes sexual orientation (see Waaldijk (1986–87 Eur)) was confirmed by the Amsterdam Court of Appeal in a decision of 10 Dec. 1987, NJCM–Bulletin 14 (1989), p. 305 at 315.

I have done so by examining three arguments for interpreting each instrument as implicitly containing a prima facie prohibition of sexual orientation discrimination. If I have succeeded, my analysis should have shown that strong arguments can be made that sexual orientation discrimination is a prima facie violation of these instruments, thus placing a heavy onus of justification on those who would defend such discrimination. At the very least, I hope that I have shown that this is a complex question once one looks beneath its surface, and that the widely held perception in Canada that the answer is obvious, requiring no reasons, is not warranted.

However, as Part I.C. of this chapter suggested, it must be acknowledged that there is no necessary connection between the existence or use of strong arguments that sexual orientation discrimination prima facie violates a principle of constitutional and international human rights law and a court's concluding that such a violation has occurred. Where there exists a political consensus against such discrimination (as in Canada), a court may reach that conclusion regardless of which argument is used, or whether any argument is used at all. Where there does not exist a sufficient political consensus (as in the US and the Council of Europe countries), a court may reject that conclusion, in spite of intellectually rigorous arguments that a principle of constitutional and international human rights law compels it.

Why has it taken so long for a political consensus to develop against sexual orientation discrimination (as opposed to discrimination based on race, religion or sex)? There are probably many reasons for this. The gay, lesbian, and bisexual minority is small and relatively invisible, unlike women, and its history of discrimination is not as well known as the worst instances of discrimination against racial or religious minorities (and majorities), i.e. the tragedies of slavery, the Holocaust, and apartheid. It is a minority in every country in the world, unlike particular racial or religious minorities, which are usually the majority in at least one country. This may reduce the potential for empathy on the part of the heterosexual majority, who cannot imagine the tables being turned.

The greatest difficulty is perhaps the fact that prohibiting sexual orientation discrimination requires the protection of a new area of individual choice or freedom. Sex discrimination and fundamental choice arguments present same-sex or bisexual sexual orientation (as direction of conduct) as a choice of which any person is theoretically capable, and therefore as a 'subversive idea' rather than a 'contagious affliction'. They therefore call for an expansion of the freedom that is protected by constitutional and international human rights law into new territory. Although recognizing a narrowly defined 'freedom of sexual orientation' might seem to be a logical extension of 'freedom of religion' and 'freedom of political opinion', it must be remembered that the latter freedoms came to be protected only after centuries of bloody repression of dissenters. And a major obstacle to the recognition of an analogy between sexual orientation and religion (both of which could be seen as fundamental choices) is the opposition of religious persons, who are among the main advocates of sexual orientation discrimination in many countries.[67]

The opposition of religious persons is objectionable in that it often amounts to an attempt to impose their religious beliefs on others. But it is also somewhat ironic, in that they would quickly invoke the freedom of religion provisions of human rights instruments if a majority sought to interfere with their religious practices. Yet when the gay, lesbian, and bisexual minority seeks similar protection against discrimination by the heterosexual majority, religious persons are often the first to oppose it, and fail to see how their arguments could easily be used to justify discrimination based on religion. For example, John Finnis informs same-sex couples that their relationships are 'the pursuit of an illusion', are 'deeply hostile to the self-understanding of [married opposite-sex couples]', and are 'an active threat to the stability of existing and future [opposite-sex] marriages'.[68] If it were suggested that the beliefs of a Roman Catholic (or Jewish) minority were 'the pursuit of an illusion' and were 'deeply hostile' and 'an active threat' to a Protestant (or Roman Catholic) majority, many would respond that it is for Roman Catholics (or Jews) to decide whether their beliefs are 'an illusion' and that the fact that Roman Catholics (or Jews) practise their religion does not prevent Protestants (or Roman Catholics) from practising their religion. A same-sex couple would respond to Professor Finnis's perception of the 'threat' to married opposite-sex couples in the same way: it is for a same-sex couple to decide whether their relationship is 'an illusion', and their relationship does not prevent heterosexual persons from entering into opposite-sex marriages.

It may be possible to persuade religious persons that living in a plural society means accepting and respecting the differences of your neighbours. For religious persons, this will mean living, working, and shopping beside neighbours they believe will burn in hell for eternity because of the way their neighbours live their lives, but accepting that it is their neighbours' choice and that they must respect it. Perhaps a situation of mutual respect between religious persons and gay, lesbian, and bisexual persons could be achieved. This would require gay, lesbian, and bisexual persons to respect freedom of religion by not asking the law to intervene to change the internal doctrines of religions (as to who may be a religious leader, or who may enter a religious marriage). On the other hand, it would require religious persons to respect freedom of sexual orientation by not asking the law to impose their beliefs regarding sexual orientation on gay, lesbian, and bisexual persons.

If a court, such as the US Supreme Court, the European Court or the Canadian Supreme Court, were to adopt a new, general principle that sexual orientation

---

[67] On the opposition of conservative Christians in Canada, see Herman (1994 Can), 77–127. See also Richards (1994 US).

[68] Finnis (1994 Eur), 1065, 1069–70. Indeed, he argues (at 1054) that prohibiting sexual orientation discrimination 'would work significant discrimination and injustice against (and would indeed damage) [traditional] families . . .'

discrimination prima facie violates the constitution or treaty which it interprets, whether because it agreed with one of the three arguments I have used, or with another argument (e.g. that gay, lesbian, and bisexual persons are a 'disadvantaged group'), or because it did not require any argument, what legal consequences would this have? First, it would require that each instance of such discrimination be justified. Assuming that the court imposed a standard of justification as strict as that applied to race or sex discrimination, it is likely that findings of justification would be no more frequent than for race, and less frequent than for sex (i.e. sex distinctions that exclude all women or all men).

Second, assuming that most asserted justifications were rejected, it could lead to the substantial elimination of overt sexual orientation discrimination by the legislature or other public sector actors in the jurisdiction in question. The check on the legislature would be semi-permanent, in that it would require an amendment to the constitution or treaty to remove it,[69] unlike anti-discrimination legislation, which could more easily be repealed. The substitution of global, judicially mandated change for piecemeal, voluntary change would be particularly marked in multi-jurisdictional, federal systems like the US and Canada. This effect has been seen in the US in the areas of school segregation and abortion, while in Canada, the decision in *Haig* could lead to the inclusion of sexual orientation in all thirteen human rights acts (only seven having included it before the decision). But such global change probably could not occur to the same extent in the Council of Europe countries, because, by requiring 'European consensus', the European Court of Human Rights only imposes change on a relatively small minority of member states.

Third, a new principle of constitutional and international human rights law could also affect sexual orientation discrimination in the private sector. This would depend on how strictly the requirement of 'government action' is applied (in the US and Canada), and on the extent of the horizontal effect or *Drittwirkung* of the European Convention (i.e. can member states be held responsible for failing to prohibit discrimination by private parties?).[70] In *Haig*, the Ontario Court of Appeal effectively held that the Charter requires Canadian legislatures to include sexual orientation in their anti-discrimination legislation, which applies both to the public and private sectors. Even if amendment of anti-discrimination legislation applying to the private sector is not required, a constitutional and international principle would probably have a strong, persuasive influence on legislatures considering change. And if constitutional and international protection were achieved through acceptance of a sex discrimination argument, it

---

[69] A Canadian legislature could theoretically invoke Section 33 of the Charter to override a Supreme Court decision on sexual orientation discrimination. This could not be done by US or Council of Europe legislatures or governments (except in very narrow circumstances under Article 15 of the Convention). See MacKay (1986 Can), 47 n. 37 (threat of Nova Scotia's attorney-general 'to use Section 33 if the courts interpreted the Charter to include the right of homosexuals to serve in the police forces'); Bruner (1985 Can), 468, 491–2.

[70] See generally Clapham (1993 Other); van Dijk and van Hoof (1990 Eur), 15–20.

could lead courts to interpret 'sex' in an anti-discrimination law applying to the private sector as including 'sexual orientation'.

Greater protection under constitutional and international human rights law would not be a panacea for the problems of gay, lesbian, and bisexual persons. It might often be difficult to enforce, because of the expense of litigation or lack of evidence (where discrimination is not overt), and could not immediately remove the prejudice and hostility of many heterosexual persons towards them. Indeed, many closeted gay, lesbian, and bisexual persons might choose not to exercise a right to equal treatment, believing that it is safer to remain invisible rather than 'rock the boat'. But such protection would have tremendous symbolic value, by recognizing that discrimination based on sexual orientation is as wrongful as that based on race, religion, and sex, and that the right to be free from sexual orientation discrimination is a human right on a par with the right to be free from those other kinds of discrimination. And it could have great practical value for those gay, lesbian, and bisexual persons who would like to live their lives as openly as heterosexual persons, and have the same choices as heterosexual persons regarding employment, marriage, immigration, and having or raising children, but are blocked only by overtly discriminatory rules. Protection against sexual orientation discrimination under constitutional and international human rights law has begun. Its extension and completion is a matter of time.

III. EPILOGUE: *EGAN* V. *CANADA*

The Supreme Court of Canada rendered its decision in *Egan* v. *Canada* on 25 May 1995.[71] The Court split 4–1–4. One group of judges, Justices Cory, Iacobucci, L'Heureux-Dubé, and McLachlin (the 'discrimination' group) held that a distinction between same-sex couples and unmarried opposite-sex couples is based on an analogous ground (sexual orientation), is 'discrimination' contrary to Section 15(1), and cannot be justified under Section 1. A second group of judges, Justice La Forest, Chief Justice Lamer, and Justices Gonthier and Major (the 'no discrimination' group) agreed that sexual orientation is an analogous ground, but held that such a distinction is not 'discrimination' contrary to Section 15(1), and that even if it were 'discrimination', it would be justified under Section 1. Justice Sopinka was in the middle. He agreed with the 'discrimination' group that sexual orientation is an analogous ground and that the challenged distinction is 'discrimination' contrary to Section 15(1), but he held, like the 'no discrimination' group, that the 'discrimination' could be justified, at least temporarily, under Section 1. His position was thus 'discrimination but justification'.

The net effect of these three positions was as follows. The Court held: (1) by

---

[71] [1995] 2 SCR. For the facts, see Ch. 7, notes 43–45 and accompanying text.

9–0, that sexual orientation is an analogous ground of discrimination under Section 15(1) of the Charter; (2) by 5–4, that a distinction between same-sex couples and unmarried opposite-sex couples in relation to a benefit provided by government is based on sexual orientation and is 'discrimination' contrary to Section 15(1) (a sex discrimination argument was not discussed); and (3) by 5–4, that the 'discrimination' and prima facie violation of Section 15(1) can be justified, at least temporarily, under Section 1. Thus, the majority (consisting of the 'no discrimination' group plus Justice Sopinka) voted to dismiss the appeal of James Egan and John Nesbit, who had been living together for 46 years,[72] and deny their Charter claim to a benefit made available to unmarried opposite-sex couples who have been living together for one year. What reasons did the Court give on the three issues it decided?

A. Is Sexual Orientation an Analogous Ground Under Section 15(1)?

The unanimous decision on this point was once again assisted by the federal government's conceding it.[73] Justice La Forest (writing for the 'no discrimination' group) had no difficulty accepting that 'whether or not sexual orientation is based on biological or physiological factors, which may be a matter of some controversy, it is a deeply personal characteristic that is either unchangeable or changeable only at unacceptable personal costs, and so falls within the ambit of s. 15 protection as being analogous to the enumerated grounds'.[74]

Justice Cory (writing with the substantial agreement of the 'discrimination' group[75] and Justice Sopinka) began by observing that '[t]he fundamental consideration underlying the analogous grounds analysis is whether the basis of distinction may serve to deny the essential human dignity of the Charter claimant', and that a group's being a 'discrete and insular minority' lacking political power, or suffering 'economic disadvantage', is not essential.[76] He then cited '[t]he historic disadvantage suffered by homosexual persons', including public harassment and verbal abuse, crimes of violence, discrimination in employment and services, exclusion from the armed forces, being forced to conceal their sexual orientation because of stigmatization and hatred, a higher teenage suicide rate, criminalization of same-sex sexual activity, and labelling of 'homosexuality' as

---

[72] Although the length of the Egan-Nesbit relationship seemed to make it a 'perfect case' to present to the Supreme Court, Justice Cory stressed (in dissent) that a publicly represented relationship of one year (as required by the statute) would have been sufficient. Reasons of Justices Cory and Iaccobucci at 169 (paragraph number in SCR; same for all citations in notes 72–107).

[73] Reasons of La Forest J. at 5.

[74] Ibid., citing his dicta in *Ward* (see Ch. 7, note 19).

[75] In her Reasons (at 46–54, 82), Justice L'Heureux-Dubé expressed her view that the 'analogous grounds' approach is not the best way to give effect to the purpose of Section 15(1). But she did not seem to suggest that sexual orientation is not such a ground, if such an approach is used. She described sexual orientation (at 89) as 'an aspect of "personhood" that is quite possibly biologically based and that is at the very least a fundamental choice'.

[76] Reasons of Justices Cory and Iacobucci at 171–2.

a psychiatric disorder. '[H]omosexuals, whether as individuals or couples, form an identifiable minority who have suffered and continue to suffer serious social, political and economic disadvantage.'[77] Because of the emerging consensus amongst Canadian legislatures that sexual orientation should be included in human rights legislation as a prohibited ground of discrimination,[78] and because 'judicial opinion [in the lower courts] has overwhelmingly recognized that [it] is an analogous ground' under the Charter, 'there can be no doubt that sexual orientation is indeed a ground of discrimination analogous to those enumerated in s. 15(1)'.[79]

B. Is Discrimination Against Same-sex Couples 'Discrimination' Contrary to Section 15(1)?

Justice Cory wrote with the substantial agreement of the other justices in the majority of five on this point (the 'discrimination' group plus Justice Sopinka). He considered (1) whether there was a distinction denying the plaintiffs the 'equal benefit of the law', (2) whether the distinction was based on the analogous ground of sexual orientation, and (3) whether the distinction gave rise to 'discrimination'. On the first question, he observed that the challenged statute (which 'makes no reference to children' and 'is not concerned with benefiting those who have raised . . . children')[80] is not facially neutral. Rather, it draws a clear distinction between opposite-sex couples and same-sex couples and therefore 'presents a situation of direct discrimination'.[81] This distinction 'denies equal benefit of the law to homosexual couples',[82] by denying them both an economic benefit and the right to choose 'to be publicly recognized as a common law couple'. 'The law confers a significant benefit by providing state recognition of the legitimacy of a particular status. The denial of that recognition may have a serious detrimental effect upon the sense of self-worth and dignity of members of a group because it stigmatizes them even though no economic loss is occasioned.'[83]

On the second question, Justice Cory held that the distinction between opposite-sex couples and same-sex couples is not based on 'spousal status', but 'is a differentiation which must be based upon sexual orientation', because the

---

[77] Ibid. at 173–5.   [78] See Appendix II.

[79] Reasons of Justices Cory and Iacobucci at 176–8.

[80] Reasons of Justices Cory and Iacobucci at 143.   [81] Ibid. at 139.

[82] Because the plaintiffs 'must demonstrate that homosexual couples *in general* are denied equal benefit of the law, not that they themselves are suffering a particular or unique denial of a benefit', the fact that they may have been entitled to greater benefits under other federal or provincial programmes was irrelevant. Ibid. at 152–7 (Cory J.), 199–208 (Iacobucci J.). See also Reasons of Justice La Forest at 12.

[83] Reasons of Justices Cory and Iacobucci at 158–63, citing *Brown* v. *Board of Education*, Ch. 2, note 205.

'[t]he sexual orientation of the individual members cannot be divorced from the homosexual couple'.[84] Indeed, he went on to state that:

Sexual orientation is more than simply a 'status' that an individual possesses. It is something that is demonstrated in an individual's conduct by the choice of a partner. The Charter protects religious beliefs and religious practice as aspects of religious freedom. So, too, should it be recognized that sexual orientation encompasses aspects of 'status' and 'conduct' and that both should receive protection. Sexual orientation is demonstrated in a person's choice of a life partner, whether heterosexual or homosexual. It follows that a lawful relationship which flows from sexual orientation should also be protected.[85]

As for the third question, Justice Cory found 'discrimination' because the opposite-sex definition of 'spouse' 'reinforces the stereotype that homosexuals cannot and do not form lasting, caring, mutually supportive relationships with economic interdependence in the same manner as heterosexual couples',[86] and reinforces consequent prejudical attitudes. This effect 'is clearly contrary to s. 15's aim of protecting human dignity'.[87]

Justice La Forest, writing for the minority of four on this point (the 'no discrimination' group), agreed that the challenged law (1) drew a distinction between the plaintiffs and others, and (2) did not provide them with a benefit which it grants others. But it also had to be shown (3) that the distinction is based on an enumerated or analogous ground which represents an 'irrelevant personal characteristic'. There is thus no 'discrimination' if the distinction is relevant to 'the functional values underlying the law'.[88] Here, the distinction was relevant and not arbitrary because the law's purpose is to support the 'heterosexual couple', married or unmarried, which is 'the social unit that uniquely has the *capacity* to procreate children and generally cares for their upbringing'. Same-sex couples are not 'capable of meeting the fundamental social objectives . . . sought to be promoted by Parliament'. Their adopting or bringing up children 'is exceptional and in no way affects the general picture'. Nor should the courts 'attempt to require meticulous line drawing that would ensure that only [opposite-sex] couples that had children were included'.[89] Same-sex couples do not differ from other excluded 'couples' (e.g. siblings). The fact that '[o]ther excluded couples . . . do not have to be described by reference to sex or sexual preferences . . . is of no moment'. 'The distinction . . . is relevant, indeed essential, to . . . differentiate [opposite-sex couples] . . . from all couples that do not serve the social purposes for which the legislature made the distinction.

[84] Ibid. at 164–70.
[85] Ibid. at 175, citing the European Parliament's 1994 'Resolution on equal rights for homosexuals and lesbians in the EC' (see Ch. 5, notes 88–89 and accompanying text).
[86] Ibid. at 180 (noting that the plaintiffs' relationship 'vividly demonstrates the error of that approach').
[87] Ibid.   [88] Reasons of Justice La Forest at 9–14.
[89] Ibid. at 25–6.

Homosexual couples are not, therefore, discriminated against; they are simply included with these other couples.'[90]

C. Is the Discrimination Justified Under Section 1?

Justice Sopinka cast the deciding vote. Although he agreed with Justice Cory that the legislation infringed Section 15(1), in his opinion the infringement was saved under Section 1. He noted that the Court could not 'assume that there are unlimited funds to address the needs of all', and that 'it is legitimate for the government to make choices between disadvantaged groups'.[91] Here, 'the legislation was addressing itself to *those in greatest need*' (i.e. financially needy opposite-sex couples rather than financially needy same-sex couples), and could be regarded as 'a substantial step in an incremental approach to include all those . . . in serious need of financial assistance due to the retirement . . . of a supporting spouse'. There was thus 'proportionality between the effects of the legislation on the protected right and the legislative objective'.[92] He concluded by addressing the argument that the federal government could no longer justify a delay since 1975 (when the benefit was extended to unmarried opposite-sex couples) in extending the benefit to same-sex couples: 'Given the fact that equating same-sex couples with heterosexual spouses, either married or common law, is still generally regarded as a novel concept, I am not prepared to say that by its inaction to date the government has disentitled itself to rely on s. 1 of the Charter.'[93] Justice Sopinka and the four justices in the 'no discrimination' group formed the majority of five that decided the case. Justice La Forest (writing for the 'no discrimination' group) would have upheld any infringement of Section 15(1) under Section 1, for reasons similar to those of Justice Sopinka, and for his reasons for finding no 'discrimination' under Section 15(1).

Justice Iacobucci wrote with the substantial agreement of the other three dissenting justices in the minority of four (the 'discrimination' group). In applying the *R.* v. *Oakes* test,[94] he identified the objective of the 'spous[e's] allowance' the plaintiffs were seeking as 'the mitigation of poverty among "elderly households" ', and agreed that this objective is 'of pressing and substantial importance'.[95] However, the exclusion of same-sex couples, 'an equally deserving group', is not a 'reasonable limit' on Section 15(1) rights under Section 1, because it 'is simply not rationally connected to the goal of alleviating poverty among elderly couples. . . . A more rationally connected means to the end would be to assist the entire group [of elderly couples] . . .'[96] Even if the federal government's estimates of up to 30,000 eligible same-sex couples across Canada,

---

[90] Ibid. at 26–7.   [91] Reasons of Justice Sopinka at 103–5.
[92] Ibid. at 106–10.   [93] Ibid. at 111.
[94] See Ch. 6, notes 13–16 and accompanying text.
[95] Reasons of Justices Cory and Iacobucci at 184–9.
[96] Ibid. at 190–1.

and an annual cost of up to C$37,000,000,[97] were correct, 'they do not justify the denial of the [plaintiffs'] right to equality'.[98] And whatever the patterns of economic interdependence among same-sex couples, '[t]he spous[e's] allowance is provided to heterosexual couples regardless of the existence of a dependency pattern in their relationships'.[99]

Had the goal of the legislation been 'ameliorating the situation and fostering the existence of *elderly heterosexual couples only*', the goal would itself have been discriminatory and therefore constitutionally impermissible under Section 1.[100] As for the proportionality of such a goal, Justice Iacobucci said:

[I]t eludes me how according same-sex couples the benefits flowing to opposite-sex couples in any way inhibits, dissuades or impedes the formation of heterosexual unions. Where is the threat? In the absence of such a threat, the denial of the s. 15 rights of same-sex couples is anything but proportional to the policy objective of fostering heterosexual relationships.[101]

He then noted that the issues of same-sex marriage and adoption by same-sex couples, like the issue of the treatment of 'other cohabitation arrangements (brother-sister, two friends, uncle-nephew)', were not before the Court.[102]

Justice Iacobucci described Justice Sopinka's approach to Section 1 as 'extremely deferential', and his '[p]ermitting discrimination to be justified on account of the "novelty" of its prohibition or on account of the need for government "incrementalism" [as] introduc[ing] two unprecedented and potentially undefinable criteria into s. 1 analysis'.[103] His approach 'permits s. 1 to be used in an unduly deferential manner well beyond anything found in the prior jurisprudence of this Court', and could allow governments 'to uphold legislation that . . . discriminatorily allocates resources'. 'This would undercut the values of the Charter and belittle its purpose.' Instead Justice Sopinka's concerns 'ought to inform the remedy'.[104] Justice Iacobucci, applying the criteria laid down in *Schachter*,[105] would have extended the benefit to same-sex couples, but would have allowed a 'grace period' of one year to permit the federal and provincial governments to 'co-ordinate and harmonize their approaches to same-sex benefits'.[106] He would thus have ordered that a modified version of the definition of 'spouse' (deleting 'of the opposite sex') be inserted into the legislation by the Court one year from the date of the decision, unless Parliament acted in the mean time to ensure the legislation's constitutionality.[107]

This is not the place to comment on the Supreme Court's reasoning. I hope

[97] This sum represents 'between two and four percent of the total cost of the old age supplement program'. Reasons of Justice L'Heureux-Dubé at 99.
[98] Reasons of Justices Cory and Iacobucci at 192–4.
[99] Ibid. at 195–7.   [100] Ibid. at 210.   [101] Ibid. at 211.   [102] Ibid. at 212.
[103] Ibid. at 213–16. See also Reasons of Justice L'Heureux-Dubé at 100 ('[t]here is a first time to every discrimination claim').
[104] Reasons of Justices Cory and Iacobucci at 216.
[105] Ch. 8, note 112.   [106] Ibid. at 226–7.   [107] Ibid. at 231.

to do so in a Canadian law journal later this year. In *Egan*, the Court came very close to deciding that Section 15(1) of the Charter requires that governments treat same-sex couples and unmarried opposite-sex couples equally in allocating benefits. The majority's finding of 'discrimination' under Section 15(1) means that all government discrimination against same-sex couples must be justified under Section 1. Litigation by same-sex couples will thus continue and the Court will no doubt soon have an opportunity to reconsider its decision under Section 1 in *Egan*. The Supreme Court of Canada may yet provide the comprehensive protection against sexual orientation discrimination I optimistically predicted at the end of Chapter 8. But patience will definitely be required.

1 June 1995

Appendix I—Principal Cited Provisions of the United States Constitution, the European Convention, the Canadian Charter, and the International Covenant

A. UNITED STATES CONSTITUTION[1]

First Amendment (1791)

Congress shall make no law respecting an establishment of religion, or prohibiting the free exercise thereof; or abridging the freedom of speech, or of the press; or the right of the people peaceably to assemble, and to petition the Government for a redress of grievances.

Fifth Amendment (1791)

No person shall . . . be deprived of life, liberty, or property, without due process of law; . . .

Fourteenth Amendment (1868)

Section 1. . . . No State shall . . . deprive any person of life, liberty, or property, without due process of law; nor deny to any person within its jurisdiction the equal protection of the laws. . . .

Equal Rights Amendment (passed by Congress in 1972; not ratified by three-fourths of the states by the 30 June 1982 deadline)[2]

Section 1. Equality of rights under the law shall not be denied or abridged by the United States or by any State on account of sex. . . .

B. EUROPEAN CONVENTION ON HUMAN RIGHTS[3]

Article 3

No one shall be subjected to torture or to inhuman or degrading treatment or punishment.

Article 8

1. Everyone has the right to respect for his private and family life, his home and his correspondence.

---

[1] United States Code, Vol. 1, pp. LIII–LXVII (1988 ed.). Signed on 17 Sept. 1787; entered into force on 4 Mar. 1789.
[2] Ibid. at p. LXVI.
[3] Eur. T.S. 5, 213 U.N.T.S. 221. Signed on 4 Nov. 1950; entered into force on 3 Sept. 1953.

2. There shall be no interference by a public authority with the exercise of this right except such as is in accordance with the law and is necessary in a democratic society in the interests of national security, public safety or the economic well-being of the country, for the prevention of disorder or crime, for the protection of health or morals, or for the protection of the rights and freedoms of others.

Article 10

1. Everyone has the right to freedom of expression. . . .
2. The exercise of these freedoms . . . may be subject to such . . . restrictions or penalties as are prescribed by law and are necessary in a democratic society, . . . for the prevention of disorder or crime, for the protection of health or morals, for the protection of the reputation or rights of others, . . .

Article 12

Men and women of marriageable age have the right to marry and to found a family, according to the national laws governing the exercise of this right.

Article 14

The enjoyment of the rights and freedoms set forth in this Convention shall be secured without discrimination on any ground such as sex, race, colour, language, religion, political or other opinion, national or social origin, association with a national minority, property, birth or other status.

C. CANADIAN CHARTER OF RIGHTS AND FREEDOMS[4]

Section 1

The Canadian Charter of Rights and Freedoms guarantees the rights and freedoms set out in it subject only to such reasonable limits prescribed by law as can be demonstrably justified in a free and democratic society.

Section 2

Everyone has the following fundamental freedoms:

(a) freedom of conscience and religion;

(b) freedom of thought, belief, opinion and expression, including freedom of the press and other media of communication;

(c) freedom of peaceful assembly; and

(d) freedom of association.

Section 7

Everyone has the right to life, liberty and security of the person and the right not to be deprived thereof except in accordance with the principles of fundamental justice.

[4] RSC 1985, Appendix II, Nos. 44–45 (Part I of the Constitution Act, 1982, enacted as Schedule B to the Canada Act 1982 (UK), 1982, c. 11). Proclaimed in force on 17 Apr. 1982.

Section 15

(1) Every individual is equal before and under the law and has the right to the equal protection and equal benefit of the law without discrimination and, in particular, without discrimination based on race, national or ethnic origin, colour, religion, sex, age or mental or physical disability.

(2) Subsection (1) does not preclude any law, program or activity that has as its object the amelioration of conditions of disadvantaged individuals or groups including those that are disadvantaged because of race, national or ethnic origin, colour, religion, sex, age or mental or physical disability.

Section 28

Notwithstanding anything in this Charter, the rights and freedoms referred to in it are guaranteed equally to male and female persons.

Section 33

(1) Parliament or the legislature of a province may expressly declare in an Act of Parliament or of the legislature, as the case may be, that the Act or a provision thereof shall operate notwithstanding a provision included in section 2 or sections 7 to 15 of this Charter. . . .

(3) A declaration made under subsection (1) shall cease to have effect five years after it comes into force or on such earlier date as may be specified in the declaration. . . .

D. INTERNATIONAL COVENANT ON CIVIL AND POLITICAL RIGHTS[5]

Article 2

1. Each State Party to the present Covenant undertakes to respect and to ensure to all individuals within its territory and subject to its jurisdiction the rights recognized in the present Covenant, without distinction of any kind, such as race, colour, sex, language, religion, political or other opinion, national or social origin, property, birth or other status. . . .

Article 17

1. No one shall be subjected to arbitrary or unlawful interference with his privacy, family, home or correspondence, nor to unlawful attacks on his honour and reputation. . . .

Article 19

. . .

2. Everyone shall have the right to freedom of expression. . . .

3. The exercise of the rights provided for in paragraph 2 . . . may . . . be subject to certain restrictions, but these shall only be such as are provided by law and are necessary:

(a) For respect of the rights or reputations of others;

(b) For the protection of national security or of public order (*ordre public*), or of public health or morals.

[5] 999 U.N.T.S. 171. Signed on 16 Dec. 1966; entered into force on 23 Mar. 1976.

Article 26

All persons are equal before the law and are entitled without any discrimination to the equal protection of the law. In this respect, the law shall prohibit any discrimination and guarantee to all persons equal and effective protection against discrimination on any ground such as race, colour, sex, language, religion, political or other opinion, national or social origin, property, birth or other status.

Appendix II—Constitutions and Legislation Expressly Prohibiting Sexual Orientation Discrimination[1]

A. CONSTITUTIONS

Brazil[2]

Mato Grosso—Constitution, 1989, Article 10.III (*'orientação sexual'*)
Sergipe—Constitution, 1989, Article 3.II (*'orientação sexual'*)

Germany

Brandenburg—Constitution, 1992, Article 12(2) (*'sexuelle Identität'*)
Thuringia—Constitution, 1993, Article 2(3) (*'sexuelle Orientierung'*)

South Africa

Constitution of the Republic of South Africa Act, No. 200 of 1993, Section 8(2) ('sexual orientation')

B. LEGISLATION

Australia

Australian Capital Territory—Discrimination Act 1991, No. 81, s. 7(1)(b) ('sexuality')
New South Wales—Anti-Discrimination Act 1977, No. 48, as amended by Anti-Discrimination (Amendment) Act 1982, No. 142, s. 5, Schedule 2, Anti-Discrimination (Amendment) Act 1994, No. 28, s. 3, Schedule 4 ('homosexuality' added in 1982)
Northern Territory—Anti-Discrimination Act 1992, No. 80, s. 19(1)(c) ('sexuality')
Queensland—Anti-Discrimination Act 1991, No. 85, s. 7(1)(l) ('lawful sexual activity')
South Australia—Equal Opportunity Act, 1984, No. 95, ss. 5(1), 29(3), as amended by Equal Opportunity Act Amendment Act, 1989, No. 68, Schedule ('sexuality' included in 1984)
Victoria—Equal Opportunity Act 1995, No. 42, s. 6(d) ('lawful sexual activity')

Canada

British Columbia—Human Rights Act, SBC 1984, c. 22, ss. 3–6, 8–9, as amended by SBC 1992, c. 43, ss. 2–7 ('sexual orientation')
Manitoba—Human Rights Code, SM 1987–88, c. 45, s. 9(2)(h) ('sexual orientation')

---

[1] Or prohibiting discrimination based on a similar (and often broader) ground which is intended to cover sexual orientation (or same-sex sexual orientation). The ground was added by the later law, where more than one is listed, unless otherwise indicated.

[2] See also Ch. 1, note 9.

New Brunswick—Human Rights Act, RSNB 1973, c. H-11, as amended by SNB 1992, c. 30, ss. 1–8 ('sexual orientation')

Nova Scotia—Human Rights Act, RSNS 1989, c. 214, s. 5(1)(n), as amended by SNS 1991, c. 12, s. 1 ('sexual orientation')

Ontario—Human Rights Code, RSO 1990, c. H.19, ss. 1–3, 5–6 (originally added by SO 1986, c. 64, s. 18) ('sexual orientation')

Québec—Charte des droits et libertés de la personne, RSQ c. C-12, s. 10 (originally added by SQ 1977, c. 6, s. 1) ('*orientation sexuelle*')

Saskatchewan—Saskatchewan Human Rights Code, SS 1979, c. S-24.1, ss. 9–19, 25, 47(1), as amended by SS 1993, c. 61, ss. 4–15, 18 ('sexual orientation')

Yukon Territory—Human Rights Act, SYT 1987, c. 3, ss. 6, 34 ('sexual orientation')

Denmark

Law of 9 June 1971, nr. 289, as amended by Law of 3 June 1987, nr. 357 ('*seksuelle orientering*')

France

Nouveau Code pénal, arts. 225–1, 225–2, 226–19, 432–7; Code du travail, arts. L. 122–35, L. 122–45 (originally added by Loi No. 85–772, 25 July 1985, Loi No. 86–76, 17 January 1986) ('*moeurs*' or 'morals, manners, customs, ways')[3]

Ireland

Unfair Dismissals Act, 1977, No. 10, s. 6(2)(e), as amended by Unfair Dismissals (Amendment) Act, 1993, No. 22, s. 5(a) ('sexual orientation')

Israel

Equal Opportunities in Employment Act 1988 s. 2(a), as amended by Book of Laws, No. 1377 of 2 Jan. 1992 ('*neti'ya minit*' or 'sexual orientation')

Netherlands

Penal Code, arts 137f, 429 *quater* (inserted by Law of 14 Nov. 1991, Staatsblad 1991, nr. 623); General Equal Treatment Act, arts 1, 5–7 (Law of 2 March 1994, Staatsblad 1994, nr. 230) ('*hetero- of homoseksuele gerichtheid*' or 'hetero- or homosexual orientation')

New Zealand

Human Rights Act 1993, No. 82, s. 21(1)(m) ('sexual orientation')

Norway

Penal Code, para. 349a, Law of 8 May 1981, nr. 14 ('*homofile legning, leveform eller orientering*' or 'homosexual inclination, lifestyle or orientation')

Sweden

Criminal Code, c. 16, para. 9, Law of 4 June 1987, SFS 1987:610 ('*homosexuell läggning*' or 'homosexual inclination')

[3] All translations are unofficial.

United States

California—Cal. Labor Code s. 1102.1 (added in 1992) ('sexual orientation')

Connecticut—Conn. Gen. Stat. ss. 4a–60a, 45a–726a, 46a–81b to 46a–81r (added in 1991) ('sexual orientation')

District of Columbia—D.C. Code Ann. ss. 1–2501 to 1–2533 (originally added in 1973) ('sexual orientation')

Hawaii—Haw. Rev. Stat. ss. 378–1, 378–2 (added in 1991) ('sexual orientation')

Massachusetts—Mass. Gen. Laws Ann. ch. 151B, ss. 3, 4 (added in 1989) ('sexual orientation')

Minnesota—Minn. Stat. Ann. ss. 363.01(45), 363.03 (added in 1993) ('sexual orientation')

New Jersey—N.J. Rev. Stat. ss. 10:5–5.hh.-kk., 10:5–12 (added in 1991) ('affectional or sexual orientation')

Vermont—Vt. Stat. Ann. tit. 1, s. 143; tit. 21, s. 495 (added in 1991) ('sexual orientation')

Wisconsin—Wis. Stat. Ann. ss. 101.22, 111.31 to 111.36 (added in 1982) ('sexual orientation')

Major US cities with prohibitions extending to private sector employment include Baltimore, Boston, Chicago, Denver, Detroit, Kansas City, Los Angeles, Minneapolis, New Orleans, New York, Philadelphia, Pittsburgh, Portland, Saint Louis, San Diego, San Francisco, and Seattle. See National Gay and Lesbian Task Force (1994 US); Harvard Note (1993 US) at 1923–25; Hunter, Michaelson, & Stoddard (1992 US), 204–8.

Appendix III—United States: States Without and with[1] Laws Prohibiting Private, Adult, Consensual, Oral or Anal Intercourse[2]

Alaska	repealed in 1978
California	repealed in 1975
Colorado	repealed in 1971
Connecticut	repealed in 1969
Delaware	repealed in 1973
District of Columbia	repealed in 1993
Hawaii	repealed in 1972
Illinois	repealed in 1961
Indiana	repealed in 1976
Iowa	repealed in 1976, after *State* v. *Pilcher*, 242 NW 2d 348 (Iowa 1976)
Kentucky	invalidated in *Commonwealth* v. *Wasson*, 842 SW 2d 487 (Ky 1992) (same-sex only)
Maine	repealed in 1975
Nebraska	repealed in 1977
Nevada	repealed in 1993 (same-sex only)
New Hampshire	repealed in 1973
New Jersey	repealed in 1978, after *State* v. *Saunders*, 381 A 2d 333 (NJ 1977)
New Mexico	repealed in 1975
New York	invalidated in *People* v. *Onofre*, 415 NE 2d 936 (NY 1980)
North Dakota	repealed in 1977
Ohio	repealed in 1972
Oregon	repealed in 1971
Pennsylvania	invalidated in *Commonwealth* v. *Bonadio*, 415 A 2d 47 (Pa 1980)
South Dakota	repealed in 1976
Vermont	repealed in 1977
Washington	repealed in 1975
West Virginia	repealed in 1976
Wisconsin	repealed in 1983
Wyoming	repealed in 1977

[1] As of 31 December 1994.

[2] Opposite-sex and same-sex unless otherwise indicated.

[3] See Rivera (1979 US), 950–51; Hunter, Michaelson, and Stoddard (1992 US), 148–75; [1993] *Lesbian/Gay Law Notes* 18, 48, 75.

B. STATES WITH SUCH LAWS (22)[4]

Alabama	Ala. Code ss. 13A-6-65(a)(3), 13A-6-60(2)
Arizona	Ariz. Rev. Stat. Ann. ss. 13-1411, 13-1412
Arkansas	Ark. Code Ann. s. 5-14-122 (same-sex only)
Florida	Fla. Stat. Ann. ch. 800.02
Georgia	Ga. Code Ann. s. 26-2002
Idaho	Idaho Code s. 18-6605
Kansas	Kan. Stat. Ann. ss. 21-3501, 21-3505 (same-sex only)
Louisiana	La. Rev. Stat. Ann. s. 14:89
Maryland	Md. Ann. Code art. 27, ss. 553–54
Michigan	Mich. Comp. Laws Ann. ss. 750.158, 750.338, 750.338a, 750.338b
Minnesota	Minn. Stat. Ann. s. 609.293
Mississippi	Miss. Code Ann. s. 97–29–59
Missouri	Mo. Ann. Stat. ss. 566.010, 566.090 (same-sex only)
Montana	Mont. Code Ann. ss. 45-2-101(20), 45-5-505 (same-sex only)
North Carolina	N.C. Gen. Stat. s. 14-177
Oklahoma	Okla. Stat. Ann. tit. 21, s. 886
Rhode Island	R.I. Gen. Laws s. 11-10-1
South Carolina	S.C. Code Ann. s. 16-15-120
Tennessee	Tenn. Code Ann. s. 39-13-510 (same-sex only)
Texas	Tex. Penal Code Ann. ss. 21.06, 21.01 (same-sex only)
Utah	Utah Code Ann. s. 76-5-403
Virginia	Va. Code Ann. s. 18.2-361

NOT CLEAR (1)

Massachusetts Mass. Gen. Laws Ann. ch. 272, s. 34, arguably invalidated by *Commonwealth* v. *Balthazar*, 318 NE 2d 478 (Mass 1974)

[4] Including laws that have not been invalidated by the state's highest court. See also art. 125 of the federal Uniform Code of Military Justice, 10 USCA s. 925.

Appendix IV—Council of Europe: Member States[1] with Equal and Unequal Ages of Consent[2] to Sexual Activity

A. Member States with Equal Ages (22)

Member State	Male–Female	Female–Female	Male–Male
Andorra	16	16	16
Belgium	16	16	16
Czech Republic	15	15	15
Denmark	15	15	15
France	15	15	15
Germany	14	14	14
Greece[3]	15	15	15
Iceland	14	14	14
Italy	14	14	14
Luxembourg	16	16	16
Malta	12	12	12
Netherlands	12	12	12
Norway	16	16	16
Poland	15	15	15
Portugal	12	12	12
San Marino	14	14	14
Slovakia	15	15	15
Slovenia	14	14	14
Spain	12	12	12
Sweden	15	15	15
Switzerland	16	16	16
Turkey[4]	15/18	15	15/18

[1] As of 10 Feb. 1995. I would like to thank Helmut Graupner, Alecos Modinos, and Peter Tatchell for their assistance with the preparation of this Appendix.

[2] Lowest ages shown. A higher age may apply in certain circumstances: e.g. where the younger person or their parent complains or where the older person is in a position of trust or authority.

[3] See Ch. 5, note 93.

[4] 18 for vaginal and anal intercourse.

B. Member States with Unequal Ages or Total Bans (9)

Member State	Male–Female	Female–Female	Male–Male
Austria	14	14	18
Bulgaria	14	18	18
Cyprus	16	16	18[5]
Finland[6]	16	18	18
Hungary	14	18	18
Ireland[7]	15/17	15	17
Liechtenstein	14	14	18
Romania	14	illegal	illegal
United Kingdom	16 (17 in Northern Ireland)	16 (17 in Northern Ireland)	18

Not Clear (3)

Estonia
Latvia
Lithuania

[5] Under legislation expected to be passed in 1995.
[6] An equal age of 15 has been proposed.
[7] See Ch. 5, note 93.

Bibliography

Sources cited in the footnotes have been indicated with the author's name, year of publication, and an abbreviation (US, Eur, Can, or Other) indicating in which of the four main parts of this bibliography the source can be found: A. United States Materials (US); B. European Convention and Other European Materials (Eur); C. Canadian Materials (Can); D. Other Materials (Other). Part A is highly selective, in view of the enormous literature on sexual orientation discrimination and US constitutional law. Parts B and C contain most of the material I came across that relates to sexual orientation discrimination and the European Convention or the Canadian Charter. Part D is a list of miscellaneous cited sources that are international in focus, relate to other jurisdictions, or contain scientific or other non-legal material. Part E indicates the city of publication (or the address) of the gay, lesbian, and bisexual community publications that are frequently cited in the footnotes.

A. UNITED STATES MATERIALS

Ackerman, Bruce (1985), 'Beyond *Carolene Products*' 98 *Harvard Law Review* 713

Adams, William (1994), 'Pre-Election Anti-Gay Ballot Initiative Challenges: Issues of Electoral Fairness, Majoritarian Tyranny, and Direct Democracy' 55 *Ohio State Law Journal* 583

Babcock, Barbara et al. (1975), *Sex Discrimination and the Law: Cases and Remedies* (Boston: Little, Brown)

Badgett, Lee (1995), 'The Wage Effects of Sexual Orientation Discrimination' 48 *Industrial and Labor Relations Review* 726

Barnett, Walter (1973), *Sexual Freedom and the Constitution* (Albuquerque: University of New Mexico Press)

Bibliography (1994), 'Sexual Orientation and the Law: A Selective Bibliography on Homosexuality and the Law, 1969–1993' 86 *Law Library Journal* 1

Bowman, Craig, and Cornish, Blake (1992), 'A More Perfect Union: A Legal and Social Analysis of Domestic Partnership Ordinances' 92 *Columbia Law Review* 1164

Brest, Paul (1976), 'Foreword: In Defense of the Antidiscrimination Principle' 90 *Harvard Law Review* 1

Burke, Craig (1993), 'Fencing Out Politically Unpopular Groups From the Normal Political Processes: The Equal Protection Concerns of Colorado's Amendment Two' 69 *Indiana Law Journal* 275

Byrne, Jeffrey (1993), 'Affirmative Action for Lesbians and Gay Men: A Proposal for True Equality of Opportunity and Workforce Diversity' 11 *Yale Law and Policy Review* 47

Cain, Patricia (1993), 'Litigating for Lesbian and Gay Rights: A Legal History' 79 *Virginia Law Review* 1551

Capers, Bennett (1991), 'Sex(ual Orientation) and Title VII' 91 *Columbia Law Review* 1158

Chaitin, Ellen, and Lefcourt, Roy (1973), 'Is Gay Suspect?' 8 *Lincoln Law Review* 24

Chang, David (1987), 'Conflict, Coherence and Constitutional Intent' 72 *Iowa Law Review* 753

Cole, David, and Eskridge, William (1994), 'From Hand-Holding to Sodomy: First Amendment Protection of Homosexual (Expressive) Conduct' 29 *Harvard Civil Rights–Civil Liberties Law Review* 319

Conkle, Daniel (1987), 'The Second Death of Substantive Due Process' 62 *Indiana Law Journal* 215

Cox, Barbara (1994), 'Same-Sex Marriages and Choice of Law: If We Marry in Hawaii, Are We Still Married When We Return Home?' [1994] *Wisconsin Law Review* 1033

Dickey, Todd (1993), 'Reorienting the Workplace: Examining California's New Labor Code Section 1102.1 and Other Legal Protections Against Employment Discrimination Based on Sexual Orientation' 66 *Southern California Law Review* 2297

Duncan, Richard (1994), 'Who Wants to Stop the Church: Homosexual Rights Legislation, Public Policy, and Religious Freedom' 69 *Notre Dame Law Review* 393

Dworkin, Ronald (1984), 'Reagan's Justice' *The New York Review of Books* (8 November 1984) 27

Dworkin, Ronald (1987), 'The Bork Nomination' *The New York Review of Books* (13 August 1987) 3

Ely, John (1980), *Democracy and Distrust* (Cambridge, Mass.: Harvard University Press)

Eskridge, William (1993), 'A History of Same-Sex Marriage' 79 *Virginia Law Review* 1419

Ettelbrick, Paula (1992), 'Since When Is Marriage a Path to Liberation?' in Sherman (1992 US)

Fajer, Marc (1992), 'Can Two Real Men Eat Quiche Together? Storytelling, Gender-Role Stereotypes, and Legal Protection for Lesbians and Gay Men' 46 *University of Miami Law Review* 511

Fiss, Owen (1976), 'Groups and the Equal Protection Clause' 5 *Philosophy and Public Affairs* 107

Foss, Robert (1994), 'The Demise of the Homosexual Exclusion: New Possibilities for Gay and Lesbian Immigration' 29 *Harvard Civil Rights–Civil Liberties Law Review* 439

Friedman, Joel (1979), 'Constitutional and Statutory Challenges to Discrimination in Employment Based on Sexual Orientation' 64 *Iowa Law Review* 527

Garrow, David (1994), *Liberty and Sexuality: The Right to Privacy and the Making of Roe* v. *Wade* (New York: Macmillan)

Goldberg, Suzanne (1993), 'Give Me Liberty or Give Me Death: Political Asylum and the Global Persecution of Lesbians and Gay Men' 26 *Cornell International Law Journal* 605

Goldberg, Suzanne (1994), 'Facing the Challenge: A Lawyer's Response to Anti-Gay Initiatives' 55 *Ohio State Law Journal* 665

Goldstein, Anne (1988), 'History, Homosexuality and Political Values: Searching for the Hidden Determinants of *Bowers* v. *Hardwick*' 97 *Yale Law Journal* 1073

Grey, Thomas (1980), 'Eros, Civilization and the Burger Court' 43:3 *Law and Contemporary Problems* 83

Grider, Stuart (1994), 'Sexual Orientation as Grounds for Asylum in the US' 35 *Harvard International Law Journal* 213

Halley, Janet (1989), 'The Politics of the Closet: Towards Equal Protection for Gay, Lesbian and Bisexual Identity' 36 *UCLA Law Review* 915

Halley, Janet (1993), 'Reasoning About Sodomy: Act and Identity In and After *Bowers* v. *Hardwick*' 79 *Virginia Law Review* 1721

Halley, Janet (1994), 'Sexual Orientation and the Politics of Biology: A Critique of the Argument from Immutability' 46 *Stanford Law Review* 503

Harvard Case (1986), 'Leading Cases: *Bowers* v. *Hardwick*' 100 *Harvard Law Review* 100, 210–20

Harvard Case (1993), 'Recent Case: *Commonwealth* v. *Wasson*' 106 *Harvard Law Review* 1370

Harvard Note (1985), 'The Constitutional Status of Sexual Orientation: Homosexuality as a Suspect Classification' 98 *Harvard Law Review* 1285

Harvard Note (1989), 'Custody Denials to Parents in Same-Sex Relationships: An Equal Protection Analysis' 102 *Harvard Law Review* 617

Harvard Note (1991), 'Constitutional Barriers to Civil and Criminal Restrictions on Pre- and Extramarital Sex' 104 *Harvard Law Review* 1660

Harvard Note (1993), 'Constitutional Limits on Anti-Gay-Rights Initiatives' 106 *Harvard Law Review* 1905

Harvard Survey (1969), 'Developments in the Law: Equal Protection' 82 *Harvard Law Review* 1065

Harvard Survey (1989), 'Developments in the Law: Sexual Orientation and the Law' 102 *Harvard Law Review* 1508

Hayes, John (1990), 'The Tradition of Prejudice vs. the Principle of Equality: Homosexuals and Heightened Equal Protection Scrutiny After *Bowers* v. *Hardwick*' 31 *Boston College Law Review* 375

Henderson, Lynne (1987), 'Legality and Empathy' 85 *Michigan Law Review* 1574

Henson, Deborah (1993–94), 'Will Same-Sex Marriages Be Recognized in Sister States?' 32 *University of Louisville Journal of Family Law* 551

Hohengarten, William (1994), 'Same-Sex Marriage and the Right of Privacy' 103 *Yale Law Journal* 1495

Hovermill, Joseph (1994), 'A Conflict of Laws and Morals: The Choice of Law Implications of Hawaii's Recognition of Same-Sex Marriages' 53 *Maryland Law Review* 450

Hunter, Nan (1992), 'Life After *Hardwick*' 27 *Harvard Civil Rights–Civil Liberties Law Review* 531

Hunter, Nan, Michaelson, Sherryl, and Stoddard, Thomas (1992), *The Rights of Lesbians and Gay Men: The Basic ACLU Guide to a Gay Person's Rights* (Carbondale, Ill.: Southern Illinois University Press)

Karst, Kenneth (1977), 'Foreword: Equal Citizenship Under the Fourteenth Amendment' 91 *Harvard Law Review* 1

Karst, Kenneth (1980), 'The Freedom of Intimate Association' 89 *Yale Law Journal* 624

Karst, Kenneth (1991), 'The Pursuit of Manhood and the Desegregation of the Armed Forces' 38 *UCLA Law Review* 499

Keane, Thomas (1995), 'Aloha, Marriage? Constitutional and Choice of Law Arguments for Recognition of Same-Sex Marriages' 47 *Stanford Law Review* 499

Koppelman, Andrew (1988), 'The Miscegenation Analogy: Sodomy Laws as Sex Discrimination' 98 *Yale Law Journal* 145

Koppelman, Andrew (1994), 'Why Discrimination Against Lesbians and Gay Men Is Sex Discrimination' 69 *New York University Law Review* 197

Law, Sylvia (1988), 'Homosexuality and the Social Meaning of Gender' [1988] *Wisconsin Law Review* 187

Leonard, Arthur (1993a), *Sexuality and the Law: An Encylopedia of Major Legal Cases* (New York: Garland Publishing)

Leonard, Arthur (1993b), 'Sexual Orientation and the Workplace: A Rapidly Developing Field' 44 *Labor Law Journal* 574

Marcosson, Samuel (1992), 'Harassment on the Basis of Sexual Orientation: A Claim of Sex Discrimination Under Title VII' 81 *Georgetown Law Journal* 1

Miami Note (1986), 'Survey on the Constitutional Right to Privacy in the Context of Homosexual Activity' 40 *University of Miami Law Review* 521

Michigan Note (1974), 'The Constitutionality of Laws Forbidding Private Homosexual Conduct' 72 *Michigan Law Review* 1613

Miller, Harris (1984), 'An Argument for the Application of Equal Protection Heightened Scrutiny to Classifications Based on Homosexuality' 57 *Southern California Law Review* 797

Mohr, Richard (1988), *Gays/Justice: A Study of Ethics, Society and Law* (New York: Columbia University Press)

Murphy, Arthur (1993), 'Homosexuality and the Law: Tolerance and Containment II' 97 *Dickinson Law Review* 693

National Gay and Lesbian Task Force (1994), *Lesbian, Gay and Bisexual Civil Rights in the US: A Chart of States, Cities, Counties, and Federal Agencies Whose Civil Rights Laws, Ordinances, and Policies Bar Discrimination Based on Sexual Orientation* (February 1994)

Niblock, John (1993), 'Anti-Gay Initiatives: A Call for Heightened Judicial Scrutiny' 41 *UCLA Law Review* 153

Nowak, John (1974), 'Realigning the Standards of Review Under the Equal Protection Guarantee—Prohibited, Neutral and Permissive Classifications' 62 *Georgetown Law Journal* 1071

Nowak, John, and Rotunda, Ronald (1991), *Constitutional Law*, 4th ed. (St. Paul, Minn.: West Publishing Co.)

Pearl, Mitchell (1988), 'Chipping Away at *Bowers* v. *Hardwick*: Making the Best of an Unfortunate Decision' 63 *New York University Law Review* 154

Penn Note (1979), 'Homosexuals' Right to Marry: A Constitutional Test and a Legislative Solution' 128 *University of Pennsylvania Law Review* 193

Perry, Michael (1979), 'Modern Equal Protection: A Conceptualization and Appraisal' 79 *Columbia Law Review* 1023

Polikoff, Nancy (1993), 'We Will Get What We Ask For: Why Legalizing Gay and Lesbian Marriage Will Not "Dismantle the Legal Structure of Gender in Every Marriage"' 79 *Virginia Law Review* 1535

Posner, Richard (1992), *Sex and Reason* (Cambridge, MA: Harvard University Press)

Richards, David (1986), 'Constitutional Legitimacy and Constitutional Privacy' 61 *New York University Law Review* 800

Richards, David (1994), 'Sexual Preference as a Suspect (Religious) Classification: An Alternative Perspective on the Unconstitutionality of Anti-Lesbian/Gay Initiatives' 55 *Ohio State Law Journal* 491

Rivera, Rhonda (1979), 'Our Straight-Laced Judges: The Legal Position of Homosexual Persons in the United States' 30 *Hastings Law Journal* 799

Rivera, Rhonda (1980–81), 'Recent Developments in Sexual Preference Law' 30 *Drake Law Review* 311

Rivera, Rhonda (1985–86), 'Queer Law: Sexual Orientation Law in the Mid-Eighties' (1985) 10 *University of Dayton Law Review* 459, (1986) 11 *University of Dayton Law Review* 275

Roberts, Eric (1993), 'Heightened Scrutiny Under the Equal Protection Clause: A Remedy to Discrimination Based on Sexual Orientation' 42 *Drake Law Review* 485

Rosales Arriola, Elvia (1988), 'Sexual Identity and the Constitution: Homosexual Persons as a Discrete and Insular Minority' 10 *Women's Rights Law Reporter* 143

Rubenfeld, Jed (1989), 'The Right of Privacy' 102 *Harvard Law Review* 737

Rubenstein, William (1993), *Lesbians, Gay Men, and the Law* (New York: The New Press)

Samar, Vincent (1991), *The Right to Privacy: Gays, Lesbians, and the Constitution* (Philadelphia: Temple University Press)

Schacter, Jane (1994), 'The Gay Civil Rights Debate in the States: Decoding the Discourse of Equivalents' 29 *Harvard Civil Rights–Civil Liberties Law Review* 283

Sherman, Suzanne (1992) (ed.), *Lesbian and Gay Marriages: Private Commitments, Public Ceremonies* (Philadelphia: Temple University Press)

Sinisalco, Gary (1976), 'Homosexual Discrimination in Employment' 16 *Santa Clara Law Review* 495

Stoddard, Thomas (1987), '*Bowers* v. *Hardwick*: Precedent by Personal Predilection' 54 *University of Chicago Law Review* 648

Stoddard, Thomas (1992), 'Why Gay People Should Seek the Right to Marry' in Sherman (1992 US)

Strasser, Mark (1991a), 'Family, Definitions and the Constitution: On the Antimiscegenation Analogy' 25 *Suffolk University Law Review* 981

Strasser, Mark (1991b), 'Suspect Classes and Suspect Classifications: On Discriminating, Unwittingly or Otherwise' 64 *Temple Law Review* 937

Sunstein, Cass (1988), 'Sexual Orientation and the Constitution: A Note on the Relationship Between Due Process and Equal Protection' 55 *University of Chicago Law Review* 1161

Sunstein, Cass (1994), 'Homosexuality and the Constitution' 70 *Indiana Law Journal* 1

Thomas, Kendall (1992), 'Beyond the Privacy Principle' 92 *Columbia Law Review* 1431

Tribe, Laurence (1978), *American Constitutional Law*, 1st ed. (Mineola, NY: Foundation Press)

Tribe, Laurence (1980), 'The Puzzling Persistence of Process-Based Constitutional Theories' 89 *Yale Law Journal* 1063

Tribe, Laurence (1988), *American Constitutional Law*, 2d ed. (Mineola, NY: Foundation Press)

Tribe, Laurence, and Dorf, Michael (1990), 'Levels of Generality in the Definition of Rights' 57 *University of Chicago Law Review* 1057

Trosino, James (1993), 'American Wedding: Same-Sex Marriage and the Miscegenation Analogy' 73 *Boston University Law Review* 93

Vieira, Norman (1988), '*Hardwick* and the Right of Privacy' 55 *University of Chicago Law Review* 1181

Wilkinson Harvie, and White, Edward (1977), 'Constitutional Protection for Personal Lifestyles' 62 *Cornell Law Review* 563

Wilkinson, Harvie (1975), 'The Supreme Court, the Equal Protection Clause, and the Three Faces of Constitutional Equality' 61 *Virginia Law Review* 945

Yackle, Larry (1993), 'Parading Ourselves: Freedom of Speech at the Feast of St. Patrick' 73 *Boston University Law Review* 791

Yale Note (1973), 'The Legality of Homosexual Marriage' 82 *Yale Law Journal* 573

B. EUROPEAN CONVENTION AND OTHER EUROPEAN MATERIALS

Blackburn, Catherine (1982), 'Human Rights in an International Context: Recognizing the Right of Intimate Association' 43 *Ohio State Law Journal* 143

Bradley, David (1989), 'The Development of a Legal Status for Unmarried Cohabitants in Sweden' 18 *Anglo-American Law Review* 322

British Medical Association (1994), *Age of Consent for Homosexual Men* (January 1994 report)

Buquicchio-de Boer, Maud (1985), 'Sexual Discrimination and the European Convention on Human Rights' 6 *Human Rights Law Journal* 1

Castberg, Frede (1974), *The European Convention on Human Rights* (Leiden: A.W. Sijthoff)

Clapham, Andrew, and Weiler, Joseph (1993), 'Lesbians and Gay Men in the European Community Legal Order' in Waaldijk and Clapham (1993 Eur)

Connelly, A.M. (1982), 'Irish Law and the Judgment of the European Court of Human Rights in the *Dudgeon* Case' 4 *Dublin University Law Journal* 25

Connelly, A.M. (1986), 'Problems of Interpretation of Article 8 of the European Convention on Human Rights' 35 *International and Comparative Law Quarterly* 567

Council of Europe (1981), Parliamentary Assembly, Committee on Social and Health Questions, 'Report on discrimination against homosexuals', *Parliamentary Assembly Documents* 4755 (8 July 1981)

Council of Europe (1994), 'Text of Protocol No. 11 and Explanatory Report' 15 *Human Rights Law Journal* 86

Crane, Paul (1982), *Gays and the Law* (London: Pluto Press)

Criminal Law Revision Committee (UK) (1984), *Fifteenth Report: Sexual Offences*, Cmnd. 9213

Danish National Organization for Gays and Lesbians (1990), 'Report of the Study-Conference on the possibilities of expanding the European Convention on Human Rights to eliminate discrimination based on sexual orientation' (Copenhagen, 26–27 May 1990)

Delmas-Marty, Mireille (1992) (ed.), *The European Convention for the Protection of Human Rights: International Protection vs. National Restrictions* (Dordrecht, NL: Martinus Nijhoff)

Dillon, Kathleen (1989), 'Divorce and Remarriage as Human Rights: The Irish Constitution and the European Convention on Human Rights At Odds In *Johnston* v. *Ireland*' 22 *Cornell International Law Journal* 63

Doswald-Beck, Louise (1983), 'The Meaning of the "Right to Respect for Private Life" Under the European Convention on Human Rights' 4 *Human Rights Law Journal* 283

Drzemczewski, Andrew (1983), *European Human Rights Convention in Domestic Law: A Comparative Study* (Oxford: Clarendon Press)

Drzemczewski, Andrew (1985), *The right to respect for private and family life, home and correspondence as guaranteed by Article 8 of the European Convention on Human Rights* (Strasbourg: Council of Europe)

Dubber, Markus (1990), 'Homosexual Privacy Rights Before the United States Supreme Court and the European Court of Human Rights: A Comparison of Methodologies' 27 *Stanford Journal of International Law* 189

Duda, Alexandra (1995), 'Comparative Survey of the Legal and Societal Situation of Homosexuals in Europe' in National Danish Organisation for Gays and Lesbians, *Euro-Letter No. 31* (February 1995), pp. 12–15

Duffy, Peter (1982), 'The Protection of Privacy, Family Life and Other Rights under Article 8 of the European Convention on Human Rights' 2 *Yearbook of European Law* 191

Eide, Asbjorn, and Opsahl, Torkel (1994), 'General Report on Equality and Non-Discrimination' in Council of Europe, *7th International Colloquy on the European Convention on Human Rights* (Kehl am Rhein: N.P. Engel), 97–132

Eissen, Marc-André (1990), 'L'interaction des jurisprudences constitutionnelles nationales et de la jurisprudence de la Cour européenne des Droits de l'homme' in Dominique Rousseau and Frédéric Sudre (eds.) *Conseil constitutionnel et Cour européenne des droits de l'homme: Droits et libertés en Europe* (Paris: Editions des Sciences et des Techniques Humaines)

Ermanski, Robert (1992), 'A Right to Privacy for Gay People Under International Human Rights Law' 15 *Boston College International and Comparative Law Review* 141

Evrigenis, Dimitrios (1982), 'Recent Case-Law of the European Court of Human Rights on Articles 8 and 10 of the European Convention on Human Rights' 3 *Human Rights Law Journal* 121

Finnis, John (1994), 'Law, Morality, and "Sexual Orientation"' 69 *Notre Dame Law Review* 1049

Forder, Caroline (1990), 'Legal Protection Under Article 8 ECHR: *Marckx* and Beyond' 37 *Netherlands International Law Review* 162

Gearty, Conor (1983), 'Homosexuals and the Criminal Law—The Right to Privacy' 5 *Dublin University Law Journal* 264

Girard, Philip (1986), 'The Protection of the Rights of Homosexuals Under the International Law of Human Rights: European Perspectives' 3 *Canadian Human Rights Yearbook* 3

Glendon, Mary Ann (1991), *Rights Talk: The Impoverishment of Political Discourse* (New York: The Free Press)

Hansen, Bent, and Jorgenson, Henning (1993), 'The Danish Partnership Law: Political Decision Making in Denmark and the National Danish Organization for Gays and Lesbians' in Hendriks, Tielman and van der Veen (1993 Other)

Helfer, Laurence (1990), 'Finding a Consensus on Equality: The Homosexual Age of Consent and the European Convention on Human Rights' 65 *New York University Law Review* 1044

Helfer, Laurence (1991), 'Lesbian and Gay Rights as Human Rights: Strategies for a United Europe' 32 *Virginia Journal of International Law* 157

Helfer, Laurence (1993), 'Consensus, Coherence and the European Convention on Human Rights' 26 *Cornell International Law Journal* 133

Hendriks, Aart and Ruygrok, Willemien (1993), '"Strangers" in the Netherlands: Dutch Policy toward Gay and Lesbian Aliens' in Hendriks, Tielman and van der Veen (1993 Other)

Henson, Deborah (1993), 'A Comparative Analysis of Same-Sex Partnership Protections: Recommendations for American Reform' 7 *International Journal of Law and the Family* 282

Home Office (UK) (1957), *Report of the Committee on Homosexual Offences and Prostitution*, Cmnd. 247

Honoré, Tony (1978), *Sex Law* (London: Duckworth)

Kane, Daniel (1988), 'Homosexuality and the European Convention on Human Rights: What Rights?' 11 *Hastings International and Comparative Law Review* 447

Kimble, Jennifer (1988), 'A Comparative Analysis of *Dudgeon* v. *United Kingdom* and *Bowers* v. *Hardwick*' 5 *Arizona Journal of International and Comparative Law* 200

Kingston, James (1994), 'Sex and Sexuality under the European Convention on Human Rights' in Liz Heffernan (ed.) *Human Rights: A European Perspective* (Dublin: Round Hall Press)

Lester, Anthony (1988), 'The Overseas Trade in the American Bill of Rights' 88 *Columbia Law Review* 537

Loucaides, L.G. (1990), 'Personality and Privacy Under the European Convention on Human Rights' 61 *British Year Book of International Law* 175

Macdonald, Ian, and Blake, Nicholas (1991), *Immigration Law and Practice in the United Kingdom*, 3rd ed. (London: Butterworths)

Martin, Jorge (1994), 'English Polygamy Law and the Danish Registered Partnership Act: A Case for the Consistent Treatment of Foreign Polygamous Marriages and Danish Same-Sex Marriages in England' 27 *Cornell International Law Journal* 419

Michael, James (1988), 'Homosexuals and Privacy' 138 *New Law Journal* 831

Nielsen, Linda (1990), 'Family Rights and the "Registered Partnership" in Denmark' 4 *International Journal of Law and the Family* 297

Nielsen, Linda (1992–93), 'Denmark: New Rules Regarding Marriage Contracts and Reform Considerations Concerning Children' 31 *University of Louisville Journal of Family Law* 309

Norrie, Kenneth (1994), 'Reproductive Technology, Transsexualism and Homosexuality: New Problems for International Private Law' 43 *International and Comparative Law Quarterly* 757

Norris, David (1993), 'The Development of the Gay Movement in Ireland: A Personal and Political Memoir' in Hendriks, Tielman and van der Veen (1993 Other)

O'Donnell, Thomas (1982), 'The Margin of Appreciation Doctrine: Standards in the Jurisprudence of the European Court of Human Rights' 4 *Human Rights Quarterly* 474

Pannick, David (1985), *Sex Discrimination Law* (Oxford: Clarendon Press)

Parliamentary Assembly of the Council of Europe (1992), 'The Geographical Enlargement of the Council of Europe' 13 *Human Rights Law Journal* 230

Pedersen, Marianne (1992), 'Denmark: Homosexual Marriages and New Rules Regarding Separation and Divorce' 30 *Journal of Family Law* 289

Pinto, Roger (1965), *Les Organisations européennes*, 2nd ed. (Paris: Payot)

Policy Advisory Committee on Sexual Offences (UK) (1981), *Report on the Age of Consent in relation to Sexual Offences*, Cmnd. 8216

Rendel, Margherita (1991), 'Abortion and Human Rights' 141 *New Law Journal* 1270

Saldeen, Ake (1988–89), 'Sweden: More Rights for Children and Homosexuals' 27 *Family Law Journal* 295

Saldeen, Ake (1990–91), 'Sweden: Changes in the Code on Marriage and Plans for Reform in the Areas of Adoption, Child Custody and Fetal Diagnostics' 29 *Journal of Family Law* 431

Self, Janet (1988), *'Bowers* v. *Hardwick*: A Study of Aggression' 10 *Human Rights Quarterly* 395 (discusses *Dudgeon*)

Storey, Hugo (1990), 'The Right to Family Life and Immigration Case Law at Strasbourg' 39 *International and Comparative Law Quarterly* 328

Tatchell, Peter (1992), *Europe in the Pink: Lesbian and Gay Equality in the New Europe* (London: GMP Publishers)

van der Veen, Evert, Hendriks, Aart, and Mattijssen, Astrid (1993), 'Lesbian and Gay Rights in Europe: Homosexuality and the Law' in Hendriks, Tielman and van der Veen (1993 Other)

van Dijk, Pieter (1993), 'The Treatment of Homosexuals under the European Convention on Human Rights' in Waaldijk and Clapham (1993 Eur)

van Dijk, Pieter, and van Hoof, G.J.H. (1990), *Theory and Practice of the European Convention on Human Rights*, 2nd ed. (Deventer, NL: Kluwer)

Vincineau, Michel (1979), 'Les homosexuels devant la Commission européenne des Droits de l'Homme' 59 *Revue de droit pénal et de criminologie* 83

Waaldijk, Kees (1986–87), 'Constitutional Protection Against Discrimination of Homosexuals' 13 *Journal of Homosexuality* 57

Waaldijk, Kees (1991), *Tip of an Iceberg: Anti-Lesbian and Anti-Gay Discrimination in Europe* (Utrecht: Department of Gay and Lesbian Studies, University of Utrecht)

Waaldijk, Kees (1993), 'The Legal Situation in the Member States' in Waaldijk and Clapham (1993 Eur)

Waaldijk, Kees, and Clapham, Andrew (1993) (eds.), *Homosexuality: A European Community Issue* (Dordrecht, NL: Martinus Nijhoff)

Warbrick, Colin (1989), '"Federal" Aspects of the European Convention on Human Rights' 10 *Michigan Journal of International Law* 698

Warbrick, Colin (1990), 'Coherence and the European Court of Human Rights: The Adjudicative Background to the *Soering* Case' 11 *Michigan Journal of International Law* 1073

Wintemute, Robert (1994), 'Sexual Orientation Discrimination' in Christopher McCrudden and Gerald Chambers (eds.) *Individual Rights and the Law in Britain* (Oxford: Clarendon Press)

Yourow, Howard (1987), 'The Margin of Appreciation Doctrine in the Dynamics of European Human Rights Jurisprudence' 3 *Connecticut Journal of International Law* 111

C. CANADIAN MATERIALS

Alberta Human Rights Commission (1992), *A Study of Discrimination Based on Sexual Orientation* (4 December 1992)

Baker, David (1987), 'The Changing Norms of Equality in the Supreme Court of Canada' 9 *Supreme Court Law Review* 497

Bankier, Jennifer (1985), 'Equality, Affirmative Action, and the Charter: Reconciling "Inconsistent" Sections' 1 *Canadian Journal of Women and the Law* 134

Bayefsky, Anne (1985), 'Defining Equality Rights' in Bayefsky and Eberts (1985 Can)

Bayefsky, Anne (1990), 'A Case Comment on the First Three Equality Cases Under the Canadian Charter of Rights and Freedoms: *Andrews, Workers' Compensation Reference* and *Turpin*' 1 *Supreme Court Law Review* (2d) 503

Bayefsky, Anne, and Eberts, Mary (1985) (eds.), *Equality Rights and the Canadian Charter of Rights and Freedoms* (Toronto: Carswell)

Bender, Paul (1983), 'The Canadian Charter of Rights and Freedoms and the United States Bill of Rights: A Comparison' 28 *McGill Law Journal* 811

Bergeron, Jacques (1980), 'New Categories in Québec Analyzed' 1 *Canadian Human Rights Reporter* C/17

Black, William (1979), '*Gay Alliance Toward Equality* v. *Vancouver Sun*' 17 *Osgoode Hall Law Journal* 649

Black, William (1986), 'Intent or Effects: Section 15 of the Charter of Rights and Freedoms' in Weiler and Elliot (1986 Can)

Black, William, and Grant, Isabel (1990), 'Equality and Biological Differences' 79 *Criminal Reports* (3d) 372

Black, William, and Smith, Lynn (1989), '*Andrews* v. *Law Society of British Columbia*' 68 *Canadian Bar Review* 591

Brodsky, Gwen, and Day, Shelagh (1989), *Canadian Charter Equality Rights for Women: One Step Forward or Two Steps Back?* (Ottawa: Canadian Advisory Council on the Status of Women)

Brudner, Alan (1986), 'What Are Reasonable Limits to Equality Rights?' 64 *Canadian Bar Review* 469

Bruner, Arnold (1985), 'Sexual Orientation and Equality Rights' in Bayefsky and Eberts (1985 Can)

Canada (1981), *Minutes of Proceedings and Evidence of the Special Joint Committee of the Senate and of the House of Commons on the Constitution of Canada*, 1st Sess., 32nd Parl., Issue No. 48

Coffey, M.A. (1986), 'Of Father Born: A Lesbian Feminist Critique of the O.L.R.C. Recommendations on Artificial Insemination' 1 *Canadian Journal of Women and the Law* 424

Commission des droits de la personne du Québec (1994), *De l'illégalité à l'égalité: Rapport de la consultation publique sur la violence et la discrimination envers les gais et lesbiennes* (May 1994)

Demers, Robert (1984), 'De la lex scantinia aux récents amendements du Code criminel: homosexualité et droit dans une perspective historique' 25 *Cahiers de Droit* 777

Department of Justice (Canada) (1986), *Toward Equality: The Response to the Report of the Parliamentary Committee on Equality Rights*

Duclos, Nitya (1991), 'Some Complicating Thoughts on Same-Sex Marriage' 1 *Law and Sexuality* 31

Duplé, Nicole (1984), 'Homosexualité et droits à l'égalité dans les Chartes canadienne et québécoise' 25 *Cahiers de Droit* 801

Eberts, Mary (1985), 'Sex-Based Discrimination and the Charter' in Bayefsky and Eberts (1985 Can)

Elliott, David (1989), 'Comment on *Andrews* v. *Law Society of British Columbia*' 35 *McGill Law Journal* 235

Flanagan, William (1989), 'Equality Rights for People With AIDS: Mandatory Reporting of HIV Infection and Contact Tracing' 34 *McGill Law Journal* 530

Freeman, Jody (1994), 'Defining Family in *Mossop* v. *DSS*: The Challenge of Anti-Essentialism and Interactive Discrimination for Human Rights Litigation' 44 *University of Toronto Law Journal* 41

Gairdner, William (1990), *The Trouble With Canada* (Toronto: Stoddart Publishing)

Gall, Gerald (1986), 'Some Miscellaneous Aspects of Section 15 of the Canadian Charter of Rights and Freedoms' 24 *Alberta Law Review* 462

Gibson, Dale (1991a), 'Analogous Grounds of Discrimination Under the Canadian Charter: Too Much Ado About Next to Nothing' 29 *Alberta Law Review* 772

Gibson, Dale (1991b), 'Equality for Some' 40 *University of New Brunswick Law Journal* 2

Girard, Philip (1986), 'Sexual Orientation as a Human Rights Issue in Canada 1969–1985' 10:2 *Dalhousie Law Journal* 267

Girard, Philip (1987), 'From Subversion to Liberation: Homosexuals and the Immigration Act 1952–1977' 2 *Canadian Journal of Law and Society* 1

Gold, Marc (1989), 'Comment: *Andrews* v. *Law Society of British Columbia*' 34 *McGill Law Journal* 1063

Gold, Richard (1989), 'From Right to Remedy' 14 *Queen's Law Journal* 214

Green, Richard (1987), 'Give Me Your Tired, Your Poor, Your Huddled Masses (of Heterosexuals): An Analysis of American and Canadian Immigration Policy' 16 *Anglo-American Law Review* 139

Grey, Julius (1988), 'Equality Rights: An Analysis' 19 *Revue de Droit, Université de Sherbrooke* 183

Harris, David (1987), 'Equality, Equality Rights and Discrimination Under the Charter of Rights and Freedoms' 21 *University of British Columbia Law Review* 390

Hawkins, Robert (1990), 'Interpretivism and Sections 7 and 15 of the Canadian Charter of Rights and Freedoms' 22 *Ottawa Law Review* 275

Herman, Didi (1990), 'Are We Family?: Lesbian Rights and Women's Liberation' 28 *Osgoode Hall Law Journal* 789

Herman, Didi (1994), *Rights of Passage: Struggles for Lesbian and Gay Legal Equality* (Toronto: University of Toronto Press)

Hickling, M.A. (1988), 'Employer's Liability for Sexual Harassment' 17 *Manitoba Law Journal* 124

Hogg, Peter (1985), *Constitutional Law of Canada*, 2nd ed. (Toronto: Carswell)

Hogg, Peter (1990), 'Interpreting the Charter of Rights: Generosity and Justification' 28 *Osgoode Hall Law Journal* 817

Hogg, Peter (1992), *Constitutional Law of Canada*, 3rd ed. (Scarborough, Ont.: Carswell)

Hughes, Patricia (1985), 'Feminist Equality and the Charter: Conflict with Reality?' 5 *Windsor Yearbook of Access to Justice* 39

Jefferson, James (1985), 'Gay Rights and the Charter' 43:1 *University of Toronto Faculty of Law Review* 70

Kinsman, Gary (1987), *The Regulation of Desire: Sexuality in Canada* (Montréal: Black Rose)

Kopyto, Harry (1980), 'The *Gay Alliance* Case Reconsidered' 18 *Osgoode Hall Law Journal* 639

Leopold, Margaret, and King, Wendy (1985), 'Compulsory Heterosexuality, Lesbians, and the Law: The Case for Constitutional Protection' 1 *Canadian Journal of Women and the Law* 163

Lepofsky, David, and Schwartz, Hart (1988), 'An Erroneous Approach to the Charter's Equality Guarantee: *R.* v. *Ertel*' 67 *Canadian Bar Review* 115

MacKay, Wayne (1986), 'Judging and Equality: For Whom Does the Charter Toll?' 10:2 *Dalhousie Law Journal* 35

MacLauchlan, Wade (1986), 'Of Fundamental Justice, Equality and Society's Outcasts: A Comment on *R.* v. *Tremayne* and *R.* v. *McLean*' 32 *McGill Law Journal* 213

McEvoy, J.P. (1994), 'The Charter and Spousal Benefits: The Case of the Same-Sex Spouse' 2 *Review of Constitutional Studies* 39

McLellan, Anne (1985), 'Marital Status and Equality Rights' in Bayefsky and Eberts (1985 Can)

Moon, Richard (1988), 'Discrimination and Its Justification: Coping with Equality Rights Under the Charter' 26 *Osgoode Hall Law Journal* 673

Ontario Law Reform Commission (1993), *Report on the Rights and Responsibilities of Cohabitants under the Family Law Act* (Toronto)

Petersen, Cynthia (1991), 'A Queer Response to Bashing: Legislating Against Hate' 16 *Queen's Law Journal* 231

Petter, Andrew (1989), 'Legitimizing Sexual Inequality: Three Early Charter Cases' 34 *McGill Law Journal* 358

Pothier, Dianne (1993), 'Charter Challenges to Underinclusive Legislation: The Complexities of Sins of Omission' 19 *Queen's Law Journal* 261

Proulx, Daniel (1988), 'L'objet des droits constitutionnels à l'égalité' 29 *Cahiers de Droit* 567

Richstone, Jeff and Russell, Stuart (1981), 'Shutting the Gate: Gay Civil Rights in the Supreme Court of Canada' 27 *McGill Law Journal* 92

Rogers, Peter (1986), 'Equality, Efficiency and Judicial Restraint: Towards a Dynamic Constitution' 10:2 *Dalhousie Law Journal* 139

Ross, June (1986), 'Levels of Review in American Equal Protection and Under the Charter' 24 *Alberta Law Review* 441

Rusk, Peter (1993), 'Same-Sex Spousal Benefits and the Evolving Conception of the Family' 52 *University of Toronto Faculty of Law Review* 170

Russell, Stuart (1982), 'The Offence of Keeping a Common Bawdy-House in Canadian Criminal Law' 14 *Ottawa Law Review* 270

Ryder, Bruce (1990), 'Equality Rights and Sexual Orientation: Confronting Heterosexual Family Privilege' 9 *Canadian Journal of Family Law* 39

Sanders, Douglas (1994), 'Constructing Lesbian and Gay Rights' 9 *Canadian Journal of Law and Society* 99

Sheppard, Colleen (1989), 'Recognition of the Disadvantaging of Women: The Promise of *Andrews* v. *Law Society of British Columbia*' 35 *McGill Law Journal* 206

Smith, Lynn (1984), 'Charter Equality Rights: Some General Issues and Specific Applications in British Columbia to Elections, Juries and Illegitimacy' 18 *University of British Columbia Law Review* 351

Smith, Lynn (1988), 'Judicial Interpretation of Equality Rights Under the Canadian Charter of Rights and Freedoms: Some Clear and Present Dangers' 23 *University of British Columbia Law Review* 65

Smith, Lynn (1991), 'The Equality Rights' 20 *Manitoba Law Journal* 377

Spitz, Stephen (1986), 'Litigation Strategy in Equality Rights: The American Experience' in Weiler and Elliot (1986 Can)

Stychin, Carl (1995), 'Essential Rights and Contested Identities: Sexual Orientation and Equality Rights Jurisprudence in Canada' 8 *Canadian Journal of Law and Jurisprudence* 49

Tarnopolsky, Walter (1982), *Discrimination and the Law in Canada* (Don Mills, Ont.: Richard De Boo)

Turnbull, Lorna (1989), '*Brooks, Allen & Dixon* v. *Canada Safeway Ltd.*—A Comment (*Bliss* Revisited)' 34 *McGill Law Journal* 172

Vagelos, Ellen (1994), 'The Social Group That Dare Not Speak Its Name: Should Homosexuals Constitute a Particular Social Group for Purposes of Obtaining Refugee Status? Comment on *Re: Inaudi*' 17 *Fordham International Law Journal* 229

Veitch, Edward (1976), 'The Essence of Marriage—A Comment on the Homosexual Challenge' 5 *Anglo-American Law Review* 41

Weiler, Joseph, and Elliot, Robin (1986) (eds.), *Litigating the Values of a Nation: The Canadian Charter of Rights and Freedoms* (Toronto: Carswell)

Williams, Wendy (1983), 'Sex Discrimination Under the *Charter*: Some Problems of Theory' 4 *Canadian Human Rights Reporter* C/83–1

Wintemute, Robert (1994), 'Sexual Orientation Discrimination as Sex Discrimination: Same-Sex Couples and the Charter in *Mossop, Egan* and *Layland*' 39 *McGill Law Journal* 429

Woehrling, José (1985), 'L'article 15(1) de la Charte canadienne des droits et libertés et la langue' 30 *McGill Law Journal* 266

D. OTHER MATERIALS

Allen, Laura and Gorski, Roger (1992), 'Sexual Orientation and the Size of the Anterior Commissure in the Human Brain' 89 *Proceedings of the National Academy of Sciences of the U.S.A* 7199

Amnesty International (1994), *Violations of the Human Rights of Homosexuals: Extracts from Amnesty International Action Materials* (AI Index: POL 30/01/94)

Bailey, Michael, and Pillard, Richard (1991), 'A Genetic Study of Male Sexual Orientation' 48 *Archives of General Psychiatry* 1089.

Bailey, Michael, Pillard, Richard, et al. (1993), 'Heritable Factors Influence Sexual Orientation in Women' 50 *Archives of General Psychiatry* 217

Bamforth, Nicholas (1996, forthcoming), *Sexuality, Morals and Justice: A Theory of Lesbian and Gay Rights and the Law* (London: Cassell)

Boswell, John (1980), *Christianity, Social Tolerance and Homosexuality: Gay People in Western Europe from the Beginning of the Christian Era to the Fourteenth Century* (Chicago: University of Chicago Press)

Boswell, John (1994), *Same-Sex Unions in Premodern Europe* (New York: Villard Books)

Cameron, Edwin (1993), 'Sexual Orientation and the Constitution: A Test Case for Human Rights' 110 *South African Law Journal* 450

Clapham, Andrew (1993), *Human Rights in the Private Sphere* (Oxford: Clarendon Press)

Croome, Rodney (1992a), 'Australian Gay Rights Case Goes to the United Nations' 2 *Australasian Gay and Lesbian Law Journal* 55

Croome, Rodney (1992b), '"Out and About": The Public Rights of Lesbians and Gays in Tasmania' 2 *Australasian Gay and Lesbian Law Journal* 63

Grau, Günter (1995), *Hidden Holocaust? Gay and Lesbian Persecution in Germany 1933–45* (London: Cassell)

Green, Richard (1988), 'The Immutability of (Homo)sexual orientation: Behavioral Science Implications for a Constitutional (Legal) Analysis' [Winter 1988] *Journal of Psychiatry and Law* 537

Green, Richard (1992), *Sexual Science and the Law* (Cambridge, Mass.: Harvard University Press)

Grossfeld, Bernhard (1990), *The Strength and Weakness of Comparative Law* (Oxford: Clarendon Press)

Hamer, Dean, and Copeland, Peter (1994), *The Science of Desire: The Search for the Gay Gene and the Biology of Behavior* (New York: Simon and Schuster)

Hamer, Dean, et al. (1993), 'A Linkage Between DNA Markers on the X Chromosome and Male Sexual Orientation' 261 *Science* 321

Hart, John (1993), 'Gay and Lesbian Couple Immigration to Australia: Pressure Group Compromises and Achievements' in Hendriks, Tielman and van der Veen (1993 Other)

Heger, Heinz (1980), *The Men with the Pink Triangle* (London: Gay Men's Press)

Heinze, Eric (1995), *Sexual Orientation: A Human Right* (Dordrecht, NL: Martinus Nijhoff)

Helfer, Laurence, and Miller, Alice, 'Human Rights and Sexual Orientation: Developments in the United Nations, the United States and Around the World' (1995, forthcoming in a US law journal)

Hendriks, Aart, Tielman, Rob, and van der Veen, Evert (1993) (eds.), *The Third Pink Book: A Global View of Lesbian and Gay Liberation and Oppression* (Buffalo, NY: Prometheus Books)

Kahn-Freund, Otto (1974), 'On Uses and Misuses of Comparative Law' 37 *Modern Law Review* 1

Kinsey, Alfred, et al. (1948), *Sexual Behavior in the Human Male* (Philadelphia: W.B. Saunders)

Kinsey, Alfred, et al. (1953), *Sexual Behavior in the Human Female* (Philadelphia: W.B. Saunders)

Levay, Simon (1991), 'A Difference in Hypothalamic Structure Between Heterosexual and Homosexual Men' 253 *Science* 1034

Levay, Simon (1993), *The Sexual Brain* (Cambridge, Mass.: MIT Press)

Marie, Jean-Bernard (1994), 'International Instruments Relating to Human Rights' 15 *Human Rights Law Journal* 51

McCormick, Cheryl, Witelson, Sandra, and Kingstone, Edward (1990), 'Left-handedness in Homosexual Men and Women: Neuroendocrine Implications' 15 *Psychoneuroendocrinology* 69

McCormick, Cheryl, and Witelson, Sandra (1991), 'A Cognitive Profile of Homosexual Men Compared to Heterosexual Men and Women' 16 *Psychoneuroendocrinology* 459

McGoldrick, Dominic (1994), *The Human Rights Committee: Its Role in the Development of the International Covenant on Civil and Political Rights* (Oxford: Clarendon Press)

Morgan, Wayne (1993), 'Sexuality and Human Rights: The First Communication by an Australian to the Human Rights Committee under the Optional Protocol to the International Covenant on Civil and Political Rights' 14 *Australian Year Book of International Law* 277

Nowak, Manfred (1993), *UN Covenant on Civil and Political Rights: CCPR Commentary* (Kehl am Rhein: N.P. Engel)

Parliamentary Research Service (Australia) (1994), *Strange Bedfellows: The U.N. Human Rights Committee and the Tasmanian Parliament* (Current Issues Brief No. 6)

Plant, Richard (1987), *The Pink Triangle: The Nazi War Against Homosexuals* (Edinburgh: Mainstream Publishing)

Rich, Adrienne (1983), 'Compulsory Heterosexuality and Lesbian Existence' in Ann Snitow, Christine Stansell and Sharon Thompson (eds.) *Powers of Desire: The Politics of Sexuality* (New York: Monthly Review Press)

Ruse, Michael (1988), *Homosexuality: A Philosophical Inquiry* (Oxford: Basil Blackwell)

Sherman, Martin (1979), *Bent* (Oxford: Amber Lane Press)

Stewart, Blair (1993), 'New Zealand Immigration Law and Gay and Lesbian Couples' 3 *Australasian Gay and Lesbian Law Journal* 30

Stewart, David (1993), 'US Ratification of the Covenant on Civil and Political Rights: The Significance of the Reservations, Understandings and Declarations' 14 *Human Rights Law Journal* 77

Stychin, Carl (1995), *Law's Desire: Sexuality and the Limits of Justice* (London: Routledge)

Tasker, Fiona, and Golombok, Susan (1991), 'Children Raised by Lesbian Mothers: The Empirical Evidence' 21 *Family Law (UK)* 184

Tielman, Rob, and Hammelburg, Hans, 'World Survey on the Social and Legal Position of Gays and Lesbians' in Hendriks, Tielman and van der Veen (1993 Other)

United Nations (1995), 'Human Rights: International Instruments: Chart of Ratifications as at 31 December 1994', UN Publication No. ST/HR/4/Rev.11

Weinberg, Martin, Williams, Colin, and Pryor, Douglas (1994), *Dual Attraction: Understanding Bisexuality* (New York: Oxford University Press)

E. GAY, LESBIAN, AND BISEXUAL COMMUNITY PUBLICATIONS

Capital Gay, London

Gay Times, London

GO Info, Ottawa

Lesbian/Gay Law Notes, Lesbian and Gay Law Association of Greater New York, 799 Broadway, Rm. 340, New York, NY 10003, USA

Perceptions, Saskatoon

Pink Paper, London

The Advocate, Los Angeles

The Native, New York

The Washington Blade, Washington, DC

Xtra, Toronto

Index

abortion
  Canada 184–6
  European and US consensus on 138–9
  prohibition as sex discrimination 211–12
  US 43–6, 48–9
adoption and fostering, *see* parental rights
affection, public displays of 13, 49, 83, 130,
    168, 177–8, 203, 208
affirmative action 12–13, 65, 161
age of consent to sexual activity
  Canada 165, 168, 235–6
  European Convention and 92–3, 95
    discrimination under Article 14 and
      119, 121–2
    European consensus on 134–8, 270–1
    justifications for higher 107–9, 127
anal intercourse, *see* sexual activity
'anti-gay' initiatives, *see* right to participate
    equally in the political process
armed forces
  Canada 169, 222–3
  Colombia 5
  lack of privacy in 79–80, 216–19
  UK 96, 109–10, 123–4, 136
  US 29, 54–5, 70–2, 76, 78–82, 89–90
associations of gay, lesbian and bisexual
    persons 49–52, 88, 100, 117, 151, 169,
    239–40

blasphemous libel 114, 116, 124
Bowers v. *Hardwick* 30–46
  application of fundamental right tests 44–5
  application of general privacy principle
    40–4
    formulations 41–2
    'intimate association' 41–2
    'personhood' 41–3
    'zone of privacy' 40–1
  application of *Griswold* and other privacy
    cases 33–9
  application of *Stanley* v. *Georgia* 39–40
  contraception cases 33–6
  criticism of 31–2
  decision 30–2
  limitations of right of privacy 47–9
  married vs. unmarried persons 37–8
  'morality' as rational basis 45–6
  oral or anal intercourse laws after 46–7
  potential levels of protection under 73–4,
    81–2
  religious beliefs and 45

'second death of substantive due process'
    43–4
suspect classification argument and 68–78,
    88–90

Canada, success of Charter litigants and
    consensus in 248–50
Canadian Charter of Rights and Freedoms 4,
    150–228, 254–60
  anti-discrimination (human rights)
    legislation and 223–4
  assessment of protection under 222–8,
    254–60
  criteria for identifying analogous grounds
    154–62
    Andrews v. *Law Society of B.C.* 154–5
    'disadvantaged groups' 157–61, 255–6
    'fundamental choices' 161–2, 255
    'immutable statuses' 161–2, 255
    'nature of ground' vs. 'use of ground'
      criteria 156–7, 161–2
    'personal characteristics' 158–9, 162
  disability discrimination 198
  'discrimination', third requirement for
    162–3, 256–8
  'equality' (Section 15(1)) 151–3
  family status discrimination 198–9, 227
  'liberty' (Section 7) 151–3
  marital status discrimination 182, 184,
    198–9
  Oakes requirements (Section 1) 154,
    258–60
  pregnancy discrimination 184, 208–14
  sexual harassment 208–14
  sexual orientation as an analogous ground
    163–73, 254–6
    court decisions 164–8, 254–6
    criteria that are satisfied 168–72, 255–6
    'discriminatory impact' 166–7, 256–8
    economic and social disadvantage 171,
      255
    identifiability or visibility 170
    intention of drafters 171–2
    response of Canadian legal community
      163–8, 254–6
  sexual orientation as a fundamental choice
    183–97, 255
    attraction-conduct distinction 194–7,
      256–7
    freedom of expression, association or
      religion and 193–4